Also by Thomas R. Flagel

THE HISTORY BUFF'S GUIDE TO THE CIVIL WAR

THE HISTORY BUFF'S GUIDE TO WORLD WAR II

· KEY PEOPLE, PLACES, AND EVENTS ·

The HISTORY BUFF'S™ GUIDE to GETTYSBURG

THOMAS R. FLAGEL & KEN ALLERS JR.

CUMBERLAND HOUSE

NASHVILLE, TENNESSEE

THE HISTORY BUFF'S GUIDE TO GETTYSBURG
PUBLISHED BY CUMBERLAND HOUSE PUBLISHING, INC.
431 Harding Industrial Drive
Nashville, Tennessee 37211

Cover design by Gore Studio, Inc., Nashville, Tennessee

Library of Congress Cataloging-in-Publication Data

Flagel, Thomas R., 1966–
   The history buff's guide to Gettysburg / Thomas R. Flagel and Ken Allers Jr.
      p. cm.
   Includes bibliographical references and index.
   ISBN-13: 978-1-58182-509-1 (pbk. : alk. paper)
   ISBN-10: 1-58182-509-9 (pbk. : alk. paper)
   1. Gettysburg, Battle of, Gettysburg, Pa., 1863—Miscellanea. I. Allers, Ken, 1950– .
II. Title.
E475.53.F58 2006
973.7'349—dc22   2006004431

Printed in Canada

1 2 3 4 5 6 7 8 9 10—10 09 08 07 06

To the Loras College Department of History
and
To Deb,
I owe her so much

Contents

Prologue

DAYS AFTER A TERRIBLE battle, Daniel Holt, an exhausted Union surgeon, slumped down on a log somewhere near Turner's Gap, just inside the northern border of Maryland. Draping his torso over the head of a drum, his back aching, legs sapped, arms leaden after repeatedly lifting bodies and sawing limbs, the doctor slowly reached for pen and paper and tried to explain what he had just seen: "The battle of the 1st, 2nd, and 3rd July will ever be known as one of the hardest fought, most destructive of human life and most decided in its results of any on record. What the *name* of the battle will be I do not know, nor is it important, but inasmuch as it was fought near Gettysburg."

Eyewitnesses to massive disasters often assume they have experienced something unparalleled in history. Their reactions are understandable, considering that any tempest viewed from within might look like the world coming to an end. Such was the tendency in the American Civil War as officers, soldiers, and diarists described nearly every nasty engagement as "the decisive moment of the war" or "the bloodiest contest ever waged." Within the tales of battles, hyperbole reigned supreme.

Yet in his case, the 121st New York Infantry Regiment's Dr. Holt may have been correct. Never before or since in the history of the North American continent had so many people died in combat during so brief a period of time. The battle of Gettysburg remains the largest and deadliest military engagement ever fought in the Western Hemisphere. In comparison, a later generation of American, British, and Canadian troops launched an invasion of occupied Europe with the same number of troops and suffered fewer casualties.

Holt was just one of a thousand surgeons caring for more than 20,000 maimed out of 150,000 combatants thrown against one another for sixty unspeakable hours. The consequences were such that both commanding generals later offered their resignation. The good doctor survived, but seven thousand of his countrymen did not, and thousands more would soon follow their lost comrades into premature death. More blood had soaked into the soil of south central Pennsylvania in three days than had been lost in any other week of any other campaign in the entire war. The dead lost in the Wheatfield, the Peach Orchard, and Pickett's Charge exceeded the number of Americans killed in action during the War for Independence, the War of 1812, and the Mexican War combined.

In the years after the Brother's War, as citizens looked back at their costly crime of fratricide, many viewed that battle among the thousands to be the turning point, the moment when a nation had fully paid for its offenses and had finally started its march toward a new birth of freedom. Though fought in Pennsylvania, the battle was a national conflict. Men from every state in the Union and regiments from all eleven states in the Confederacy met on that great battlefield. For a brief period, quite involuntarily, Gettysburg was the ninth most populous city in the nation, holding a greater number of citizens than either Richmond or Washington. Among its combatants were descendants and forefathers of scholars, governors, artists, generals, and presidents.

Gettysburg came to be known as "the symbolic center of American history," "the grand mausoleum of our patriot dead," a euphemism for noble sacrifice. Yet, in its exaltation, the enigma has been heavily wrapped in nostalgia, subjectivity, and myth. Held aloft, this intricate and pivotal episode drifts back into the musket fire and cannon smoke from whence it came to reside as somehow separate and above all other events around it. Gettysburg simultaneously embodies the Altar of Freedom and the Lost Cause, a High Tide, where the foremost size of the battle was simply emblematic of its premier historic significance. In an attempt to understand this great event, historians both amateur and scholastic, military tacticians, novelists, reenactors, and millions of like-minded devotees have analyzed the topic to the point of atomization. In short, the subject is either nurtured or nitpicked. Consequently, a clear image of Gettysburg is lost.

The purpose of *The History Buff's Guide* series is to examine past events through the looking glass of top-ten lists, to search the vast middle ground between the glorifying monuments and the trifling minutiae. The goal is to make history comprehensive and comprehendible to the newcomer, yet engaging and enlightening to the aficionado. Every list overtures with background information and criteria for the respective topic. Some are chronological to illustrate progression. Others are quantitative or qualitative. Where appropriate, names and words appear in SMALL CAPS to indicate a subject appearing in another list. All rankings are a result of thousands of hours of research, confirmations, consultations, and analysis.

In ranking the key people, places, and events of Gettysburg, a very different image of the battle emerges, one where most of the dying occurred away from the high ground, where the town and Culp's Hill played greater roles than either Devil's Den or Little Round Top, and where the smaller states made the greater sacrifices. Foremost, the lists indicate that the battle was indeed a pivotal event in the course of American history, but not for reasons popularly held.

As a military phenomenon, the engagement was not particularly unique, nor did it appreciably alter the pervasive stalemate in the East. But in its aftermath, Gettysburg was unlike any other place or time. Its destruction of life was unprecedented, as was the manner in which it recovered. Whereas most battle sites remained under threat or occupation for months or years, Gettysburg was essentially "liberated" overnight. As both armies departed, they also liberated the region of ambulances, doctors, medicines, supplies, and food while abandoning more than thirty thousand dying and dead men. The scenarios both enabled and mandated a great civilian migration *into* the area, the exact opposite effect of most battles. The end result was a massive fusion of philanthropy and pilfering, of repairing and relic hunting. Months later a dedication ceremony produced a singular address, one that came to define the war more than any battle ever could.

☆ ☆

THOUGH TWO surnames appear on the cover of the book, hundreds of individuals brought this work to fruition. Thomas Flagel wishes to extend heartfelt gratitude toward the Prairie Writers of Iowa; Kevin Peterson; Dr. David Salvaterra of Loras College; William D. Thomas, Steve Olsson, Michael Bryant of the U.S. Department of Education; Glenn Janus of Coe College; and Mary Elworth of Chicago. He is also grateful to Larry Trujillo for his Web engineering, to Joel Shrader for his marketing savvy, to Bev Finnegan of the Sidney (Iowa) Library, to Josephine Elworth for her encouragement, and to his parents and siblings for their support. As always, countless thanks go to Ed Curtis, Ron Pitkin, Tracy Ford, and the rest of the patient and professional staff at Cumberland House.

A note from Ken Allers: One can never truly understand the battle of Gettysburg without walking the field. It has been a long journey of forty-four years of countless days on the battlefield. One person has made the battlefield come alive and helped make sense of it all. His patience with questions and enthusiasm in explanation were beyond my humble requests: Howie Frankenfield, licensed battlefield guide. Thanks also to my parents, Ken and Lorna Allers, for igniting the small flame of Gettysburg in 1961; to Matt and Amy for their forbearance of my lifelong study of Gettysburg; to all of the members of the Civil War Round Table of Cedar Rapids; to the staff at the Brickhouse Inn at Gettysburg; to Lucille Lettow of the University of Northern Iowa; to Phil Lucas of Cornell College; to Don Montgomery from Prairie Grove State Battlefield Park in Arkansas; to Dick Pohorsky; to Noel Harman; to Jim Kern; to Norm and Carolyn McElwain; to my "Civil War buddy," Maureen McElwain; and to my sister, Nancy Owens (for one of the best trips I ever had in 1971). A special note must be made of the late Clyde Putnam, who was the first person to urge me to write on Gettysburg. Despite his long absence from my life, I have finally fulfilled my promise. Last, but not least, thank you to the most important person in my life, my best friend, wife, and love of my life for the last thirty-plus years, Deb.

1

COMING TO THE CROSSROADS

TOP TEN EVENTS PRIOR TO GETTYSBURG

When the war began, the balance sheet blatantly favored the Union. The North possessed more than twice the population of the South, sixfold the number of engineers, tenfold as many seagoing vessels, and more than thirty times the guns, great and small. All the pieces were available to construct a capital war machine, if needed. But the Confederates owned the daunting weapons of home-field advantage and time, two powerful levers their forefathers had used to great effect against the British Empire.

As the war unexpectedly stretched into a second year, clearly neither side was faring well. The South was losing most of Arkansas, Kentucky, Missouri, northwest Virginia, and western Tennessee. By April 1862 New Orleans was gone, and with it the South's most populous city and strongest anchor to the seven seas. Likewise the North could make no reasonable progress toward Richmond, the blockade leaked like a carpetbag, and foreign powers were contemplating intervention. For blue and butternut, hopes for a short war had faded, but that only fueled aspirations on both sides for a knockout blow to end it all.

Following in chronological order are the ten most prominent political, economic, and military events in the months leading up to the clash at Gettysburg. Viewed in this dark light, the battle truly appears to be more of a mutual low point than a glorious high tide, when desperate times mandated a most desperate measure.

1.   THE BATTLE OF FREDERICKSBURG (DECEMBER 13, 1862)

Newly appointed head of the Army of the Potomac was bright, humble, honest Maj. Gen. Ambrose E. Burnside. Gone for lack of aggression was the beloved Maj. Gen. George B. McClellan. Looking to validate Lincoln's unsolicited faith in him, Burnside aspired to deliver a quick blow upon the doggedly persistent Army of Northern Virginia and, with luck, end the war by Christmas.

By early December Burnside prepared to cross the Rappahannock River—the dividing line between Union- and Confederate-held territory. He envisioned a sprint through the city of Fredericksburg, after which he could wedge his troops between the Army of Northern Virginia and their capital. But a critical delay doomed the scheme. Pontoon boats, necessary for traversing the icy flows of the wide river, arrived more than a week late, allowing Robert E. Lee and sixty thousand soldiers plenty of time to dig in and wait for Burnside's "surprise" attack.

On December 11 the Federals finally crossed the river into largely deserted Fredericksburg. On their right wing loomed Marye's Heights, a wide and steep ridge, upon which stood battery after Confederate battery, each one capable of hitting any target that dared present itself on the open acres below. A half-mile stone wall skirted the hill's base, sheltering rows of infantry. Burnside correctly surmised this would be the last place his adversary would expect him to attack, so he foolishly did. Wave after wave, Federal brigades moved forward. None came closer than a hundred yards to the wall. Gales of rifle fire and artillery washed away their advance.

The picturesque river city of Fredericksburg was the setting of the second bloodiest day in American military history.

LIBRARY OF CONGRESS

In the hills and woods south of Marye's Heights, the Union scored a fleeting breakthrough, led by a division under Maj. Gen. GEORGE GORDON MEADE. Overestimating this small success on his left flank, Burnside threw still more men at Marye's Heights on his right, firmly convinced he was on the verge of victory.

The piling bodies of Union infantry spoke otherwise. Not until thousands had died and several officers begged an end to the sacrifice did Burnside halt the offensive. Enraged by his own failure, tears running down his face, the shattered general swore to lead one last charge himself, until subordinates forcibly detained him.

Union dead and wounded exceeded thirteen thousand, outnumbering Confederate losses nearly three to one, making Fredericksburg one of the most lopsided battles in the entire war. Federal soldiers blamed their government, their officers, and Burnside. Their commander in turn tried to sack four reluctant generals and stated a willingness to hang their suspected ringleader, Joseph "Fighting Joe" Hooker. In the North, rumors claimed that Lincoln's entire cabinet would resign, and perhaps the president as well. The normally patriotic *Chicago Tribune* wondered whether "nothing is left now but to fight for a boundary." The tragic litany prompted Lincoln to say, "If there is a worst place than Hell, I am in it."[1]

Robert E. Lee knew the Fredericksburg area intimately. Years before the battle, he had courted the young, wealthy, and beautiful Mary Custis at nearby Chatham Manor.

---

2. EMANCIPATION PROCLAMATION (JANUARY 1, 1863)

The war clearly demonstrated that the country was less a melting pot and more a bubbling cauldron, stoked in large part by lingering issues of race. Often set apart and whitewashed, the Gettysburg campaign was no exception.

In 1863 Maryland contained nearly 90,000 slaves. The Old Line State also contained 80,000 free blacks, and its neighbor Pennsylvania was home to 60,000, the first and second highest populations of free blacks North and South. Gettysburg alone contained nearly 190 African Americans, about 8 percent of its inhabitants. Some residents were former slaves, including Clem Johnson, who in his youth was the property of one

In July 1862, Lincoln announces his plan to free the slaves, a radical shift in policy. Most agree, but William Seward (seated center-right) counsels that the Union must first win a major military engagement before the pronouncement should be made.

LIBRARY OF CONGRESS

Francis Scott Key. Frederick Douglass had spoken here, and militant John Brown attempted to recruit area residents for his doomed 1859 raid on Harpers Ferry. Also, the town had likely been a stop on the Underground Railroad.[2]

While little is known of how Gettysburg's "citizens of color" responded to Lincoln's Emancipation Proclamation when it went into effect New Year's Day, 1863, other groups eagerly voiced judgment. Copperheads and hard-line Confederates viewed the decree as proof that the war was "an abolitionist conspiracy." In turn, the small but growing abolitionist camp in the North, including Union Gens. Oliver O. Howard and Carl Schurz, saw Lincoln's act as an all-important first step toward attaining the moral high ground.

Many Union soldiers found no comfort in adding yet another dimension to an already complicated war. Desertions rose. Whole regiments threatened mutiny. A member of the 9th New York fumed, "We thought we were fighting for the stars and stripes, but we find out it is for the d— n[—]." Another soldier in the 15th New Jersey observed with dejection, "I never before seen so much discontent in the army."[3]

While the North wrestled for months with the task of freeing slaves in Confederate-held territory, the South brought the slavery issue to the North, compliments of Lee's Pennsylvania raid. The Army of Northern Virginia brought with it thousands of bondsmen who gathered supplies, cooked meals, drove wagons, and performed general labor. Evidently, scores of African Americas living in the North were captured and taken south. Whether this was done by direct order has never been determined, but on June 18, 1863, Maj. Charles Blacknall of the 23rd North Carolina wrote of gathering blacks "for southern exportation." In a July 1 dispatch, JAMES LONGSTREET informed division commander GEORGE E. PICKETT, "The captured contraband [i.e., blacks] had better be brought along with you for further disposition."[4]

James Getty, founder of the borough that bears his name, was a slave owner.

3. THE FIRST UNION DRAFT (MARCH 3, 1863)

By 1862 both sides experienced military losses far beyond their most fatalistic estimations. The April battle of Shiloh brought the first harsh lesson, producing twenty thousand dead and wounded, five times worse than the losses of First Manassas. Larger and deadlier contests followed. Costlier still were the year-round diminutions of expiring enlistments, desertions, dysentery, malaria, pneumonia, and typhoid.

To reduce the effusion, the Richmond Congress enacted in April 1862 the first draft in American history. Their Washington counterparts long assumed that no such draconian device would ever be needed in the North, as its largely free population contained nearly four times the white males of military age as the South. But by March 1863, the Republican Congress also recognized that the Union was hemorrhaging, and enacted its own conscription in hopes of finding new blood. The operation proved exceedingly unpopular.

When the law went into effect in July 1863, violence erupted in cities across the North. Crowds of mostly poor, young, foreign-born males

Names are drawn for the draft in New York City, calling forth the first wave of conscripts and prompting a backlash of widespread violence.

LIBRARY OF CONGRESS

ransacked draft offices and harassed conscription agents. Lives were lost. Corruption and evasion flourished. Over time Union conscription netted only forty-six thousand of more than seven hundred thousand eligible. The rest paid commutation fees of three hundred dollars, found substitutes, were given exemption, or simply went into hiding. The draft did coerce thousands to volunteer, landing them lucrative cash bounties in the process and allowing the Union to maintain a numerical advantage at places like Antietam, Chancellorsville, and Gettysburg.[5]

> Ulysses S. Grant, Rutherford B. Hayes, James Garfield, and William McKinley all volunteered and served in the Union army. Another future president, Grover Cleveland, was drafted and hired a substitute.

4. BREAD RIOTS IN THE SOUTH (APRIL 1863)

The leanest months were always springtime, a.k.a. the "starving season," when harvests of the preceding year were nearing depletion. For Southerners, war exacerbated the problem thoroughly. Invading armies trampled crops, disintegrated rail lines, devoured draft animals, and generally disrupted every link between farmers and the famished. Worst hit were the cities, as swarms of refugees distended their prewar populations beyond critical mass. In two years, Richmond alone ballooned from forty thousand to one hundred thousand inhabitants.

Inflation outpaced population. From 1861 to 1863, the cost of wheat tripled while milk and butter quadrupled. Salt, the age's only practical meat preservative, could hardly be found at any price. For many families of modest means, food bills soon consumed every penny they made.[6]

Reminiscent of the French Revolution, women began to protest the exorbitant price of bread. They believed a negligent government and hoarding merchants were to blame, and to enunciate their displeasure, many of the "fairer sex" turned to violence. In Macon, Augusta, and Atlanta, armed mobs attacked warehouses and shops. Salisbury, North Carolina, witnessed the destruction of grocery and dry goods stores as well as jewelry and clothing shops. In the Confederate capital a small peaceful protest grew into a gang of several thousand women, men, and children, who subsequently let loose on ten square blocks of the commercial district. The local militia, the mayor, the governor, and President Jefferson Davis himself begged the crowd to disperse, with no success. Only when Davis ordered militiamen to line up and load their weapons did the rioters desist.[7]

Protesters in Mobile, Alabama, were succinct in their demands. They carried signs that read simply, "Bread or Blood."

---

5. CONFEDERATE CONGRESS PASSES TAX-IN-KIND (APRIL 24, 1863)

Though 98 percent of Confederate congressmen owned slaves, and 90 percent of Confederate soldiers did not, all could rally around the war cry of "states' rights." Powerful was the provincial draw, with its notion of local rule for local interests. Central governments, so the states' rights message went, were prone to becoming tyrannical and therefore could never be trusted.

However strong this ideological kinship, the legislature had to face economic reality. Growing inflation and shrinking revenues threatened to implode the war effort. To keep the ship of state afloat, Richmond abruptly and perhaps insensitively imposed a broad taxation program in the spring of 1863.

Southern citizens, for the first time in their lives, had to pay a national income tax. Any purchase of food, cloth, iron, or alcohol would include a 10 percent sales tax. Like the hated Stamp Tax preceding the American Revolution, the plan also imposed fees on professional licenses of every variety.

Worst of the lot was the "Tax-in-Kind" authorizing the government to seize 10 percent of all agricultural crops and livestock. Designed to resolve food and supply shortages, the levy merely intensified the crisis. Three thousand government collection agents scoured the countryside, arbitrarily determining what constituted 10 percent of a family's animals and crops. To defend themselves, farmers hid their harvests or sold them on the black market. Much of what was confiscated never reached intended recipients, as bureaucratic backlogs and fragile transport systems left untold tons of corn, cotton, bacon, and beef to rot in depots.

As supplies decreased and more farmland was lost to occupation, a Confederate general began to formulate his own tax-in-kind program, designed to collect grain and livestock from Pennsylvania. The South's political elite, under heavy pressure to reduce levies at home, proved receptive to the officer's plan.[8]

Under strict interpretation of Confederate law, the tax-in-kind measure was almost certainly unconstitutional.

---

6. THE BATTLE OF CHANCELLORSVILLE (MAY 1–4, 1863)

"May God have mercy on General Lee, for I will have none." Hooker's boast appeared to have some credence in late April, when he instigated a rather brilliant strategy against an opponent he outnumbered two to one. Feigning an attack at Fredericksburg with a sizable force of forty thousand, he sent seventy thousand far upstream along the Rappahannock to swoop down on Lee's flank—a hard left jab followed by a deadly right hook. In Hooker's view, "Our enemy must ingloriously fly, or come out from behind his defenses and give us battle on our own ground, where certain destruction awaits him."[9]

It was all quite logical, and by all odds the engagement should have transpired as predicted. Yet in an inspired and desperate move to counter the Union assaults, Lee divided his greatly outnumbered force in half, blunting the advance at Fredericksburg with ten thousand men under JUBAL A. EARLY and hitting Hooker's main force with fewer than fifty thousand men.

Shocked by Lee's surprising audacity, Hooker mysteriously and submissively withdrew to the "safety" of a crossroads near the Chancellor house, an area shrouded by thick woodlands known ominously as the

JOHN ESTEN COOK, A LIFE OF GEN. ROBERT E. LEE (1871)

Some historians consider Chancellorsville to the be high tide of the Confederacy, when Lee was at his best and Jackson was still among the living.

Wilderness. Hooker could have attacked anywhere and broken the Confederate spine. Suddenly lacking one himself, he waited for Lee to move again. It was his undoing.

After conferencing with Thomas J. "Stonewall" Jackson on the night of May 1, Lee decided to divide his strength once more, sending Jackson and thirty thousand on a rapid twelve-mile end run around the Union right. Shortly after 5 p.m. on May 2, 1863, the Confederate 2nd Corps burst from the Wilderness and sent thousands of Federals reeling back on themselves. Only nightfall stemmed the surging gray tide.

On May 3 the Confederates renewed the attack, digging their talons into the right and left flanks of the blunted Union spearhead and beginning to pinch off two entire corps. Viewing his position as untenable, Hooker quickly withdrew his forces northwest, from whence they came, handing the South a most unexpected albeit inconclusive victory.

> Had all troops on the Union side been engaged, Chancellorsville and not Gettysburg would have been the largest battle ever in the Western Hemisphere, yet Hooker failed to utilize nearly a third of his men.

7. THE DEATH OF STONEWALL JACKSON (MAY 10, 1863)

As Lee vexed over what might have been at Chancellorsville, one incident in particular caused him immeasurable grief. While conducting reconnaissance on the night of May 2, Thomas Jackson rode back toward his lines with other members of his staff, and a wave of friendly fire crashed into them. Two men died outright. The hail of bullets also struck Jackson's

An operatic rendition of a fatal accident. Jackson's mortal wounding verified the great risks of night combat—especially for commanding officers.

LIBRARY OF CONGRESS

right hand and shattered his left arm at the elbow. Early the next morning the crushed limb was amputated.

Weakened from loss of blood and the operation, Jackson was brought to a plantation near Guinea Station, Virginia, to recuperate in peace. On May 7 his wife, Anna, arrived from Richmond, along with their infant daughter, Julia. Though heartened by their arrival, the patient soon became nauseous, feverish, and feeble, his face appeared drawn and sunken, his pulse turned erratic—telltale signs of pneumonia.

Treated today with antibiotics, there was no known cure in the nineteenth century. Inflammation of the lungs claimed thirty-seven thousand soldiers during the war, and Jackson was about to become one of them. The general's attending physician, Dr. Hunter McGuire, had seen the malady's lethal performance countless times before, and he knew when death was imminent. Shortly after noon on Sunday, May 10, Jackson was informed that he had two hours left. "Thank God," whispered the general, "my wish is fulfilled. I have always desired to die on a Sunday." Ninety minutes later he slipped into hallucinations, began to relive moments of past battles, and passed away.[10]

Lee once said of him: "Such an executive officer the sun never shown on. I have but to show him my design, and I know that if it can be done, it will be done." Virtually unknown to each other before the war, the two men quickly established a rapport. Jackson became in time Lee's "right arm," his confidant, and perhaps the only subordinate who could correct Marse Robert and be heard. An Old Testament zealot, Stonewall pushed mortals to superhuman marches of thirty miles a day on half rations. Brutally aggressive, he also knew when to fight on the defensive, all elements that might have served Lee well in Pennsylvania.[11]

Devastated by the loss, Lee surmised that his corps were too big for anyone but Jackson to handle. At thirty thousand men each, they were nearly three times as large as a corps in blue. He resolved to turn his two columns into three, keeping JAMES LONGSTREET at the head of the 1st Corps. The other two would go to RICHARD S. EWELL and A. P. HILL, neither of which had led a unit of such size.

As Jackson's body lay in state at the Confederate Capital, more than twenty thousand people came to pay their last respects. The number would have been even higher had Lee permitted front-line troops to attend.

---

8. LEE STARTS HIS CAMPAIGN (JUNE 3, 1863)

The Army of Northern Virginia was in motion a month before Gettysburg proper. In that time Lee's veterans tangled with portions of the Army of the Potomac in no fewer than two battles, three heavy actions, and thirty-eight separate skirmishes. Eleven recorded skirmishes occurred in Pennsylvania alone.

In the early going, Union authorities were largely in the dark as to Lee's intentions. Confederate-held Fredericksburg seemed quieter than normal. When Hooker received word that thousands of mounted Confederates were collecting near Brandy Station twenty-five miles northwest of Fredericksburg, he surmised it was the spearhead of an eastward offensive. Hooker immediately amassed nearly all of his own cavalry, more than seven thousand troopers, plus three thousand of his best foot soldiers. He sent them forward with the explicit order to "disperse and destroy." It marked the first and only offensive Hooker launched against his adversary during Lee's invasion.[12]

At 4 a.m. on June 9, two great columns of Union horsemen came roaring into JAMES EWELL BROWN "JEB" STUART's encampment and caught his ten thousand men completely off guard. To stem the rush, many of Stuart's men rode into battle without saddles, shirts, and in some cases pants. After nearly twelve hours of a long and intense battle, with surprisingly few casualties, the contest ended in a draw. Brandy Station fully embarrassed the otherwise attentive Stuart and gave Federal horsemen their first taste of success against the previously feared Rebel cavalry.

Jeb Stuart was caught unawares at Brandy Station. Just the day before, his horsemen performed a mock battle on the same ground for a crowd of delighted civilians and dignitaries.

HARPER'S WEEKLY

Brandy Station also revealed that Lee was on the move. Days later, his infantry retook the north Virginia city of Winchester plus 4,000 Union prisoners. Lincoln rightly suspected imminent invasion and called out 100,000 state militia from Pennsylvania, West Virginia, Ohio, and Maryland, to remain activated for six months.[13]

June 17 brought news of Confederates crossing the Potomac into Maryland. Somehow, Hooker hypothesized something other than an invasion was taking place. "Has it ever suggested itself to you," the general telegraphed Washington, "that this cavalry raid may be a cover to Lee's re-enforcing [Braxton] Bragg or moving troops to the West?" Hooker had made a similar assessment right before his implosion at Chancellorsville, where he construed Jackson's wide left flanking maneuver as a wholesale retreat.[14]

While the general pondered, Union civilians panicked. From Pittsburgh to Philadelphia, roads clogged with bankers toting bags of money, farmers driving livestock, white and black families pushing cartloads of belongings. Not a few cursed the White House for leaving them defenseless as wild rumors and a very real invasion metastasized northward.

By June 26 the bulk of Lee's army had crossed the Potomac and were well into Pennsylvania. Points of his columns were nearing the state capital of Harrisburg, forty miles northeast of the town of Gettysburg and two hundred miles from where they had started near Fredericksburg.

With combined forces of seventeen thousand horsemen, the battle of Brandy Station was and remains the largest cavalry conflict ever fought in North America. Currently, the only posterity of its location is a single historical marker posted along U.S. Highway 15.

---

9. THE OUSTING OF HOOKER (JUNE 27–28, 1863)

 Time and again Hooker refused to move with haste until he received reliable intelligence from Washington. Time and again Lincoln and General in Chief Henry W. Halleck reminded him that he was closer to Lee than they were. But Fighting Joe held to caution like a drunk to a bottle. "It must be borne in mind," he telegraphed Washington on June 26, "that

I am here with a force inferior in numbers to that of the enemy." In truth Hooker outnumbered his foe by at least twelve thousand.[15]

The last straw fell over Harpers Ferry, the Federal arsenal tucked into the deep valley confluence of the Shenandoah and Potomac rivers. In Hooker's view, its garrison of four thousand troops was a sitting duck, better to be added to his mobile force than left to capture or annihilation. Both Lincoln and Halleck denied the request, unwilling to give ground without a fight. The following day Hooker shot back, "I beg to be understood, respectfully, but firmly, that I am unable to comply with this condition with the means at my disposal, and earnestly request that I may at once be relieved from the position I occupy."[16]

Lincoln's response was quick and to the point: "By direction of the President, Maj. Gen. Joseph Hooker is relieved from command of the Army of the Potomac, and Maj. Gen. George G. Meade is appointed to the command of that army, and of the troops temporarily assigned to duty with it."[17]

Meade received the appointment because he was highly recommended by fellow officers, some of whom outranked him. He was also a resident of Pennsylvania and would likely be motivated to fight well on home soil. An additional factor may have influenced Lincoln's decision, one highlighted by the *New York Times:* "We may all feel devoutly thankful. He was born in *Spain,* and consequently, is not eligible for the office of President of the United States. . . . There is no danger, that the approaching campaign will be political as well as military."[18]

Meade learned of his "promotion" at 3 a.m. on June 28. Col. James A. Hardie of the War Department found Meade asleep in his tent near Frederick, Maryland. Stirred awake, his head in a fog, Meade initially believed he was being arrested, perhaps for being falsely accused of conspiring against Hooker. Hearing instead that he had been named head of the Army of the Potomac seemed only slightly less troubling, for he never wanted the position. In a letter to his wife, Meade surmised, "I've been tried and condemned without a hearing, and I suppose I shall have to go to the execution."[19]

Among the generals rumored to be Hooker's replacement were Winfield Scott Hancock, George B. McClellan, John F. Reynolds, William S. Rosecrans, John Sedgwick, and Daniel E. Sickles.

---

10. THE HARRISON REPORT (JUNE 28, 1863)

The early stages of their Pennsylvania march were halcyon days for the soldiers of the South—plenty of fresh wells, ripe fruit trees, and fat farm hogs upon which to feast. The only nuisances seemed to be sore feet and a few pockets of easily intimidated militia. For their commander, invasion was a different experience altogether. His eyes and ears—Jeb Stuart's cavalry—were missing in action.

Normally the embodiment of composure, Lee frayed into agitation. The Federals were probably still nibbling at the bait of Fredericksburg, but without Stuart, he could not be sure. His lumbering infantry continued to spread across the soft underbelly of Pennsylvania, steadily advancing, yet increasingly vulnerable. "Preparations were now made to advance upon Harrisburg," Lee wrote to Richmond, "but, on the night of the 28th, information was received from a scout."[20]

The man in question was one dust-covered and exhausted HENRY THOMAS HARRISON. Lee had never before met nor heard of him, yet the spy came compliments of JAMES LONGSTREET, who had known the man since the siege of Suffolk, Virginia, earlier in the year. Longstreet's chief of staff said with confidence that Harrison "always brought us true information."[21]

Evidently, the news Lee heard that night was plausible enough to halt his entire army. Harrison reported that the Army of the Potomac had left Fredericksburg and was advancing steadily northward, which was indeed true. He also stated, incorrectly, that "the head of the column had reached the South Mountain."[22]

South Mountain was the last link of the Appalachians, Lee's cloak and protector on the march northward. His army had by that time sifted through its narrow passes and was well east of its protective peaks. Believing Harrison's report to be fully accurate, and working without the aid of Stuart's cavalry, Lee felt compelled to drastically alter his course. Believing his line of retreat was in danger, he did not dare advance any farther. Yet to order a sudden withdrawal might incite panic among his widely scattered troops.[23]

The commander quickly sent couriers into the night, telling all his forces to converge on Gettysburg. He also stated a desire to avoid a general engagement. After hearing the disturbing news from this mysterious spy, Lee later insisted, "A battle thus became, in a measure, unavoidable."[24]

To maintain the loyalty of his prized spy, Longstreet routinely paid Harrison
in U.S. gold coins and greenbacks.

TOP TEN REASONS WHY THE SOUTH
INVADED PENNSYLVANIA

On May 15, 1863, Lee came to Richmond from the Chancellorsville area
to confer with Jefferson Davis on future strategies. Though pleased to see
each other, neither man was feeling well. Davis continually struggled with
clinical depression and blinding neuralgia. Lee had probably suffered a
mild heart attack during the Chancellorsville campaign, for he was beginning to feel a perpetual shortness of breath and a gradual lowering of
stamina. Without question, both men were still mourning the loss of their
mutual friend, the irreplaceable Stonewall Jackson.

Ailing though they were, Davis and Lee both knew that the Confederacy was slowly but surely turning blue. As the two sat down in the
Confederate White House to discuss options with Secretary of War
James A. Seddon, Lee proposed an aggressive if not radical operation.
He would again cut northward with his army, this time pushing deep
into lush and expansive Pennsylvania. The general had been contemplating the maneuver since February, when he secretly asked Jackson's
chief engineer to create a detailed map of the state's southern reaches,
including Philadelphia and the capital, Harrisburg. Davis and Seddon
expressed reservations but agreed to discuss the idea with the cabinet
the following day.[25]

All who attended the daylong meeting responded with trepidation.
They had heard many justifications for the offensive but few specifics. By
nightfall the weary cabinet granted tacit approval.

Following are the primary reasons why the Confederate high command consented to a Pennsylvania offensive. As events unfolded, it was
evident no one had any idea what was about to transpire. On July 1, 1863,
the *New York Times* predicted that a clash would occur at Shippensburg,
whereas Lee's advanced columns envisioned a pitched battle outside
Philadelphia. Just before contact, Gettysburg resident SARAH BROADHEAD
wrote in her diary that a great confrontation was probable, but she added,
"There is no telling where it will be."[26]

1. THE SIEGE OF VICKSBURG

In early 1863, of all the Confederacy's troubled waters, the mighty Mississippi was most in jeopardy. All but two hundred miles of its length was back in Federal hands, and its last firm holdout was under attack from all sides. Perched upon high bluffs on a tight bend, standing guard over the Father of Waters, the town of Vicksburg was what Jefferson Davis called the "nailhead that [holds] the South's two halves together." For months Union armies and gunboats had clawed at the nailhead with no measurable success. Then the iron began to give way.[27]

As defiant Vicksburg residents attended a gala ball on a moonlit April night, their festivities came to a crashing halt when Federal gunboats made the first successful run downriver past the city, with heavy deck guns blazing. Soon after, news arrived of a Union cavalry force of unknown size barreling down from Mississippi's northern border and making fifty miles a day. Clouds darkened further when, weeks later, divisions of infantry under Ulysses S. Grant floated across from Louisiana, landed south of the citadel, and began to move inland.[28]

Awaiting this combined force of more than sixty thousand was a main garrison of just over thirty thousand poorly equipped and feebly led Confederates. A relief party was already on its way, but it totaled perhaps seven thousand. Leading them slowly westward was stoic Gen. Joseph E. Johnston, whom Jefferson Davis viewed as the most vain and least aggressive of his chieftains.

The consensus in Richmond was that Vicksburg could not hold out, not without help from Lee. Yet when asked, Lee refused to ship as much

For forty-seven days Union troops laid siege to the defenses of Vicksburg. For his part, Lee insisted the only way to save the citadel was to attack the North in kind.

LIBRARY OF CONGRESS

as a company to the West, citing distance and the insecure patchwork of the Southern rail system as too precarious. Any troops dispatched, he claimed, would arrive too late and too few in number to make a difference. He added that the Confederacy had enough troops to protect either the southwest around Vicksburg or the southeast around Chattanooga, but not both. The only way to rescue the South, at that point, Lee reasoned, was to push north, threaten the Union's vitals, and force Grant into the transfer game.[29]

The Confederate commander at Vicksburg was Maj. Gen. John C. Pemberton. Though trusted by Jefferson Davis, Pemberton had a difficult time instilling confidence in others, largely because he had limited combat experience, and he was born and raised in Pennsylvania.

---

2.   LEE'S VIRGINIA FIXATION

In the Confederate cabinet, the only Virginian was Secretary of War James A. Seddon, and he initially championed the idea of sending part of Lee's army to Vicksburg. Yet Lee eventually convinced Seddon and most of the cabinet that a Virginia-based offensive was the quickest option available, and it had the most potential. The one dissenting vote came from Postmaster General John H. Reagan, who suspected that Lee, in focusing so heavily on one piece of the puzzle, was using something other than logic.

Lee had a history of positioning his home state above all others. Since 1862 he had bolstered Old Dominion's defenses by plucking troops from endangered South Carolina and Georgia. By May 1863 his "Army of Northern Virginia" (a title he imposed) contained regiments from every state in the Confederacy, and the general busied himself with packing in even more troops from outside. When Mississippi was invaded and Vicksburg besieged, Lee refused to release any of his Mississippi soldiers, including a battery, a cavalry squadron, and eleven infantry regiments. Ten days into his march northward, he wrote his war department and all but demanded cavalry from Georgia and Alabama and insisted on bringing all available North Carolina forces up into Virginia to protect Richmond. His president once asked him where the next line of defense should be if Richmond were lost. He responded that there would be no other line.[30]

Lee could say that by fighting for his home, he was also defending the Confederacy's most industrialized, wealthiest, and most populous state (in both slaves and free citizens). Certainly he was also protecting the South's national capital and preoccupying Union forces that would otherwise have attacked elsewhere. Yet by all indications, in both word and deed, Lee never seriously considered his "country" as anything other than Virginia.

His excuses for neglecting other regions were weak at best. Vicksburg was supposedly too far away to send troops, yet in the same breath he demanded reinforcements from Florida and Texas.[31] He assured his colleagues that the annual yellow fever outbreaks in the Deep South would keep the Federals at bay, while saying Richmond was all but doomed unless he received every battery and regiment he requested. As for Vicksburg, he claimed that a summer campaign in sweltering Mississippi was physically impossible for troops from the colder North, but at the same time he argued that a prolonged campaign in the North for his threadbare Southern troops was perfectly feasible.[32]

No matter the flaws of his arguments, with the passing of Stonewall Jackson and Albert Sidney Johnston before him, Lee had become the last great leader of the Confederate warrior class. Davis and his staff had grown to trust anything the general said, and this faith had become virtually boundless after Chancellorsville.[33]

Though remembered as a man of his word, Robert E. Lee accepted a generalship in the Confederate army not five weeks after he renewed an oath of allegiance to the United States.

---

3. "CHANCELLORSVILLE FEVER"

Every Confederate victory brought a surge of devotion in the Southern cause, but the miracle of Chancellorsville converted even the most skeptical. Emphatically outnumbered, under attack, and with no prospect of escape, Lee devised and his troops executed a most daring and complex battle plan—and prevailed. Normally averse to exaggeration, and personally regarding the victory as unfinished business, Lee displayed a growing sense of invincibility in his troops as well as himself. "There never were such men in an army before," he surmised. "They will go anywhere and do anything if properly led."[34]

Subordinates agreed. They bragged of being able to march twice as fast and fight twice as hard on half the rations and half the pay of Northern "shop keeps" and "scallywags." A Georgian in gray proclaimed: "This is the best army in the world. We are all satisfied with Gen. Lee and he is always ready for a fight." Young artillery Col. E. Porter Alexander admitted in late June, "We looked forward to victory under him as confidently as to successive sunrises."[35]

Lee knew this bounty was perishable. His army was approaching its apex while his opponent was suffering an intense bout of indecision. Armed with vastly superior morale, the commander refused any notion of staying on the defensive, as his top lieutenant JAMES LONGSTREET suggested. Success in the past had come to Lee because he knew precisely when to strike. He would come to rely on that gift one more time in an attempt to determine the future.

When hearing the news of Chancellorsville, Republican Senator Charles Sumner exclaimed, "Lost, lost, all is lost!"

---

4. THE WANT OF A DECISIVE BATTLE

History celebrates Chancellorsville as Lee's masterpiece, but the artist himself believed otherwise. As his countrymen celebrated, Lee admitted, "I on the contrary, was more depressed. . . . Our loss was severe, and again we had gained not an inch of ground and the enemy could not be pursued." The general tempered other triumphs with the same frustration. Wins he had achieved. It was a knockout blow he needed.[36]

The outlook does much to explain why he chose to go on the offensive. Victories such as Fredericksburg, won almost totally on the defensive, did nothing to push the Union from his beloved Virginia, which was suffering through a plurality of the war's military engagements. A week into his march, Lee told Seddon that any defensive stand could only end in "catastrophe."[37]

Maj. Gen. Isaac R. Trimble, who was fated to lose a leg, his freedom, and much of a division in Pickett's Charge, recalled a conversation he had with the general when they were moving through Pennsylvania. When hearing that the Army of the Potomac was in pursuit, Lee reportedly said: "I shall throw an overwhelming force on their advance, crush it . . . and virtually destroy the army. . . . And if God gives us victory, the war will be over and we shall achieve the recognition of our independence."[38]

Lee's wartime record on the attack: five wins, eleven losses.

Lee's wartime record on the defensive: fourteen wins, eight losses.

---

5. THE RAPPAHANNOCK STALEMATE

Midway between Richmond and Washington, the Rappahannock River functioned as a dividing line. It was what one Confederate soldier called the "Dare Mark." From Fredericksburg onward, every major contest in the eastern theater transpired within twenty miles of its banks. One-fifth of a million men spent seven months either staring down or shooting at each other across this previously tranquil vein. After Lee's victory at Chancellorsville, this mark was beginning to look permanent.[39]

In pushing "On to Richmond," a visibly ineffective Army of the Potomac had advanced barely forty-five miles in two years, losing battles with pathetic frequency. Their effort had cost them one hundred thousand men killed, wounded, captured, or missing—literally one casualty for every two feet of "progress."

Likewise, Lee concluded that waiting along the Rappahannock gained the Confederacy nothing. The eastern fifth of the state, including Lee's Arlington home, was firmly under Federal control. Hundreds of costly engagements had wrested not a league of it back. The wide Rappahannock protected the Army of the Potomac as much as it did the Army of Northern Virginia.

Once more, during the protracted stalemate, the North's immensely superior industry, economy, and population truly started to mobilize, like some colossal engine slowly churning up to speed. Lee feared that it would only be a matter of time before sheer mass, and not terrain or élan, would decide battles. In troop strength alone, Federals outnumbered Lee's men by fifteen thousand at Second Manassas, thirty thousand at Antietam, forty thousand at Fredericksburg, and sixty thousand at Chancellorsville. In writing to his president, Lee insisted, "We should not, therefore, conceal from ourselves that our resources in men are constantly diminishing, and the disproportion in this respect between us and our enemies, if they continue united in their efforts to subjugate us, is steadily augmenting."[40]

In late May, while standing in Fredericksburg and observing the Federal army milling about on the opposite side of the river, Marse Robert confessed, "I wish I could get at those people over there." Days later, the high command granted the general's wish, agreeing that Lee could neither outlast Joe Hooker nor cross the Rappahannock and attack him. Thus, "it was determined," said Lee, to "draw him from it [and] transfer of the scene of hostilities north of the Potomac."[41]

The National Cemetery at Fredericksburg contains more than fifteen thousand graves, which is 50 percent more than the U.S. Military Cemetery overlooking Omaha Beach in France.

---

6. A SHORTAGE OF FOOD

When marching toward a group of tentative Pennsylvanians, a column of Louisiana infantry explained the reason for their visit: "We had Eat up the last mule we had and had come over to get some beef & bacon."[42]

Lee's men were certainly a lean force, described as "gaunt" by Northern observers. Seemingly everything conspired to keep a Confederate's belly empty. Federals occupied the breadbasket of the Shenandoah, and thus Virginia wheat production was down 50 percent from 1861. Lost to the Union were most of Kentucky and Tennessee and, with them, large supplies of pork and grain. Mississippi and Georgia had plenty of corn, but the few connecting rail lines were hauling guns before butter. The Federal naval blockade was starting to work its black magic, while Union infantry regiments were raiding the coastal areas of the Palmetto State. Nothing compared to the loss of the South's principle trading partner—the North. Wheat, oats, milk cows, mutton, barley, and salt were North-dominated commodities.[43]

Such was a main motivation for "reentering the Union." Lee's army was in danger of starving to death. Thin rations caused an increase in illnesses, exhaustion, night blindness, and worst of all, desertions. So too the cities of the South were running out of provisions and patience, as illustrated by the number of BREAD RIOTS sprouting up in every major urban center.

The march was to produce, with luck and hard work, more than just an opportunity to eat through the Keystone State. Surplus was the goal.

Though they knew a long train meant slower progress, the advancing army brought along hundreds of empty wagons in anticipation of a big haul, and they were not disappointed. Pennsylvania awed one Confederate soldier in particular: "I have never yet seen any country in such a high state of cultivation. Such wheat I never dreamed of, and so much of it." Pvt. John C. West of the 4th Texas echoed the sentiment: "Apples, cherries, currants, pears, quinces, etc., in the utmost profusion, and beehives *ad infinitum*. The barns were, however, the most striking feature of the landscape, for it was one bright panorama for miles."[44]

In addressing the issue of scarcity, Lee also revealed that he was quite interested in a prolonged stay in the North, if feasible. Among his stated goals was a desire to see the farmers of Virginia have enough time and serenity to grow and harvest what they had planted.[45]

> When a Northern woman chastised Lt. Gen. James Longstreet for letting his troops confiscate everything in sight, Longstreet responded, "Yes, madam, it's very sad—very sad; and this sort of thing has been going on in Virginia more than two years—very sad."

7. A SHORTAGE OF SUPPLIES

More than its reliance on Northern farmers for food, the South had been utterly dependent on Northern factories for almost everything else. This patent craving was a major reason why the great split occurred in the first place. Planters were beginning to feel at the whim and mercy of mighty industrialists up yonder. It was a somewhat reasonable phobia. The Singers, McCormicks, Morses, and Colts, plus the Rothschilds and Vanderbilts that financed them, operated almost exclusively above the Mason-Dixon Line. Northern states produced 95 percent of the country's steel, 97 percent of its boots and shoes, and 98 percent of its weapons, leaving the cash-poor South wondering if it could ever be anything beyond the North's most needy customer.[46]

Separation only exacerbated the South's industrial impotence through internal shortages, crippling inflation, and a tightening Union embargo by land and sea. Lee reasoned, and the high command agreed, that a large raid was a good way to assuage the weakness. Confronting the Union head on certainly had paid off in the past. Pushing the Army of the Potomac away from Richmond in the Seven Days' battles had netted some thirty thousand shoulder arms, Second Manassas brought twenty thousand, and Fredericksburg added nine thousand more. The majority of Confederate cannons were formerly owned by Federal batteries and forts.[47]

Invasion provided the chance to collect not only weapons but also anything of industrial or military value, including boots, lead, lathes, medicines, cloth, tents, and wagons. Failing that, the troops could at least destroy this otherwise undisturbed wealth the North held in abundance.

In 1863, Pennsylvania produced twice as much in manufactured goods as every state in the Confederacy combined.

8. THE PEACE DEMOCRATS

A week into his march northward, Lee wrote to Jefferson Davis, "We should neglect no honorable means of dividing and weakening our enemies, that they may feel some of the difficulties experienced by ourselves. It seems to me that the most effectual mode of accomplishing this object, now within our reach, is to give all the encouragement we can, consistently with the truth, to the rising peace party in the North."[48]

The general was referring to a broad spectrum of citizenry—anti-abolitionists, pacifists, Confederate sympathizers, but mostly "Peace Democrats," a growing faction within the country's oldest party. They called themselves copperheads for the copper "Liberty head" pennies they wore upon their lapels. Their detractors thought the name fit, because it reminded them of the venomous serpent.

Even the most patriotic Northerners began to question a war that was costing an average of two hundred lives a day, and that rate was climbing. Heartbreaking accounts of corrupt contractors, widowed mothers, camp epidemics, and military defeats, on top of a new invention called the Internal Revenue Service, did nothing to stem the mounting anguish. From the East Coast to Iowa, peace campaigners grew in decibels. A rally in New York City drew thousands of marchers. Dissent, it appeared, was reaching a hide tide.[49]

While raising the Confederate flag over York, Pennsylvania, Maj. Gen. JUBAL A. EARLY fomented this groundswell, telling his captive audience, "We do not war upon women and children, and I trust the treatment you have met with at the hands of my soldiers will open your eyes to the monstrous iniquity of the war waged by your government upon the people of the Confederate States, and that you will make an effort to shake off the revolting tyranny under which it is apparent to you are yourselves groaning."[50]

However hopeful Early and Lee may have been to promote the gospel of the Peace Democrats, the invasion almost immediately produced the opposite effect. The normally objective *New York Times* calculated: "Whatever else Gen. Lee may achieve, one thing is certain—if he keeps on, he is bound to make an end of the Peace party. . . . This party will be as dead as Julius Caesar." Two weeks into the campaign, Joe Hooker called Lee's raid "an act of desperation on his part, no matter in what force he moves. It will kill copperheadism in the North."[51]

> A volunteer nurse from New Jersey was rather open about her feelings concerning the peace movement in the Union. In a pleasant letter home she closed with cordial farewells and a succinct request: "Kill the copperheads."

9. REVENGE

Lee admirers point to his Order Number 72 as proof that his infamous temper could never outflank his sense of decency. Issued on June 21, while the last of his army entered Pennsylvania, the order strictly forbade the confiscation or destruction of private property. Purchases were allowable, provided soldiers paid with Confederate scrip.

Of course grayback currency was worthless in the Union. In addition to endorsing this virtual method of theft, Lee all but declared open season on anything thought to be owned by the U.S. government. Thus instructed, Confederate soldiers set torches and pickaxes to railroads, bridges, and Federal warehouses. Jubal A. Early's men threatened to ransack the town of York unless given $100,000 in gold and greenbacks. The townspeople handed over $28,600, plus thousands of socks, hats, and shoes. Near Greenwood, Pennsylvania, Lee's enlisted burned an ironworks to the ground, much to the anger and financial setback of its principle owner, ardent abolitionist and former Gettysburg resident Thaddeus Stevens. A Louisiana soldier wrote home about his take: "Our soldiers were just turned lose & told to go [to] it. I have as many nice clothing as I want Sugar & coffee, rice & Everything. . . . I am writing to you on Yankee paper, pens, ink & envelopes."[52]

Popular is the notion that Lee rarely called Northerners his "enemies," preferring instead the more reserved term of "those people." In reality the general frequently used "enemy" and much harsher terms, including "vandals" and "cowardly persecutors." Responding to destructive raids waged upon South Carolina in 1862, Lee lashed back, "No civilized nation within my knowledge has ever carried on war as the United States government has against us."[53]

Whether Lee ever read of Sparta, the Roman Empire, or Genghis Khan is immaterial. His hyperbole was not without provocation, and he wanted his former countrymen to know that invasions could run both ways. Essentially R. E. Lee orchestrated the original "March to the Sea," sowing fear and reaping property as fast as his forces could move. Driving through enemy territory and toward the Atlantic, Lee was aiming to break the civilian will to fight.

During their march northward, the 1st and 3rd North Carolina were inspired to further remuneration. One night they bivouacked near Sharpsburg, Maryland, and discovered by the light of their campfires that they were sleeping next to the skulls of comrades lost in the battle of Antietam.

---

10. HOPE FOR INTERNATIONAL RECOGNITION

At the start of the war, Jefferson Davis and much of the South assumed that, sooner or later, cotton-hungry European nations would officially sanction the Confederacy. London and Paris initially encouraged this notion by declaring the Confederacy a belligerent—a de facto government engaged in a war that was not illegal. Such a declaration was one step shy of granting de jure status—full diplomatic recognition of the Richmond government as a sovereign nation state.[54]

Southern hopes for international endorsement dulled with the defeat at Antietam and Lincoln's subsequent EMANCIPATION PROCLAMATION. Though critical of the Lincoln administration, British prime minister Lord Henry Palmerston and his foreign minister, Lord John Russell, disdained

slavery more. The largely indifferent French emperor Napoleon III refused to move unless Whitehall moved first.

Yet resolute Confederate victories at Fredericksburg and Chancellorsville, and six months without a major defeat, rekindled Southern aspirations. Several of Europe's prominent papers certainly agreed. The London
Times insisted the Union was in the spring of 1863 "irreparably divided."[55]

While both Lee and Davis hypothesized that victory in the North
might bring recognition, or at least improve their credit among international banks, the issue was not forefront among their operational goals.
Better to see how well the campaign progressed, they surmised, and then
make an assessment. As fate would affirm, Britain and France would also
wait and see, closely watching the eastern theater, where most of their
correspondents, military observers, and diplomats operated.[56]

James M. Mason, the Confederacy's minister to Britain at the time of
Gettysburg, was a graduate of the University of Pennsylvania.

TOP TEN MILITARY FIGURES
ENTERING THE BATTLE

Atop the high command of both sides were a select few who were well
known throughout the country. Among their shared traits, none were
generals before the war, but all had served the United States for many
years. Unlike the great majority of citizens they were leading, these were
predominantly professional soldiers, trained in military institutes, experienced in warfare, but part of a national army that rarely exceeded sixteen
thousand men and officers.

Now they were at the upper echelons of two immense armies, among
the largest the world had ever seen. How they would manage their mammoth forces at Gettysburg depended largely on what they personally
brought to the engagement, including talents, assumptions, state of
health, and aspirations.

In three days some of these men would see their reputations made or
broken, their bodies spared or mangled, and their qualities exposed in a
supreme test of will. Following are the ten most prominent among them.
Each was to play a leading role in this tragedy. Each is listed in order of
his arrival on the grand stage.[57]

1.   MAJ. GEN. JOHN F. REYNOLDS (U.S., PENNSYLVANIA, AGE 42) ARRIVED ON THE FIELD—JULY 1, 9:00 A.M.

 Pennsylvania-born John Fulton Reynolds was the highest-ranking Union officer in the Army of the Potomac and among the most famous. Stalwart and tall, with dark locks and darker eyes, he was refinement on horseback, and his valiant appearance matched his reputation. A West Point graduate trained in artillery, he served with the army in Florida, Louisiana, Maine, Maryland, New York, Oregon, South Carolina, Texas, and the Utah Territory. Quick and perceptive, he could "read" a battle instantly, a fact verified at Buena Vista in the Mexican War, when his guns twice thwarted dangerous flank attacks from fast-charging cavalry. Grateful for his levelheaded leadership, enlisted men reportedly called him "Old Common Sense."

Commandant of cadets at his alma mater at the start of the Civil War, Reynolds bounced from appointment to appointment as superiors fought for his services. Not until the 1862 Peninsula campaign would he lead a fighting brigade, yet his stint at the front was brief. Reynolds was captured in combat and shipped to the infamous Libby Prison. Exchanged for a Confederate officer, he was back in the army and promoted to the head of a division.

At Second Manassas in August 1862, Reynolds continued his reckless habit of gallantry, leading from the front. When the Union line started to fall back, Reynolds personally led a counterattack down Henry Hill, near where Thomas Jackson earned the nickname "Stonewall" the previous year. His brazen act slowed the Confederate pursuit and prevented the Union retreat from becoming a rout.

Reynolds led the 1st Corps at FREDERICKSBURG, where his subordinate George Gordon Meade spearheaded his nearly successful attacks on the Confederate right flank. At CHANCELLORSVILLE, Joe Hooker inexplicably held his corps in reserve, which angered the aggressive Reynolds immeasurably. While voicing his concerns personally to his commander in chief, Reynolds was asked if he wished to pilot the Army of the Potomac. Knowing he could never lead without political interference, he rejected the idea.

Weeks later his new superior, Meade, ordered him to take command of the left, or lead, wing of the Army of the Potomac as it made contact with Lee on the outskirts of Gettysburg. Suddenly in charge of thirty thousand men, facing an unknown number of Confederates deep in Union territory, Reynolds quickly read the situation and determined the terrain and town as worthy of defending, thus committing himself and his army to fight where they stood.[58]

When he applied for admission to West Point, he was only seventeen and not a stellar student, but the academy accepted John Reynolds nevertheless, thanks to the influence of family friend and future president of the United States, James Buchanan.

2. LT. GEN. RICHARD S. EWELL (C.S., WASHINGTON DC, AGE 46) ARRIVED ON THE FIELD—JULY 1, NOON

Bald, bug-eyed, beak-nosed, Dick Stoddard Ewell had all the esthetic charm of a flightless fowl. He also suffered from ulcers, migraines, and insomnia. In spite of his sorrowful maladies, he was an exceptionally likable figure, generous with praise, readily approachable, and armed with a saber-sharp wit. After graduating from West Point in 1840, he fought Santa Anna's army in Mexico before resigning his captain's bars for a Confederate colonelcy.

A veteran of First Manassas, the Shenandoah campaign, the Seven Days, Second Manassas, and Chancellorsville, he grew to be a popular and effective commander. Attentive to the welfare of his men, open to advice from subordinates, he never shirked from a fight yet avoided placing his men in undue peril. Attesting to his courage were three horses shot from beneath him (with a fourth to come on the first day of Gettysburg) and a leg shot off during the Second Manassas campaign. Such was his reputation that Ewell had the honor of being a pallbearer in Thomas Jackson's funeral. Unfortunately for "Old Dick," he also had the unenviable task of being Stonewall's replacement. Though Robert E. Lee appointed him to the position, Lee viewed him with suspicion, disliking his affinity for swearing and drinking and loathing his tendency to swing from hope to dread in an instant. In turn, Ewell detested Lee's extremely vague orders, something he called "indefinite phraseology."[59]

Their inability to understand each other only worsened during the Gettysburg campaign. Just as Ewell prepared to capture the capital of Pennsylvania, and with it perhaps everlasting fame, Lee told him to reverse course, "to join the army at Cashtown or Gettysburg as circumstances might require."[60]

Incensed at yet another ambiguous request, especially while on the verge of glory, Ewell grudgingly informed his staff of the unwelcome change in plans. But true to his style, Ewell responded quickly and ably, driving his widely dispersed corps back south, where the Army of the Potomac and another set of unclear orders awaited.

The man who removed Ewell's leg was the same doctor who amputated Stonewall Jackson's arm. Hunter McGuire was chief surgeon of the 2nd Corps of the Army of Northern Virginia and a graduate of the University of Pennsylvania.

---

3. LT. GEN. AMBROSE POWELL HILL (C.S., VIRGINIA, AGE 37) ARRIVED ON THE FIELD—JULY 1, 12:30 P.M.

Gettysburg marked the first time A. P. Hill commanded such a large force of men, but his superior officer believed he was up to the task. After nominating the fellow Virginian to head the newly formed 3rd Corps, Lee told Jefferson Davis, "I consider A. P. Hill the best commander with me."[61] Intelligent, hard working, and studious, Ambrose Powell Hill was a product of the West Point Class of 1846 that included Thomas J. Jackson, George E. Pickett, and Cadmus M. Wilcox. His closest companions were Henry Heth, Ambrose E. Burnside, and roommate George B. McClellan. Like senior classmate U. S. Grant, the freshman Hill drank bourbon. Unlike Grant, he made friends easily, perhaps too easily. While on furlough, A. P. contracted gonorrhea. The protracted illness forced him to graduate a year late.

Amiable though he was, Hill became a different man in combat. Always sporting a red "battle shirt" for the occasion, Hill fought fiercely, marched his men with lighting speed, and often beat stragglers with the flat of his sword. Arguably his finest moment came at Antietam, where, after capturing Harpers Ferry to secure Lee's rear, Hill sped to Sharpsburg and threw his division against his old friend Burnside, just as the luckless Union general was about to destroy the Confederate right flank.

Hill was again with an old friend at the onset of another great battle, telling Henry Heth to head into Gettysburg for the purpose of reconnaissance. His last orders to Heth were, "Do not bring on an engagement."[62]

Perhaps Hill could have prevented the escalation that transpired, but he awoke on July 1 with a painful ailment, probably dysentery, and remained in bed at Cashtown for much of the morning. When reports came that Heth had stumbled into a fight, Hill believed, as did Lee, that the Federal presence was a modest one and that the main Union body was still days away. Riding eastward on horseback, his stomach in knots, Hill called up the rest of his corps and vowed "to push the attack vigorously," expecting it to be quick and easy work. Despite his strong words, his iron willpower was absent. It was an irregularity he hoped would pass as he dragged his tired and sickly body eastward.[63]

In the Revolution, A. P. Hill's grandfather Henry fought under the command of Col. Richard "Light-Horse Harry" Lee, father of Robert E. Lee.

---

4.   GEN. ROBERT E. LEE (C.S., VIRGINIA, AGE 56)
ARRIVED ON THE FIELD—JULY 1, 2:00 P.M.

Although his father, Richard "Light-Horse Harry" Lee, abandoned the family while Robert was a young boy, Lee grew up to graduate second in his class at West Point. He survived a near fatal wound in the Mexican War to become superintendent of his alma mater. Offered the post of general in chief of the Union armies in April 1861, he resigned and joined the Confederacy. Celebrated as the South's great hope, he abruptly lost northwestern Virginia in a series of unsettling defeats.

Relegated to supervising coastal defenses in the Carolinas and later moved to Richmond as a military adviser, Robert E. Lee was on track to be a tertiary name in a short-lived rebellion. Then, on June 1, 1862, Gen.

Joseph E. Johnston was seriously wounded during the Peninsula campaign. Riding from the capital to assume command, Lee reformed the struggling army as its nemesis approached within sight of Richmond's church spires. Renaming his force the Army of Northern Virginia, he soon engaged in what became known as the Seven Days' battles. From June 25 to July 1, outnumbered nearly two to one, he lost five of seven contests outright, but he pushed the Army of the Potomac back seventeen miles and stunted the confidence of its brash commander, George B. McClellan, for months to come.

The Virginian of knightly self-denial and impeccable moral stature had become the savior of Richmond and a new hope for a desperate Confederacy. He had also revealed an ability to induce and withstand a tremendous number of casualties. Taken in total, the Seven Days produced nearly thirty-seven thousand dead, wounded, captured, and missing (generations later, Americans would lose fewer men in six weeks at Iwo Jima).

To try and stop him, the Union kept sending new generals. Lee kept driving them off—defeating John Pope at Second Manassas in August 1862, drawing even with McClellan at Antietam the following month, dismembering Ambrose E. Burnside that December at FREDERICKSBURG, and finally pulling off a stunning upset against "Fighting Joe" Hooker at CHANCELLORSVILLE in May 1863.

Inspired by his successes and an eerie ability to anticipate his adversaries, he moved into Union territory for a second time in June 1863. Though his army was in dire need of provisions and accoutrements of war, their morale and numbers were at their highest ever, and their faith in Lee bordered on absolute reverence. Yet the man came to Gettysburg in a personal state of weakness. He was visibly drawn and pale from the fluxes—a severe case of diarrhea. The "Marble Man" was also suffering from the onset of cardiovascular disease as he rode into Pennsylvania.

Lee's battle record before Gettysburg: seven wins, eleven losses.

5. MAJ. GEN. WINFIELD SCOTT HANCOCK (U.S., PENNSYLVANIA, AGE 39) ARRIVED ON THE FIELD—JULY 1, 2:30 P.M.

Few men could boast of equal or greater experience than career officer Winfield Scott Hancock, veteran of the Mexican War, the frontier, the

Seminole Wars, and the Kansas border conflicts. Tall, barrel-chested, with light brown hair and a jawline as strong as his credentials, he was charismatic and talkative, confident yet kind. Professional in appearance and demeanor, his imposing stature earned him innumerable admirers and friends.

Most outstanding was his ability to keep a clear head in times of great confusion. McClellan labeled him "Hancock the Superb" for his performance in the Peninsula campaign, in which the brigadier general was told to attack and then retreat from a key Confederate fort. Hancock simply followed the first order and ignored the latter, driving the Confederates out of the stronghold.

At Antietam he took over a division when its commander was mortally wounded. Injured during the fight at Chancellorsville, Hancock nonetheless stayed on the field and helped cover the massive Union retreat. A major general and head of the 2nd Corps at Fredericksburg, he openly criticized Ambrose E. Burnside's plans for frontal assault. The commanding general verbally reprimanded him, but Hancock proved the wiser, as he lost all but a third of his fifty-seven hundred men in the pointless assaults against Marye's Heights.

Mired in deep depression from the ensuing chain of Federal losses, Hancock recovered when the Army of Northern Virginia invaded his home state. In the early afternoon of July 1, as bluecoats reeled back from an overwhelming Confederate offensive, Brig. Gen. John Buford reported to headquarters: "In my opinion there seems to be no directing person. . . . We need help now." Ten minutes later Hancock arrived with orders to take charge of the 1st, 3rd, and 11th Corps, even though the commanding officer at the scene, Maj. Gen. Oliver O. Howard, outranked him.[64]

Immediately Hancock concurred with Howard to hold Cemetery Ridge and ordered the seizure of undefended Culp's Hill. He then reported back to Meade, saying Gettysburg was fine ground for a fight, calling it "the strongest position by nature upon which to fight a battle that I ever saw."[65]

In the 1850s Hancock was assigned to duty in California, but his wife, Almira, balked at moving so far west. She was eventually convinced to join her husband through the comforting advice of one of his superior officers: Col. Robert E. Lee.

---

6. MAJ. GEN. JUBAL EARLY (C.S., VIRGINIA, AGE 46)
ARRIVED ON THE FIELD—JULY 1, 3:30 P.M.

Scheming, womanizing, selfish, unforgiving, the six-foot, black-bearded Jubal Anderson Early was quite possibly the most detested general officer in Lee's army. The Virginian agreed with his detractors, admitting, "I was never blessed with a popular or captivating manner."[66] Fellow officers often quarreled with him. His men loathed him, stung too many times by his severe and often arbitrary punishments. From his smirking lips came alternating streams of sarcasm and spittle, for he chewed more tobacco than Stonewall did fruit, and he perpetually sloshed the chaw in his irreverent, volatile mouth. Not surprisingly, "Old Jube" never married. Yet he possessed the two qualities necessary for promotion in the Confederacy: he fought like a tempest, and he expressed absolute loyalty to Robert E. Lee.

A West Point classmate of D. H. Hill, Joe Hooker, JAMES LONGSTREET, and John Sedgwick, Early was very much an outsider and not a model soldier. Lax were his appearance and demeanor, but he possessed a superior intellect. Serving in the Mexican War, Early displayed a talent for training and drilling soldiers, which won him the admiration of fellow officer Jefferson Davis.

Later selected as a delegate to the Virginia convention on secession, Early voted against leaving the Union and begged his statesmen to give the newly elected Abraham Lincoln more time. But when his words failed to sway enough votes and Union troops began deploying against his native state, Early volunteered for service and quickly became one of the most combative officers in gray.

At First Manassas his regiment helped turn the Federal right flank, scaring the men in blue into full retreat. Receiving a general's star, he then led a brigade in the 1862 campaign to push McClellan from the Peninsula, where Early was badly wounded and mistakenly reported as killed in action. Surviving to fight in the Seven Days, Second Manassas,

Antietam, and Fredericksburg, he often led critical flank positions with audacity and skill. Promoted to major general before Chancellorsville, Early held back nearly three times his number on the Union left flank while Jackson smashed the Federal right.

At the start of the Gettysburg campaign, Early again took a prominent position, commanding the lead division across southern Pennsylvania. He reached as far as Wrightsville, forty-five miles east of Gettysburg, before being called back to join Ewell. His arrival on the afternoon of the first day produced dramatic results.

Jubal A. Early's West Point classmate Lewis Armistead was expelled from the academy for smashing a dinner plate over the head of a fellow cadet. The battered noggin belonged to none other than the sour, confrontational Early.

7. LT. GEN. JAMES LONGSTREET (C.S., SOUTH CAROLINA, AGE 42) ARRIVED ON THE FIELD—JULY 1, 5:00 P.M.

If Lee had a favorite general, it was probably his second in command, for James Longstreet exuded more confidence than Richard S. Ewell, more prudence than Jeb Stuart, greater composure than Jubal A. Early, and courage unequalled in the entire Confederacy. A six-foot-two-inch solidly built frame added to his stature as a steady and unshakable commander. Consequently, Lee entrusted nearly half his army to the amiable and quiet West Pointer, whom he called "my old war-horse."

For twenty years Longstreet had served in the U.S. Army on the frontier and in the war with Mexico. Reluctantly following his home state from the Union, he comprehended, perhaps better than any other Southern commander, the precious limit of Confederate numbers. He preferred counterattacks, unleashing assaults only after his adversaries spent themselves against his well-planned defenses. As much of a stone wall as any other general at First Manassas, he led the massive counterblow that decimated John Pope at Second Manassas. At Antietam it was his wing that held the Confederate right against vastly superior numbers. At Fredericksburg he orchestrated a lethal defensive stand at Marye's Heights, rendering four Union casualties for every one of his.

Because of his loyalty and reliability, "Old Pete" enjoyed Lee's almost limitless faith. The level of trust was remarkable, considering Longstreet was an outsider, a South Carolinian leading the 1st Corps of the Army of Northern Virginia. The lieutenant general also had strong Union connections, including family ties by marriage to U. S. Grant. Longstreet was in fact the best man at Grant's wedding.

Gettysburg would severely test Lee and Longstreet's bond, as Longstreet did not share his superior's desire for an offensive operation. Differences became acute early on, when Longstreet rode up to Seminary Ridge to join his commander late in the afternoon of July 1. In the distance the South Carolinian could see Union guns and infantry atop solid high ground (Cemetery Hill and Cemetery Ridge). Longstreet recommended moving to the southeast, to try and get between the Union men and their capital. Lee feared such a maneuver might be considered a withdrawal and snapped at his suddenly defeatist friend with a strangely inflexible pledge: "If the enemy is there tomorrow, we must attack him."

Longstreet replied, "If he is there, it will be because he is anxious that we should attack him—a good reason, in my judgment, for not doing so."

Unmoved, Lee dismissed Longstreet's evaluation and opted for engagement, filling his second in command with unalterable dread.[67]

Longstreet came to Pennsylvania with a heavy heart. In the previous year, three of his four children died in a scarlet fever epidemic. They were buried in Hollywood Cemetery in Richmond. The cemetery would later become the final resting place for three thousand Confederates killed at Gettysburg.

---

8. MAJ. GEN. DANIEL E. SICKLES (U.S., NEW YORK, AGE 43) ARRIVED ON THE FIELD—JULY 1, 9:00 P.M.

Extrovert extraordinaire Dan Sickles was neither a West Pointer nor a college graduate, but he was fluent in several languages, and he had a talent for translating politics into power. By the late 1850s the New Yorker was a hefty cog in the political machinery of Tammany Hall, and he was once considered a contender for the White House. Yet his star never rose quite as high as his appetite for intrigue and prostitutes.

When the secession crisis emerged, Congressman Sickles defended the right of separation, and for a time he considered leading the Empire State out of the Union. But the bombardment of Fort Sumter turned him full astern, and he began recruiting volunteers by the thousands. Concerning the Republican Lincoln, the Democrat Sickles adopted a patriotic stance, proclaiming, "I will trust him everywhere, and pray for him night and day."[68]

For Sickles's conspicuous bipartisan loyalty, Lincoln appointed him brigadier general of volunteers in spite of the fact Sickles had no military experience whatsoever. Surprisingly, the neophyte proved to be a quick study. On the Peninsula campaign his men performed defensive operations well. A division commander during the Seven Days, Antietam, and Fredericksburg, he allowed his able subordinates a degree of latitude and praised those who performed with initiative. With officers of superior rank, however, he seemed to invite confrontation.

Leading the 3rd Corps to Chancellorsville, Sickles again found himself at odds with command. At the height of battle, he insisted on holding a piece of high ground known as Hazel Grove. His commander, Joe Hooker, overruled him, arguing the position was too exposed to be practical. Hooker instead ordered a withdrawal, which precipitated a collapse of the entire Union line. Seething at an opportunity lost, Sickles firmly believed he alone could have won the day, and he let people know it.

Not a few feared his rogue streak. When hearing that Sickles was under consideration for command of the Army of the Potomac, Maj. Gen. Oliver O. Howard bereaved, "If God gives us Sickles to lead us I shall cry with vexation and sorrow and plead to be delivered."[69]

As fate would have it, Howard was the very officer who called Sickles to Gettysburg. On July 1 at 3:15 p.m., while protecting Union supply lines at Emmitsburg, Sickles and his 3rd Corps received orders from Howard to come to the front at once. With admirable dispatch, Sickles obeyed. But along with his corps of more than ten thousand, he also brought himself, sporting an inflated sense of self-worth and a desire to capture the glory that had eluded him at Chancellorsville, come hell or high water.[70]

In 1859 Sickles went on trial for killing his wife's lover, the son of Francis Scott Key. He successfully pleaded "temporary insanity," the first use of that defense in U.S. legal history. Attorney for the defendant happened to be Edwin M. Stanton, future U.S. secretary of war under Abraham Lincoln.

9. MAJ. GEN. GEORGE GORDON MEADE (U.S., PENNSYLVANIA, AGE 47) ARRIVED ON THE FIELD—JULY 2, 2:00 A.M.

His hooked nose, dark eyes, peppered beard, and worn countenance made him look like a brooding gargoyle with an intense cold stare, an image in perfect step with his nature. In announcing his appointment to head the most powerful fighting force on earth, his words were typical George Gordon Meade: "By direction of the President of the United States, I hereby assume command of the Army of the Potomac. As a soldier, in obeying this order—an order totally unexpected and unsolicited—I have no promises or pledges to make."[71]

Trained in engineering at West Point, he built lighthouses along the Atlantic Coast and surveyed the Great Lakes before heeding the call in 1861. A veteran of the Mexican War but without any experience in field command, Meade used an engineer's eye for practicality and his training in artillery to become a quietly effective officer. His qualities were on display at Second Manassas and Antietam, where his division successfully stunted fierce attacks. At Fredericksburg, Meade cursed the poor choice of ground, yet he hit the South's right flank hard and nearly brought Stonewall Jackson to grief before a lack of support forced him back. His army's timid performance at Chancellorsville sickened him.

Unexpectedly appointed head of the Army of the Potomac, he vowed that no similar vacillation would occur during his tenure. As he spurred his newly acquired command forward, Meade clarified what awaited those who hesitated: "Corps and other commanders are authorized to order the instant death of any soldier who fails in his duty at this hour."[72]

George Gordon Meade was severely wounded at the 1862 battle of White Oak Swamp. The bullet entered near his hip, grazed his liver, and exited within inches of his spine. Meade kept fighting until blood loss forced him to relinquish his command.

10. MAJ. GEN. J. E. B. STUART (C.S., VIRGINIA, AGE 30)
ARRIVED ON THE FIELD—JULY 2, NOON

Detractors and admirers alike labeled him cavalier, immature, cocky. Many diluted his achievements as grandiose acts of foolish youth. West Point graduate James Ewell Brown "Jeb" Stuart indeed pushed luck to its natural limits, but he did so with an industrious and well-managed staff, disciplined and motivated men, and a gift for gathering priceless intelligence at minimal cost.[73]

He often made his greatest contribution on the eve of battle. Before Lee attacked McClellan in the Peninsula campaign, Stuart ran reconnaissance. More precisely, Stuart and a thousand troopers rode completely around McClellan's army, destroyed supply lines, captured hundreds of Federals, and exposed the Army of the Potomac as a timid Goliath. Before Second Manassas, Stuart and fifteen hundred horsemen snatched three hundred prisoners, tens of thousands in gold and greenbacks, plus Union commander John Pope's dress coat, personal baggage, and dispatch ledger, which contained information on the Union army's strength and disposition. For both endeavors, Stuart suffered a grand total of three casualties.[74]

Praised as a cavalry genius, he also led artillery and footmen. On the vulnerable Confederate left flank at Fredericksburg, Stuart used his horse artillery to scald a potentially lethal Federal attack. At Chancellorsville, he took over the twenty-thousand-man 2nd Corps of the wounded Jackson and used its infantry and guns to force Hooker into full retreat.[75]

Stuart never induced the body counts of a Lee or Jackson, but he also never faltered in his duty, until the battle of BRANDY STATION. Publicly he declared the colossal cavalry duel a great victory, but privately he chomped at the bit, eager for any opportunity to reimburse the Army of the Potomac for tarnishing his stellar record.

Jeb Stuart's paternal ancestors came over from Ireland and initially settled in Pennsylvania.

THE BATTLE

TOP TEN REASONS WHY THE CONFEDERATES WON THE FIRST DAY

Riding hard from the south, a Union corps commander galloped to the Lutheran seminary west of Gettysburg and shouted to an officer in the cupola high atop the building. The time was 9 a.m.

"How goes it, John?"

A terse, deep voice shouted back, "The devil's to pay!"

The commander queried, "I hope you can hold out until my corps comes up."

"I reckon I can," came the response.[1]

Brig. Gen. John Buford and a division of cavalry would indeed hold out just long enough for Maj. Gen. John F. Reynolds to pull the lead brigades of his U.S. 1st Corps into place and receive the first major Confederate assault at the battle of Gettysburg.

Often noted is the irony that the South came in primarily from the north, and the North came up from the south. Frequently downplayed is the Confederacy's complete dominance of the first day. Viewed from hindsight, July 1 often appears to be the preliminary phase of a Union victory. To the participants, the initial hours closely resembled Second Manassas or Chancellorsville, where vicious skirmishing quickly escalated into a large-scale engagement and ended with a large-scale Union retreat. Watching events unfold from atop Seminary Ridge, A. P. Hill believed that by late afternoon the Federal army had been "entirely routed." An adversary viewing the same scene from the perspective of Cemetery

Ridge was inclined to agree. "Matters do not appear well," reported Maj. Gen. HENRY W. SLOCUM. "I hope the work for the day is nearly over."[2]

While the engagement would last longer than either man expected, Union reversals were undeniable. In many respects the damages were worse than previous contests. In eight hours the South would capture thirty-five hundred prisoners, kill the Union's second in command, induce more than 40 percent casualties on the two corps, and occupy a Northern town. Following are the chief factors that enabled the lead elements of the hard-fighting Army of Northern Virginia to achieve these gains against an equally diligent vanguard of the Army of the Potomac. Reasons are listed by the sequence in which they entered the picture, though their respective effects would reverberate for many days.

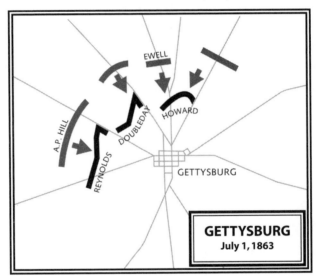

1.   THE ROADS

On average, a thousand infantrymen would occupy a half mile of road. Adding horses, cannons, caissons, commissary wagons, ammunition wagons, ambulances, rolling livestock, not to mention laborers, reporters, and stragglers of every sort made any column of infantry two or three times longer. When dealing with armies in excess of sixty thousand pairs of feet, the importance of good avenues of approach was readily apparent.

In this regard, the Army of Northern Virginia had a supreme advantage when it came to Gettysburg. Situated at a convergence of ten roads, the town was an unusually sturdy wheel, the best focal point of byways for forty miles in any direction. When receiving word from the spy Harrison that the Union army was in pursuit, Lee consciously chose the hub as the most expedient point of convergence for his dispersed columns, even though some of them were up to thirty miles away. When learning of Lee's concentration on the town, GEORGE GORDON MEADE reportedly said, "Good God! If the enemy get Gettysburg, we are lost!"[3]

Though starting from farther away, Lee could make better time. His 2nd Corps under Lt. Gen. RICHARD S. EWELL came down on the Harrisburg road from the northeast and the Carlisle road from the north. The 3rd Corps under A. P. HILL moved in from the west on the Chambersburg road, with JAMES LONGSTREET's 1st Corps farther back on the same route.

The Union had two of its seven infantry corps in the vicinity, the 1st and the 11th, but they had to share the Emmitsburg road on their way in. To worsen the situation, the avenue angled northeast into Gettysburg, skewing away from John Buford's beleaguered division.

As the 11th continued into town, the 1st stepped off the fast macadam surface just past a modest homestead known locally as the Codori farm and headed overland. While Buford was running out of time and ammunition, the 1st Corps were weaving through fields, fences, and pastures, traversing the mile of broken ground as fast as their heavy legs could move.

As if in some Norse saga, the U.S. 1st Corps entered the battle of Gettysburg swinging axes. In order to make better time through the fields, their pioneers led the way, hacking down fences as they went.

---

2. MANPOWER

Superiority in numbers does not guarantee success, a fact demonstrated time and again by the Army of the Potomac. In the four major battles preceding Gettysburg, the boys in blue held clear majorities only to be matched or beaten each time. Yet with all other variables being equal, an army of greater mass has greater leverage via width, depth, and firepower.

For one day, Johnny Reb enjoyed the infrequent pleasure of outweighing his opposite. Altogether, the Army of Northern Virginia brought forth more than twenty-seven thousand men, while the Army of the

Potomac could assemble no more than nineteen thousand infantry plus three thousand cavalry.[4]

The South's greatest advantage came on the western front, where the Confederate 3rd Corps eventually brought 16,000 soldiers against fewer than 9,000 troops in the Union 1st Corps. A. P. Hill's corps actually lost more casualties—approximately 6,300 to 5,500. But because of their numerical advantage, Hill's delegation was able sustain their losses and continue fighting.[5]

On the northern side of town, the Confederate 2nd Corps and the Union 11th were nearly level at approximately 6,000 apiece. Yet through quick deployment and a lightning attack, Ewell's troops were able to kill, wound, or capture a larger number of their opponents in a few hours. By the end of the day, the 11th Corps had only 60 percent of its effectives remaining, whereas the Confederate 2nd Corps had 86 percent of its men still standing.[6]

At around noon, the 150th Pennsylvania Regiment positioned west of town received a volunteer from the town. Elderly resident John Burns, armed with an archaic flintlock musket and angered by the lingering battle, offered his services. Shorthanded, the regiment accepted his help, and Burns fought until successive wounds forced him to quit.

---

3. ARTILLERY

On July 1 the South held the majority of field guns. Not unlike their upper hand in manpower, the South's advantage in artillery was uncommon, brief, but influential. At the outset of the contest, John Buford tried to hold the western front with the only crew available to him at the time, Battery A, 2nd U.S. Artillery: seventy-five men firing six guns. Pitched against him were twenty pieces from Maj. Gen. Henry Heth's division. Union odds improved slightly when three Confederate tubes jammed with oversized ammunition, yet constant pressure from long-range infantry volleys reduced Battery A's efficiency and pushed them back.[7]

With more Confederate infantry came more artillery, as every division possessed a battalion of twenty guns. From the west and north, commensurate with their growing numbers, the South brought an increasing amount of brass and iron. Situated on Oak Hill northwest of town, eight

Confederate pieces under Maj. Gen. ROBERT E. RODES poured shots into the 1st Corps as it clung to the length of Seminary Ridge. North of town on Blocher's Knoll, Battery G, 4th U.S. Artillery tried desperately to fend off twenty rival guns and thousands of charging foot soldiers with six Napoleon smoothbores only to lose its position and commanding officer in the ensuing fight.

By the end of the day, more than one hundred Confederate tubes faced sixty Union. As with their advantage in bayonets, Lee's supremacy in field guns was temporary. Early the next morning, the sum of Federal cannon caught and passed their adversaries, swinging the ratio from 3:5 to 4:3.[8]

> At the base of John Buford's statue on McPherson's Ridge, west of Gettysburg, are four artillery tubes. One of them is the cannon that fired the first Union artillery shot in the battle.

4. THE TERRAIN

To the west of Gettysburg swelled a series of land waves, rising and falling every few hundred yards as they neared the edge of the town. From farthest to nearest they were Knoxlyn Ridge, Herr Ridge, McPherson's Ridge, and Seminary Ridge. The latter two joined to the northwest at Oak Hill. Next came the Gettysburg plain and then nothing of tactical worth for a mile. Armed with greater numbers and firepower, Lee's army was able to push the Union off each successive rise and onto the plain, where the only option left to Billy Yank was to run until he could reach the next high ground.

Knoxlyn marked the point of first contact, where at 7:30 a.m. Lt. Marcellus E. Jones of the 8th Illinois Cavalry fired off a carbine round at the approaching 13th Alabama Infantry. Jones hit no one, but the ground upon which he was standing was no longer tenable. Loss of the following Herr Ridge provided far more grief for the Union defenses. In height and width, the rise was far superior to McPherson's, just to the east, granting the Confederates better lines of fire for artillery and a perfect shelter behind which they could amass their building infantry. It was from this position that two of A. P. Hill's divisions launched into John F. Reynolds's 1st Division of the 1st Corps. As the Union fell back, the two Confederate corps linked together near Oak Hill, the highest point of terrain within several miles and an effective platform for long-range artillery.

Outnumbered, outgunned, and outpositioned, the Union had a marginal chance of maintaining a stand on McPherson's and Seminary ridges. The 1st Corps relinquished both elevations that afternoon, but not before losing nearly half of its officers and men in defense.

> McPherson's Ridge was named after the Edward McPherson family who owned the main farm on the rise. Edward McPherson himself was out of the area at the time of the battle, working as the clerk of the U.S. House of Representatives.

5.   THE DEATH OF REYNOLDS

Minutes after John Reynolds assembled a portion of his infantry along the eastern slope of McPherson's Ridge, a brigade of Confederates under Brig. Gen. James J. Archer came bounding up from the west and into the shelter of Herbst Woods. "Forward men," screamed Reynolds, "forward for God's sake and drive those fellows out of those woods." Turning back toward the seminary for more support, the general received a single fatal bullet wound to the back of the head.[9]

As Reynolds's lifeless body slid off his horse and crashed face first onto the ground, the Union lost its second in command and their de facto leader on the battlefield. Not only was the Pennsylvanian in charge of the 1st Corps, he also directed the Union left wing, a position he had ac-

The single shot that struck Reynolds killed him instantly. Witnesses said they had never seen a man die so quickly.

cepted by request from Joseph Hooker weeks earlier and continued under the grateful insistence of GEORGE GORDON MEADE. Three corps totaling thirty thousand men were suddenly without one of the most respected and senior officers in the Union.

Naturally, there is no way to know exactly what Reynolds would have done next. What can be said is that his early departure caused an immediate ripple effect through the Union chain of command, creating several hours of confusion and readjustment. Wing command temporarily passed to Maj. Gen. Oliver Otis Howard, the pious yet generally uninspiring commander of the 11th Corps. He was busy at the other end of the battlefield, herding his men north and into the streets of Gettysburg. The 1st Corps fell to Maj. Gen. ABNER DOUBLEDAY, a capable officer who nonetheless had decidedly poor relations with both Howard and Meade. In moving up the chain, Doubleday left his post as 3rd Division commander to the care of Brig. Gen. THOMAS A. ROWLEY, who subsequently suffered a type of mental breakdown (see WORST PERFORMING COMMANDERS).[10]

By midafternoon Maj. Gen. WINFIELD SCOTT HANCOCK reached the field and, by order of Meade, assumed control of the wing. Solidifying a defensive position on Cemetery Hill, Hancock labored to restore order. Yet much damage had transpired, and the front lines were nearing the point of implosion.

When Reynolds was a prisoner of war in 1862, he regained his freedom after he was exchanged for Confederate Brig. Gen. William Barksdale. A year later both men would fight at Gettysburg and die in the process.

---

6. THE CONFEDERATE WILL TO ENGAGE

Difficult to measure yet impossible to overlook, the morale of the Army of Northern Virginia was near an all-time high on July 1. Coupled with harsh contempt for their opponent, the troops were willing to take part in any reasonable scrap, and their recent successes against sparse bands of Pennsylvania militia only cemented their confidence. Perhaps few expressed a greater want for action than members of the officer class, particularly at the brigade and division levels, where opportunities for glory and promotion were generally welcomed.

Maj. Gen. Henry Heth's headlong rush into Gettysburg may have sparked the battle, but it also brought greater numbers than John Buford and a division of Union horsemen could withstand. Setbacks did not prevent further aggression, as Maj. Gen. ROBERT E. RODES demonstrated with his uncoordinated assaults from Oak Hill. Regiments nearly fought themselves into oblivion while slashing away at the Union's Iron Brigade, which clutched to the woodlots of McPherson's Ridge. Three miles east, Maj. Gen. JUBAL A. EARLY did not wait for explicit permission to hit the thin line of the U.S. 11th Corps as it reached the north of town. All three of his brigade commanders performed with considerable ferocity, in particular the cocky and dogged Brig. Gen. John B. Gordon with his regiments of Georgians.

Any Confederate officer could have found a reason not to push forward—lack of information, no cavalry support, and most of all, orders from Lee to avoid a large engagement. But a consistent use of quick strikes characterized an army willing to live and die on the offensive. For the first day of Gettysburg, that mentality reaped considerable rewards.[11]

Confederate Col. Abner Perrin went into battle heading a brigade for the first time. By the end of the day, his South Carolina regiments had captured four Union battle flags, including the banner of the U.S. 1st Corps.

---

7. THE TOWN

Ordered to protect the north side of Gettysburg, the U.S. 11th Corps had to first get through the town's narrow and askewed avenues. Often described as a "sleepy village," the burg was closer to the U.S. Census definition of a "city" at that time. Only 20 percent of the American population, North or South, lived in towns larger than Gettysburg.

There were metal shops, limekilns, five multistory hotels, a score of tanneries, forty flour mills, dry goods merchants, warehouses, clapboard homes, town mansions, and dozens of churches. Pocketed with dead-end alleyways, divided by vertical-board fences, and possessing few signs and no street addresses, the cross-connecting radial hub of streets was a maze to out-of-towners, especially a pack of eight thousand in a bit of a hurry.

Slowing the 11th Corps even further were the townspeople, who came out to thank and cheer their assumed saviors. A few citizens offered ladles of cool well water, to which the trotting and overheated flocked. Irate officers kicked over buckets and hurried troops along, as they had been doing all morning, trying to reach their objective before it was too late. The 11th soon discovered it indeed was too little and too late.[12]

> When his division rode through town the previous day, John Buford knew how to keep his men moving. He stated, quite emphatically, that the saloons were off-limits.

8.   THE 11TH CORPS' ELEVENTH HOUR

If there ever was a military unit looking for redemption, it was the snake-bitten U.S. 11th Corps. A collection of three divisions that were thoroughly routed at Second Manassas, the 11th Corps marched into Chancellorsville with the honor of being the Union's right flank. That flank collapsed the moment Stonewall Jackson and thirty thousand graybacks slammed into it.

A second wave of attacks came after the battle, when their own comrades leveled the most hateful condemnations, accusing them of carelessness before Jackson's assault and cowardice after. Said one bluecoat, "They run like sheep."[13]

It did not help their cause that the majority of the corps' troops were German, including division commanders Carl Schurz and Alexander Schimmelfennig. Hating the Deutsch almost as much as they hated the Irish, xenophobes and the native born spared no slur in roasting the scapegoats. One soldier felt compelled to say, "We think but very little of

Late deployment, poor leadership, an aggressive adversary, and a collapsing flank encouraged the men of the Union 11th Corps to run for their lives.

LIBRARY OF CONGRESS

the dutch [expletives]. . . . They do not fight worth [expletive] under Howard."[14]

Oliver Otis Howard, a native of Maine, certainly found his job as corps commander difficult. Pious, serious, studious, far from charismatic, he at least shared his corps' underlying courage and overwhelmingly bad luck, receiving two wounds and losing an arm in the 1862 Peninsula campaign. For him, the enlisted were not as much a problem as his officers, lamenting, "Everybody who is to blame tries to shift the responsibility upon somebody else's shoulders."[15]

But when Howard's multinationals were one of the first two Union corps to march into Gettysburg, many started to believe their chance for redemption had come. Sprinting with great difficulty through the tight corridors of the city, they reached the town's northern edge and began to spread out. A sergeant of the 26th Wisconsin noted, "Everyone's blood flows quicker, every pulse beats louder, every nerve is more sensitive, and every one feels that he is living faster than he was half an hour since."[16]

Aspirations quickly faded. Slowed by the maze of town streets, troops did not have time to deploy well. Officers did not have enough wisdom to create a strong defensive position and stretched their lines far too thin. Howard failed to bring up all of his brigades to assist. In a final and fatal mistake, Brig. Gen. FRANCIS C. BARLOW unwisely pulled the right flank of the corps forward and onto an unsupportable hill, creating an appealing gap between the town and its defenders. Onto the hill and into the gap came a division of Confederate troops superbly led by Maj. Gen. JUBAL A. EARLY, sending the 11th reeling once again.[17]

Delayed, unorganized, uncoordinated, and fragile, the corps cemented its pitiful reputation on July 1 by surrendering the inroads to Gettysburg. But the defeat was more from a lack of leadership than from a lack of courage. Fifty percent of its losses came from capture, many of them snared within the labyrinth of the town that slowed their deployment hours earlier. But there was a silver lining. The narrow streets that plagued them also decelerated the hard-chasing Confederates and prevented Ewell's victorious corps from organizing a late-day attack on the key defensive position of Cemetery Hill.

It was not all that strange for the 11th Corps to be heavily German. One out of every four Union soldiers in the Civil War was foreign-born.

9. THE UNION TURTLE: HENRY W. SLOCUM

Four miles southeast of Gettysburg, along the hard-surface road to Baltimore, sat the diminutive village of Two Taverns. Resting there for the moment was the bulk of the Union 12th Corps with its steady, unexcitable commander, Maj. Gen. Henry W. Slocum. Having marched just six miles from their morning campsite farther south, the men were not particularly tired nor were they in a hurry. It was lunchtime. Up ahead was the left wing of the Union army, but the 12th Corps was part of the right. To keep moving would tangle them up with 1st, 3rd, and 11th Corps and take them too far west to maintain their starboard position. Slocum and his staff figured that they would hear something if they were needed. They did.

Breezing over the horizon were the murmurs of field guns. Slocum believed it was horse artillery voicing its authority in some far-off skirmish. Sometime later a civilian passed by and reported there was a battle up ahead. Around 1 p.m. officers swore they could hear the sounds of rifles shooting in unison, and Slocum sent a man to investigate. Smoke began to rise to the northwest. Couriers arrived from 11th Corps commander Howard reporting a fight but not explicitly asking for help. The two corps commanders exchanged dispatches back and forth to the point that Howard was essentially ordering him forward.[18]

Finally, Slocum had his nine thousand men on the road and moving. It was 4 p.m., precisely when Howard's 11th Corps was beginning to collapse for lack of support.

At the same time Henry W. Slocum was shepherding his 12th Corps toward Gettysburg, Confederates north of the town were carrying away wounded Brig. Gen. Francis C. Barlow of the 11th Corps. Barlow would get his revenge. After the war, the two men ran against each other for New York secretary of state. In a tight race, Barlow won.

---

10. LEE'S DECISION TO CONTINUE

When Robert E. Lee reached the field at 2 p.m., his 3rd Corps had been fighting for more than five hours. His 2nd Corps was bearing down from the north and was preparing to pounce. Yet his orders to "avoid a general engagement" were still in effect.

He was reluctant to commit until all of his army was available. The size and disposition of the enemy was unknown, except for the fact that a corps directly in front of him was offering exceptional resistance. Lacking information, he waited. It soon became apparent that Longstreet's entire corps was not going to make it in time. Then word came that the missing Jeb Stuart and his four thousand horsemen, the one group that could tell him exactly how much of the enemy lay behind the hills, were still thirty miles away.[19]

In spite of the bad news, Lee took measure of the situation. He had valid reason to pull back and use the protection of the mountains in a defensive stand. Yet he had come this far. It appeared as if he had a temporary edge in numbers and artillery. The terrain favored him. Troop morale was never higher. Eager to consolidate his gains, Lee decided to press home the attack. At 4:30 p.m., in the company of sickly 3rd Corps commander A. P. Hill, Lee watched from atop Seminary Ridge as his general assault resulted in the implosion of the Union line. Within hours, the town would be his, as well as thousands of captives. A distant and pronounced hill capped with headstones appeared to be the next logical objective, but for the moment, he looked to have made the correct decision.[20]

Famous was R. E. Lee's favorite horse Traveller, which he brought with him on the Gettysburg campaign. The mount was originally named Jeff Davis. As the general did not wish to straddle anything that would embarrass his president, Lee changed the name.

TOP TEN REASONS WHY THE SECOND DAY ENDED IN A DRAW

By the morning of July 2, Lee had approximately forty-five thousand men at his disposal. Meade had amassed at least an equal amount. Both believed they were outnumbered, and neither commander knew much of the other's disposition. The Union may have taken a beating during the previous day's fight, but Meade himself was not around to see it. The newly appointed commander arrived on the battlefield around midnight, and from his belated vantage, his side appeared to be in a strong position.

Lee also had cause to feel confident. Despite getting snarled in a large engagement, one he had hoped to avoid until better conditions arose, his men had done well. A day's hard work earned him a number of key ridges, four major roads, and more than three thousand prisoners. Foremost in his mind was the momentum gathered. A true believer in seizing the initiative, Lee had dedicated himself at the end of the first day to staying on the offensive. His army was nearly collected, and it curled tightly around a badly battered adversary. The next logical step was to close the hand and finally crush the enemy that had too often avoided a decisive battle.

While each man contemplated his next move, the morning passed. Both armies conducted reconnaissance and brought up their remaining corps. The situation was tense but uneventful. Journalists on the scene, in a hurry to meet their deadlines, reported that the day would see no action.

By late afternoon, however, Lee was finally ready to go. As Ewell and Hill held the north side of the Union line firmly in place, Longstreet was to maneuver in stealth toward the southern end (which Lee assumed to be Cemetery Ridge) and, with an upward motion, hammer against the line with extreme force, shattering it in total. But what should have been an abrupt surgical procedure soon went horribly wrong. July 2 would become the bloodiest day of the bloodiest battle of the war. It would also end in stalemate. As events would illustrate, the chief surgeon was operating on a less than cooperative patient. Listed below, in the general order

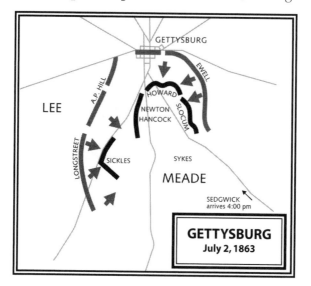

of their occurrence, are the main circumstances that led to the tactical draw between South and North and a major reallocation in morale.

1.   EFFECTIVENESS OF "THE FISHHOOK"

However pressured Meade may have felt on the morning of day two to push the Confederacy from the North, he found security in the basic shape of things. The position of his front formed an inverted J, commonly referred to as "the fishhook." By bending back on itself, the Federal posture gave Meade the tactical panacea of interior lines. Lee had used the configuration to survive multiple Union attacks at Antietam. Now Meade was going to take full advantage of the shield to survive Lee.

By holding a convex shape, the Union forced the Confederates to spread themselves along the whole front, thereby making their line twice as long and twice as thin. Should Lee attempt to retract either end, he would offer his adversary an easy avenue to his backside.

Just as significant, the geometry condensed the Union area of operation. Whereas Lee had to maneuver around a wide orbit, Meade directed from the core, giving him comparatively much shorter distances of travel for everything of military importance. Ammunition, rations, infantry, artillery, and information shifted faster and with less effort within the arc.

On the second day, the Gettysburg battle line reached from Culp's Hill to Little Round Top. For Meade, this was a distance of two miles. For Lee, it was a circumnavigation of nearly seven miles. Meade would be able to transfer most of his 12th Corps from Culp's Hill to Cemetery Ridge and back again in a few hours. He was also able to insert brigades of his 5th Corps to his left flank and center. The late-arriving 6th Corps was never needed but stood at the ready to the center rear, capable of moving to any place in the line if needed.

On the other side, Lee's thin line did not have the surplus for a substantial reserve. When he did attempt to shift units from point to point, their deployments proved to be perilously slower than whatever Meade offered in response.

Situated in interior lines, George Gordon Meade's headquarters were on average three times closer than Lee's headquarters to every major point of engagement on the battlefield.

2.   UNION SECURITY ON THE HIGH GROUND

The general retreat on the first day may have been the best move the Federals could have made. In succumbing to the Confederate tide, they washed ashore along the best high ground of the region. Viewed three-dimensionally, the Union fishhook resembled a human femur. On the ball joint of wooded and rocky Culp's Hill stood the 12th Corps. Remnants of the 11th Corps manned the large hip bend of Cemetery Hill. Running south along the shaft of Cemetery Ridge were the 1st, 2nd, and 3rd Corps, with the 5th Corps in reserve and the 6th Corps within a half-day's march. The knee joint of Little Round Top initially stood barren but within reach.

An added advantage to the Union arrangement, the centrally situated Cemetery Hill was nearly devoid of trees or cumbersome vegetation, which created a nearly ideal defensive platform for artillery. Except for the far side of Culp's Hill, nearly every point of the Union line was in full view of cannon muzzles bristling the crown of Cemetery Hill.

Facing these highlands were the Confederate positions within the town and along Cemetery Ridge. Formidable locales on their own, they were separated from the Union line by open ground, a no-man's-land ranging from a half mile to a mile in any direction. As the day would demonstrate, every Confederate attempt to bridge this chasm would turn into an uphill battle.

The four highest points of elevation in the Gettysburg area were Big Round Top at 785 feet above sea level, Little Round Top at 650 feet, Cemetery Hill at 628 feet, and Culp's Hill at 620 feet.

A sketch of the 3rd Division of the 2nd U.S. Corps readying itself for the impending action on Cemetery Ridge.

LIBRARY OF CONGRESS

3. LEE'S POOR RECONNAISSANCE

"Intelligence" is an ideal euphemism for information. Without it, an army is prone to slow progress and big mistakes. Neither Lee nor Meade had access to an abundance of intelligence on the morning of July 2, but the Virginian struggled with a greater number of handicaps. For starters, Lee was no longer on home soil. Familiar landscapes that had served his divisions so well at Fredericksburg and Chancellorsville were more than a hundred miles south. Also far away were cooperative civilians, who in a pinch functioned as guides and lookouts. Most unsettling was the continued absence of Jeb Stuart and his main body of cavalry. Stuart had left behind two brigades, neither of which Lee trusted to attain the information he needed. Lee had a vague concept of where his opponent stood but no idea of how many troops were at Meade's immediate disposal.

Few battles revealed how much Lee's modus operandi depended on detailed and timely information. His was a lax command style, based on imprecise orders and open strategies, allowing for maximum flexibility. Working deaf and blind at Gettysburg, his tactics suddenly turned very rigid. In short, Lee knew he wanted to attack, but without knowing the full picture, he chose to guess where the Union was most vulnerable. With minimal intelligence, he spent much of the second day stumbling into rough topography, heavy defenses, and visible lines of approach, the very conditions he consciously avoided in most contests.

For a brief moment the Army of Northern Virginia held Little Round Top. At approximately 5:30 a.m. on July 2, minutes after a Union brigade left the hill, Confederate Maj. J. J. Clarke and Capt. S. R. Johnston climbed to the summit while running reconnaissance. Spotting nothing of significance, the party rode farther south and away from the high ground.

4. LONGSTREET'S LONG MARCH

Just as the lack of roads slowed the Union to a crawl on the first day, Lee's army would face the same problem on the second. At 11 a.m. the general ordered James Longstreet to attack the Union left flank. On a two-dimensional map the request seemed reasonable. In three dimensions, the approach was less inviting.[21]

Sidestepping, backtracking, and overlapping his men's deployment on day two was the epitome of James Longstreet's inefficiency at Gettysburg. And a late start did not help.

LIBRARY OF CONGRESS

Much of Longstreet's trailing corps had to funnel along the Chambersburg road coming in from the northwest. Not until noon did Longstreet feel he had adequate numbers to proceed. Next came a long, southerly trudge, mostly over open terrain and dusty roads. The procession came to an abrupt halt when it was discovered they could not advance across a small ridge, lest the assault force show themselves in full view of Union signalmen stationed on Little Round Top. A lengthy countermarch ensued, almost to the starting point, just as the sun began to administer a most wretched heat. By the time 1st Corps units finally reached the front and were in place for the attack, five hours had passed, and the Union presence was far stronger than anticipated.[22]

Much has been written on Longstreet's dour mood at the time. Assumptions pervade that his poor attitude, brought on by Lee's refusal to disengage at Gettysburg, poisoned his initiative and was the major cause of the long delay. Taken in context, Longstreet's lethargy may have been from an inability more than an unwillingness to carry out orders, and he was definitely not the only man on the march greatly vexed by the troubles encountered.[23]

Four miles southwest of Gettysburg stood Black Horse Tavern. Some of Longstreet's troops would see the stone building three times on July 2—first on their march toward the Union left, a second time on their countermarch to avoid Union detection, and last when it became a hospital after the day's fighting. More than two hundred severely wounded men were brought to the tavern, scores of whom died.

5.   THE MONKEY WRENCH OF SICKLES'S SALIENT

While Longstreet was trying to get his 1st Corps in motion, Maj. Gen. DANIEL E. SICKLES was contemplating how he could make his U.S. 3rd Corps immovable. Most of the Union line sat on stable high ground. Sickles's troops did not. His ten-thousand-man corps occupied the southern tail of Cemetery Ridge, where the earthen spine sank into the earth before it reached Little Round Top. Lacking the numbers to elongate his line up the rocky slope, he sent his men forward to take and hold slightly elevated positions along Devil's Den to his left, the Peach Orchard to his front, and the Emmitsburg road to his right.

The move surprised his own side as well as the Confederates. Both Meade and Lee worked under the assumption that the Union left would remain along Cemetery Ridge, and their plans for the day depended on it. Suddenly faced with a drastic alteration of his formation, and with no time to change it back, Meade resolved to stabilize the weak salient with reinforcements from the 2nd and 5th Corps. Whatever grand strategy he was entertaining would have to wait until this uninvited advance resolved itself.[24]

At least Meade knew of the change. Lee was not yet aware of the bulge until his grand attack was well under way. Marse Robert incorrectly believed that the Peach Orchard had but a few regiments and a single battery of six cannons, the fields and woods behind were relatively clear, and the Round Tops were nearly empty. Any foreseeable resistance would come from the Union stronghold of Cemetery Hill much farther north, which he planned to hit while coming up from the south along Cemetery

The Peach Orchard marked the apex of Sickles's salient and the depths of misery for both sides during the afternoon of July 2.

LIBRARY OF CONGRESS

Ridge. Lee surmised his troops would be marching up the ridge by mid-day. Instead his men would spend the better part of July 2 getting into position and then addressing the salient for four long hours.[25]

> Daniel E. Sickles's headquarters within the salient stood next to a large tree just northwest of the Trostle farm. To the present day, the farm and the tree are still standing.

6. LONGSTREET'S ROUGH APPROACH

"General Longstreet is to blame for not reconnoitering the ground, and for persisting in ordering the assault when his errors were discovered." Confederate Maj. Gen. Lafayette McLaws had reason to be angry. It was his division with its prized brigades under WILLIAM BARKSDALE and JOSEPH B. KERSHAW that were deployed across the Peach Orchard. Told he was to make a flank attack against "a small force of the enemy in front," McLaws instead saw that he was about to go head to head against a strong line of Federal infantry that had plenty of artillery at their disposal. Beyond them were more troops positioning along a little mountain overlooking the entire area.[26]

Maj. Gen. John Bell Hood, whose division stood to the right of McLaws's, expressed even greater frustration. An extremely aggressive commander, Hood nonetheless balked at his assignment. Ahead of him were acres of rocky and uneven ground punctuated by monstrous boulders of what would become known as Devil's Den. All of it seemed to crawl with Union artillery and infantry. He too would be walking into the enemy head on, and if he made any ground, his reward would be shells and bullets raining down from the Round Tops.

Hood recommended an alternative plan. His scouts had discovered an open route to the south of Sugarloaf Mountain (Big Round Top) where they could travel unhindered until they reached the back of the Union line. Twice he pleaded with Longstreet to consider the idea, and twice Longstreet rejected him, in part because "Old Pete" had tried several times to change the mind of his superior and was soundly rebuked. At 4 p.m. members of the Confederate 1st Corps went forward into the hardscrabble landscape, urged onward by Longstreet's command—"We must obey the orders of General Lee."[27]

Among the thousands of Confederate casualties in the assault upon Devil's Den and the Round Tops was John Bell Hood, whose left arm was mangled by Union artillery. Hood also lost three of six infantry brigade commanders, plus the regimental leaders of the 2nd and 20th Georgia, the 4th and 5th Texas, and the 3rd Arkansas.

---

7. THE FAILURE OF *EN ÉCHELON*

If Lee's line of attack was poor, his method of assault was worse. *En échelon* was a pet tactic among Confederate commanders. French for "rung of a ladder," a more fitting term would have been *sur échelonner* ("to stagger"). In principle, the process was simple. Troops lined up side by side in groups, for example, in brigades of two thousand men. Starting from one end, a brigade would begin to march, then the next brigade would go, then the next, until the whole formation was moving forward as a diagonal line. The maneuver was supposed to mimic the slanted blade of a guillotine, driving down upon its victim until it sliced from one side to the other.

In practice the tactic was extremely complicated and rarely worked. Should any one section falter, whether from heavy fire or natural obstacles, the line would break apart, with trailing units often stopping altogether. Fearing a loss of support, officers and men often concentrated too much on comrades over their shoulder and not enough on the enemy to their front.

These tendencies, along with the broken terrain facing him, did not deter Lee from trying an unprecedented, two-mile-wide *en échelon* on the Union left. Starting southwest of the Peach Orchard in a grand south-to-north surge, the entire operation was supposed to link twelve brigades. It fell apart after two.

Units still moved forward, but they did so in isolation. Farmhouses, hills, tree lines, and brutal close-quarter fighting split brigades apart. The greatest progress came from the commands of Barksdale and Kershaw in the Peach Orchard, plus Cadmus M. Wilcox and Ambrose R. Wright farther north. All four outfits became separated from the main line in the early moments of engagement, and all endured casualties greater than 30 percent. Others traveled piecemeal into the fray and were turned back early or torn apart after several hours of marginal success.[28]

In the nineteenth century, much of American military thinking was done en français. For example, while the batteries in the artillery fired their Napoleons, the generals, colonels, captains, and lieutenants marched their corps, divisions, brigades, and regiments en échelon to fire muskets loaded with minié bullets en enfilade into the bastions.

8. THE INFLEXIBLE LITTLE ROUND TOP

There is a reason why Meade overlooked the mountain when deploying his troops on July 2 and why Lee never once considered the rise as critical to his operation. With prohibitively steep slopes, woods to the east and south, Devil's Den to the west, and pervasively rocky terrain covering the entire area, Little Round Top was not suited for military operations. The split-second arrival of Union troops, the harrowing attacks from Hood's Confederates, and Col. Joshua Lawrence Chamberlain's charge of bayonets makes the site one of the epic stories of Gettysburg, but for all intents, the fight for the crest was not unlike the brawl in the salient: an oscillating slugfest over ground of marginal tactical worth.[29]

Nothing demonstrated this more clearly than the Union's struggle to turn the rugged elevation into an artillery platform. While Cemetery Hill held scores of cannons, Battery D of the 5th U.S. Artillery Brigade struggled to carry six tubes up the rocky inclines of Little Round Top. Upon reaching the crest, gunners discovered they could not defend the hill itself. Unable to fire downward, their pieces simply lofted volleys over the heads of approaching Confederates. Battery D sacrificed several members of

Union gunners discovered what the infantry already knew: rugged Little Round Top was not suited for offensive operations.

HARPER'S WEEKLY

their crew in a largely symbolic gesture, unable to do much more than probe the crags of Devil's Den or launch shots into Sickles's salient.[30]

For the Confederates, blocked by a mile of trees, creek beds, and the boulder-strewn Valley of Death, moving artillery up the hill was never a viable option. Little Round Top came down to a test of endurance between infantry regiments. On the extreme Union flank, the 20th Maine underwent at least three frontal attacks over the course of ninety minutes from the 15th Alabama before leading a counterassault downhill to neutralize the Southern threat. On the west side, the Federal line started to give way, and only a last-second arrival and suicidal charge of the 140th New York stopped a Confederate breakthrough (see BLOODIEST FIELDS OF FIRE).

From beginning to end, the fight for Little Round Top lasted approximately two hours. The elevation was destined to play a marginal role the following day, with Battery D's rifled guns tossing long-range potshots toward Pickett's Charge, but neither side placed much stock in the rise before or after the deadly contest for its possession. It is possible that the abrupt Union defense of Little Round Top prevented any further bloodshed upon its slopes. Whereas Lee's marginal successes on Culp's Hill and against Cemetery Ridge enticed him into trying his luck for yet another long and costly day, the Union left flank appeared far too strong for any further Confederate consideration.

> The 20th Maine, though fighting effectively and heroically on Little Round Top, lost a lower percentage of men killed in action than the 3rd and 4th Maine in the salient or the 19th Maine on Cemetery Ridge.

9. THE SALIENT SLAUGHTERHOUSE

Along with time, terrain, and manpower, the fight for the salient was destined to end in a stalemate because of the extreme losses incurred by both sides. Already fighting fatigue from long deployments, lack of water, and rising heat and humidity, troops Confederate and Union rendered hours of brutal damage upon each other with no sign of sustainable progress. Fundamentally, the contest over the Union left ended in mutual exhaustion.

Many soldiers, having fought back and forth for many hours, found themselves hopelessly separated from their outfits and out of ammunition. Deaths and injuries fractured the officer class, leaving chains of

The plateau of the Peach Orchard erupts as Joseph Kershaw's South Carolinians plow into the Union 3rd Corps.

LIBRARY OF CONGRESS

command irreparably broken. Even the most belligerent of fighters discovered that their units were "fought out," no longer capable of conducting offensive or defensive operations of any kind.

Most destructive were the overall reductions. Of Meade's thirteen brigades involved, the majority experienced casualties surpassing 30 and 40 percent. Col. P. R. Guiney brought his 9th Massachusetts up from guard duty to assist their brigade, only to discover the brigade was effectively no more, that it "had been fought nearly to extinction." Maj. Gen. David B. Birney reported that the whole U.S. 3rd Corps had been "used up." On the Confederate side, out of twelve brigades involved, five lost their commanders. Several outfits lost more than 40 percent casualties.[31]

Taken as a whole, July 2 losses in the Peach Orchard, Devil's Den, the Rose and Trostle farms, and the Wheatfield far exceeded the casualties of Pickett's Charge. Combined dead and wounded neared fourteen thousand. And although junior officers were still calling for reinforcements as the sun was setting, most senior officers surmised that any continuation would have been pointless.[32]

Longstreet sent twelve thousand men into Pickett's Charge. More than eighteen thousand Confederates were involved in the fight for the salient.

10. AN UNSUPPORTED ATTACK ON THE UNION RIGHT

An assault upon Cemetery Hill and Culp's Hill was supposed to commence much earlier in the day. Lee had instructed Richard S. Ewell to make a demonstration on this far end of the Union line while Longstreet hit the other flank. If the 1st Corps made any substantial progress, Ewell's 2nd Corps was to push ahead with a "real attack."[33]

Old Pete's long delay meant a similar wait for Old Dick, and nothing came to pass for hours on end. Longstreet broke the silence at 4 p.m. with an artillery volley on the Peach Orchard. Ewell immediately let loose with a barrage of his own, hammering tightly packed Federal cannons lined up along the east side of Cemetery Hill. At that moment, Lee's army appeared to be of one mind, synchronized and attacking in lockstep. It would be their last harmonious act of the day.

As Hood's division pushed into Devil's Den and up the Round Tops, Ewell simply continued rattling off artillery rounds. While his first shots were impressively accurate, a quick Union response diluted all subsequent efforts. Owning no high ground of significance, Ewell's gunners were forced to huddle on Brenner's Hill, a modest elevation nearly a mile away to the northeast and more than a hundred feet lower than Cemetery Hill. Only about half of the 2nd Corps' eighty available guns could fit on the rise, and despite more than two hours of hard work, their effect was marginal.[34]

Not until 8 p.m. did the lieutenant general send his infantry forward, well after the sun had begun to fall into the horizon and Longstreet's assault had died out. Running toward the eastern side of Culp's Hill, a division under Maj. Gen. Edward Johnson first had to cross Rock Creek, most of which was waist deep. As his sodden men emerged from the muddy banks, they weaved into the trees up along the rocks and cliffs and were greeted by the exceptional defensive log works constructed by Brig.

Nighttime simply accentuated the shadowed and unforgiving terrain of Culp's Hill. Conditions virtually guaranteed close-quarter fighting and casualties from friendly fire.

BATTLES AND LEADERS

Gen. GEORGE S. GREENE of the U.S. 12th Corps. Meanwhile, a half mile to the west, part of Maj. Gen. JUBAL A. EARLY's division swung into the east side of Cemetery Hill.

Impressively, both offensives made headway despite the darkness. Johnson's men broke through the southern end of Greene's defenses and proceeded up the southern crest of Culp's Hill. Early's headlong push into the steepest part of Cemetery Hill sent parts of the hapless Union 11th Corps on the run once again. Some of the "flying Dutchmen" were so frightened that they ran into their own cannon fire.[35]

Despite some of the harshest combat to occur at Gettysburg, including incidents on Cemetery Hill in which men were clubbing each other with fence rails, all the Confederate gains were doomed to be lost. Darkness, exhaustion, and lack of artillery support weakened the engagement. Lack of infantry support killed it. Ewell still had a division left to use, but it was under the direction of Maj. Gen. ROBERT E. RODES, who wasted time aligning his men against the west side of Cemetery Hill and never moved them forward. Johnson went into Culp's Hill without his lethal Stonewall Brigade, which was wrestling with Union cavalry farther east under Brig. Gen. DAVID GREGG. Most significant, Richard S. Ewell, fellow corps commander A. P. Hill, and Robert E. Lee never coordinated forces of the 2nd and 3rd Corps and never defined a unified plan of attack. All the courageous work of their subordinates went to waste while the Union right, holding the interior lines, inserted reinforcements at will and halted every advance.

> At one point during the dark fight for Cemetery Hill, the 6th North Carolina and 9th Louisiana planted their regimental flags alongside Federal cannons atop the hill. The banners were torn down by fierce counterattacks from Union reinforcements.

TOP TEN REASONS WHY THE UNION WON THE THIRD DAY

There was no dawn on July 3. Night simply turned into lighter shades of gray as a heavy overcast sky suppressed the rising sun. Many soldiers had not yet slept—enlisted assigned to skirmish lines, officers preparing for the coming fight, doctors operating by lamplight, the wounded fighting the misery of frayed bones. Others managed to find a few hours of much needed rest. Confederate Col. E. Porter Alexander, in charge of James Longstreet's artillery, was lucky enough to find two hours before a long day's work. Brig. Gen. Alpheus S. Williams, acting commander of the Union 12th Corps, caught thirty minutes of sleep after readying defenses on Culp's Hill.

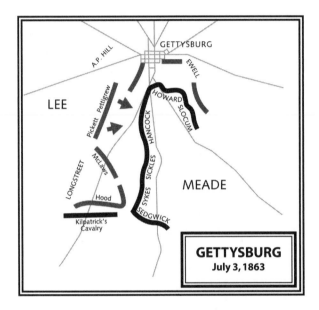

Lee and Meade maybe slept a combined eight hours. The former, convinced he was on the verge of victory, would again go on the offensive. The latter conferred with his corps commanders. The Union would remain in place, except for a dawn attack down the southern side of Culp's Hill to secure the entire rise.[36]

Surrounding them all were four thousand dead. Some had been hastily buried. Most were still awaiting any kind of internment as they lay front and center in no-man's-land or as yet unseen in some dark crevice, their bodies slowly bloating, their skin turning murky hues of black.

One individual who was very much alive and eager was Maj. Gen. George E. Pickett. Pompous, haughty, prone to tantrums, Pickett was a glory-starved man. Severely wounded in the Seven Days' battles, positioned in the only quiet section of Fredericksburg, absent from Chancellorsville, the Virginian believed he had missed the show once again at Gettysburg. Yet when Lee sought a fresh division to lead a frontal assault, Pickett's moment with destiny had arrived. Confidant his troops could win the battle, and with it perhaps the war, Picket left the shade trees of Seminary Ridge on the early afternoon, firmly convinced that he was undertaking the chance of a lifetime.

Following is an account of what happened to Pickett's dream, Lee's plan, and the Confederacy's hope of victory in the North, a sequential breakdown of how the South failed and the Union prevailed on July 3.

1. THE UNION VICTORY ON CULP'S HILL

Having failed to take all of Culp's Hill on the night of July 2, Lee ordered a renewed assault on the morning of July 3. This was not to be a feint or sideshow. Curling around the hill from the west and up to a lower peak on the south side, seven Confederate brigades (including the legendary Stonewall Brigade) were ordered to take the entire hill and surrounding area. Standing in their way were six Union brigades around the peak and several Federal batteries stationed to the west. In total there were well over twelve thousand combatants, all resigned to an all-or-nothing contest for the Federal anchor.[37]

Spoiling Lee's design for a surprise attack, the Union artillery opened first. At 4:30 a.m. twenty-six guns launched shots from the Baltimore pike to the west, hurling shells from a half mile into the Confederate left flank. When silence resumed fifteen minutes later, Southern infantry returned the favor and charged up the slopes.

Both sides intended on taking all of Culp's Hill on July 3. The Union struck first, using overwhelming reinforcements and artillery support to maximum effect.

LIBRARY OF CONGRESS

Back and forth the lines surged, rifle fire ebbing then swelling again. The desperate fight resembled the struggle for Little Round Top the previous day, including a Union downhill bayonet charge to clear an imperiled summit. Yet this day's fight lasted twice as long, involved three times the troops, and killed three times as many men. By 11 a.m. the Confederates withdrew, losing all the ground they had gained the night before.

Prior to the battle, Culp's Hill was a favorite destination for picnickers.

---

2. STUART'S FINAL FAILURE AT GETTYSBURG

Just before noon, with exceptional stealth, Jeb Stuart led a brigade of more than one thousand horsemen several miles east of town. Two more brigades were to follow, making a total of four thousand saddles and sabers. He was to wait for the trailing horsemen and then attack the rear of the Union army. His intention was to pull Federal reserves away from the point of Pickett's attack and cause damage at will.

The Union signal corps had spotted a fair amount of movement among the distant swales and tree lines, but spotters saw nothing to cause appropriate alarm. Then for some unknown reason, perhaps to create confusion among Federal positions within earshot, Stuart unlimbered a single cannon and blasted a few random rounds over the treetops. Rather than strike fear into his opponents, the cavalry commander simply alerted the Federals to his presence. Stuart worsened his chances by proceeding without his support brigades, turning his great force into two modest ones, which were never synchronized in the ensuing fight.[38]

Atypical of his usual practice, Jeb Stuart attempted piecemeal charges through narrow fields east of Gettysburg, making his cavalry an easy target for Union troopers and horse artillery.

BATTLES AND LEADERS

At first glance the arena three miles east of Cemetery Ridge seemed well suited for an old-fashioned cavalry dogfight, the kind a traditionalist like Stuart enjoyed most. But the generally level ground and sparse wood-lots were crisscrossed with a tight weave of sturdy fencerows. The grid work killed almost every charge attempted. When a final, gallant rush of fifteen hundred Confederate troopers ran headlong toward the heart of the Union cavalry, a funnel of fencing compressed the stampede. The charge turned into a solid and sluggish target for Federal artillery, dismounted troops, and a vicious counterassault by Brig. Gen. George Armstrong Custer and his Michigan squadrons.

In the end both sides claimed victory, though both lost more than three hundred casualties and failed to dominate the field. True to form, Stuart stated his assaults would have been decisive had his men conducted more and larger charges.[39]

One of George Custer's key advantages in the battle—his men were armed with Spencer seven-shot repeating rifles. Custer would miss these fine weapons years later, when his 7th U.S. Cavalry rode into the valley of Little Big Horn carrying meager Springfield single-shot carbines.

---

3. THE LONG SHOT: FAILURE OF THE CONFEDERATE ARTILLERY BARRAGE

The South brought some 280 field guns to Gettysburg. The 1st Corps artillery officer E. Porter Alexander was able to gather at least half of them for the massive bombardment meant to emasculate the Union center. Lining them up from west of town all the way south to the PEACH ORCHARD, a distance of nearly two miles, Alexander issued each crew a specific target. The young colonel was about to unleash the largest salvo the continent had ever seen—and one of the least effective.

To start with, the martial assembly was far from uniform. Forced to use whatever was available, the Confederates used nine different models of field artillery, each with a different caliber requiring its own ammunition. Largest of the collections were the trustworthy smoothbore Napoleons, but they constituted less than 40 percent of the mix. In addition, fuses, gunpowder, and shells were of poor quality. Crews loading the same ammo into the same gun rarely achieved the same trajectory twice.[40]

Again the terrain granted no favors. With the Federals owning the high ground, Lee's cannons had to work from considerable distances, ranging from a thousand yards to one and a half miles. Also, the air was warm, heavy, and still, keeping the artillery wrapped in its own smoke. The crews, unable to clearly see the effect of their shots, were unaware that nearly all were flying at least twenty feet above their intended targets, shattering headstones on Cemetery Hill, gutting horses tethered far to the rear, and knocking out trees and shrubs rather than limbers and guns.[41]

The event was unquestionably terrifying and spectacular. A Southern journalist wrote in amazement: "The very earth shook beneath our feet and the hills and rocks seemed to reel like a drunken man. . . . [T]he heavy muttering from the valley between the opposing armies, the splash of bursting shrapnel, and the fierce neighing of artillery horses, made a picture terribly grand and sublime." A fellow reporter on the opposite side watched the incoming missiles with far greater horror, confessing: "The air seemed literally filled with screaming messengers of death."[42]

One Union soldier, perhaps emboldened by survival, found a shred of amusement in the long but fruitless volleys. The mighty cannonade, he said, was "the biggest humbug of the season."[43]

On average, 50 percent of Confederate shells used in the Civil War were duds.

---

4.   A WEAKENED FORCE

In looking across the great divide of Seminary Ridge to Union-occupied Cemetery Ridge, James Longstreet lamented, "No fifteen thousand men ever arranged for battle can take that position." His cynicism might have sharpened had he known the true figures involved. At hand for the impending assault were not fifteen thousand Confederates but twelve thousand.[44]

Of the three divisions going forward, Maj. Gen. George E. Pickett's constituted the right side, Brig. Gen. James Johnston Pettigrew's moved on the left, with Maj. Gen. Isaac R. Trimble's division close behind. Pickett's men were relatively fresh but not at full strength. One of their four brigades was absent, assigned by Jefferson Davis to guard Richmond, and thereby rendering Pickett two thousand men short.

LIBRARY OF CONGRESS

In many respects, Lee's force had already spent itself before embarking on Pickett's Charge.

Pettigrew and Trimble led two very tired, ravaged assemblies. Each division had lost a third of its men during the carnivorous engagements of the first day. A day of sporadic rest did little to rectify the weakening.[45]

Once more, the entire construction was fragile at the top. Much has been made of how Pickett's Charge decimated Lee's officer class. Far less print acknowledges the loss of leaders before the assault was ever made. At every level, from corps to companies, most of the infantry units in the Army of Northern Virginia were "under new management" from the outset of the campaign. Considerable losses along the way simply accelerated the game of musical chairs. Pettigrew himself inherited his lofty position on the battle's first day, when the original division commander, Maj. Gen. Henry Heth, was struck in the head with a spent bullet. Trimble's division originally belonged to Maj. Gen. William D. Pender, until an artillery shell sliced open his leg during the second day's fighting. The well-liked commander eventually died from his wounds, but not before the much less qualified Trimble took his place. With few exceptions, nearly every officer involved in Pickett's Charge either had little or no experience at his existing level of command.[46]

The famous assault on Cemetery Ridge marked the first time George E. Pickett, a man who graduated dead last in his class at West Point, ever led a division into combat.

5. THE PATH OF ATTACK

"The point selected and the method of attack would certainly have been chosen for us by the enemy had they had the choice," reflected artillerist E. Porter Alexander. "I can only account for their allowing our visible preparations to be completed without interference by supposing that they appreciated in what a trap we would find ourselves. It seemed like madness to undertake such an attack."[47]

Aside from a few subtle declines and swells of the earth, there was virtually no protection for a mile. Unlike Second Manassas and Chancellorsville, there would be no element of surprise. Out in the open, the men were exposed to artillery fire the whole of the way.

There were two farms to negotiate. The Bliss house, owning perhaps the most ironic name on the battlefield, stood halfway and in the center. It was a sniper's nest until Union skirmishers burned it to the ground that morning. To the right and near their destination, the Codori home remained generally intact. Both farms functioned as obstacles rather than shields, breaking the infantry's unison, forcing them to slow and realign.

Most unsettling were the strong lumber fences along the way. The last was especially treacherous. Parallel to the Emmitsburg road that ran away from town to the southwest, the solid railings nearly touched the Union line on its north side and pulled gradually away to where it was a quarter mile back on the south. Too sturdy to pull down in a reasonable amount of time, the lumber net forced gear-toting soldiers to squeeze through or climb over, presenting a steady belt of inviting and easy targets.[48]

The final dash was all open ground, up a slight rise, to a finish line of stacked fence rails, shallow trenches, piled knapsacks filled with soil. Unbeknown to Lee and his men, across the center stood three hundred yards of a solid stone wall. Behind it all were the stalwart rises of Cemetery Ridge and Cemetery Hill, providing excellent platforms for the rows upon rows of Union artillery. It was to be Fredericksburg in reverse.

Part of the famous stone wall that shielded the Union infantry was built long before the battle—four score and seven years before.

---

6. CONFEDERATE LOSS OF ARTILLERY SUPPORT

The Confederate artillery bombardment stands as one of the most famous episodes of the battle. Often overlooked is that Lee intended the big guns to move up and keep firing throughout the life of the assault. He later recalled, "The batteries were directed to be pushed forward as the infantry progressed, protect their flanks, and support their attacks closely."[49]

Lee's reasonable order was in fact wishful thinking, as the gun crews expended far more ammunition than anticipated. The bombardment was supposed to last fifteen minutes. It went on for more than an hour. Unable to confirm any appreciable effect on his targets, E. Porter Alexander kept pounding away in hopes of improving the odds. The Confederate artillery arm was already low on missiles, having used a large portion of their cache during the firefights of the previous afternoon.[50]

Wary of a possible shortage and its ramifications, Longstreet counseled Alexander: "If the artillery fire does not have the effect to drive off the enemy or greatly demoralize him, so as to make our efforts pretty certain, I would prefer that you should not advise General Pickett to make the charge." Alexander, perhaps unwilling to countermand Lee's order for an assault, hurried Pickett forward with an urgent message: "For God's sake, come quick, or we cannot support you. . . . Ammunition nearly out."[51]

For all practical purposes the ammunition was gone. Only eighteen guns rolled forward with the charge. They popped out a few rounds, mostly solid shot, which had virtually no effect except by direct hit. Aside from five guns finding a moment of success on the extreme right side of the charge, almost nothing was hit. With no cavalry in the rear and no

Too little, too late, Confederate artillery gallops forward to assist the infantry's big push against Cemetery Ridge.

BATTLES AND LEADERS

artillery up front, Lee's infantry were going forward unprotected, out-gunned, and very much on their own.

The Confederates brought to Gettysburg two Whitworth breech-loading rifles, capable of launching a bolt three miles. As with most long-range artillery at the time, it was excessively inaccurate and almost useless in close-quarter fighting.

---

7. EFFECTIVE UNION ARTILLERY

Peering into the limber chests of the 1st Volunteer Artillery Brigade stationed on Cemetery Ridge, Union artillery commander Brig. Gen. HENRY J. HUNT noticed that the rounds were running low. Previously, for fear of this very situation, he had instructed all of his batteries to fire slowly and with great deliberation. As the Confederate guns kept pounding relentlessly but with minimal effect, Hunt decided to reduce firing altogether and to pull back several crews to safety in preparation for the infantry assault he was sure would come. His superior, GEORGE GORDON MEADE, had come to the same conclusion almost simultaneously. Confederate observers deduced incorrectly that this reduction meant the end of opposition from Federal gunners. The lull, however, only reflected better management.[52]

Numerically, the South held the edge. Though the Union brought somewhere around 80 more cannons to Gettysburg, the duel across the Emmitsburg road found the Confederates in the majority. Roughly 150 Southern guns faced not more than 120 Northern pieces.[53]

What the Union conceded in quantity, they more than superceded through quality. By firing tubes of higher tolerances and using more dependable gunpowder and shells, the industrial giant of the United States demonstrated its technological advantage in no uncertain terms. In addition, the Union guns were nearly uniform. Overall, nearly every Federal tube was either a smoothbore Napoleon or a three-inch rifled "Ordnance Gun," greatly simplifying the task of ammo supply and distribution.[54]

Hunt exploited this uniformity, placing large reserves of highly compatible guns and ammunition within a thousand yards of the front line. When the time came, he was able to bring everything necessary to the fore, and in the process, benefit from the last and most decisive advantage over his opponents. Confederate guns were still shooting at scattered targets a mile or more in the distance. Hunt and his gunners were training their sights on a solid object, moving closer and closer to the muzzle of their lethal devices. Across the divide, a reporter from the *Augusta Constitutionalist* watched in horror as the Union tactic went into effect. "There is Pickett and Pettigrew half across the valley; the enemy have run up new guns and are pouring a deadly fire into their ranks. . . . And our guns, will they not re-open?"[55]

As the Confederates came within paces of the stone wall, several Union batteries ran out of ammo but not gunpowder, so they loaded their cannons with stones, bullets, and bayonets, and kept firing.

---

8.   THE DEADLY ENFILADE

To fire upon an enemy line from the side can be brutally effective. Shots falling long or short are still likely to hit part of the target, and only the opponent's flank can fire in response. Pickett's Charge had the misfortune of being hit with enfilade fire on both its left and right sides.

Significantly, the Confederate line was more than a mile wide when it started, but Lee ordered Pickett and Pettigrew to gradually bunch together and concentrate their attack on a six-hundred-yard-wide section of the Union line, centering on a solitary copse of trees. This compaction created a dense, slow, and easily enveloped spearhead. However strong their front was, the Confederates exposed their sides, making themselves ripe for the feast of enfilade.

The lethal Angle: Confederates who reached this point were subjected to fire from three sides.

BATTLES AND LEADERS

First to falter was the Confederate left. Oddly, Lee allowed the critical position to be manned by Col. John M. Brockenbrough's brigade. The Virginia unit was at one time formidable, but not this day. Hard fighting over the previous months had whittled away its strength, and the brigade came to Gettysburg with an anemic eight hundred men—the size of a regiment. By day two they were down to five hundred, the weakest brigade on the field. Scarcely ten minutes into the march they wavered, taking hits from long-range artillery on Cemetery Hill and the 8th Ohio Infantry Regiment on their front left. By the halfway mark, the Brockenbrough shield had fallen away, exposing the Confederates' left ribcage to murderous crossfire. The farther Pettigrew's men went, the deeper they walked into the chasm. To their front, blasting muskets were protected by a formidable stone wall. On their left stood the shooting gallery. First they had to walk past the 8th Ohio, then the 1st Massachusetts, the 126th New York, the 108th New York, and finally the 1st U.S. Artillery. The final slaughter at the foot of the wall was a mere formality, as Confederates alive and dead were ripped to shreds from three directions.[56]

On Lee's extreme right marched Brig. Gen. James Kemper's brigade, once commanded by a young James Longstreet. Moving ever to their center left to form the spearhead Lee desired, Kemper's men nearly turned their backs to the fire coming from their right, issued at almost point-black range from a brigade of Vermonters under Brig. Gen. George J. Stannard. A desperate countercharge pushed the Vermont men back, but not until they had captured a battle flag, gunned down untold piles of men, and snatched hundreds of prisoners.[57]

The 13th Vermont Infantry, in attacking the right flank of Pickett's Charge, reportedly killed, wounded, or captured more Confederates than the number of men on the muster roll of the 13th that day.

---

9. ONLY ONE SIDE SENT REINFORCEMENTS

Before the assault began, Confederate brigade commander Ambrose R. Wright contemplated the task set before him and his men. The great distance was not his main concern, nor the lack of natural cover or artillery support. "The real difficulty," he surmised, "is to stay there after you get there."[58]

A breakthrough was probable in Wright's mind, but any infiltration would melt in minutes if successive waves were not close behind. A few units tried to hold their untenable position, in hopes that a wave of reserves would come and push the effort home. Several officers pinned down on the front sent couriers running back, begging for assistance. Clutching the ground, trying to survive the firestorm, a soldier in Kemper's brigade looked back at the empty spaces behind him and shouted, "Why don't they support us?" Most desperate was George E. Pickett, who sent repeated demands for "vigorous and immediate support."[59]

It was Longstreet's responsibility to send reinforcements. Thousands of soldiers stood ready, awaiting the much-anticipated order to finish off the Union line. Maj. Gen. JUBAL A. EARLY and his division were staged to strike from inside Gettysburg proper. Maj. Gen. ROBERT E. RODES prepared his North Carolina and Georgia boys to follow the footsteps of the leading troops from Seminary Ridge. Maj. Gen. RICHARD H. ANDERSON was in the process of sending the rest of his division from the ridge. Anderson later stated, "I was about to move forward . . . when Lieutenant-General Longstreet directed me to stop the movement, advising that it was useless, and would only involve unnecessary loss, as the assault had failed."[60]

To what extent an additional wave would have affected the outcome will forever be unknown. According to several prominent witnesses to the attack, including Robert E. Lee, the failure to send more bodies forward was the single most important reason why the charge did not accomplish its objective.[61]

Pickett's Charge contained less than a third of the able-bodied troops present in the Army of Northern Virginia.

10. SOMETHING TO DO WITH THE UNION ARMY

After the war, a journalist asked George E. Pickett why his famous Gettysburg assault had failed so spectacularly. His answer: "The Union army had something to do with it."

In examining any lopsided military result such as Gallipoli, Pearl Harbor, or Stalingrad, the standard operating procedure is to place blame on the vanquished. Many Confederates did so with Gettysburg, viewing the final charge in particular as an issue of internal wrongdoing. Such condemnation was paradoxically a show of patriotism, insinuating that the Yankee foe was unworthy of any measurable credit.

Pickett's minority opinion was nonetheless astute. The Army of the Potomac, well practiced at pulling defeat out of the jaws of victory, brought its higher qualities to bear in Pennsylvania. Reverses on the first day alone might have broken it in earlier contests. The Union retreated two full miles and lost more than five thousand killed and wounded, plus more than three thousand captured—a beating worse than the first day of either Second Manassas or Chancellorsville. Gettysburg's second day brought more setbacks along the center and casualties in excess of ten thousand. Falsely believing themselves outnumbered, with the recent and dismal performances of Chancellorsville and Fredericksburg fresh in their minds, Federal soldiers watched in awe as the Confederates came at them in plain sight, twelve thousand bayonets dead ahead and closing. But this time, the Northerners would stand firm.[62]

Riflemen obeyed orders to wait until the first lines were well within reach. Artillery batteries also refrained, their tubes loaded with short-range canister. As Confederates started to breach the fence rails along the Emmitsburg road, the grievous fire slowly grew until all was a fusion of blinding smoke and earsplitting volleys. Yet in this terrible fog, as lead flew in clouds, skulls opened like eggshells, and confusion expanded across the field, Union lines executed their work with newfound determination. With uncanny repetition, as holes opened, reserves quickly plugged the gaps. Gunners fired well past the point of escape. Infantry regiments fell en masse. Situated at the angle of the stone wall, every member of Company F of the 69th Pennsylvania became a casualty. But the wall held, as did the entire Union line.[63]

Embodying the absolutism of resolve, Battery A of the 4th U.S. Light Artillery lost four of its six guns. Exploding caissons killed or maimed much of its crew, prompting one dying private to end his own suffering with a pistol shot to the brain. Instead of falling back, the lieutenant in charge advanced the two remaining guns to the stone wall, where he coolly administered their fire. Brought down by several gunshot wounds, Alonzo Cushing stood again and continued his work until a rifle shot entered his mouth and blew out the back of his head. But before the Confederates could rush the silent guns, a regiment of Pennsylvanians abruptly closed the line and shot the advancing grays to pieces.[64]

In only one instance during Pickett's Charge was there a conspicuous Union breakdown. Fragmented by conflicting orders and the intense fighting, a portion of a single regiment broke and ran for the rear. Adding to the embarrassment of their fearful act, the perpetrators were from Pennsylvania.

TOP TEN BEST PERFORMING COMMANDERS

When dissecting the battle and its results, the incentive is to concentrate on the decisions of a few men and heap credit and blame accordingly. Such analysis is done with the luxury of hindsight, copious amounts of information, and freedom from consequences, all of which were not available to any of the mortals present in the crisis.

It is debatable how much leverage any individual actually has upon a conflagration, especially one involving 150,000 heavily armed warriors fighting for their lives. Add unalterable variables—such as the strength and actions of the opposition, existing terrain, available troops, supply base, technology, unit health, and weather—and any given tactic may succeed marvelously one day and fail miserably the next. Yet, ultimately, officers are responsible for the way in which they execute their given orders, the ingenuity with which they utilize available resources, and the condition, discipline, and actions of their troops.

Whether the following are worthy of adoration is up to the devotee, but all were able to produce measurable gains under excessively hostile conditions. Listed are the best individual performances in command during the fight for Gettysburg based on their application of tactics, effect on morale, clarity in communication, and above all, the degree to which they personally contributed to the success of their respective side in a given engagement.

1. MAJ. GEN. WINFIELD SCOTT HANCOCK (U.S., PENNSYLVANIA, AGE 39)

While advancing to Gettysburg in front of his ten-thousand-strong 2nd Corps, Winfield Scott Hancock inherited his army's left wing by order of Maj. Gen. GEORGE GORDON MEADE. The assignment had a few challenges. At that very moment, most of the left wing was engaged in a large and escalating firefight, the original senior officer had just been killed, and the second in command outranked Hancock. Adding to the difficulties, Hancock had never led so many troops at one time, he had no concept of the terrain at the scene, and he was miles away from all of it.

Regardless, he hurried to the front, riding partway in an ambulance wagon so he could study maps of the area. Reaching his senior officer, the pious and proud Maj. Gen. Oliver O. Howard, Hancock acknowledged the awkwardness of replacing a superior but took control anyway. He agreed with the offended Howard that the rise upon which they were standing, known locally as Cemetery Hill, would make the best available rallying point for the already retreating wing.

Immediately ordering reinforcements while sending word back to Meade of the situation, Hancock also instructed every available body to occupy a tree-shrouded rise a half mile to the right called Culp's Hill. After Meade's arrival, Hancock returned to his 2nd Corps and moved it forward to a ridge stretching south from Cemetery Hill.[65]

The following day presented another challenge. While Union forces collected along Cemetery Ridge and the morning passed without incident, Maj. Gen. DANIEL E. SICKLES and his 3rd Corps, positioned to Hancock's left, ventured out unannounced in front of the Union line. Perplexed, Hancock knew it was a mistake.

When Sickles's salient started to crack that afternoon from a massive Confederate attack, Hancock requested permission to send one of his own divisions to stem the tide. Meade said yes. When Sickles fell wounded, Hancock asked if he could assume control of both his own and Sickles's dying corps. Meade again said yes. Maneuvering along the thin Union line, rallying each regiment in person, "Hancock the Superb" was also capable of being ruthless, as illustrated by his order to the 1st Minnesota to charge straight into an advancing brigade.[66]

July 3 brought no respite. Hancock's 2nd Corps would receive the spearhead of Pickett's Charge. Atop his horse to inspire his men, Hancock refused to dismount, claiming that there were times when a corps commander's life did not matter. He still had the wisdom to apply crossfire when the chance presented itself, and he instructed his Vermont regiments to fold in from the left and shoot along the length of the advancing Confederates.[67]

Only twice did he lose his composure, but for valid reasons. When Union batteries reduced their rate of fire to save ammunition, Hancock furiously demanded they resume. The decision was not his to make, and one battery did deplete their stores, but the gesture may have steadied the nerves of his regiments. He knew from experience that soldiers felt most vulnerable when they could not fire back.

He also displayed a great deal of panic at the height of the Confederate attack. As he was shouting to his men, Hancock was hit in the leg, and the projectile traveled upward into his hips. Spurting blood and in excruciating pain, he begged for others to come help him. Shaking and ashen, he pleaded, "Don't let me bleed to death." He survived, and due to his efforts throughout the battle, so did his army.[68]

Hancock's wound during Pickett's Charge would plague him for the rest of his life, but it wasn't a bullet that struck him. A rifle shot hit the horn of his saddle, sending a tanner's nail and debris deep into the general's body.

---

2. BRIG. GEN. GEORGE S. GREENE (U.S., RHODE ISLAND, AGE 62)

He was a West Point graduate and a civil engineer. At age sixty-two, he was also the oldest general at Gettysburg and one of the finest. Since 1862 George Sears Greene had held the reins of a brigade. At Second Bull Run and Antietam, when his superiors fell wounded, Greene temporarily took charge of their divisions and stepped down after each fight. He was still "just a brigadier" when he came to Gettysburg at the head of five New York regiments, but his experience at the upper levels would prove invaluable and earn him the title "Savior of Culp's Hill." More accurately, he saved the Union right flank.

Deployed to secure the rise with the rest of the 12th Corps in the early hours of July 2, the former engineer immediately set to constructing substantial breastworks along the corps' entire line. His superior officers, Maj. Gen. HENRY W. SLOCUM and Brig. Gen. John W. Geary, insisted he was wasting his time. They initially appeared to be correct. Hours passed without incident. Then word came of a Confederate breakthrough two miles to the southwest. Every brigade but Greene's was sent as reinforcements, and the bluecoat population defending the hill went from 9,000 to 1,300.[69]

To maintain the line, Greene ordered his men to extend along the works as thin as they would dare. Night was falling, and he wanted no surprises. One came nonetheless.

His men began to hear the rustle of leaves and the snapping of twigs on the lower west slopes. Minutes later, a rush of 4,500 Confederates slammed against the cordons. As regiments from the U.S. 1st and 11th Corps came to his assistance, Greene coolly directed his troops to use the tall log defenses to their advantage and to move wherever the threat was worst. He also instructed his troops to rotate to the back every thirty to ninety minutes to rest and refill their cartridge boxes. The tactic also gave the Confederates the impression that the Union was continually receiving reinforcements.[70]

By midnight, the Southern assaults had abated, and the rest of the 12th Corps were returning to reinforce Greene's lines. For nearly four hours, outnumbered more than three to one, behind defenses of his construction, the aged Greene had saved the critical high ground on the Union's far right. His casualties exceeded three hundred. In turn, he and his regiments induced fifteen hundred casualties among the Confederates.

The fight for the hill resumed four hours later, this time initiated by the Union. As testimony to the strength of the Confederate opposition present, the entire 12th Corps required six hours to tame Johnson's division, something Greene effectively accomplished in nearly half the time with a fraction of the troops.[71]

George Greene studied civil engineering at West Point. One of his many prewar projects was the Central Park Reservoir in New York City.

---

3. MAJ. GEN. GEORGE GORDON MEADE (U.S., PENNSYLVANIA, AGE 47)

For Union commanders in the East, standard procedure was to talk a big game and then proceed with extreme caution. George B. McClellan, John Pope, Ambrose E. Burnside, and Joseph Hooker did as much over the course of two years. When unexpectedly appointed as head of the Army of the Potomac, George Gordon Meade abruptly broke the pattern, preferring action over words. Six days later, he and his associates would achieve the first great Federal victory in the eastern theater.

His challenges were daunting from the outset. Appointed to the job while an invasion was in progress, he was working on scant information. Due to the secretive command style of his predecessor, Meade did not initially know the exact whereabouts or troop strength of his fellow corps leaders. He was barely known outside his 5th Corps, and he was inheriting an army low in morale and not of his design. Plus, he was about to go up against the same man who had ruined more careers and had won more primary battles than the rest of the Confederacy's generals put together.

Pausing momentarily along meandering Pipe Creek on the northern border of Maryland, Meade assessed the situation and adhered to the basics. He reestablished communications among the senior officers, condensed his forces, and calmly directed them to proceed northward until contact was made and then engage the opposition. To simultaneously protect the East Coast and find his adversary, he set forth his army along a wide berth, consisting of two wings, twenty miles across. Cavalry would act as extending tentacles, feeling ahead for any sign of Lee's infantry.[72]

Once contact was made, he immediately granted the highest authority to his most trusted and capable officers, regardless of rank. Throughout the battle, Meade openly courted the idea of attacking, and came to Gettysburg with that purpose in mind. Seeing no conspicuous opportunity present itself, he waited, for fear of committing himself to a reckless and costly charge. Though maintaining a defensive posture over the two days he was present on the field, his headquarters were closer to the fighting than was his adversary's. Most of his subsequent decisions were sound until he removed too many 12th Corps troops from Culp's Hill—a

Meade's council of war on the night of July 2, where he established a unified plan among his chief field commanders.

U.S. ARMY MILITARY HISTORY INSTITUTE

mistake rectified by the hard work of George Greene and the unbreakable pieces of three corps.

The one move he never would have advocated, Daniel E. Sickles's forward deployment into the Peach Orchard, proved to be the area in which his side sustained its highest casualties. He can simultaneously be accused of not keeping a tighter reign on his most impetuous officer and be credited for inserting enough reinforcements to prevent the line from imploding. Throughout the day, he stayed in close contact with the front. While Lee sat on a tree stump far behind the lines, sending and receiving exactly one dispatch during the whole of the afternoon, Meade was often on horseback along Cemetery Ridge. In his fifth day at the head of affairs, the major general nearly became a casualty when a bullet hit and severely wounded his mount.[73]

On the night of July 2, Meade's council of war gave his corps chieftains the opportunity to assess the situation, share information, and create a single strategy for the following day. His adversary invited no such meeting nor entertained dissenting opinion at the battle. While leadership by definition is less democratic than autocratic, Meade was dealing with an officer class wounded by infighting and politics. Complicating matters further, a number of the gentlemen in his service outranked him by seniority. On several occasions, Meade's diplomacy almost jeopardized the chain of command, as exemplified by Sickles (who by the time of the council meeting was in a field hospital and minus a leg). Yet through the use of popular consensus, Meade provided a temporary truce, allowing for better communication and singularity of purpose. That unity would be tried to the fullest the next day, when his side would undergo the largest artillery bombardment of the war, followed by a massed, direct assault.

George Gordon Meade died in 1872 from the same ailment that killed Stonewall Jackson, Richard S. Ewell, and James Longstreet: pneumonia.

---

4. BRIG. GEN. WILLIAM BARKSDALE (C.S., MISSISSIPPI, AGE 42)

A graduate of the University of Nashville, an attorney, a Democrat, a Mexican War veteran, and a U.S. Congressman, Barksdale achieved success through impulsiveness and pure zeal. As the war progressed, his fiery nature won him undying respect among his Mississippi troops, at least

 from the ones who survived his battles. He was also esteemed among the Confederate high command as a reliable and swift sword. Predictably, on the afternoon of July 2, the brigade deployed directly across from the Peach Orchard was his. To his right were the South Carolinians of JOSEPH B. KERSHAW.

While Longstreet took a few hours to situate the line, Barksdale begged to be sent forward, asking for just a few minutes so that he could forcefully remove the Federal cannon staring in his direction. The requests were denied. His brigade would move *en échelon* like the other eleven. Waiting his turn, the general carefully explained to his officers what the next hour or so would bring for them and the eighteen hundred men under their direction. Speed and confusion would be their weapons. There would be no hesitating.

Sometime after 5 p.m. it began, and as instructed, Barksdale's men moved from their positions and sped into the Union lines. Pushing just north of the peach trees, his brigade smashed through one Union brigade and captured its general, but then his own brigade started to split apart. Knowing that to stop and realign would endanger them all, he allowed his 21st Mississippi to continue straight ahead, for the regiment was making good ground and overrunning a bevy of artillery in the process. Meanwhile Barksdale swung to the left with his other three regiments, ramming into the side of a second Union brigade manning the Emmitsburg road.[74]

Wheeling right and heading east again, his troops started to slow against the fresh brigade of Col. George L. Willard. Fatigue began to set in. Some of his men started to fade backward. Furious, Barksdale ordered them to return, and he himself was struck in the chest and leg by a fusillade of bullets.[75]

The shock tactics of Barksdale's brigade achieved exceptional results. Against heavy resistance, his men broke through a fortified line, knocked out two brigades, damaged a third, captured 250 soldiers (including a general officer), took nine artillery pieces, and pressed a large part of the Union line back one mile. The price, however, was exorbitant. Of 1,400 men to go forward, only half returned. Lost among them was Barksdale himself, who would die from his wounds in a Union field hospital the following day.[76]

William Barksdale's Civil War record did not start well. He was court-martialed for drunkenness at First Manassas, but he was reinstated when he swore never to touch another drop until the war was over.

5. BRIG. GEN. HENRY J. HUNT (U.S., MICHIGAN, AGE 43)

 It was no secret between the armies that the Union artillery was the superior of the two. Meade's gunners had more ammunition, better powder, and healthier draft horses. From July 2 onward, they also deployed a greater number of guns. An additional and perhaps decisive edge came by way of leadership. Whereas Confederate Chief of Artillery WILLIAM PENDLETON was an indecisive second fiddle, his Union counterpart was the master of a prodigious orchestra.[77]

A West Pointer, a veteran of the Mexican War, and a firm believer in training and self-discipline, Henry Hunt had served with distinction since First Manassas, where he was one of the few Federal battery officers to maintain his composure and continue fighting. A firm believer in deliberate, unhurried accuracy over sheer firepower, he handed Robert E. Lee one of the general's worst defeats, blasting away his impetuous frontal assault up Malvern Hill during the Seven Days' battles in 1862.

Advising divisional batteries and directing the artillery reserve, Hunt preferred to lead in person. Wherever his guns were, Hunt was there scouting positions, checking trajectories, boosting morale, ensuring a steady supply of ammunition. After checking on a crew stationed in Gettysburg's Devil's Den, he was nearly gored by a stampede of frightened cattle, but neither horns nor bullets appeared to concern him when he was at work. When Meade held his council of war on the night of July 2, Hunt begged off, opting instead to labor through the darkness, attending to his guns.[78]

On the third day, the great Confederate cannonade began while Hunt was on Little Round Top. Deducing that the barrage was essentially telegraphing the imminence and location of an assault, he hurried to the artillery reserve to bring up fresh batteries and ordered the guns of the 2nd Corps to cease fire and conserve ammunition.

Unlike his adversaries, who left their ordnance wagons far out of reach, he placed his gun park eight hundred yards from the front line. Unlike Pendleton, who stayed far to the rear, Hunt personally directed the placement and rotation of gun crews on Cemetery Ridge. And unlike the more famous work of Col. E. Porter Alexander's artillery barrage of more than 150 guns, the Federal gunners achieved more with fewer. Drawing steady beads on Lee's frontal attack, Hunt was able to ensure a repeat of Malvern Hill, where Lee suffered nearly the same number of casualties in an assault launched a year almost to the day of Pickett's Charge.[79]

Gunners North and South worked from a prewar army manual on artillery. One of the manual's coauthors was Henry Hunt.

---

6. BRIG. GEN. JOHN BUFORD (U.S., KENTUCKY, AGE 37)

 Roughhewn, businesslike, with a low and deliberate manner of speech, John Buford drove his men almost as hard as he pushed himself, and on the last day of June, they were all riding hard through the streets of Gettysburg. Many Union officers claimed they were the first to recognize the area's favorable ground, but long before they ever set eyes on the place, Buford was already betting his life that it was land worth keeping.

The deduction was unremarkable. The town contained a hub of ten roads, and the hills and ridges immediately to the south were too prominent to be missed. Foremost, the area's strategic location was self-evident by June 30. In the ever-narrowing gap between two great hunting parties, Gettysburg stood right in the middle. It would take a particularly witless individual to overlook the region's recently elevated stature. Regardless, Buford was still brilliant for the way in which he secured the place, giving his army the two things it needed most: space and time.

Rather than lodge in the high hills and ridges to the south, Buford positioned his two thousand troopers far west and north of Gettysburg. By nightfall he had created a breakwater of nearly twenty square miles.

Outermost were his "videttes," pockets of lookouts stationed four miles distant. Closer in were intermediaries in larger numbers, reaching back to his headquarters in town. When lookouts made contact along the

Chambersburg pike early the next morning, Buford hurried to Seminary Ridge and began a methodical, regressive defense. Sending couriers south to hurry Maj. Gen. John F. Reynolds and the Union left wing along, he placed his six cannons astride the pike, and condensed his dismounted troops along the ridges farther west.[80]

Being mindful of his ammunition and vulnerable flanks, Buford offered resistance, then retracted his frontline little by little. Facing long-range rifles with short-range carbines, outgunned in artillery, outnumbered two to one, then three to one, and finally four to one, Buford still managed to buy nearly three hours at the price of two miles and 130 dead, wounded, or captured. Just as his lines were about to break, the Union 1st Corps appeared and replaced his troops along McPherson's Ridge.[81]

Exhausted and out of ammunition, Buford's division spent the rest of the day conducting reconnaissance for the still outnumbered Union. The next morning they were ordered away from the front to rest for several days. As was his nature, Buford was soon chomping at the bit to return.

John Buford had something in common with Abraham Lincoln. He was born in Kentucky and raised in Illinois.

---

7. THE SAVIORS OF LITTLE ROUND TOP

Who was the savior of Little Round Top? The answer varies from generation to generation. Since the 1993 release of the motion picture *Gettysburg*, the front-runner has been a Maine professor of ancient and modern languages. In truth, the hill's timely defense involved several pieces fitting together. Remove any one of them, and the battle might have progressed quite differently.

First on the scene was Meade's chief engineer, Gouverneur K. Warren. With the unauthorized introduction of Sickles's salient, Meade ordered the brigadier general to ascend Little Round Top to assess the condition of his new left flank. While scanning the fields below, Warren saw what looked to be an imminent attack upon the very rise where he was standing. Sounding the alarm to his commander and every nearby officer, Warren demanded immediate help in securing the position.

First to respond was Col. Strong Vincent, a brigade leader in the U.S. 5th Corps stationed near the base of the hill. Looking up at the potential

Gouverneur Warren (left), Strong Vincent (middle), Joshua Lawrence Chamberlain (right)

catastrophe, Vincent risked court-martial for failing to enter the salient as instructed and instead led his men up the slopes of the rocky top and over to its southwest side. His brigade—consisting of the 83rd Pennsylvania, 44th New York, 16th Michigan, and 20th Maine—arrived just in time to blunt the first Confederate attack.[82]

First to bring the big guns were Capt. Augustus Martin and Lt. Charles Hazlett of the 5th Corps artillery brigade. Ascending the rocky slope, fighting for every yard of elevation, their crews dragged the beastly pieces to the summit. Loading and firing directly, they stayed their ground but lost Hazlett.

The first reinforcements came from Col. Patrick O'Rorke, leading his 546 men of the 140th New York at a sprint, up and over the rise, and directly into the line of battle. Within moments, O'Rorke fell dead from a spray of bullets, yet his regiment sustained the Union's defensive stand.[83]

Col. Joshua Lawrence Chamberlain's actions on the extreme left flank epitomized calm under fire. Working with his depleted regiment of Maine men, Chamberlain withstood several assaults upon his critical position. Running low on ammunition, with his left flank about to give way, he personally led a countercharge down the hill and into the approaching Confederates, initiating an end to Southern assaults upon the south side of the rise.[84]

Taken individually, Union senior officers on Little Round Top displayed no more courage or initiative than many of their allies and adversaries at the lower elevations. Collectively, they fashioned a timely and successful defense of Meade's neglected left flank.

At the summit of Little Round Top is the statue of Maj. Gen. G. K. Warren perched on a stone, said to be the very platform upon which he stood and saw the approaching Confederate attack. It is the only rock in Gettysburg National Military Park that visitors are forbidden to stand on.

---

8.   BRIG. GEN. JOSEPH B. KERSHAW (C.S., SOUTH CAROLINA, AGE 41)

Indicative of the generally mediocre performance among Confederate senior officers, the most impressive demonstrations of leadership are found not at the corps or division levels but among the brigades. In addition, two outstanding examples are found on the second day right next to each other.

The refined and educated Joseph B. Kershaw of Longstreet's 1st Corps was a veteran of Second Manassas, Fredericksburg, and Chancellorsville. Known as a "devout man of high character," he was also a willing fighter and an officer not afraid to innovate under fire. He would call upon all of his talents when entering Sickles's salient with nearly two thousand men. His brigade was the first to break through, and his men would reach the farthest.

Lining up to go into the Peach Orchard, Kershaw noticed the area did not hold the few regiments and guns he was told. Upon the squat plateau were something more like thirty cannon, several brigades, plus more artillery and infantry on the slopes and hills to the rear. Adding to the unpleasantness, the terrain was a mix of woodlots and rocky slopes plus several stone buildings (the Rose farm) directly in his path. After passing this information up the chain of command, Kershaw received word from Longstreet that the orders were to be obeyed. Kershaw would move ahead, but he had no idea how long his men could endure the impending nightmare. As it turned out, they would last more than two hours.[85]

On the signal to advance, Kershaw directed his men up a slope and into the guns. Shells splattered the ranks. Men who survived recalled the odd sound of shrapnel bouncing off the stone barns and the unnerving sensation of cannon shots passing between their legs.

After entering the orchard, Kershaw swung them to the left, sweeping two brigades of Union infantry from atop the aptly named Stony Hill. As Federal artillery advanced to his right, the general bent his line back to meet them head on. A lieutenant misunderstood the order and turned his section into an awaiting row of Federal cannon. The ensuing gust of shrapnel leveled the lieutenant and his men, and yet the lethal blunder failed to rattle Kershaw or break the brigade.

Eventually forced back, and relinquishing Stony Hill in the process, the general started to pull his men away, until reinforcements appeared from the rear, inspiring him to move his troops forward yet again. Pushing past the hill and into the Wheatfield beyond, mowing over Federal resistance in their path, Kershaw and the remains of his regiments advanced all the way to the northwest base of Little Round Top, until a Union countercharge threw them back yet again.

In total, Kershaw's outfit fought against five Union brigades and progressed more than a mile through the most heavily contested terrain of the battlefield. While others halted or broke, he used time, terrain, and superior discipline to his advantage. The maneuvers of his troops were so precise as to be called "majestic," a feat accomplished despite an overall loss of one out of every three men along the way. For his cool and deliberate performance under fire, and through several hours of close-quarter fighting, Kershaw was cited for gallantry by Longstreet, the very man who sent him into the fray.[86]

Brigade commander Joseph B. Kershaw found work early after the war. In 1866 he was elected to the state senate of South Carolina.

---

9. BRIG. GEN. ALEXANDER S. WEBB (U.S., NEW YORK, AGE 28)

A former mathematics professor at West Point and junior grade artillery officer at the beginning of the war, the hardworking and highly respected Alexander S. Webb was a Civil War Dwight Eisenhower. He was so proficient and highly regarded in staff operations that he never had the opportunity to personally lead men into battle. At the start of Lee's campaign, he was serving as Meade's chief of staff in the U.S. 5th Corps. But Webb's luck, for better or worse, would change three days before Gettysburg.

Due to an arrest of its previous commander, Webb inherited the 2nd Brigade of the 2nd Division of the 2nd Corps, the so-called Philadelphia

Brigade. Consisting of four regiments with low morale and a tough reputation, the men and their new caretaker marched along Cemetery Ridge and took up their assigned spots. One of the regiments, the 69th Pennsylvania, positioned itself behind a stone wall bent at a ninety-degree angle to the right and shaded by a copse of trees to the left.[87]

That afternoon the 69th faced a hard-charging pack of Georgia bulldogs led by Brig. Gen. AMBROSE R. WRIGHT. Webb strengthened his vanguard by coolly sending another of his regiments in at the double quick, then his third and fourth to finish the work. As the Georgians halted and began to fall back, Webb's troops could not help themselves. With newfound determination, they bounded over the wall and gave chase, returning with a brighter step and three hundred prisoners.[88]

July 3 began with Webb's 69th back at the wall, his 71st and 72nd Pennsylvania fifty paces farther back and to the right, and his 106th divided between skirmish duty and guarding Cemetery Hill to the rear. Although his day began quietly, the early afternoon brought the Confederate bombardment, pushing everyone to the ground and bringing forth an assault aimed right for his men. From then on Webb was in motion, sending the spare guns of Lt. Alonzo Cushing to the wall and filling gaps in the line with companies from his 71st. He tried to push his 72nd to the front, even grabbing their standard in an attempt to lead the way. They refused their new senior officer, firing into the Confederates from a distance.

Turning back into the storm, Webb returned to the wall and shouted encouragement to his bravest 69th, who were frantically laying down fire into their front and to their right, where a crowd of gray infantry had

Alexander Webb's brigade and Alonzo Cushing's battery withstand the apex of Lee's final assault.

passed the Angle. In grinding crossfire, Webb and his dying regiment refused to move. Supporting them from the back were the two skirmishing companies of the 106th, standing, loading, and firing over the heads of their comrades. Soon after, the wall was breached, and fighting turned hand-to-hand. The regimental commander fell dead. Every member of Company F became a casualty. Webb himself was struck in the hip but survived.

In the words of Winfield Scott Hancock: "In every battle and on every important field there is one spot . . . the spot upon which centers the fortunes of the field. There was but one such spot at Gettysburg and it fell to the lot of General Webb to have it and hold it." For his actions and for those of his men at the Angle, Webb immediately received accolades from his peers and would eventually be awarded the Medal of Honor.[89]

Years after Gettysburg, Alexander Webb became president of the New York City College, a post he would maintain for thirty-three years.

10. BRIG. GEN. DAVID M. GREGG (U.S., PENNSYLVANIA, AGE 30)

 With the flashy dress and matching personalities of Alfred Pleasonton, George Custer, and Judson Kilpatrick in the U.S. Cavalry, it is little wonder why the reserved and studious David Gregg was not the most well-known Union horseman at Gettysburg. Nor did he stand out at West Point, where his upperclassmen included Jeb Stuart, and the commandant from his second year onward was Robert Edward Lee.

By Gettysburg, Gregg was at the head of a cavalry division, positioned with his brigades east of town. Soon after arriving, his men were involved in a heavy skirmish with the famous Stonewall Brigade of Lee's 2nd Corps, aided by a batch of troopers under Gregg's former classmate Stuart. Gregg won the fight, but Stuart would be back.[90]

Assigned to remain in the area and protect the Union's right flank, Gregg was also instructed early the next morning to move his division closer to the Federal line. He resisted vehemently, knowing that such a maneuver would bind the end too tightly, allowing any competent cavalry a wide-open avenue to the Baltimore pike, the main artery connecting the Army of the Potomac to all points east, including the national capital.[91]

Bending his instructions, he stretched his brigades farther east to act as a shield, in case the Confederates would try an end run. Around noon that day, Stuart did in fact arrive to stab at the Federal back with four thousand horsemen in tow. Nearly matching Stuart's numbers, Gregg used artillery, dismounted troops, natural cover, and precisely applied countercharges upon his attacker. After three hours of tangled fighting, Stuart departed, leaving the Union road to Washington intact, and losing for the second time in two days to an unassuming underclassman.[92]

In February 1865 David Gregg suddenly resigned and left the army. His exact reason for doing so has never been determined.

TOP TEN WORST PERFORMING COMMANDERS

After reflecting some time on the subject, Richard "Baldy" Ewell said to a fellow officer that it took "a dozen blunders to lose at Gettysburg." Perhaps the 2nd Corps general was looking to deflect a growing din of criticism against his spotty leadership in the contest, but his basic argument was still correct. No one person or incident could decide the outcome of this or any battle. The monster is simply too colossal and erratic a beast to be so easily directed.[93]

Although scrutinized like no other, Gettysburg possessed no more failures or laxity than most major battles in the Civil War. On the contrary, by July 1863 many of the habitually poor leaders had resigned, were replaced, or had died from illness or through their own incompetence. The battle is sometimes referred to as a "soldiers' fight," where high-level decisions meant little compared to the resolve of the enlisted men in the field. This position may be applicable to a Chickamauga or a Wilderness, where contact and order quickly melted into the dense underbrush. Yet the escalation at the Pennsylvania crossroads, with its critical sites of high ground, demanded the utmost precision of deployment. The multiple cases of extended fighting that ensued also required an officer's direct supervision of reinforcements, repositioning, and resupply.

Strangely, some of the least impressive officers in the engagement possessed some of the most enviable war records. But the finest reputations do not preordain success. It is one thing to make a calculated risk and fall short. It is quite another to make a mistake and run with it. Following are the worst performances in command during the battle, based on the degree to which these commanders squandered resources, undermined communications, failed to collaborate, and generally neglected intelligence. Foremost, they are ranked by the degree to which they personally jeopardized the success of their side.

1. LT. GEN. JEB STUART (C.S., VIRGINIA, AGE 30)

From beginning to end, the Gettysburg campaign was a series of faults and false starts for this otherwise exceptional leader. His series of capital mistakes began with the shame of Brandy Station and continued through to the end of the battle. Most of the lasting failures arose for his unwise and desperate attempts to make amends for the first. In a fit of denial, Jeb Stuart called the June 9 surprise of seven thousand Federal troopers bounding through his camp a Confederate "victory." Though technically a draw, Brandy Station challenged the long-held assumption that Union cavalry was inferior to Stuart and his Southern horsemen.

Three weeks into the Pennsylvania campaign, the tarnished Stuart requested permission from Lee to launch a raid around the Army of the Potomac and strike its supply lines at will. The tactic worked miracles during the Peninsula campaign and Second Manassas, primarily because Stuart also collected a feast of information concerning the enemy's whereabouts.[94]

Lee approved the plan—with stipulations. First, Stuart was to leave two thousand of his eight thousand riders behind to protect Lee's infantry. Second, the paternal Marse Robert insisted, "You will, however, be able to judge whether you can pass around their army without hindrance." Should any problem arise, Stuart was to return at once. The Army of Northern Virginia was heading into unknown territory. More than ever it needed the eyes and ears of its cavalry to monitor the opposition. As instructed, Stuart shed two brigades and set off eastward on June 24. And then he disappeared.[95]

On the very first day of his ambitious outing, Stuart ran into the Union 2nd Corps marching northward. Rather than head back, as ordered, Stuart simply rode farther south and out of the campaign. For nearly a week he wandered through Maryland, often within closer range of the Atlantic Ocean than Lee. Meanwhile Lee wandered too, blind and deaf to the closing Army of the Potomac.

On June 28 Stuart ran into more than a hundred Union supply wagons loaded down with corn, ham, and whiskey. Rather than destroy the collection or let it trail behind as he sped back to his army, Stuart dragged the lumbering booty with him, slowing him down even further. He was nearly one hundred miles from the nearest Confederate foot soldier.[96]

Not until noon on July 2 did he find his commander at Gettysburg, bringing wagons, mules, and whiskey, thousands of exhausted and unusable troopers and horses, and almost no decent intelligence. Normally stern but forgiving, Lee lashed out at him, deriding his lateness, silence, and negligence. Lee would later report, "The movements of the army preceding the battle of Gettysburg had been much embarrassed by the absence of the cavalry."[97]

At Chancellorsville, Lee knew he could launch his crushing left hook because Stuart's reconnaissance had told him it was possible. Now the chance to probe the Union flanks, or to check the feasibility of Longstreet's idea of an end run, were long gone.

A paltry cavalry battle east of Gettysburg on July 3, against an inferior number of Union horsemen, only confirmed that Stuart had ridden his men into the ground and rendered one of Lee's sharpest weapons nearly useless.

Two months after Gettysburg, R. E. Lee elevated his cavalry to the status of a corps, but he did not give its commander, Maj. Gen. Jeb Stuart, the promotion that normally accompanied the post.

---

2. MAJ. GEN. DANIEL E. SICKLES (U.S., NEW YORK, AGE 43)

By 1863 Daniel E. Sickles had a full résumé—lawyer, Tammany Hall insider, U.S. Senator, womanizer, murderer, Democrat, and major general in the Union army. Through a lifetime of practice, he knew how to promote himself and how to get into trouble. At Gettysburg he did both. His unilateral decision to push his entire corps forward in the early part of day two was an extremely brash and ultimately costly mistake. Whether the tactic actually benefited his side is a question for debate (see CONTROVERSIES). The manner in which he executed the plan was unquestionably a prime example of poor generalship.

Sickles had mentioned the idea in passing to artillery chief Brig. Gen. HENRY J. HUNT, but he never consulted Meade or any of the nearby corps commanders before leading his troops forward. Meade arrived on Cemetery Ridge hours later to find that the 3rd Corps and its commander were gone. Acrimonious, Meade called for the major general, who arrived some time later with the claim that his command had moved to higher ground . . . a mile away. Better terrain or not, Sickles did not have the manpower to hold this new position. His troops were standing on an arch a mile and a half long and were completely detached from the rest of the army.

The rationale for a chain of command is to enable decisions to flow from the top down. On July 2 Sickles reversed the current. By overcommitting his troops, not only did he bend the 3rd Corps to his own will, he also forced every corps nearby to cooperate without soliciting the consent of a single fellow officer. Above all, the advance of his corps (that contained nearly as many men as Pickett's Charge), completely negated Meade's battle plans, which included the proposition of launching an offensive the following day.[98]

Just when Sickles offered to pull his men back, the battle over the bulge commenced. Confederate cannon began to discharge in the distance, telling both Sickles and Meade that the time to realign had passed. The ensuing engagement, though it may have disrupted Lee's plans as much as Meade's, revealed that Sickles's choice of ground was tactically worthless. Fully exposed on the sides, internally segmented by woodlots and homesteads, far too distant from the rest of Meade's army to be quickly reinforced, the salient was an eggshell begging to be smashed. Yet Sickles would be largely spared of recrimination because of two subsequent events: he would become one of the thousands to fall within the salient, and his side would eventually prevail.

After the battle, the eternal attorney Daniel E. Sickles argued that it was perfectly within his rights to order his corps forward at Gettysburg, because no one ordered him not to.

---

3.   GEN. ROBERT E. LEE (C.S., VIRGINIA, AGE 56)

Without question the Marble Man was one of the most committed and talented commanders in the war. Since 1862 he had invented ways to drive off his enemies again and again, despite being outnumbered and outgunned continually. By 1863 he had become the last best hope to a nation collapsing on all fronts except his. Popular is the premise that the immortal general performed all the more valiantly at Gettysburg, only to be thwarted by the inherent limitations of lesser men beneath him.

Taken in context, the situation at Gettysburg was not necessarily all that different from preceding campaigns. The battle commenced without his consent and long before he was able to bring up Longstreet's divisions—precisely the scenario of Second Manassas. Gettysburg was not ground of his choosing, nor was Chancellorsville. During the contest, Lee's aggression nearly matched his ruthless tenacity in the Seven Days' battles.

In Pennsylvania, Lee also continued his practices of testing well-defended heights and issuing nebulous orders. But he pressed his luck on each to a greater extent and with more frequency than ever before. His indulgences backfired nearly each and every time.

On his willingness to attack strong defensive positions on high ground, sometimes it worked, such as his grand assault against Chinn Ridge at Second Manassas, where Longstreet unhinged the Union army and sent it hurling back to Washington. Sometimes it did not, as with the Seven Days' battle of Malvern Hill, where Lee lost nearly twice as many men as the Federals and never took the heights. At Gettysburg, it never worked. Not against rocky Little Round Top. Not against Cemetery Hill in a poorly coordinated night attack. Not against Culp's Hill in a series of vain charges against boulders and bulwarks. The tactic failed decidedly against Cemetery Ridge on the third day, despite Lee's using twelve thousand soldiers and almost as many rounds of artillery in the attempt.

As stated before, many of these setbacks were blamed on subordinates for failing to match his initiative. Thus, the issue of his ambiguous command technique arises. Lee rarely bothered with particulars, preferring instead to rule by deputation. In theory, the policy allowed his lieutenants all the latitude they needed to fulfill his wishes. In reality, his wishes were often as vague as his instructions.[99]

It could be argued that Jeb Stuart's wandering folly at the beginning of the campaign was due in part to Lee's indistinct and somewhat contradictory orders. Stuart rode off without knowing exactly when he was supposed to return or if his primary duties were to collect supplies or to gather information.

The battle itself ignited west of town and escalated rapidly on the north side because several officers could not differentiate between Lee's conflicting orders to "drive the enemy" and "avoid a general engagement." Concerning his instructions for Ewell to take Cemetery Hill on day one, he coupled his request with "if practicable" (see CONTROVERSIES). It may have been difficult for Ewell to read Lee's mind on the matter, considering the two men had not seen each other face to face since the start of the campaign nearly a month past. As for A. P. Hill's poor troop deployment on day two, Lee never interjected. Nor did he tell Longstreet exactly how or when to initiate Pickett's Charge.[100]

After the battle, there was speculation that Lee's lieutenants failed him by failing to commit themselves fully. Lee himself was among their accusers. Such allegations seem out of place when viewed next to the casualty lists. In addition, if the subordinates failed to obey the orders of their commander, than the commander himself had evidently lost control of his men.

At Gettysburg, R. E. Lee lost some ten thousand dead and wounded trying to take defensive positions. Before he commanded the Army of Northern Virginia, he was in charge of the Confederacy's Carolina coastline, where he specialized in defensive strategies and the construction of bastions and earthworks.

---

4. BRIG. GEN. FRANCIS C. BARLOW (U.S., NEW YORK, AGE 28)

Bright, handsome, and driven, Francis Barlow was a successful Manhattan lawyer in his twenties when the war broke out. He volunteered as a private, and despite having no formal military training, he climbed through the ranks via hard work and an aptitude for combat. A colonel at the Seven Days' battles, he was given a star after leading his men at Antietam, where he was wounded. At Gettysburg he was head of the

1st Division of the U.S. 11th Corps, a post he had held for just two months.

As July 1 awoke, the escalations rolled into motion with the 11th Corps rushing to the front. Marching hard from Emmitsburg, Maryland, twelve miles distant, through the streets of Gettysburg, and into the fields north of town, the "boy general" spotted a prominent mound called Blocher's Knoll four hundred yards in front of his position. Longing for the high ground, he ordered his division forward but neglected to tell his corps commander.[101]

The movement disconnected Barlow from the divisions to his left. There were no divisions to his right. Barlow's perch represented the extreme flank of the entire corps, and his unfortunate soldiers were like ripe concords on a thin vine. At approximately 3:15 p.m., coming down hard from the west and north, Maj. Gen. JUBAL A. EARLY's Confederate division proceeded to trample out the vintage.[102]

The 1st Division, nearly surrounded, was unable to withstand the pressure and broke under the onslaught. Barlow himself was severely wounded, hit in the side by a stinging bullet. He tried to walk to the rear, fell into shock, and within minutes became a prisoner.

Unhinged, the entire 11th Corps started to collapse, and the inspired Confederate 2nd Corps began to hammer in unison upon the whole of the line. The abrupt loss of the 11th quickly doomed the Union 1st Corps to the west. With sudden deflation, the entire Federal front retracted southward, surrendering more than three thousand troops and the city of Gettysburg to Lee's army.

Whether the Union could have held the northern border of the town is unknown. But the opportunity to organize a defense of the city or the chance to fall back in good order to places farther south was abruptly lost the moment Barlow made the most faulty decision of his military career.[103]

Francis Barlow received his law degree from Harvard, where he graduated first in his class.

---

5. LT. GEN. AMBROSE POWELL HILL (C.S., VIRGINIA, AGE 37)

The final count listed five thousand soldiers of the Army of Northern Virginia as missing in action. It may have been fair to count among them

Ambrose Powell Hill. At age thirty-seven Hill was the youngest corps commander in the Confederate army, a position he inherited by being one of the most decisive and unflinching division commanders in Lee's thinning arsenal. But he had come to Gettysburg gravely ill, completely unable to hold a morsel in his bowels or a thought in his head. Rather than step down, or at least confess to his weakened state, he retained his position, albeit doubled over and incontinent.

Hill and Lee were of one mind at the battle's inception. When reports came back of light resistance west of Gettysburg, neither general believed it could be the tip of something much bigger. Both endorsed an aggressive push of two divisions to clear away the Union troopers and take possession of the town just beyond.[104]

Yet, for the remainder of the day and well into the second, Hill displayed minimal initiative. While he stood back, his 3rd Corps became the center of the Confederate line, the palm of the hand trying to crush the Army of the Potomac. In the fading daylight of July 2, the hand began to close along the Emmitsburg road, aiming to catch Cemetery Ridge in its fist. Rather than direct the reach in person, Hill left most of the work to his division commander, Maj. Gen. Richard H. Anderson, who in turn left the decision making to his brigade commanders. Preoccupied with charging into the Army of the Potomac, the brigade commanders did not have the luxury of watching each other. Had Hill stood closer to the front, he could have seen the beginning of the breakdown rather than hear of it later. By the time he felt compelled to send another division into the plan, the efforts of the first had already disintegrated.[105]

Day three brought little change. Though Pickett's Charge would involve two of his three divisions, Hill would not be directing the affair. Nor would he raise the issue with Lee that none of his men were in condition to stage such an assault. His one interjection proved to be a mistake. In order to clear the Bliss farm of Federal snipers, Hill ordered a useless artillery assault. The ineffective volleys simply wasted precious ammunition. As the charge commenced, the left side, his side, began to fold inward from crossfire. But the general was too far back, and not even among his own reserve troops, to offer assistance. He watched from a battery connected to Ewell's 3rd Corps, and when the gunners asked if they could open fire to support his wing, Hill mysteriously refused, allowing the Federals to continue shooting undisturbed into the front and sides of his infantry.[106]

Many may wonder if Gettysburg would have been different if the great Stonewall Jackson were present. The same might be asked of Ambrose Powell Hill.

Legend states that both Stonewall Jackson and Robert E. Lee called out for A. P. Hill on their deathbeds.

6. MAJ. GEN. RICHARD H. ANDERSON (C.S., SOUTH CAROLINA, AGE 41)

 He was a popular figure in the army. Unlike other generals who sought any opportunity to advance their career, Richard Anderson took no part in such self-promotion. Though noted for his "modesty, amiability and unselfishness," the division commander may have been too keen to express his affable nature on July 2, when the fighting was reaching its apex. At the very moment he should have been most conspicuous, the general was far behind the front lines, resting in the tree shade on the west side of Seminary Ridge.

Anderson's five brigades were supposed to march *en échelon* and roll up the Union line stationed along the Emmitsburg road. By 6 p.m. two of his brigades were doing just that. Alabama regiments under the admirable Cadmus M. Wilcox, attacking just north of the Peach Orchard, were forcing their way east and toward Cemetery Ridge. Farther to their left, nearer to town, Ambrose R. Wright's Georgia boys were within yards of the ridge, enduring close-range rifle and artillery fire. Both brigades were painfully aware that they were far ahead of the rest of their division.

Their linking brigade of Floridians was being torn apart much farther back, having walked up a steep slope and into a hidden line of Union artillery and infantry. A brigade of Mississippi regiments to their left was busy fighting off snipers and skirmishes nested in the Bliss farmstead. Brig. Gen. WILLIAM MAHONE's brigade, assigned to protect everything from the left, never went forward with the division, citing conflicting orders as the reason for its stasis.[107]

Also missing was the one man who could have addressed the situation. The desperate Wilcox, wondering what he should do next as his troops were falling left and right, sent an aide running back to find Anderson. The messenger came upon the genial division commander a mile away, behind the safety of Seminary Ridge, engaging in conversation with his staff. The friendly general was apparently unaware that a crisis was at hand and seemed relatively undisturbed by the bad news. While Anderson contemplated his options, his two courageous brigades at the step of Cemetery Ridge began to fall back, half ruined and totally unsupported.[108]

After the battle, a Georgia journalist investigated the cause of the collapse. In his own defense, Richard Anderson answered, in so many words, that the attack was under the direction of his immediate superior A. P. Hill, and that he had no authority to interfere.

The general never explained why he sent his troops forward as one thin line rather than support them with reserves or why he did not supervise his division in person. In the last year of the war, by way of attrition, Anderson was promoted to lieutenant general and given the newly formed 4th Corps. His laissez-faire style fared no better in later engagements, and he lost nearly his entire corps during the retreat to Appomattox. He was relieved of duty a day before Lee's surrender.[109]

A slacker in war, Richard Anderson continued to lack initiative in civilian life. He died in 1879 in abject poverty.

---

7. BRIG. GEN. WILLIAM MAHONE (C.S., VIRGINIA, AGE 36)

Richard Anderson's apathy on July 2 was made all the more damaging by one of his own brigade commanders, who was normally one of his most competent officers. "Little Billy" Mahone, a graduate of the Virginia Military Institute, started the war as a lieutenant colonel and had worked his way to brigadier general by the summer of 1863. A veteran of the Seven Days' battles, Second Manassas, Antietam, and Chancellorsville, he extracted exceptional esprit de corps from his brigade. He had also earned the implicit trust of many outside of his outfit, including Robert E.

Lee. By the time of Gettysburg, Mahone enjoyed a reputation that far outweighed his diminutive one-hundred-pound body.[110]

Yet Mahone's performance at Gettysburg was wholly frozen and dormant. For nearly the entire battle, he refrained from activity, citing ambiguous orders from his equally idle superiors Richard H. Anderson and A. P. Hill. As his fellow brigade commanders risked their troops and their lives along the Emmitsburg road, Billy sat far to the rear. When his beleaguered comrades begged for help, Mahone claimed that his was a reserve unit only, and he would not go forward unless given direct orders from Hill. When Anderson sent an aide to spur Mahone forward, he again refused, insisting that Hill had appointed him as the division's reserve.[111]

As if the sacrifice of his comrades was not enough, Mahone's inaction prompted division commander Maj. Gen. William D. Pender to ride to the front and investigate the breakdown of Anderson's division in person. During his recon, Pender was struck in the thigh by a shell fragment, a wound that would remove the capable general from command and end his life sixteen days later. If there was a positive to be mined from Mahone's lethargy, it was that his men experienced an overall casualty rate of 6.6 percent at Gettysburg, the lowest of any infantry brigade in Lee's army.[112]

When informed that "Little Billy" had suffered a flesh wound at Second Manassas, his wife said, "Now I know it is serious, for William has no flesh whatever."

---

8. MAJ. GEN. ROBERT E. RODES (C.S., VIRGINIA, AGE 34)

Maj. Gen. Robert E. Rodes was a sun on the ascent. A brigade commander twice wounded, he served in the battles of the Seven Days, Antietam, and Fredericksburg. His superior officer, Richard S. Ewell, asserted there were two heroes of Chancellorsville—Stonewall Jackson and the man who led Jackson's grand attack on the Union right flank, Robert E. Rodes. Heading a division at Gettysburg, Rodes had apparently reached the limits of his promise.

On July 1 Rodes led his division south from Carlisle and landed on Oak Hill northwest of Gettysburg (site of the current PEACE LIGHT ME-

MORIAL). The natural platform gave him a full view of the surroundings. Far off to the right, A. P. Hill's 2nd Corps stood on the superior elevation of Herr Ridge. Standing perpendicular not a half mile away was the U.S. 1st Corps, its right flank completely exposed. The only section out of view was to his center left, blocked by the elevation of Oak Ridge. Not bothering to investigate the dark side of the rise, he assumed there were few if any Federals tucked at its base. He assumed incorrectly.[113]

At 2 p.m. Rodes sent two brigades forward, intent on hammering the Union nail to his front. He neglected to coordinate with Ewell or Hill. He also failed to notice that his two brigades were not moving in unison. On the left, Col. Edward O'Neal's Alabama brigade ran into unexpected rifle fire and stopped. On the right, Brig. Gen Alfred Iverson's brigade of North Carolinians headed down along the west side of Oak Ridge, without reconnaissance, without support, and without Iverson, who was busy looking for O'Neal. After marching a quarter mile, Iverson's brigade decided to swing over the ridge in hopes of finding O'Neal's men on the other side. They instead came upon a long stone wall. Stepping within eighty yards of the wall, they found themselves staring into a rising line of rifles, five regiments of Union 1st Corps soldiers that Rodes never saw. After a sudden explosion, a North Carolinian remembered being "sprayed by the brains of the first rank." Unable to go forward or back, five hundred of Rodes's troops were killed or wounded in five minutes.[114]

The next day Rodes was assigned to support a late-night attack upon Cemetery Hill. But he marched his remaining troops to the area cautiously and then procrastinated in readying his men for the assault. When Jubal A. Early's division attacked the northeast slope of the hill after 8 p.m., Rodes crawled toward the northwest side, slowly enough to ponder his options. A bright moonlight revealed that the hill was well defended. While Rodes conferred with his subordinates, Early's men had reached the Union line and proceeded to fight hand-to-hand for rifle pits and artillery placements. Impressed by the heavy combat, Rodes concluded that to support them would be "a useless sacrifice of life" and pulled his division back.[115]

> Robert Rodes was an instructor at VMI but quit in frustration when the
> school did not promote him to a position he wanted. Though Rodes was
> probably a better teacher, VMI felt that the other candidate, Thomas J.
> Jackson, had better credentials.

9.   BRIG. GEN. WILLIAM N. PENDLETON (C.S., VIRGINIA, AGE 53)

 He began his spotty career at West Point, graduating
in 1830. After three years in the service, wracked by
illnesses, William Pendleton resigned to teach mathematics in various colleges. In 1838 he became an Epis-
copalian minister. With the outbreak of the war,
Pendleton was elected captain of a Virginia artillery
unit, though he had no combat experience. Rising
through the ranks, essentially by default, he eventually
became chief of artillery for the Army of Northern Virginia, having never
before distinguished himself in battle. By the time of Gettysburg, however, it looked as if he would never get the chance.

Six weeks earlier, when Lee fractioned his infantry into three corps, he
also distributed the guns of Pendleton's artillery reserve to various divisions
and brigades. Pendleton was a general without a command. But he still had
his title plus the tacit authority to collect and distribute batteries that were
not in use. Unfortunately for the Confederacy, in a battle that required decisive action, Pendleton chose to be timid.

Arriving with Lee on July 1, Pendleton had guns in position to fire on
Cemetery Hill just as retreating Union forces began to use the rise as a
rallying point. For some unknown reason, Pendleton let the opportunity
pass. The following day Pendleton ran reconnaissance for Lee to help determine where best to strike at the Union left flank. After examining
lower Cemetery Ridge and the Round Tops, he saw nothing of note, possibly because the minister was looking at the positions from nearly two
miles away, behind his own lines.[116]

During the grand bombardment preceding Pickett's Charge, conducted by the young Col. E. Porter Alexander, Pendleton only gave a cur-
sory review of the arrangements and offered no concrete suggestions. He
also failed to provide more than fifty guns stationed nearby. In addition,

he allowed ammunition chests to be positioned more than a mile away from Alexander's guns, making resupply nearly impossible.[117]

In an odd display of selective authority, the general did loan Alexander nine short-range howitzers to accompany the infantry. But just as Alexander was about to send the howitzers forward, they disappeared. Pendleton had taken back four without explanation, and the other five were dragged by their crews to "safer positions."[118]

Pendleton was never formally investigated for his actions and inactions at Gettysburg. He instead remained Lee's indecisive and ineffective chief of artillery until the termination of the war.

William Pendleton looked so much like Robert E. Lee that soldiers often mistook one for the other.

---

10. BRIG. GEN. THOMAS ROWLEY (U.S., PENNSYLVANIA, AGE 54)

Thomas Rowley may have been a brave man, or at least tolerant of exceptional pain. During the 1862 battle of Seven Pines outside Richmond, while leading the 102nd Pennsylvania, Rowley suffered a fractured skull, compliments of a bullet to the head. Yet he remained on the field and in command. Rising to brigadier thereafter, he saw little action until Gettysburg. When his superior officer, Maj. Gen. Abner Doubleday, took over the 1st Corps upon the death of Maj. Gen. John F. Reynolds, Rowley jumped from brigade to division command. Although he had minimal experience leading a few hundred troops, the Pennsylvanian was suddenly in charge of several thousand.[119]

Petty and uncooperative by nature, Rowley won few friends on the first day of battle when, according to several accounts, he got drunk. While his infantry fought without direction on McPherson's Ridge, at times marching in front their own artillery for lack of leadership, Rowley was far to the rear, incoherent. Acting belligerent to everyone but the Confederates, he somehow convinced himself, and tried to inform everyone within earshot, that he was in charge of the entire 1st Corps. The charade was rather unconvincing, considering he was having a hard time recognizing his fellow officers. Stumbling to Cemetery Hill late in the day, "raving and storming and giving wild and crazy orders," according to a witness, Rowley was placed under arrest at bayonet point.[120]

Court-martialed in April 1864, Rowley was charged with drunkenness while on duty and while in battle, negligence of discipline, conduct unbecoming an officer, and insubordination. Due to lack of evidence and conflicting testimonies, he was found not guilty on all charges but the last. Contending his innocence on all counts, Rowley retired from the army and became a lawyer.[121]

In defense of his friend and subordinate, Abner Doubleday cited Thomas Rowley for "gallantry in action" at Gettysburg.

THE LAST FULL MEASURE

TOP TEN BLOODIEST FIELDS OF FIRE

Before Gettysburg the costliest battle in the war had been Antietam, when in September 1862 more than 23,000 were killed or wounded in eleven hours. Close behind was Chancellorsville in May 1863, where 21,000 fell over four days.

As the Army of Northern Virginia marched into Pennsylvania, the impending contest with the Army of the Potomac displayed all the signs of becoming yet another bloodbath. The combined number of combatants entering the area exceeded 150,000. Also present was the exceptionally aggressive Lee. Of the war's six deadliest battles preceding Gettysburg, Marse Robert was involved in four of them.

In every battle of the Civil War, some portions of the field saw little fighting whereas other areas became literally soaked with blood. The "death zones" of Antietam included the West Woods, Burnside's Bridge, and Bloody Lane. Chancellorsville had its Crossroads, Salem Church, and Marye's Heights, a position already infamous from the preceding battle of Fredericksburg.

So, too, Gettysburg would bring forth its own ghastly offspring, a manifest of sites peculiar in their butchery. Following are the battle's most lethal areas of combat, based on the approximate number of killed and wounded.

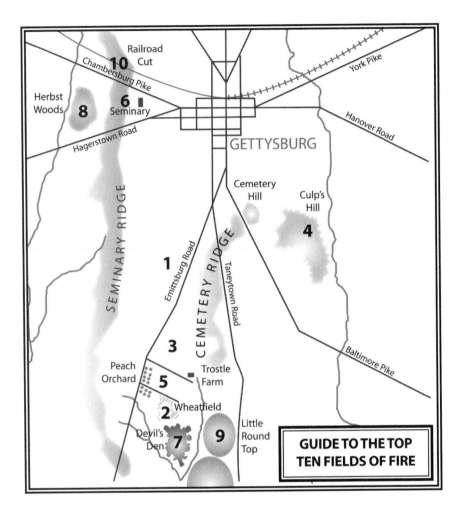

1. PICKETT'S CHARGE (6,640 KILLED OR WOUNDED)

The dying began before the march was ever made, with the artillery barrage from both sides killing at long distance. The destruction simply intensified with the introduction of Confederate infantry. The most famous assault of the war involved nearly twelve thousand men, stretching a mile from end to end, moving forward en masse across nearly a mile of open ground. Many who witnessed the spectacle confessed it was one of the most beautiful sights they had ever seen, a parade of martial grandeur, rows upon rows of bayonets gleaming in the afternoon sun.

This great adventure of three divisions began on a false assumption. Contrary to their commander's insistence, the distant Cemetery Ridge was neither dispossessed of Union artillery nor lacking in Union infantry.

At half distance, Union artillery opened fire, taking random chunks from whole men. At three hundred yards the Confederates quickened their pace, only to meet a slowly swelling rain of rifle fire. The advancing troops crouched forward, as if walking against a terrible wind, while bullets hissed and buzzed about them. A thickening crossfire started to wash away their numbers with disturbing efficiency. Diagonally across the Confederate approach stood a rail fence tracing along the Emmitsburg road. Nearly every man who climbed over or pushed through the rails was about to become a casualty.

At two hundred yards the tempest unleashed in full fury, and a deafening roar enveloped the entire front. Union artillery, its gun tubes blackened with soot, spouted squalls of lead, severing limbs, tearing bodies, and cracking skulls. Rows of Union infantry delivered successive volleys from rifles and smoothbores. At one hundred yards the Confederates finally started to shoot back. The exchange produced a peculiar trembling of the air, resultant from a combined rate of small-arms fire nearing two hundred shots per second. A Confederate colonel recalled, "There was a hissing sound, like the hooded cobra's whisper of death, a deafening explosion . . . and when I got to my feet again there were splinters of bone and lumps of flesh sticking to my clothes."[1]

At fifty yards the Confederates rushed with the bayonet, breaching the Federal line at the Angle in the stone wall. Troops fired at each other from point-blank range, swung their muskets like clubs, pushed their

As if on parade, the mile-wide saunter of Pickett's Charge steadily advances and constricts against Cemetery Ridge.

bayonets deep into bodies and faces. Low ground began to fill with pools of blood. In less then ten minutes, every soldier in the immediate area of the Angle, North and South, either surrendered, fell wounded, or died. After ten minutes of contact, the great Southern wave finally ebbed away, barely half the size of when it began. In the successful standoff, the Union lost approximately fifteen hundred dead, wounded, and missing.

> Of George E. Pickett's division, all three of his brigade commanders and every one of his thirteen colonels were either wounded or killed in the charge.

2.   THE WHEATFIELD (4,400 KILLED OR WOUNDED)

If the impetuous Maj. Gen. DANIEL E. SICKLES had not sent his 3rd Corps forward on the second day, this secluded corner of the Rose family farm would have remained as anonymous as any other plot of American countryside. Instead, this shaded cropland became one of the deadliest pieces of real estate in U.S. military history, costing as many dead and wounded as Omaha Beach in the Second World War.

The area was no place to stage a fight. It was nearly surrounded by thick woods, a "Stony Hill" on its west edge, and a rock wall along its southern side. Anyone entering the fringe of trees would be walking into close-quarter fighting. Anyone trying to occupy the open field would be mowed down in minutes. Support was bound to be slow, as the woodlands cloaked the area from outside observers.

Father William Corby grants absolution to the Irish Brigade before they step into the Wheatfield. Hundreds would soon die. Corby would live on to become president of Notre Dame.

LIBRARY OF CONGRESS

The Union held the field first, mostly from the stalwart shooting of the 17th Maine, well protected behind the southern rock wall. But when supporting columns inexplicably abandoned Stony Hill, the Maine men fell back under the pressure of Brig. Gen. JOSEPH B. KERSHAW's South Carolina brigade.

To recapture the field, Federal units entered the fray piecemeal, including the famed Irish Brigade, marching forward after their priest, Father William Corby, had stood upon a high rock and absolved them of their sins. One by one the brigades entered and then fell from successive waves of Confederate rifle fire, which also scythed the wheat and reddened the soil.

For nearly every Union push, the Confederates answered with a countermarch of their own, each time turning the scenery into "a whirlpool of death." And so it went, brigades were killed nearly as fast as they appeared. Only nightfall stopped the bloodshed.

Fourteen brigades in all took part, and the field changed hands six times over three hours, yet ultimately the area was of no military value. The Confederates held the cropland, but the Union still held the nearby high ground of Little Round Top and Cemetery Ridge.[2]

Union Col. Edward Cross always wore a red bandana in combat. Before entering the Wheatfield with his brigade, Cross donned a black headcloth instead and proclaimed, "This is my last battle." True to his prediction, Cross was mortally wounded soon after.

---

3. EMMITSBURG ROAD TO CEMETERY RIDGE—THE SECOND DAY (3,200 KILLED OR WOUNDED)

The Trostle farm road formed the base of a tall triangle, with its west side made up of the Emmitsburg road and the east rise of Cemetery Ridge converging over a mile to the north. On July 2, DANIEL E. SICKLE's brittle right flank occupied the southern half of this triangle. The Union line looked like a thin shell with nothing behind it.

After the Confederates made quick and bloody work of the Peach Orchard, they looked to this area as the next and final target. Galloping his limbered batteries north through furrowed fields along the Emmitsburg road, dodging fresh corpses the whole way, Longstreet's young and skillful

Union batteries fall back under heavy Confederate pressure along the Emmitsburg road.

LIBRARY OF CONGRESS

artillery commander, Col. E. Porter Alexander, declared the Confederacy would smash Sickle's fragile line and "finish the whole war this afternoon."[3]

Backing Alexander's words were four brigades of Maj. Gen. RICHARD H. ANDERSON's division, each intending to push the Union off the Emmitsburg road and over the critical high ground of Cemetery Ridge behind. Alexander's countrymen would have to move quickly, he reckoned. The time was nearing 7 p.m. and darkness lay in wait.

The Confederate attack failed completely on the line's southern end, repulsed by three New York regiments protected by foliage and rough terrain along Plum Run Creek. Partial success came on the northern end. Braving a series of orderly defensive stands from artillery and infantry, Brig. Gen. Ambrose R. Wright's Georgia troops nearly reached Cemetery Ridge but were thrown back with heavy losses.[4]

Right down the center, almost unopposed, pushed Brig. Gen. Cadmus M. Wilcox's brigade. Spotting the obvious danger, Union Maj. Gen. Winfield Scott Hancock ordered the 1st Minnesota to stop them—eight companies of a single regiment against an entire brigade. With bayonets fixed, spanning a paltry hundred yards, Col. William Colvill's men stepped forward. Two hundred seventy men faced nearly four times their number. Marching at the double quick, the Minnesota troops loaded and fired on the trot, advancing to the marginal dip along Plum Run, where they proceeded to make a desperate stand.

Remarkably, Wilcox's Confederates started to fall back on themselves, their advanced lines collapsing from the concentrated shooting. Getting no help from behind, and with both of his flanks exposed, Wilcox grudgingly ordered his men to disengage, leaving the 1st Minnesota victorious, albeit reduced by nearly 180 killed and wounded.[5]

Before making his near suicidal charge, Colonel Colvill shouted for other regiments on Cemetery Ridge to come and help him. Hancock told him to stop, fearing that such pleading would demoralize the handful of troops still defending the rise. Colvill obeyed and headed into the field with his lone regiment.

---

4. CULP'S HILL (2,400 KILLED OR WOUNDED)

On the evening of July 1 the Union 12th Corps and remnants of the 1st Corps managed to secure most of Culp's Hill. Afterward Confederates stationed close by could hear the constant felling of trees as Union men hurried to construct breastworks.

Nearly twenty-four hours later, bearing on 8 p.m., Maj. Gen. Edward Johnson's division launched its first major effort against the position, long after the Union men had become fully entrenched. Advancing from the northeast, Johnson's Virginia, North Carolina, and Louisiana boys struggled through the waist-deep Rock Creek at the base of the hill, then melted into the dense trees, boulders, and ravines that folded into the steep slopes. As the Confederates neared the breastworks, conditions mandated close-quarter fighting, resulting in a great many deaths from hand-to-hand combat. The intensifying darkness added to the unearthly battle, and several soldiers from both sides died from friendly fire. By 11

Little Round Top attained greater fame, but Culp's Hill resulted in 250 percent greater casualties.

p.m. the front had quieted, but not until the South had managed to secure the southern crest.[6]

At 4:30 a.m. the following day, the Union launched a massive counter-attack, slowly and steadily breaking the Confederate grip on the south hillside. The sporadic, tangled, and deadly fighting of the previous night simply repeated itself. Though it had not rained for days, soldiers found themselves slipping on rocks and logs, because their footing had become slick from accumulating blood and entrails spilt upon the ground. Of all engagements at Gettysburg, Culp's Hill achieved the purest chaos.

By late morning it was evident to Johnson that further bloodshed was untenable—he was losing men twice as fast as his adversaries. By 11 a.m. he pulled back to the northeast, just hours before Pickett's Charge began its ill-fated attack from the west.[7]

The day after the battle, Union soldiers on Culp's Hill emerged from their trenches to assess the damage. Many became physically ill at the heaps of mangled bodies they discovered. One soldier wrote: "I have just returned from being one of the 'pall bearers' in the largest funeral I ever attended . . . we dug a trench into which we piled about 200." Another looked upon a small congregation of twisted corpses and reasoned, "None but demons can delight in war."[8]

One of the many Confederates to die in the area of Culp's Hill was Pvt. John Wesley Culp, a native of Pennsylvania and a relative of the family that lent their name to the elevation.

---

5. THE PEACH ORCHARD AND TROSTLE FARM (1,950 KILLED OR WOUNDED)

In the late afternoon of July 2 the Confederates launched their one-two punch against this Union spearhead. As regiments from the Palmetto State struck the south side, they took a squall of artillery for their initiative. A soldier from the 2nd South Carolina marveled at the way the Union artillery was "cutting off large trees and plowing up the ground." Another grieved over what the guns were doing to his friends, as flying canisters seemed to be "exploding in their bodies."[9]

Driving straight into the grove and then turning north, Brig. Gen. WILLIAM BARKSDALE's Mississippi Brigade delivered the crippling body

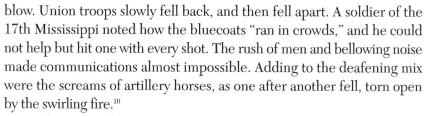

Just a few of some fifty Union artillery horses shot down during the fight at the Trostle farm.

LIBRARY OF CONGRESS

blow. Union troops slowly fell back, and then fell apart. A soldier of the 17th Mississippi noted how the bluecoats "ran in crowds," and he could not help but hit one with every shot. The rush of men and bellowing noise made communications almost impossible. Adding to the deafening mix were the screams of artillery horses, as one after another fell, torn open by the swirling fire.[10]

Inebriated with his good fortune, the audacious Barksdale drove his ranks forward in person, rushing eastward between the Wheatfield road and the Trostle farm road. Only a frantic Union artillery stand and a desperate counterattack of reserve infantry blunted the Confederate thrust.

More than seventeen hundred men lost blood or their lives in this brief fight, including William Barksdale, mortally wounded in the dying moments of his assault.[11]

Among those wounded near the Trostle farm was Daniel E. Sickles. A shell hit him in the left knee, leaving his leg dangling by a ligament. He survived the wound and ensuing surgery. After the war he visited the amputated leg often, where it was stored at the Army Medical Museum in Washington.

6. THE LUTHERAN THEOLOGICAL SEMINARY
(1,700 KILLED OR WOUNDED)

When traveling down the park road that leads to McPherson's Woods, most visitors direct their attention to the west and the site of the Reynolds death monument. Yet if they turn to the east and glance upon the unassuming fields just before the Lutheran Theological Seminary, they would see one of the deadliest areas anywhere on the Gettysburg battlefield.

On the first day of battle, as Federal troops north of town gave way to Confederate numbers, a portion of the Union 1st Corps headed for an ideal defensive position: a long row of impromptu barricades piled nearly four feet high around the seminary. Remnants of ten regiments and three batteries took up positions behind the defenses and readied themselves for an attack. They did not have to wait long.

Out of the Herbst Woods charged the brigades of Brig. Gen. Alfred Scales and Col. Abner Perrin, hungry to finish off their fleeing prey. As they drew near, Union guns let loose, hacking away in a desperate rate of fire. Scales's men came within a hundred yards of the seminary before a cloud of lead enveloped them. Perrin's brigade also took severe losses but managed to endanger the left flank of the Union position, forcing the bluecoats to resume their escape all the way to Cemetery Ridge south of town. Though successful in their goal, the two Southern brigades lost more than a thousand men in capturing the seminary grounds.[12]

The three seminary buildings survived the battle. In 2004 a fire severely damaged one. Fortunately, the structure was repairable.

---

7. DEVIL'S DEN (1,665 KILLED OR WOUNDED)

Three miles south of Gettysburg rests a bizarre gathering of enormous boulders, some nearly two stories tall. When viewing it for the first time, a

Aptly named Devil's Den lies jagged in the shadow of Little Round Top.

LIBRARY OF CONGRESS

Union soldier described it "as though nature in some wild freak had forgotten herself and piled great rocks in mad confusion together."[13]

On the battle's second day, this surreal landscape served as the linchpin between the Wheatfield to the northwest and Little Round Top to the east. The Union held the den first, but the 1st Texas and 3rd Arkansas regiments rushed its western side, moving up a ramp of open acreage that came level with the top of the boulders. A Federal volley of rifles and cannon pushed the Confederates back. The 1st Texas mounted another charge, only to be met head on by the 124th New York, who impetuously ran after its quarry and was itself gunned down in short order, losing its major and colonel in the process.[14]

Simultaneously, the bowels of the den lay open to the south, along Plum Run (soon to be renamed Bloody Run), where two Alabama regiments (the 44th and 48th) worked their way up the rock-strewn valley. Taking artillery strikes the entire way, the Alabama troops were still able to pin down the lone regiment sent to guard the den's base—the 4th Maine.

It appeared as if the Federals would hold out, until four Georgia regiments moved forward. Fearing encirclement, Union officers ordered a withdrawal. Units began to fall back, except for the 4th Maine, which either did not hear the command or was unable to move. The Confederate lines summarily massed around the Maine men and inflicted casualties exceeding 50 percent.

The entire fight lasted only ninety minutes, yet the exchange of fire was intense enough to kill or wound a combatant, on average, every three seconds. The Union sacrificed 846 officers and men in a losing effort. The Confederates lost 819 killed or maimed.[15]

There is no written evidence that this area was called Devil's Den prior to the war. A July 1863 official report called it "Devil's Cave." In October 1863 a Pennsylvania soldier referred to it as "Devil's Den." The origin is a mystery.

---

8. MCPHERSON FARM AND HERBST WOODS (1,570 KILLED OR WOUNDED)

On his visit to Gettysburg, when Lincoln took a brief tour of the battlefield, he ventured neither to the site of Pickett's Charge nor to Little Round Top. He went to the McPherson farm and Herbst Woods, where

Struggling to hold the McPherson farm and the surrounding area, the Union 1st Corps gained valuable time for its comrades and sacrificed nearly half the corps in doing so.

BATTLES AND LEADERS

the Union's famed Iron Brigade essentially died out in the course of a day and a Confederate regiment practically disappeared in thirty minutes.

It was here that the virus of the battle truly germinated, when Union dismounted cavalry clashed with Confederate infantry on the morning of July 1. Both sides committed more and more units to the fold, displaying a mutual willingness to hit hard and hit fast. At 10:30 a.m. Union Maj. Gen. JOHN F. REYNOLDS initiated the first major assault. The Confederates stemmed the attack, killing Reynolds in the process, and set a dangerous precedent of strike and counterstrike.

Heartened by their growing numbers, the South resolved to push the Federals from the protection of the five-acre Herbst Woods. Crossing the Rubicon of Willoughby Run, a shallow creek that divided the opposing forces, the Confederates walked into a blaze of cannon and rifle fire. Fully committed to the endeavor, they somehow continued to move forward. An acutely severe fight developed between the 26th North Carolina and the Iron Brigade's 24th Michigan and 19th Indiana. The opposing sides were evenly matched at eight hundred men.[16]

The Indiana boys soon found their left flank wide open. In pulling back, they exposed the flank of the unit on their right, the 24th Michigan. The Wolverines stepped back as well to realign, and so it went. Fighting bellowed uninterrupted for thirty minutes as the Union regiments broke and reassembled in a series of defensive stands, only to see the advancing Tarheels tear each one apart.[17]

Both sides faded at the same rate, persuading each to try and break the will of the other with one last push. Repeatedly outflanked, the Union finally pulled away to the protection of Seminary Ridge, and the engagement ceased with the Confederates holding the forest.

Losses were horrific North and South. The 26th North Carolina lost a phenomenal 75 percent of its troops. The 19th Indiana and 24th Michigan lost a combined 70 percent, and the immortal Iron Brigade had essentially fought its last battle of the war.[18]

Commander of the Iron Brigade was Brig. Gen. Solomon Meredith, a son of pacifist Quakers. He was wounded near the future home of Gen. Dwight David Eisenhower, also a son of Quakers.

---

9. LITTLE ROUND TOP (980 KILLED OR WOUNDED)

Foliage dictated that Little Round Top, rather than her taller sister to the south, would be the key high ground on the battle's southern edge. Big Round Top wore a thick shawl of trees. Neither artillery nor signalmen could see their way through the canopy, rendering the hill almost useless. In contrast, Little Round Top possessed an open view to the west, overlooking a vista that would soon contain a litany of unearthly nicknames—Devil's Den, the Slaughter Pen, the Valley of Death.

The contest for Little Round Top did not begin until late in the afternoon of the second day as battle lines stretched progressively southward from town. Union Col. Strong Vincent's brigade was dispatched to the stony rise scant minutes before the first Confederate advances began, leaving many Southern sympathizers wondering what might have been.

Stephen Weed's brigade clings to the western crest of Little Round Top.

LIBRARY OF CONGRESS

Vincent initially positioned his troops along the lower slopes. In hindsight, the decision was an inspired one. Had the Union only occupied the hill's crest, the compact position might easily have been surrounded. As it was, his four regiments could bend but not break from the onslaught of the South's five regiments. If viewed from the sky, the fight for the hill would have resembled a dying heartbeat, with the Union position constricting, then expanding again, meeting attacks with counterattacks as the sun slowly fell.

Late in the evening a sixth Confederate regiment joined in, threatening to crack the Federal line on its right side. With minutes to spare, Union Brig. Gen. Stephen H. Weed's brigade began to arrive from Cemetery Ridge. First on the scene was the 140th New York, pushing back the deadly thrust with a solo charge. The gamble paid off, at the price of the regimental commander's life.[19]

Back and forth, both sides slammed away at each other. Men not struck down by bullets collapsed instead from heat stroke and exhaustion. Not until the left side of the Union line initiated a last, aggressive countercharge did the fight end, with scores of Confederates taken prisoner and nearly a thousand men from both sides lying wounded or dead.

> In the fight for Little Round Top, casualties were heaviest on the extreme flank, where the 20th Maine and 15th Alabama clashed. If one were to draw a straight line between the respective capitals of those two states, it would pass almost directly over their respective regiments on Little Round Top.

10. THE RAILROAD CUT (560 KILLED OR WOUNDED)

What appeared to be good cover quickly turned into a deathtrap. On the battle's first day, the 55th North Carolina with the 2nd and 42nd Mississippi pushed back a line of Union troops southward from the Chambersburg road. Maneuvering to press their advantage, the Rebels moved into a mile-long unfinished railroad cut, a wide trench that ran shallow at the ends and twenty feet deep in the middle.

Taking heavy rifle fire from their unseen opponent, the 14th Brooklyn, 95th New York, and 6th Wisconsin charged headlong toward the cut, increasing their own losses. The ranks seemed to spread apart as they went—screaming men dashing forward, bleeding wounded falling back.

Harper's Weekly artist Alfred Waud sketched this view of the Railroad Cut from secondhand accounts. In reality, the cut was not nearly as deep, and the Confederate surrender was far less orderly.

LIBRARY OF CONGRESS

But once the blue waves reached the unfinished railbed, they summarily poured sheets of fire down upon their target. Moving to their right, the 6th Wisconsin came across the vale's eastern opening and began shooting at will down its length.

The bed instantly turned into a bedlam hive. Stunned Confederates tangled into each other. Some fought back, some attempted to surrender, and some tried in desperation to claw their way up and out.

The fight was over in fifteen minutes, yet Confederate losses neared 50 percent dead and wounded. The attacking 6th Wisconsin lost 160 men, more than a third of its force. Though no precise totals are known, the other two Union regiments may have lost similar numbers, making the Railroad Cut one of the least known but deadliest sections of the field.[20]

While walking along the Railroad Cut in 1996, a vacationer noticed bones protruding from the embankment. A formal excavation revealed the body of a soldier who died of severe head trauma. Though the deceased's army of origin could not be determined, he was buried with honors at the national cemetery in Gettysburg.

TOP TEN CORPS WITH THE HIGHEST PERCENTAGE CASUALTIES

A French innovation perfected by Napoleon, the corps was a stratum of delegation between *army* and *division*. Neither side in the American Civil War employed the system at first. There was no need. Yet by 1862 the largest of the field commands North and South were fast becoming unwieldy for one person to handle. Irvin McDowell marched into First Manassas with just five infantry divisions. John Pope entered Second Manassas with fourteen. Previously called *wings, commands,* or *grand divisions,* corps had become a part of the Army of the Potomac by the spring of 1862, and the strength of each ranged from nine thousand to fourteen thousand men. By late autumn the Army of Northern Virginia formed two massive corps of thirty thousand apiece.

After the death of the irreplaceable Stonewall Jackson, Lee partitioned his two corps into three, each numbering slightly more than twenty thousand troops, aided by a command of horsemen under Jeb Stuart. Meade chased Lee with seven infantry corps plus one cavalry corps and a grand division of guns.

In essence, the corps were their chess pieces. To better understand the strategies of the two commanding generals and why the match ended as it did requires examination of how each played the board and what happened to each piece as a result. Following are the most utilized, and consequently most damaged, corps in the battle, ranked by the percentage of their casualties. Listed with them are their commanding officers.

Missing from this table are the Union and Confederate cavalry, which sustained 7.2 and 4.7 percent casualties respectively, illustrating their relatively limited application. Also missing is the U.S. 6th Corps. The largest of Meade's contingent with 14,074 men, it arrived late on July 2 and was used primarily as a reserve unit. Critics of Meade have pointed to the 6th's low casualty rate of 1.7 percent as proof that the general was overly cautious. He could have used the unsullied corps, so the reasoning goes, to chase and crush Lee after the battle. Whether a single rook could have actually checked the grand master remains a topic of supposition.[21]

1.   U.S. 1ST CORPS (49.6%)

MAJ. GEN. JOHN F. REYNOLDS (KILLED)
MAJ. GEN ABNER DOUBLEDAY
MAJ. GEN. JOHN NEWTON

Appearing before the Congressional Committee on the Conduct of the War, U.S. 3rd Corps Gen. Daniel E. Sickles stated: "We in the army do not regard the operations of the two corps under General [John] Reynolds as properly the battle of Gettysburg." Sickles had not seen the first day's fighting, nor had the majority of the Army of the Potomac. Their absence is precisely why the 1st Corps suffered more than any other in the Union army. Meade used this advance guard to block Lee's move into Gettysburg, and 1st Corps paid dearly.[22]

The corps rushed to the northwest of Gettysburg to relieve John Buford and his dismounted cavalry. Buford's stubborn defense bought enough time for John F. Reynolds's footmen to arrive, yet Buford's tenacity also created a logjam against which the Confederate torrent began to rise. Lead regiments of the 1st Corps reached the area just in time to see the levy break and to watch their acclaimed commander die from a bullet to the head. Hundreds would soon join him in death as waves of Confederates crashed forward.

Three of the top ten BLOODIEST FIELDS OF FIRE involved the 1st Corps on the first day as it struggled to stay moored along Willoughby Run and the Herbst Woods without hope of immediate reinforcement. Dwindling brigades in blue repelled attack after attack, slowly and angrily lending ground to superior Confederate guns and numbers. Pushed out of the woods and past the McPherson farm, fighting viciously over the Railroad Cut, and finally driven away from barricades next to the seminary, the outflanked, exhausted, and depleted pawns fell back to the south and east of town. There they were ordered to defend Cemetery and Culp's hills at all costs.

The corps could have used the help of its Vermont Brigade, which was assigned to guard duty farther back. Three of the brigade's regiments eventually did help on July 3, laying brutal crossfire into the right side of Pickett's Charge. For their services, the Vermonters got off lightly, compared to their comrades in the 1st Corps—the brigade lost "only" 18 percent of its 1,950 men.

Over three days, the outfit lost 3,231 wounded, including five out of seven brigade commanders, plus 2,162 missing or captured, and 666 dead.

Fatally weakened by the losses at Gettysburg, the Union 1st Corps ceased to exist in March 1864. Remaining units were consolidated into the 2nd and 4th Divisions of the U.S. 3rd Corps.

---

2.   U.S. 11TH CORPS (41.2%)

MAJ. GEN. OLIVER O. HOWARD

MAJ. GEN. CARL SCHURZ

For the luckless 11th, the half-German, all-hard-knocks corps that hoped to redeem their flight at Chancellorsville, July 1 would not be like May 2. It would be worse.

Casualties mounted quickly when the Confederate 2nd Corps decimated their right-flank redoubt at Blocher's Knoll. Scores were killed outright. Hundreds were wounded and subsequently captured—including the severely injured Brig. Gen. FRANCIS C. BARLOW—because stretcher-bearers had to fight against a wholesale retreat. Fifteen hundred more Union men would also fall prisoner as they jammed into the narrow streets of the town. Nearly half of the day's losses would be to capture. Third Division commander Alexander Schimmelfennig would not be one of them. He accidentally ran down a dead-end alley, and to avoid getting caught, cowered in a drainage ditch. He would spend the rest of the battle in hiding.

Redemption came the next night, and with it came casualties of a ghastlier sort. While defending Cemetery Hill, the remainder of the 11th absorbed a vicious attack from Richard S. Ewell's 2nd Corps. Combat devolved into a slugfest, literally. The South broke through the first line of defense and started up the rock-strewn slope, heading straight for the artillery pieces atop the hill. As men fumbled to load their rifles in the moonlight, some chose more primitive means of defense: they grabbed stones and proceeded to bash heads. Slowly and brutally, the Confederate assault withered from overwhelming losses, exhaustion, and darkness. Just as depleted, the 11th could at least finally state that it had persevered in a fight.

Remaining on Cemetery Hill the third day, the 11th retained its track record of poor fortune, as it sustained additional casualties from the Confederate artillery barrage. Total losses for three long days of engagement were 369 dead, 1,924 wounded, and 1,514 missing.

After the Gettysburg campaign, the inauspicious and worn-out 11th Corps was dismantled. One of its divisions was stationed in Charleston Harbor at a place called Folly Island.

---

3. U.S. 3RD CORPS (39.5%)

MAJ. GEN. DANIEL E. SICKLES (WOUNDED)

MAJ. GEN. DAVID B. BIRNEY

The U.S. 3rd Corps suffered most on the second day, when its impudent commander, Daniel E. Sickles, turned its solid position on Cemetery Ridge into his infamous and fragile salient far ahead of the Union main line. The ensuing and desperate attempt to hold this advanced position immortalized a peach orchard, a wheat field, a den of giant boulders, and farmsteads owned by the Rose and Trostle families. Sickles's experiment caused most of his corps' 593 deaths, 3,029 injuries, and 589 captured or missing at Gettysburg. He had also lost 17 out of 37 regimental commanders. Had Meade not sent portions of the 2nd and most of the 5th Corps into the mix and backed them up with his artillery reserve, the 3rd Corps would have likely experienced much greater reductions.

After four hours of costly fighting within the salient, both sides concluded that Sickles's precious "high ground" in front of Cemetery Ridge was militarily untenable. Sickles evidently did not share in this view. As he was carried off the field, his left leg irreparably mangled by Confederate artillery, he calmly smoked a cigar and pondered the greatness of his achievement.

Average pay for a Union private was thirteen dollars a month, which meant the grunts of the 3rd Corps earned about 43 cents for their troubles on the second day at Gettysburg.

---

4. U.S. 2ND CORPS (38.9%)

MAJ. GEN. WINFIELD SCOTT HANCOCK (WOUNDED)

BRIG. GEN. JOHN GIBBON (WOUNDED)

Given the gravity of their assignments, it is a mystery how the eleven thousand men of the U.S. 2nd Corps did not suffer even greater losses. Their original placement on the morning of July 2 had them along the high, solid center of Cemetery Ridge. But events would have them pulled in two directions that day and bashed inward the following afternoon.

As Sickles's salient began to break down, the 2nd Corps' entire 1st Division marched into the Wheatfield to stop the bleeding—and to add to it. Of the division's four brigade commanders, three would fall wounded, two of them mortally. A half mile to the north, Brig. Gen. George Willard's brigade faced the magnificent charge of WILLIAM BARKSDALE and his Mississippi Brigade. Although successful in his mission, Willard died in the effort, as would his second in command. Still farther to the north, the twilight Confederate attack on Cemetery Hill nearly pierced the Union line. Sent to rescue the position, 2nd Corps brigade commander Col. Samuel Carroll vowed to push the Confederates back. As darkness made his visional commands worthless, Carroll simply screamed at the top of his lungs: "Front face! Charge bayonets! Forward, double-quick! March!" The ensuing fight turned hand-to-hand, with terrible losses on both sides, but the Union line held.[23]

The following day brought Pickett's Charge straight into the heart of the Union center, precisely where the 2nd Corps had reassembled. Exposed to sixty minutes of artillery fire followed by the brunt of the Southern infantry assault, the corps held its post and secured its place in the history of the battle.

Fighting apart and together, the men of the superb 2nd Corps lost 797 dead, 3,194 wounded, and 378 missing or captured. Of its score of senior officers, 9 had been hit, and 4 of them died.[24]

In the course of the war, no Union corps served longer or endured more casualties than the 2nd. Of the top one hundred Union regiments with the highest losses in the war, thirty-five served in this corps.

---

5.   C.S. 3RD CORPS (38.7%)

LT. GEN. A. P. HILL

AMBROSE POWELL HILL gave a passive performance at Gettysburg. This fact gives the false impression that his corps was the least active on the Confederate side. In reality, the month-old unit was Lee's largest, with nearly twenty-two thousand officers and men, and lost the highest ratio and largest number of soldiers in Marse Robert's army. While Lee attempted to maneuver his other two corps for maximum effect, he played this front force as his file of pawns, ramming them forward with minimal cunning.

On July 1, the Confederate 3rd Corps unintentionally detonated the battle west of town and then emaciated itself fighting head to head with the Union 1st Corps over Seminary Ridge. On day two, as its two lead divisions tried to recover from their first day of fighting, a third division, ineptly led by Maj. Gen. RICHARD H. ANDERSON, disintegrated as it attacked the Union center left. One of Anderson's brigades, the Georgians under Cadmus M. Wilcox, nearly breeched Cemetery Ridge until the suicidal charge of the 1st Minnesota and lack of support crippled their effort.

In Pickett's Charge, two of the three divisions belonged to the 3rd Corps, led by Gen. James Pettigrew on the left side of the assault, with Maj. Gen. Isaac Trimble following close behind. These were the same two divisions that fought so brutally on the first day. Of the nine infantry divisions in the Army of Northern Virginia, these experienced the highest percentage of casualties, losing more than 50 percent of their men, including the mortally wounded Pettigrew and the wounded and captured Trimble.

Adding to the corps' losses, troops from its third division, including Wilcox's bloodied brigade, were sent to rescue Pickett's men, with hundreds falling in the doomed endeavor. The corps' final tally included 1,724 dead, 4,683 wounded, and at least 2,088 missing in action or taken prisoner.

Despite their losses at Gettysburg, the 3rd Corps would be Lee's largest at Appomattox, totaling just 8,600 men.

---

6. C.S. 1ST CORPS (36.6%)

LT. GEN. JAMES LONGSTREET

Gathering west of Seminary Ridge in the late afternoon of July 1, the bulk of Lee's premier corps contained some of his most experienced, hardest-fighting brigades plus his most trusted general. Longstreet and Lee both envisioned using the 1st Corps like a knight the following day, but they disagreed on where the piece should strike.

Longstreet insisted that the craftiest move would be to drive two steps south, and then head east in an attempt to get behind the Union left side. Lee bitterly disagreed, believing that a more direct attack would take less time, contain fewer risks, and possess greater force. Angered but obedient, Longstreet acted as ordered. He took one step south and drove into the Union left side.

The affected areas would become euphemisms for hell on earth—the Peach Orchard, the Wheatfield, Devil's Den, the Slaughter Pen, the Valley of Death, Little Round Top. Remarkably, the 1st Corps took all of these positions except the last, and destroyed the Union 3rd Corps and part of the 2nd, with only two of its three divisions. Pickett and his men would not arrive until later that day.[25]

The dapper Pickett was most excited that the battle had gone on longer than expected, thus providing a chance for his troops to attain everlasting glory the following day. Effectively they would, losing one out of every two soldiers in the division in the space of roughly sixty minutes.

From the moment it moved into Sickles's salient to the ebb of Pickett's Charge, the 1st Corps was engaged at Gettysburg for approximately twenty-four hours. In that time, of nearly 21,000 men total, 1,617 died, 4,205 fell wounded, and 1,843 were missing or captured.

Lee's 1st Corps had its origins in P. G. T. Beauregard's eight Confederate brigades at First Manassas, a Confederate command known then as the Army of the Potomac.

---

7. C.S. 2ND CORPS (32.5%)

LT. GEN. RICHARD S. EWELL

Of Lee's three corps, the 2nd receives the least amount of praise. Some may argue that this stems from a lack of success or aggression, noting that "Old Baldy's" men rank last in terms of total casualties. Whether a unit's body count is a fair measure of its courage is debatable. Viewed as a percentage, however, Ewell's overall casualties were only slightly lower than his colleagues,' and the corps managed to capture the highest number of Union prisoners as well as the town of Gettysburg.

It can be said that Stonewall's old corps faced the best and worst geographic conditions. Finest was on the first day, when it swept down from the north on clear roads from York and Harrisburg while the U.S. 11th Corps had to filter through the tight weave of town streets. Throwing Brig. Gen. FRANCIS C. BARLOW's brigade off of the exposed and indefensible Blocher's Knoll, and rolling up the 11th's right flank to the northeast edge of the borough's limits, Ewell's men were shooting as fast as they could load, killing and capturing dozens at a time and having a generally euphoric time. A Georgia private beamed, "We drove them on through Gettysburg, and had them greatly confused."[26]

The worst would come soon. After reaching the south end of town, the lead elements of the 2nd Corps saw two menacing rises before them, eighty-foot-tall Cemetery Hill to their front and the even higher Culp's Hill to their left. For the next thirty-six hours, these elevations would reduce their numbers by nearly a third.

Heavy entrenchments in both locations, plus the rotating efforts of the Union's 1st, 11th, and 12th Corps, created a buzz saw effect on the Confederates, who were bereft of reinforcements. One attack on Cemetery Hill and a series of assaults into Culp's Hill gained little beyond a high casualty count.

In postbattle assessments, Lee was least critical of this corps, perhaps because it was the part of his army he failed to observe in combat. Preoccupied three miles to the west, literally on the other side of the Union army, Lee did not fully comprehend the losses the 2nd was undergoing until he heard the casualty estimates sometime later. The balance, derived from more than 20,000 effectives, proved to be 1,301 dead, 3,629 wounded, and 1,756 captured or missing in action.

These veterans of James Longstreet's 1st Corps made it halfway through Sickles's Salient only to be gunned down here at the Rose farm.

LIBRARY OF CONGRESS

At the height of its strength just before Fredericksburg, the 2nd Corps of the Army of Northern Virginia stood at thirty-two thousand men. By the end of the war it was down to six thousand.

8.   U.S. 5TH CORPS (20.0%)

MAJ. GEN. GEORGE SYKES

In many respects, George Sykes had reason to be frustrated at Gettysburg. He was never allowed to deploy his men as a single unit. Meade employed his ten thousand men piecemeal, using them to plug holes and address weaknesses as they occurred. And on July 2 they occurred everywhere.

The brigades of Col. Jacob B. Sweitzer and Col. William S. Tilton went into the Wheatfield, followed soon after by two brigades of U.S. regulars, among Sykes's best troops. Col. Strong Vincent and Brig. Gen. Stephen H. Weed received instructions to take their brigades to Little Round Top. The mission would kill them both. Finally, Sykes had to release two more brigades of Pennsylvania men into the Wheatfield.

When the Union 6th Corps made its appearance behind Sykes, the general hailed its arrival. His own men were shot up, scattered, and no longer able to play the part of Meade's stopgap pawns. Working as a "reserve" unit, Sykes corps lost 365 dead, 1,611 wounded, and 2,111 missing and captured.

Although cooperating admirably at Gettysburg, in spite of the challenges to his authority, Sykes fell out of favor with his superiors and was deemed unconvincing as a corps commander. In a not-too-subtle indication of its level of faith in him, the War Department transferred Sykes to Kansas.

9. U.S. 12TH CORPS (11.1%)

MAJ. GEN. HENRY W. SLOCUM
BRIG. GEN. ALPHEUS S. WILLIAMS

Rarely did an infantry corps inflict such serious casualties upon the opposition, over two days of heavy engagement, yet suffer such comparatively modest casualties. The U.S. 12th Corps managed the feat through the art of preparation. Smallest of the Union infantry corps at just under ten thousand soldiers, the 12th were assigned on July 2 to hold Culp's Hill, at that time barely manned by survivors of the 1st Corps.

To secure their position, Brig. Gen. GEORGE S. GREENE demanded the construction of heavier and heavier defenses. Laboring through the morning of July 2, axes and sweat piled logs and earth from the crown of the rise southward to the base at Spangler's Spring.

At 8 p.m. a Confederate division under Maj. Gen. Edward Johnson tested the fortifications to their limits. Breaching the line on his left, Johnson pressed north up the hill and secured a lower rise before halting the attack around midnight. Unknown to the Kentuckian, he was only facing a single Union brigade. The rest of the 12th were temporarily assigned to protect the Union center during the heavy fighting along Cemetery Ridge. With the help of regiments from the 1st and 11th Corps, the deepening night, the stolid bastions, and his own brilliance in command, Greene and his New York regiments held out with comparatively few losses.

By 4 a.m. the whole of the 12th was back, along with artillery support from East Cemetery Ridge. Rather than wait for another assault, which was indeed coming, the corps launched one of its own, clearing the southern slopes of the hill that had been lost in the night. Reflecting the power of strong defenses in the war of the long-range rifle, the 12th lost 204 dead, 812 wounded, and 66 missing or captured in just over two days of combat. Though considerable, their subtractions were less than a fourth issued upon their opponents.

The U.S. 12th Corps reportedly never lost a flag or an artillery piece to capture during its year and a half of existence.

---

10. U.S. ARTILLERY RESERVE (10.2%)

BRIG. GEN. ROBERT TYLER

Technically not a corps at the time, the grand division of the U.S. artillery reserve functioned very much as an independent entity, assigned to assist infantry units whenever and wherever needed. In contrast, Confederate artillery "battalions" were generally dispersed among the various infantry divisions.

The reserve system worked well for the Union at Gettysburg, as it provided punch and flexibility and prevented interdivisional fights for extra guns. These guns were Meade's bishops—few but powerful, effective in their diagonal trajectories, and able to strike from far way.

The reserve method had its drawbacks for the battery crews, namely, they were routinely sent where the action was fiercest. Even with the perks of added infantry protection and the ability to shoot from a distance, certain situations could turn deadly, as illustrated by the artillery's heavy losses at Gettysburg.

To the question of where the artillerists fell, the answer would be everywhere. From Devil's Den to East Cemetery Hill to Little Round Top and north to Blocher's Knoll, the Napoleons, rifled ordnance guns, and howitzers were commonly the main targets of other gun crews. Worst hit were the artillerists manning the stone wall and Cemetery Ridge on day three. Felled by infantry and artillery alike, some were nearly wiped out by lucky shell bursts or concentrated rifle fire. One battery lost two dozen men when a Confederate shell hit and detonated their ammunition. Out of 2,400 officers and men in the gun crews, the reserves lost at least 43 dead, 187 wounded, and 12 missing or captured.[27]

The artillery reserve was one of the most diverse units on the field. Along with gunners from the U.S. regular army, there were batteries from ten different states.

TOP TEN STATES WITH HIGHEST PERCENTAGE CASUALTIES

In this war for states' rights, much of life revolved tightly around the state for citizens North and South. Until the war, there was no such thing as a national draft, no federal paper currency, and no Internal Revenue Service. Men like Iowa Michigan Royster of the 37th North Carolina paid income taxes only to their state, used currency printed by their state, and generally knew their governor better than their president. A citizen's contact with the federal government basically began and ended at the post office. In 1860 three times as many men belonged to state militias as to the U.S. Army, which numbered fewer than seventeen thousand and operated mostly west of the Mississippi.

Throughout the war, the regular army would remain modest in number, totaling only thirty-three thousand troops at any one time. In comparison, nearly three million men would muster into state units, organized, outfitted, and armed primarily by local means. If one of these citizen-soldiers would die and be identified, his grave marker would bear his name, his unit, and his state.

Altogether, Gettysburg hosted military units from twenty-nine of the thirty-five states. Present on the field were the 1st South Carolina Cavalry, the 5th Massachusetts Light Artillery, and the 82nd Ohio Infantry. Fighting in the backyard of the Pennsylvania boys were the Bath City Grays, Company A of the 3rd Maine, who were more than 570 miles from home. Encouraging them to head back were the Porter Guards of Company H, 4th Texas, hailing from Montgomery County, some 1,500 miles distant.

Dominant in the battle's history are the units from Pennsylvania, New York, and Virginia. Yet their stories and monuments tend to overshadow the contribution of the whole. When examined by percentage of troops lost rather than sheer numbers, it is the so-called lesser states that made the greater sacrifice. Listed here are the regions that suffered the worst ratios of subtraction over the three-day battle through death, wounds, capture, and disappearance.[28]

1.   MINNESOTA (59.3%)

At the time of Fort Sumter, Minnesota had been in the Union for only three years, yet it would be the first state to join in its defense. Governor Alexander Ramsey happened to be in Washington DC when news came of South Carolina batteries shelling the federal fortress in Charleston Harbor. The very next morning Ramsey headed to the War Department and promptly offered one thousand citizens for military service. The resulting 1st Minnesota Volunteer Infantry Regiment spent nearly its entire tenure in the eastern theater.

Over the course of the war, the Army of the Potomac went through more troops than Minnesota had people, and part of that heavy rotation came by way of the state's vanguard unit. Men of the 1st Minnesota fought in nearly every major battle from 1861 to 1863. Consequently, when the regiment marched into Gettysburg as part of the 2nd Division of the 2nd Corps, the lone unit from Minnesota had gone from 1,000 strong to 378. It almost maintained its modest numbers, lasting half the battle with barely a scratch. But events of July 2 would not spare it. Part of a slender defense of Cemetery Ridge late in the afternoon, it was tossed headlong and alone against a whole brigade (see BLOODIEST FIELDS OF FIRE).[29]

Popular is the notion that the 1st Minnesota underwent the worst regimental losses in the battle. This is true and false. Of the men who went forward in that brutal charge, only 20 percent returned unharmed. Yet two of their ten companies were deployed somewhere else at the time, making the charge all the more harrowing but also reducing their total ratio of loss. Overall, its nearly 60 percent casualty rate ranks only sixteenth among the worst regimental losses North and South.[30]

Long before Gettysburg, the 1st Minnesota had established a tradition of sacrifice. The unit earned the unenviable distinction of suffering more casualties than any other Union regiment at First Manassas.

---

2. TENNESSEE (56.1%)

The Volunteer State initially rejected the prospect of secession. Even the election of a Northerner from a Northern party failed to push Tennessee south. Yet with Fort Sumter came separation, and much of it was internal.

The eastern counties, crumpled with hills and mountains where it pushed into the Appalachians, were ill suited for plantation slavery. Most of the 50,000 Tennesseans who fought for the Union came from this region. The flatter western portions contributed the majority of the 140,000 white male residents who fought for the Confederacy.

Both sides stayed close to home, fighting in and around their state, and they fought often. The people of Tennessee experienced the second-highest number of military engagements in the war, with over eleven hundred incidents to Virginia's seventeen hundred. As a result, Robert E. Lee, who received troops from Deep South states by the thousands, moved into Pennsylvania with only three Tennessee regiments in tow. There were no Tennessee outfits in Meade's contingent.

The Confederate 1st, 7th, and 14th Tennessee infantry regiments barely counted 750 officers and men total. Few though they were, they still presented a large target as the spearhead of the first wave into Gettysburg. With the help of artillery, they succeeded in folding back the carbine-wielding cavalry of Brig. Gen. JOHN BUFORD. Despite the assistance of two Alabama regiments, they were unable to conquer the Iron Brigade wedged into the HERBST WOODS. Broken down by soft lead and quick captures, their losses were unsustainable, and they fell back.

After sporadic rest on the second day, the Volunteers went right back into the fray on July 3. They were positioned next to the left flank of Maj. Gen. GEORGE E. PICKETT's division, in the middle of the Confederate advance. Gradually whittled down as they neared the enemy line, a few brave souls of the 1st Tennessee managed to touch the stone wall at the Angle, only to be brought down by successive head blows from canister, bullets, and swinging rifle butts. Of the three regiments that went forward, all were cut in half, and only the 7th Tennessee made it back with its flag.[31]

When eleven states split away from the Union, their senators in Congress all resigned and went with them, except one: Unionist, Democrat, and later president of the United States, Andrew Johnson of Tennessee.

---

3. FLORIDA (46.4%)

Third to leave the United States, Florida was the sparsest of the Confederate states in terms of overall population (140,000) and number of slaves (63,000). Some 15,000 white Floridians went to war. A third of them died.[32]

The three regiments that marched to Gettysburg suffered commensurate losses. Of 739 men engaged, only 396 were left physically unhurt. All were part of Col. David Perry's brigade in A. P. Hill's 3rd Corps.

The 2nd, 5th, and 8th Florida missed out on the first day's action. The following afternoon they headed for the Emmitsburg road and into the Union center. Flanked by Brig. Gen. Cadmus M. Wilcox's brigade on their right and Brig. Gen. Ambrose Wright's brigade on their left, they had reason to feel confident about their chances, until they stumbled into a grove filled with Union troops. Perry's men faltered and pulled back, intent on fighting another day. That day came on the morrow with Pickett's Charge.[33]

On July 3 the Florida troops aligned on the right flank. They again felt somewhat emboldened, as they were part of the assault's second tier. If all went well, they would be mopping up what the first wave had torn apart. Instead they were thrown against a losing proposition, with no artillery and minimal infantry support. More than the Federal guns and muskets, the deafening noise of the event may have been their greatest undoing. Evidently the Floridians did not hear the screaming commands to pull back, and they stayed long enough to be either shot down or rounded up.[34]

During the war, the Union army conquered and occupied every state capital in the Confederacy except for Florida's.

---

4. NORTH CAROLINA (46.4%)

As with most states in the South, North Carolina suffered from a split personality. Slave owners and secessionists lived primarily on or near the east coast, and the great majority of the state's 120,000 troops came from this area.

Second to last in joining the Confederacy, predominantly rural North Carolina did not have near the wealth or population of Old Dominion. While Virginia won most of the attention, North Carolina lost a plurality of the soldiers. No other Confederate state matched or exceeded the Tarheels' final tally of 40,275 military deaths.

The situation at Gettysburg was no different. In the Army of Northern Virginia, the Tarheels contributed the largest number of soldiers (14,182) and suffered the highest casualties (6,580). They made up a sixth of Lee's force and became a fourth of his casualties.

Of their four cavalry regiments, five batteries, and thirty-three infantry units, the last branch was the hardest hit. Seven of the thirty-three endured more than 60 percent casualties. Four more experienced losses in excess of 70 percent—the 13th, 23rd, and the 26th Infantry regiments and the 2nd Infantry Battalion. All four shed most of their blood on July 1 west of town. Most notable was the 26th North Carolina. The regiment tore itself apart against the Iron Brigade on the first day and then sent its remnants with Pickett's Charge on the third. They came to Gettysburg with more than 800 men. They left with 130.

The last major Confederate army to surrender in 1865 was not Robert E. Lee's in Virginia but Joseph E. Johnston's seventeen days later in North Carolina. In recognition of this fact, most Southern states declared their Memorial Day to be April 26th rather than April 9th.

5. NEW HAMPSHIRE (43.7%)

Support for the newborn Republican Party grew quickly in New Hampshire. Lincoln won the state by a large margin in 1860. Nearly half its men of military age would volunteer for military duty in the coming years. A total of 36,000 residents would fight for the Union, 843 of them at Gettysburg.[35]

Whereas the Confederate high command preferred to keep brigades as homogenous as possible, mostly in the interest of maintaining a "states' rights" élan, the Union was clearly not as rigorous in banding state units together. Exemplifying the Federal melting-pot method were the four units from New Hampshire.

In the infantry, the 12th New Hampshire belonged to the 1st Corps, the 5th New Hampshire ran with the 2nd Corps, and the 2nd New Hampshire was assigned to the 3rd. Their sole representative among the gunners was part of the artillery reserve. Aptly titled was the 1st New Hampshire Light, so named because of its small tube calibers, plus it hauled four guns as opposed to the Union's customary six per battery. The outfit also experienced light losses from its rearward positioning in Evergreen Cemetery, from which its guns lobbed shots at the Lutheran Seminary on the afternoon of July 2 and into the left flank of Pickett's Charge the following day.[36]

Not so fortunate were the troops in the 2nd New Hampsire. Positioned at the apex of the 3rd Corps salient in the Peach Orchard, it bore the brunt of the overlapping, overwhelming attacks and was driven back. Fighting just to the north, near the Spangler farm lane on the Emmitsburg road, were the men of the 12th New Hampshire, also thrown rearward when their left flank gave way. Worst hit was the 5th New Hampshire, trapped inside the meat grinder of the Wheatfield. In less than an hour the 5th lost its brigade commander and half its numbers until a brigade of U.S. regulars replaced it.

After the war, New Hampshire provided lasting tribute to more than its own fallen. Dozens of monuments at Gettysburg National Battlefield Park have been carved from stone excavated from the soil of the Granite State.

6. ARKANSAS (38.0%)

Arkansas was a bit like the United States. Its northern third was not exactly amiable to African Americans, but it cared not for slavery and expressed even less empathy for secession. Only its southern third called for a permanent separation, and citizens fought on both sides.

Approximately seventeen hundred Razorbacks eventually fought for the North, yet none of them fought at Gettysburg. Some seven thousand fellow statesmen died in service to the South, scores of whom fell in Pennsylvania.[37]

Of Arkansas's seventy military units in the Confederate armed forces, only one infantry regiment went with Lee on his northern excursion. The 3rd Arkansas was the only non-Texas outfit of Maj. Gen. John Bell Hood's famed Texas Brigade, reported to be the hardest-hitting weapon in Lee's arsenal. Hood utilized this force to inaugurate his second-day strike at the Union left, but the rugged terrain fractured his regiments. Going forward through the confusion, the 3rd Arkansas found itself stuck between the hellfire of the Wheatfield and the brimstone of Devil's Den. Venturing too close to the latter, the 3rd received a precise volley from its right. The Razorbacks fell back, rallied, and went forward again, only to receive another swath of shots coming from their left. The ensuing free fire, underlined by screams of dying men, made it impossible for the regiment's officers to shout loud enough to be heard. Their colonel, Van H. Manning, resorted to physically pushing and throwing his men into place, until the squall took him down as well. Though he did not know it at the time, Manning and his regiment had been outnumbered four to one and were falling farther behind as the killing became proficient.[38]

After several hours, the regiment, or what was left of it, moved southwest and out of range. It remained in the area overnight. The next day the Arkansans waited anxiously for a Union attack and chance for retribution, but it never came.

The Texas Brigade, to which the 3rd Arkansas belonged, reportedly invented the infamous, chilling screech known as the Rebel Yell.

7. WISCONSIN (37.4%)

The deep green fields and exposed rock slopes of southern Pennsylvania may have looked like home for the six Union regiments from Wisconsin. Out of the twenty-one-hundred-strong contingent, the 5th Wisconsin survived the experience quite well. Attached to the 6th Corps in reserve, it celebrated the Fourth of July with a clean casualty sheet. Members of the 3rd Wisconsin would not shoot their rifles in anger until the morning of the third day, when they assisted in dislodging Confederates from the lower slopes of Culp's Hill.

In the early afternoon of July 1, their brethren of the 26th, part of the half-Deutsch 11th Corps, were hurriedly deployed north of the town. Their wait was brief, as was the lifespan of twenty-six men in their ranks. Taking on the brunt of a crushing flank attack from Maj. Gen. JUBAL A. EARLY's division, the regiment lost more than a hundred killed or wounded in minutes. A desperate retreat through town dwindled its numbers further. As one of the last regiments to reach the relative safety of Cemetery Hill, it struggled up the eighty-foot slope in time to take on sniper fire.

The other badger units also lost blood on the first day. The bulk of the Iron Brigade, the 2nd, 6th, and 7th Wisconsin regiments were among the first Union infantry to rescue Buford's dismounted cavalry. While the 2nd and 7th Wisconsin slammed away against superior numbers in the Herbst Woods and the seminary, the 6th Wisconsin turned north into the raking fire of the RAILROAD CUT. Once the premier brigade of the Army of the Potomac, the Black Hats would never again play a prominent role in the war for the Union.

Had it not been for marginal losses sustained by the 3rd and 5th Wisconsin in later fighting, Wisconsin would have had the third highest ratio of losses among states.

Along with fifty-two infantry regiments plus artillery and cavalry units, the Badger State produced more than seventeen million pounds of lead, wool, clothing, and food for the Union cause.

8. ALABAMA (35.3%)

Montgomery served as the first capital of the Confederate States of America. Alabama's iron mines were the chief suppliers to the cause. A $500,000 loan, secured by the state's small but wealthy landowner class, funded the start of the war. In addition, Alabama sent one hundred thousand sons, collected in one hundred military units, into combat. Seventeen regiments and two batteries, totaling nearly six thousand men, would march into Pennsylvania.

They experienced heavy fighting all three days. The 5th Alabama Battalion Infantry and the unlucky 13th Alabama Regiment first charged alongside the Tennesseans and five other regiments into the Herbst Woods against the Iron Brigade in the effort to push the Union troops from the northern tip of Seminary Ridge. On day two, an all-Alabama brigade formed the extreme right flank of the Confederate line, and throughout the afternoon, the five regiments drained themselves trying to take Little Round Top. Farther to the north, Cadmus M. Wilcox's Alabama brigade nearly reached Cemetery Ridge before falling back for lack of support. Wilcox's survivors were called forth again to support the right flank of Pickett's division during the charge. In total, the state lost more than two thousand casualties in a little over thirty-three hours of fighting.[39]

> The Alabama State Monument, situated near the intersection of South Confederate Avenue and Emmitsburg Road, includes a statue that bears a striking resemblance to George Washington, symbolizing the "Second American Revolution."

9. MISSISSIPPI (35.0%)

Home of the first and only president of the Confederacy, Mississippi held the second-highest percentage of slaves, was the second state to leave the Union, and played host to the third highest number of military engagements. More than seventy-eight thousand of its men fought in the war, of whom a quarter perished.[40]

Five thousand marched into Gettysburg, filling eleven infantry regiments and two batteries. They would be involved from beginning to end and would provide some of the best and worst performances on the field. The 2nd and 42nd Mississippi offered an overture when they hit the right flank of the Iron Brigade from the safety of the Railroad Cut northwest of town, only to get caught within its walls.

Brig. Gen. WILLIAM BARKSDALE's all-Mississippi Brigade achieved the South's principal success of the second day, methodically bashing in SICKLES'S SALIENT at the Peach Orchard. The following drive into the body of the Union army swept away all opposition until complete exhaustion and a wave of Union reinforcements halted progress. Farther up the Confederate line, Brig. Gen. Carnot Posey and his four Mississippi regiments were supposed to take part in the broad assault against the Union center along Cemetery Ridge, but vague orders and a localized firefight away from their objective distracted the regiments from their appointed task. Adding to the embarrassment, the brigade tallied some of the lightest casualties of the battle, insinuating a reluctance to fight.

On the final day, in the final attack, the 11th Mississippi watched in bewilderment as a brigade assigned to protect its left flank started to peel away and head back. Continuing on, despite horrific frontal and enfilade fire, the regiment made it to the stone wall of the Union front, only to lose its battle flag and a majority of its troops.[41]

Mississippian Brig. Gen. Joseph Davis was a nephew of Jefferson Davis. This family relationship was critical in his rise to brigade command, because his military experience was very limited. Unfortunately for the men of his brigade, Joe Davis was largely incompetent.

---

10. DELAWARE (33.2%)

One of four slave states in the Union, Delaware sided with Democrat John Breckinridge in the election of 1860. Abraham Lincoln finished third. But secession was never a concern, in part because the state had led the charge of the original thirteen colonies into the Union; diminutive Delaware was first to ratify the Constitution of the United States.

Twelve thousand served, 485 of them at Gettysburg, in two regiments similar to the state's relative size. Although both units were in the Union 2nd Corps, they saw more of the opposition than of each other. The 2nd Delaware was part of the rescue operation to save Sickles's 3rd Corps from annihilation in the salient. Teamed with infantry from Connecticut, New York, and Pennsylvania, the men from the First State did what no other brigade could do: push the Confederates completely out of the Wheatfield, through the neighboring Rose Woods, up Rose Hill, and to the Rose farm. Nearly as overextended as the salient, with no support in sight, the brigade was forced to fall all the way back to the Wheatfield.[42]

The 1st Delaware fought in a brigade led by former commander Thomas Smyth. For the last two days of the battle, they became embroiled in a contest for the Bliss farm, a homestead interrupting the open landscape between Seminary and Cemetery ridges. Prized by both sides as an ideal forward post and sniper den, the modest clapboard house and outbuildings were deemed worthy of a few lives. By the morning of July 3, Smyth and his Delaware boys had secured the area only to be ordered to abandon it. Dragging bodies alive and dead from the house and barns, they set fire to everything. The 1st Delaware then withdrew to relative safety, behind a stone wall, just a few yards north of a ninety-degree bend called the Angle.

Never wavering from this position, the regiment paid a considerable price. But as its lieutenant, John M. Dunn, recalled, losses were far greater from the states who tried to assail them: "In our front lay Virginians and Mississippians, Tennesseans, Georgians, and North Carolinians by the score. I never saw dead and wounded men lay so thick. From a space about seventy-feet back to the opposite side of the pike you could walk over the dead bodies of men."[43]

> Much of the gunpowder produced for the Union war effort came from Delaware, manufactured at the mills and factories of Du Pont.

TOP TEN CAUSES OF DEATH

On average, a Civil War soldier entering a battlefield had a one-in-thirty chance of dying. At Gettysburg, his odds slipped below one in fifteen. Three days in length, the contest was longer than most pitched battles, with the exception of the Seven Days' battles, Chancellorsville, and Spotsylvania. In addition, most combatants at Gettysburg saw action, in contrast to other engagements such as Antietam or Chancellorsville, where about a quarter of all troops were left in reserve.

Most significant, Gettysburg involved multiple attacks on well-established defenses, replacing the art of maneuver with the physics of brute force. The Army of Northern Virginia did most of the attacking and consequently experienced the highest percentage of combat losses of any Confederate army ever. More than 30 percent were killed, wounded, captured, or missing. By comparison, the battle of Chickamauga reduced the Army of Tennessee by 26 percent, and the bloodbath of Shiloh cost the Army of Mississippi 24 percent.

For the Army of the Potomac, Gettysburg losses neared 25 percent. Only the smaller Army of the Cumberland experienced a similar ratio of loss during the New Year's 1863 battle of Stones River.

All told, fighting over the ridges and round tops of southern Pennsylvania eventually cost the lives of nearly ten thousand Americans. Listed below are the principle modes of their premature departures, ranked by approximate totals lost. Accurate numbers are nearly impossible to ascertain. Of those killed in action, most were buried in haste, with little attempt to record their names, let alone the nature of their fatal injuries. Fatalities after the battle were also poorly calculated, due to multiple causes, misdiagnoses, and lost or incomplete records.[44]

1. KILLED IN ACTION: RIFLE FIRE (3,800)

In the Civil War, more than 90 percent of deaths on the battlefield came by way of small-arms fire. At Gettysburg, 90 percent of these handheld weapons were muzzle-loading rifles.

Spiral-barreled firearms had been around for hundreds of years. Yet in that time, no one had developed an effective, inexpensive bullet that could load easily, fire cleanly, and still catch a gun's rifling. Then, in the mid-1800s, French Capt. Claude Etienne Minié perfected a conoidal bullet. Erroneously called a "minie ball," its cupped base expanded during firing, allowing the bullet to catch the rifling on its way out. Indented rings on its side carried away soot, reducing the amount of buildup that quickly jammed such weapons. By the late 1850s the U.S. War Department adopted the design, just in time for the Civil War.

Shooting four times farther than smoothbore muskets, rifles were effective at three hundred yards and could kill from nearly a mile away. This giant leap in ballistics made infantry assaults perilous and cavalry charges

The musket is a photographer's prop. The severed hand and cavernous abdominal wound are real, attesting to the gruesome authority of weaponry as well as scavenging wildlife.

LIBRARY OF CONGRESS

virtually pointless. Typically, a soldier felled by a Minié bullet was still 80 to 150 yards away from the shooter.

More than its range, the bullet's design drastically intensified damage. Malleable and oblong, the projectile tended to flatten and tumble as it passed through its victim, carving a fairly large tunnel of destruction. Its fraying edges would burst arteries, sever nerves, and splinter bone. With slow velocity it carried dirt, cloth, soot, and sweat into the body, contaminating the wound. An officer from the 82nd Ohio described being hit with one as an "instantaneous metamorphosis from strength and vigor to utter helplessness." Others recalled a "sharp, electric pain," a pervasive numbness, or the sensation of being pierced with a red-hot wire.[45]

Research indicates that Gettysburg was a typical battle for bullet-related fatalities. Eighty percent of the dead on the field received hits to the neck, face, or head. Fifteen percent were hit in the abdomen or chest. Five percent were struck in an artery of a limb.[46]

In its attack against the Iron Brigade on July 1, Company F of the 26th North Carolina lost ninety of ninety-one men within a span of thirty minutes, nearly all victims of rifle fire.

---

2. DIED OF WOUNDS: NO SURGERY (2,800)

Technically "died of wounds" pertained to any combatant who reached an aid station or field hospital before expiring. Massive hemorrhaging and major damage to vital organs caused most of the immediate deaths. Following were victims of acute head or neck injuries. Medics typically set these cases aside in quiet dells or shaded woods. Hospital areas had "dying wings" or "dying trees," part refuge and part refuse of the predestined. CORNELIA HANCOCK came upon such a place in her first hours on the field, "a collection of semi-conscious but still living human forms, all of whom had been shot through the head, and were considered hopeless."[47]

Of Gettysburg's numbers, an often-overlooked sum is its thirty thousand wounded, the largest total rendered in the war. Untold numbers were doomed by lack of care, an almost inescapable condition created by the size of the fight itself. For nearly a week after the shooting ceased, the Union had only one operating surgeon per nine hundred cases, with the Confederate situation even worse.[48]

Most pitiable were the wounded Confederate evacuees, nearly ten thousand in number. Their cruel journey began on the Fourth of July in darkness and pouring rain. A cavalryman recalled, "Of all the nights that I spent during the war I think this was the saddest." Stacked in ambulances like cordwood, the severely injured "shrieked often from the jolting of the vehicles."[49]

For two weeks and longer, miles of carts and wagons rattled over potholed back roads, including one stretch aptly named Pine Stump Road. Men with bullet wounds paled and faded as dust, rain, and mud wormed into their lacerations. Those with shattered bones sank into madness. Some begged to be put out of their misery, others were clearly too far gone to be moved any farther. Quietly, orderlies left hundreds of them behind in houses and barns, on the slim hope they would be captured alive and treated by Union doctors. A group of Louisiana soldiers were deposited in a barn, where they began to die one by one. They had no doctors or nurses to tend to them, but their increasing stench and number of dead soon gathered an unholy host of flies and rodents. Union troops eventually found a few survivors, but only after a week had passed.[50]

It is not yet clear how many of Lee's wounded made it back alive to the general hospital at Winchester or other points south. Conservatively, 90 percent of the evacuated wounded survived the trip.

Among the mortally wounded at Gettysburg were Pvt. George Nixon III of the 73rd Ohio, grandfather of President Richard M. Nixon, and Col. Paul Joseph Revere of the 20th Massachusetts, grandson of patriot Paul Revere.

3. DIED OF WOUNDS: POSTSURGERY (1,200)

Volunteer nurse SOPHRONIA BUCKLIN tersely recalled the fate of one young soldier: "His was an unnecessary amputation . . . his wound was that of a bullet through the fleshy part of the arm, and it seemed to be doing well as could be expected. After the amputation, which did not discharge properly, his symptoms grew fatal."[51]

Though Bucklin may have been correct, most other amputations were necessary. Catastrophic damage from soft-lead bullets left most limbs unsalvageable. Time was also of the essence. Surgery within twenty-four hours meant a 75 percent chance of survival. If a patient had to wait forty-eight hours, his chances slid to fifty-fifty. Maj. Gen. Lewis Armistead, shot in the arm as he breeched the Union defenses during Pickett's Charge, underwent amputation two days later. He did not survive.

Unfortunately, the afflicted overwhelmed the available medics. Dr. William Watson, operating at the Schwartz farm hospital site, estimated he performed fourteen amputations without a break on July 5. Incredibly, his work had just begun. "[Soon] I will turn my attention to wounded Rebels," he said a week after the battle had ended. Doctors kept sawing, and patients kept dying. Of sixty-eight Union deaths recorded at the LUTHERAN SEMINARY field hospital, more than half were from limb wounds. One hundred fifty-eight soldiers underwent leg amputations at Camp Letterman. Only fifty survived.[52]

Of course, stitching skin, picking out shrapnel, and digging for bullets could be just as deadly, since the discovery of bacteria was still years away. Using saliva-threaded sutures, dirty fingernails, unwashed scalpels, and pus-tainted probes, surgeons unknowingly added to the body count.

Some actually viewed contamination as a good thing. White pus was seen by many as the body trying to cleanse itself, although half its sufferers died. In some cases the seepage entered veins, killing by "pyemia," or blood poisoning. Erysipelas, or acute red swelling, meant severe infection and death for 80 percent. Gangrene turned skin black and putrid, signaling a need for higher amputation or invasive scraping, which rarely saved the patient. Tetanus was 100 percent fatal.

Wounds to the chest and abdomen killed a high number, as internal surgery was essentially a risk most doctors were unwilling to take. Some at Gettysburg experimented on lung punctures, trying to save the patient by hermetically sealing the holes. When no one appeared to survive the procedure for more than a few days, the medical pioneers stopped trying.[53]

> Miraculously, many soldiers lived despite the care they received. One eighteen-year-old soldier of the 22nd Georgia had the poor luck of having a bullet enter his left hip joint and pass out of his rectum. To help him recover, doctors administered quinine, acetate of lead, ipecac, and opium. Amazingly, he survived.

4. PRISON (900)

On the Fourth of July, Lee presented Meade with an offer: "In order to promote the comfort and convenience of the officers and men captured by the opposing armies in the recent engagements, I respectfully propose that an exchange be made at once." Meade abruptly declined on the grounds he had no authority from Washington to consent. Thus more than ten thousand men marched in captivity.[54]

Eager to unload their burden of fifty-two hundred extra mouths, Confederate officers repeated the offer of parole. Some fifteen hundred Federals illegally accepted and were released; the rest were marched toward Richmond. Nearly all captured Confederates were driven toward Baltimore.[55]

Most Confederates were processed at Fort McHenry, of Star-Spangled Banner fame. Maj. Gen. Isaac R. Trimble, minus a leg after Pickett's Charge, was transferred with scores of fellow officers to Camp Chase in Ohio, a stockade that soon filled to twice its capacity of four

Portions of Longstreet's Corps march interminable miles to prison. Hundreds would die in captivity, but prudent Federal record-keeping assured that most would be buried in accurately marked graves.

LIBRARY OF CONGRESS

Richmond's Libby Prison, where lice, fleas, rats, typhus, dysentery, hunger, pneumonia, and typhoid awaited Union officers captured at Gettysburg.

LIBRARY OF CONGRESS

thousand. The bulk of the enlisted, such as Sgt. Charles W. Rivenbark of the 1st North Carolina, were sent by steamer and packed with ten thousand other POWs into Fort Delaware, alias "the Death Pen," where commandant Albin Schoepf endorsed the use of beatings, forced labor, and random shootings to maintain order. Fatality rates there reached three hundred a month.[56]

To ease crowding, prisoners were transferred to Point Lookout, which eventually became the Union's largest prison camp. More than twenty thousand inmates were exposed to floods and storms from the sea, wells mucked with salt and iron, and open latrines overflowing with feces. More transfers followed, primarily to stockades of similar infamy, including Camp Douglas in Chicago and "Hellmira," New York.[57]

Union captives fared no better, as Confederate officials wedged them into Richmond warehouses and tobacco barns such as Belle Isle, Castle Thunder, and Libby Prison. Inmates became infested with lice, starved of sustenance, and tormented by rats. Commandants stripped them of their money, watches, photos, utensils, and in some cases uniforms. In February 1864, as overcrowding became chronic and the Confederate capital feared prison uprisings, most of the enlisted were transferred to a new camp in Georgia. Officially called Camp Sumter, it was better known as Andersonville. Overall, one in eight Confederates and one in six Union men who entered a prison camp did not survive.[58]

Prentiss Kirkman became one of the last Gettysburg POWs to die in prison. Held at Point Lookout, he succumbed to the ravages of scurvy just a month before the war ended. Ironically Kirkman belonged to the 26th North Carolina and was one of its few members who survived the battle of Gettysburg in one piece.

---

5. KILLED IN ACTION: ARTILLERY (600)

Civil War field guns, howitzers, and mortars accounted for only 4 percent of combat fatalities. Batteries at Gettysburg claimed a slightly higher than average ratio of combat deaths—approximately 6 percent—largely from heavy involvement near the Peach Orchard on the second day and the extended artillery duel across the Emmitsburg road on day three. Possibly 350 Confederates died from shrapnel during Pickett's Charge alone. Yet overall, the actual damage was modest. Dr. Henry Janes, director of the Union field hospitals, reported that of the 22,000 wounded under his charge, only 204 cases involved artillery. Regardless of statistics, veterans often perceived cannons as exceedingly lethal, a monster's bite to a bullet's bee sting. Much of this fear stemmed from the terrible effects of the ammunition.[59]

Solid cannon balls would pass through a body without slowing, producing a quick, wet, tearing sound. Case shot—hollow iron spheres filled with black powder—would explode and fill the air with hissing shrapnel. Spinning shells would produce the same effect over longer distances. At close range, battery commanders called for canister—essentially lead balls in a can—that transformed artillery pieces into mammoth shotguns, spitting hundreds of small lead spheres for a hundred yards or more.

For those on the receiving end of such devices, the experience was otherworldly. Several bodies hit near Cemetery Ridge actually caught fire. A Massachusetts soldier walking close to the Peach Orchard noticed "sticking among the rocks and against the trunks of trees, hair, brains, entrails, and shreds of human flesh." Col. E. Porter Alexander, whose own guns ended several Union lives, recalled a fellow Confederate who had been hit profile. The round tore off the lower part of the man's face, revealing a gurgling void where his jaw and teeth should have been: "He sat up and looked at me steadily, and I looked at him . . . but nothing, of course, could be done for him." The human suffering was not exclusive, as hundreds of animals also perished in like manner. A few men recalled the dismal spectacle of horses trying to run on three legs while red pints gushed from the stump of their missing fourth.[60]

Altogether twenty thousand Confederate and thirty-two thousand Union artillery rounds were fired during the battle of Gettysburg. On average, crews had to fire eighty-seven times to score one kill. This was rather efficient compared to shoulder arms, which typically killed one man per every thousand shots fired.

---

6.   KILLED IN ACTION: SMOOTHBORE FIRE (300)

By 1863, Northern and foreign arsenals had replaced the majority of smoothbore muskets with rifles. Yet because of sheer supply, and the exceptionally frugal nature of both war departments, a considerable count of these archaic muskets still found their way into battle.

A few regiments preferred the weapon. Smoothbores loaded a bit faster than rifles. Though their range was dismally short—less than a football field—they worked well in close-quarter scrapes. When soldiers went toe-to-toe, the ammunition of choice was "buck and ball"—three small lead shots perched upon a hefty sphere of lead that created a spread-pattern blast that could fell a horse in a single blast. Companies in the Union Iron Brigade fought for their lives with it on the first day of Gettysburg. The WHEATFIELD on the second day saw the Irish Brigade issue a heavy toll on Joseph B. Kershaw's division of South Carolinians. The 12th New Jersey used it with deadly effect near the Angle against Pickett's Charge, mowing down ranks and taking the regimental flag of the 26th North Carolina.[61]

Ironically, most of the smoothbores present were in the hands of Union men, despite their better funding and greater industrialization. Perhaps one in ten Confederate shoulder arms were smoothbores compared to one in nine for Meade's army.[62]

Relatively speaking, the guns were not especially lethal, partly because of their modest range, and partly because of their ammunition. Unlike the oddly shaped Minié bullets, spherical shots generally retained their shape after impact, rendering much less damage by comparison. Only rarely were doctors able to successfully extract rifle bullets, whereas removal of solid lead spheres was commonplace.

President Lincoln's assassin used a smoothbore pistol. Although its .44-caliber bullet entered the occipital lobe at point-blank range, more than nine hours passed before the president died from its effects. The bullet has been, since 1956, on display at the National Museum of Health and Medicine in Washington DC.

7. DISEASE (100)

It is well known that twice as many Civil War soldiers perished from disease as were killed by combat overall. Yet available records indicate astonishingly few disease-related fatalities in July 1863 for both the Army of the Potomac and the Army of Northern Virginia. Reasons for the fortunate lapse are manifold.

Primarily, the troops were neither encamped nor in winter. Contagious "camp diseases" such as measles, smallpox, and tuberculosis thrived in tight spaces but not on the open march. Illnesses that preyed on thousands in the cold and damp, especially pneumonia, lost their ravenous appetite in midsummer. Deadly malaria and yellow fever rarely appeared north of the Mason-Dixon Line. Of the sixty-eight Union deaths recorded at the Lutheran Seminary, only one came as a result of typhoid. Doctors there recorded just one additional fatality to "disease," although fourteen deaths were simply listed as "unknown."[63]

This is not to say that soldiers stayed healthy. Four thousand Confederates returned to Virginia with various forms of sickness. Perhaps as many as one thousand straggled behind in Pennsylvania. Many were captured and sent to prison camps, where their ailments only proliferated.[64]

There were soldiers who survived *because* of their ailments. Deemed unable to start or complete the march, a great many never made it to the battle. In addition to skulkers and "yellow bellies" who faked maladies to avoid a fight, thousands of legitimately sick men were either interned at base hospitals, left to recuperate along the way to Gettysburg, or discharged altogether.

Over the course of the war, 45,000 Union soldiers perished from dysentery and diarrhea. In July 1863, the Army of the Potomac recorded 5,890 acute and chronic cases of "the fluxes," but only two cases reportedly were fatal.

8. KILLED IN ACTION: FRIENDLY FIRE (80)

Battles appear on maps as neat lines and uniform arrows, but the dance of death is more like a screaming spasm than a courtly two-step. Rolling smoke blocks sight, explosions monopolize sound, trees and hills hide friend as well as foe. All clarity fades with contact. As a result, every major battle in the Civil War produced casualties from friendly fire, and Gettysburg was no exception.

A single Confederate brigade endured four separate volleys from "friendly" artillery and shoulder arms over the course of the battle. In places like the Peach Orchard and the copse of trees in Pickett's Charge, compatriots killed one another as units accidentally overlapped, shells exploded prematurely or went astray, marksmen misidentified their targets, and battery crews fatally misjudged distances.[65]

On July 1, when demarcation between sides was least evident, members of the hapless Union Iron Brigade began falling back from a series of costly reverses at the HERBST WOODS. They staggered into Company E of the 5th Maine Light Battery, who promptly opened fire. On day two, Confederate batteries accidentally hit members of the 5th Texas as they charged up Little Round Top. July 3 brought misery upon the 21st Mississippi and the 69th Pennsylvania. Both were blindsided by their own cannon during Lee's grand assault.[66]

Culp's Hill, a thickly wooded humpback nearly a mile wide, saw more night fighting than any other location on the battlefield and consequently experienced the largest amount of friendly fire. One instance involved the 1st North Carolina mistakenly firing into fellow Confederates of the 1st Maryland Infantry Battalion. Later, Union artillery blasted the 20th Connecticut so many times, the infantry regiment's commander threatened to return the favor.[67]

It is possible that, given the force and angle of the wound, the bullet that struck Maj. Gen. Winfield Scott Hancock came from a Vermont regiment.

9. KILLED IN ACTION: EDGED WEAPONS (30)

In films and other lore, swords and bayonets play leading roles in Civil War battle scenes. In reality, less than one-half of 1 percent of combat fatalities came from the point of a blade. As with artillery, flashing steel was most effective as a psychological weapon.

Phobias ran high during Pickett's Charge, when Federals had to wait and watch the approach of twelve thousand "bayonets gleaming in the sun." Leading the assault on the Confederate right, Lewis Armistead brandished his hat upon a sword and reportedly shouted, "Give them the cold steel!" as he climbed over the wall before Cemetery Ridge.

Trained incessantly to jab with their bayonet, most infantry at the Angle and elsewhere chose to use their rifles as clubs in hand-to-hand fighting. Union medical reports from Gettysburg show that the enlisted may have been on to something. Incise wounds, even to the head, were rarely mortal. Hard, blunt strikes to the cranium, which often came from the butt of a rifle, usually produced serious if not lethal harm.[68]

Evidently, most lacerations at Gettysburg came compliments of sabers, brandished with haste on the third day's cavalry engagement east of town. In stark contrast to most cavalry commanders at the time, JEB STUART still preferred the shock and awe of the old swinging saber to the new carbine or pistol, as he argued that firearms were wholly inaccurate on the gallop.[69]

True to form, Confederate riders gave and received a number of slices before the day was over, yet it was much ado about almost nothing. Swords produced scores of injuries but only one confirmed fatality. Otherwise, the closest soldiers came to an enemy blade at Gettysburg was when they were already dead, and looters used knives to cut open their pockets in search of valuables.[70]

The highest-ranking officer to die from an edged weapon at Gettysburg may have been Col. Harrison H. Jeffords of the 4th Michigan. In the fight for the Wheatfield, he attempted to wrest his captured regimental flag from a Confederate soldier and was immediately bayoneted.

---

10. DROWNING (25)

Lugging from twenty to forty pounds of equipment, donning heavy wool and flannel uniforms, troops were always in danger of sinking into any stream or river they were fording. Burdened by such weight, knowing how to swim rarely helped. A soldier was most vulnerable when severely wounded, as any standing water could easily smother him if he could not lift his head. Such was the case at the Bloody Pond at Shiloh, where thirsting men took their last breath before sinking into its muddy banks.

A day after the fighting stopped at Gettysburg, water threatened the wounded once again, this time from the sky. A storm front over southern Pennsylvania released a torrent of rain, quickly flooding cellars and low-lying areas, precisely where countless wounded had crawled to safety. SARAH BROADHEAD came upon scores of men packed within the cellar of the Lutheran Seminary and the seeping walls threatening to drown the weakest. She frantically called for help, and with the assistance of a few able-bodied nurses and walking wounded, carried every man to the upper floors.[71]

The same cloudburst swelled all streams far above their banks. In at least one field hospital, loss of life probably occurred. At the Jacob Schwartz farm south of town, where the Rock and White Run creeks converged, hundreds of shattered bodies were laid out on the low ground. Sometime during July 5, flashfloods submerged the area under two feet of rushing water. Those prostrated by their wounds soon disappeared beneath the churning surface or were swept downstream, screaming. So frantic was the effort to save these men, orderlies and soldiers were dragging them by their clothes, hair, broken limbs, anything to get them to higher ground. Accounts diverge, but several eyewitnesses claimed that at least twenty men, almost all assuredly Confederate wounded, were swept to a watery end.[72]

One of the first land battles of the war may have produced more drownings than combat deaths. Routed in the fight at Ball's Bluff, Virginia, Union soldiers panicked and fled into the Potomac. Dozens of them went under. Harbingers of the long war that lay ahead, some of their bodies floated downstream into their nation's capital.

POSTBATTLE

TOP TEN REACTIONS TO THE OUTCOME

The result of the battle took days to come into focus. Nearly all newspaper correspondents North and South completely missed the first twenty-four hours, and many spent the remainder of the battle shuttling reports to remote locations. To establish better contact, the *New York Herald* created a temporary pony express to rush dispatches to the home office.[1]

As with most Civil War engagements, news about Gettysburg arrived piecemeal, wrapped in bias, and bound with wild rumors. Some newspapers reported that Lee's men had been completely surrounded in the mountains of southern Pennsylvania. Others claimed Meade had been decisively beaten, his Army of the Potomac in full flight. Tallies of casualties varied by tens of thousands.

In the weeks and months that ensued, no real consensus emerged as to the battle's overall significance. While current generations tend to consider the contest as the decisive moment of the Civil War, most observers at the time could only agree that it was an extraordinarily large engagement resulting in a high number of casualties. Listed below, in no particular order, are ten prominent perceptions on Gettysburg, reflecting widely divergent views of the period, and the general impression that the battle was but one large piece to a very complex puzzle.

1. ABRAHAM LINCOLN

During the battle Lincoln practically lived at the War Department's telegraph office, a key portal buried in the building's second-floor library. Hour after hour he waited in agonizing silence, pacing among dusty books, buzzing wires, acidic batteries, and diligent cipher operators. Only a pair of telegraph lines connected the office with southern Pennsylvania, and they often went dead.

July 1 passed with hardly a word. The next two days brought intermittent and incomplete reports, mostly of Confederate units suddenly gone from the outskirts of Harrisburg and Carlisle and of thundering artillery duels emanating from the vicinity of "Gettysburgh."[2]

Then, in the early morning of July 4, news came that the Union had prevailed to some extent, prompting Lincoln to submit an open letter of accolades to his legions. Hoping Meade could consequently bag Lee's entire army, the president returned to the telegraph office frequently, walking unescorted from the White House to the War Department, to peer over the operators' shoulders as they transcribed incoming messages. Days passed and no word arrived of a Union counterattack. Lincoln's mood turned from apprehension to anger.

Meade had won, but he had relatively few enemy guns and prisoners to show for it. Now was the time to strike, Lincoln insisted, while the Army of Northern Virginia was bloodied and backed against the rain-swollen Potomac.

But Meade did nothing of substance, citing stormy weather and an entrenched enemy as reasons for prudence. Those close to Lincoln stated they had never seen him so furious. "They will be ready to fight a magnificent battle," fumed the commander in chief, "when there is no enemy there to fight."[3]

Lincoln was again in the telegraph office when Meade's dispatch arrived over the wires, proclaiming his army had driven the Confederates "from our soil." Days later Lincoln said to his secretary John Hay: "Will our generals never get that idea out of their heads? The whole country is our soil."[4]

The vexed president set his rage to paper, his quill nearly slitting the pages of an extremely terse letter to the general: "I do not believe you appreciate the magnitude of the misfortune of Lee's escape. He was within your easy grasp, and to have closed upon him would, in connection with our other late success, have ended the war. As it is, the war will be prolonged indefinitely. . . . Your golden opportunity is gone, and I am distressed immeasurably because of it."[5]

But rather than cast a cloud over this rare Union victory, or lose a commander who had performed well under considerable pressure, Lincoln decided not to voice his anger. He neatly folded the letter and slipped it into an envelope, upon which he inked the words: "To Gen. Meade, never sent or signed."[6]

On July 7 Gideon Welles told Lincoln that U. S. Grant had captured Vicksburg. Upon hearing the news, the president jumped up, bear-hugged the navy secretary, and shouted: "It is great, Mr. Welles! It is great!"

---

2. ROBERT E. LEE

Brig. Gen. John D. Imboden came upon Lee just after midnight on July 3. Visibly exhausted, the commander leaned against his horse, his arm draped over the saddle to keep himself upright, wearing what Imboden called "an expression of sadness that I had never before seen upon his face."

The brigadier consoled, "General, this has been a hard day for you." Lee turned to Imboden and said, "Yes, it has been a sad, sad day to us." After a pause, Lee was said to have wailed out: "Too bad! Too bad! OH! TOO BAD!"[7]

Over the following week, as was his nature, Lee began to assess not what had been lost but what had been gained. His men remained on the field all of July 4 without harassment. He had drawn the Army of the Potomac far away from the Old Dominion. Rather than retreating in a panic, his men were able to withdraw in good order. The opposition, it appeared, was in no hurry to pursue him.

In dispatches to follow, Marse Robert never mentioned Vicksburg, which was supposed to be the main beneficiary of his "diversionary" offensive. He did express awareness of the tremendous losses endured by his own army, but he insisted the Union had suffered equally. In a letter to his wife, he admitted: "The army has returned to Virginia. Its return is rather sooner than I had originally contemplated." But he added his foray into Pennsylvania had "accomplished much of what I proposed."[8]

Doubts and criticisms from the Southern public surfaced nonetheless, prompting Lee to offer his resignation on August 8. In his tender, he cited poor health. He also complained that the army was unable to do what he asked of them and stated that the Confederate public had failed to be "true and united." He closed with a request to be relieved of command. Jefferson Davis rejected the largely ceremonial offer and instead bombarded Lee with compliments.[9]

The general had only eight more years to live, but for the remainder of his days he rarely spoke of Gettysburg. When he did, Lee stated adamantly that his army had not been beaten. In a postwar letter, on one of the few instances where he voiced his opinion of the battle, Lee insisted the loss "was occasioned by a combination of circumstances. It was commenced in the absence of correct intelligence. It was continued in the effort to overcome the difficulties in which we were surrounded." He added that victory would have been achieved "could one determined and united blow have been delivered by our whole line," a suggestion that Pickett's Charge was far weaker than the united blow he had intended to deliver.[10]

Soon after Gettysburg, Lee purportedly said of the Army of the Potomac, "It will be seen for the next six months that that army will be as quiet as a sucking dove." He was too kind. It was nearly ten months before the Army of the Potomac engaged him again.

---

3. GEORGE GORDON MEADE

Meade's General Orders No. 68 summarized his impression: "The commanding general, in behalf of the country, thanks the Army of the Potomac for the glorious result of the recent operations. An enemy, superior in numbers, and flushed with the pride of a successful invasion, attempted to overcome and destroy this army. Utterly baffled and defeated, he has now withdrawn from the contest."

Despite his uncharacteristic optimism, Meade soon discovered his fight had just begun. Facing him were a series of torrential thunderstorms, a well-entrenched Lee in Maryland, and an impatient government in Washington. With military and political climates worsening by the hour, Meade saw his brief glory wash away with the never-ending downpour.

While waiting for the roads to dry, he received a telegraph from his general in chief, the paper-pushing and judgmental Henry W. Halleck, condemning him for not being "sufficiently active." Meade lashed back at the uninformed critique: "It is in my judgment so undeserved that I feel compelled most respectfully to ask to be immediately relieved from the command of this army."[11]

Halleck and Lincoln attempted damage control by suggesting they were merely offering "a stimulus to an active pursuit." Though the general stayed at his post, the experience only cemented his distaste for political meddling.[12]

When Halleck and Lincoln proved to be correct, and Lee had indeed escaped, Meade's ire turned to humility. Few were more surprised than Meade when the Army of Northern Virginia slipped over the Potomac, using nothing more than slapdash bridges made of dismantled warehouses. But he felt somewhat vindicated after examining the Confederate fortifications left behind. Gen. Oliver O. Howard said of the daunting hills and breastworks that if Meade had attacked, it was "by no means certain that the repulse of Gettysburg might not have been turned against us."[13]

On July 9, nearly a week after Gettysburg, Meade told Washington: "I think the decisive battle of the war will be fought in a few days."

---

4. JAMES LONGSTREET

For South Carolinian James Longstreet, who preferred to fight on the defensive, Gettysburg was land of marginal value. In a report to the Confederate War Department three weeks after the battle, Longstreet essentially condemned the entire campaign. He was especially critical of Pickett's Charge: "The distance to be passed over under the fire of the enemy's batteries, and in plain view, seemed too great to insure great results." Noting shortages of fresh troops and artillery ammunition, the general added, "The order for this attack, which I could not favor under better auspices, would have been revoked had I felt that I had that privilege."[14]

Illustrated by comments made later in life (see CONTROVERSIES), Lee's "Old War Horse" began to view Pickett's Charge and the entire campaign as a poor application of resources. In a letter penned in 1874,

Longstreet admitted, "I believe that mistakes were made on both sides and that I am likely to be one of those who have committed them as any one." Yet in 1878 he contributed an article to the *Philadelphia Weekly Times* entitled "The Mistakes of Gettysburg" and catalogued a multitude of allegedly wrong moves the South made in July 1863, laying the bulk of the blame at the feet of his deceased commander.[15]

Increasingly, "Old Pete" viewed the battle as the greatest of all missteps taken by the Army of Northern Virginia. In 1902 he admitted to former adversary Daniel E. Sickles that Gettysburg was "the sorest and saddest reflection of my life for many years."[16]

On April 9, 1889, a fire swept through James Longstreet's home in Gainesville, Georgia. The flames consumed his library, Civil War uniform, dress sword, spurs, personal letters, and related war mementos. The accident occurred twenty-four years to the day of Appomattox.

---

5. JEFFERSON DAVIS

Confederate president Jefferson Davis became nearly crippled with anxiety in early July 1863. Rumors swelled that the suddenly reclusive Davis was on his deathbed. The cause of Davis's racking angst was not Gettysburg but Vicksburg. Earlier in the year, the Confederacy's chief of ordnance, Josiah Gorgas, recalled an exceptionally tense meeting with his boss: "I spent an hour with the President. He is at present wholly devoted to the defense of the Mississippi and thinks and talks of little else."[17]

"We have suffered a check," the stoic Davis said of Gettysburg, whereas Vicksburg cost him three times the number of men, six times the number of guns, and control of the Mississippi. In addition, food shortages and inflation were intensifying throughout the South, Charleston had come under siege, and Federal armies were once again moving toward Richmond. To Davis, Gettysburg was a sideshow.[18]

By July 9 it was clear that Lee had to withdraw from his northern campaign. The news did not discourage the president, who still held absolute faith in the Marble Man. It was his other generals that troubled him—the reckless Braxton Bragg, the proud but cautious Joseph E. Johnston, and the failed defender of Vicksburg, John C. Pemberton. Formerly a colonel in the U.S. Army, Davis dreamed of taking their place in the field. "If I could take one wing and Lee the other," he told his wife, "I think we could between us wrest a victory."[19]

Later in life, Davis bestowed greater significance to Lee's 1863 invasion. "If we had won Gettysburg," he surmised, "the moral effect of that victory would have brought peace." Yet he added that winning required the total destruction of the Army of the Potomac. Anything shorter would have made little difference. "To have maneuvered Meade into the defenses of Washington City would not have concluded the war," Davis insisted, "and there he would have been unassailable."[20]

Among other things Jefferson Davis lost with Vicksburg were his family plantations of Brierfield and Hurricane, which were just miles downriver from the great city. Both homesteads were heavily damaged in the aftermath, and Hurricane was burned to the ground.

---

6.   GEORGE E. PICKETT

Some generals are capable of witnessing with cool dispassion the tearing of bodies and spurting of blood. George E. Pickett was evidently not one of those generals.

Pickett led his division rather ably across the open fields before Cemetery Ridge. At four hundred yards, a distance of only marginal safety, he stepped his horse aside and let his brigade commanders take over. What he saw next horrified him.

In minutes, thousands of living beings were cut down, men and animals instantly mangled into every deformation imaginable. The vile spectacle traumatized the sensitive Pickett. Looking on, he neither led his men forward nor called for a retreat. He simply begged for reinforcements, and none came.[21]

Witnesses said that Pickett was thereafter inconsolable, alternately weeping and hysterical for hours. He reportedly yelled at Longstreet, "I am ruined, my division is gone—it is destroyed." For days he wallowed in and out of shock. What may have pained him most was the conspicuous lack of support from his fellow officers. He was later quoted as saying, "If the charge made by my gallant Virginians on the fatal third day had been supported, or even if my other two Brigades had been with me, we would have been in Washington and the war ended."[22]

Pickett's postbattle reports were so critical of his own countrymen that Lee judged them to be potentially dangerous to morale. Lee ordered the reports destroyed, and Pickett apparently obeyed, as no copies are currently known to exist.[23]

After the war Pickett rarely spoke of the battle. He once referred to Gettysburg as "the awful conflict" and described how his men marched "one mile into the jaws of death." Otherwise he largely remained silent.[24]

In 1870 Pickett encountered Lee by chance in Richmond. After a cool exchange, Pickett whispered to John S. Mosby, "He had my division massacred at Gettysburg." Mosby responded, "Well, it made you immortal."

---

7. THE *NEW YORK TIMES*

Perhaps forty newspapers were represented in the area by the end of the battle. Nearly every major Northern paper sent a correspondent, including the *Boston Journal*, the *Cincinnati Gazette*, and the *New York World*. Certainly one of the most respected among them was the *New York Times*.

Editor Henry Raymond established the *Times* in 1851 as an objective counterweight to the preachy, abolitionist *New York Tribune* and the gossipy, sensationalist *New York Herald*. The excitement of Gettysburg greatly tested Raymond's commitment to impartial accuracy, and much of his print soon filled with rants of heavy conjecture and patriotic fervor.

At first the *Times* proclaimed a great Union victory after just one day's fighting, though none of its reporters were on hand to see it. Evidently, the U.S. 11th Corps had staged a gallant charge against Longstreet's brigades, in which the men in blue "rushed into the fight like infuriated demons, and the whole line of the enemy gave way before them." In reality, the 11th Corps was chased through town with Richard S. Ewell's 2nd Corps hot on their tails. Longstreet and his corps had not yet arrived.[25]

Other misconceptions followed. On July 6 the paper proclaimed: "Longstreet was mortally wounded and captured. He is reported to have died an hour afterward." Also, some twenty thousand Confederates were believed captured, with the Union cavalry encircling the rest.[26]

As the days progressed, the *Times* conceded that Longstreet was still alive and the Army of Northern Virginia "was discomfited, but not, as it must be, utterly destroyed."[27]

While the *Chicago Times* and other Democrat newspapers soon criticized Meade for allowing Lee's escape, and ultrapatriotic journals such as *Harper's Weekly* praised Gettysburg as a complete victory, the *Times* quickly regained its practice of sober objectivity. Its final assessment was most prophetic: "We must not, we repeat, look upon the invasion as a distinct episode of the war. It is part of the whole plan. . . . Meade's victory is anything but one step more toward the annihilation of the Confederate organization. So it must be vigorously followed upon Southern soil."[28]

New York Times correspondent Samuel Wilkeson may have inspired the theme of the Gettysburg Address. In his July 6 report, Wilkeson referred to the battle as a "second birth of Freedom." His words held considerable weight, since he wrote them while sitting next to the fresh grave of his son, Bayard, a Union lieutenant killed in action on the first day.

---

8. THE *CHARLESTON MERCURY*

Eight Southern newspapers accompanied the Army of Northern Virginia into Pennsylvania, only to find a dearth of information and a surplus of confusion. As most of Lee's actions were assaults, journalists found themselves miles away from the fighting, unable to get any sense of the big picture. After Pickett's Charge, officers and enlisted were notably unwilling to surrender any specifics.

After piecing a few details together, the *Richmond Examiner* surmised: "We were not entirely victorious at Gettysburg," and yet, "we are not worse off than before it began, nor is the North a whit stronger." The patriotic *Richmond Daily Dispatch* called the whole affair a triumphant raid and claimed that Lee netted tons of food and ten thousand horses.[29]

In contrast, the bombastic *Charleston Mercury* was less enthusiastic. Its editor, the secessionist fire-eater Robert Barnwell Rhett, had been passed over for the Confederate presidency. The post instead went to the moderate Jefferson Davis. Ever after, Rhett's *Mercury* stood ready to pounce upon the Richmond government for any and every misstep.

But even Rhett initially praised Lee's march north. His paper portrayed Lee's withdrawal on July 5 as an attempt to lure the Army of the Potomac from its defenses. Apparently, the plan worked, and "Hill and Longstreet turned upon them and repulsed them with great slaughter."

The paper added: "It is generally believed and conceded that we have gained a victory. Our loss, at first greatly exaggerated, has dwindled down most astonishingly. Late Yankee newspapers, it is said, acknowledge a defeat and heavy loss."[30]

But as more information became available, Rhett's print darkened. On July 20 the *Mercury* described the battle as a series of costly Confederate assaults against heavily defended "hills" and "mountains," and editors commented, "It is strange that Lee attacked Meade where he was."[31]

Two issues later, the paper branded Gettysburg a terrible defeat, "ill-timed," wasting men and material that would have been better applied anywhere else. Driving the bayonet deeper, Rhett's rag concluded, "It is impossible for an invasion to have been more foolish and disastrous."[32]

Days after Gettysburg the Union navy and army launched newborn attacks on Charleston Harbor and Battery Wagner. Lee's "folly" soon paled in comparison. Gettysburg lasted three days. The siege of Charleston would eventually span 566 days, ending with the city's surrender and causing the death of the *Mercury*.[33]

Before the war, Robert Barnwell Rhett and Jefferson Davis were both members of Congress, and both lobbied aggressively, although unsuccessfully, for the annexation of Cuba.

---

9. WILLIAM H. SEWARD

The U.S. secretary of state was a busy and troubled man. Over the course of the Civil War, France invaded Mexico and Britain stationed thousands of troops in Canada. English shipyards were covertly building sea raiders for the South. European merchants denounced the blockade. Both Napoleon III and the British cabinet openly considered diplomatic recognition of the Confederate States of America.

Sadly for the bright but abrasive William H. Seward, his credibility overseas was marginal at best. British prime minister Lord Palmerston considered him capable of little beyond "uncalculating arrogance." The editor of the London *Times* called him a man of "feeble build . . . contracted from sedentary habits." More than Lincoln and the White House,

Seward and the State Department needed a convincing Union victory in battle, and fast, or face the possibility of military incursions from Canada and on the high seas. Foreign intervention seemed all the more possible when Lee entered Pennsylvania and started toward Washington.[34]

Then the secretary learned that Lee had been stopped at Gettysburg. Days later came news that Vicksburg had fallen. The kid gloves came off.

In no uncertain terms, Seward informed Paris and London that the Union had triumphed and was ready to take on anything by land or sea, including Europeans. In a letter to the U.S. minister to England, Seward exalted his revitalized nation, saying that the recent victories "restore to us our accustomed facilities for foreign conflict."[35]

Seward made the letter public by the end of the year, thereby informing the Old World what to expect if any pushed their Confederate sympathies any further. Tempers flared, but Seward's country, if not his person, finally gained Europe's grudging respect.

The night Lincoln was shot, one of John Wilkes Booth's co-conspirators stabbed Secretary of State Seward several times and nearly killed him. The perpetrator was Lewis Paine, also known as Lewis Powell, a former private in the Army of Northern Virginia and veteran of the battle of Gettysburg.

---

10. SARAH BROADHEAD

A New Jersey native, thirty-year-old Sarah Broadhead followed her husband to Pennsylvania when he found work on the Gettysburg Railroad. Unnerved by the sudden approach of a gray tide in 1863, she started a diary on June 15. Her account is one of the most honest and candid written on the battle and an accurate representation of the civilian experience.

Broadhead, her four-year-old daughter, and several neighbors weathered the battle by hiding in the cellar of David Troxel, a harness maker. By the end of July 3, though the fight was over, its termination was far from evident to Sarah and her companions. "Who is victorious, or with whom the advantage rests, no one here can tell. It would ease the horror if we knew our arms were successful." Prospects for the Fourth of July appeared just as grim, as Broadhead noted: "The Rebels have promised us a glorious day. If it only ends the battle and drives them off it will be glorious, and I will rejoice."[36]

Rejoice she did, admitting on the holiday, "For the first time in a week I shall go to bed feeling safe." Yet her sense of security was short lived. She emerged from Troxel's cellar only to step into the putrid debris of battle. All around her were ransacked buildings, smoldering fires, wandering soldiers, and streets littered with carcasses and wounded. "Had any one suggested any such sights as within the bound of possibility," she observed, "I would have thought it madness."[37]

Immediately she discovered untapped talents for the rigors of nursing. She took food and blankets to the makeshift hospitals and tended to the wounded wherever she found them. And she found them everywhere, including in her own home. "It is heart-sickening to think of these noble fellows sacrificing everything for us, and saving us, and it out of our power to render any assistance of consequence."[38]

For her Confederate charges, she was less than forgiving. "I talked with some wounded Rebels, . . . they are very saucy and brag largely. . . . The spirit manifested by those I met was so vindictive that I believe they would, if they could, requite all the kindness shown them by murdering our citizens."[39]

For Broadhead and many like her, the battle held no special appeal. After tending to the wounded, she and her husband eventually moved back east, never to return.

Sarah Broadhead's husband, Joseph, was a member of the Pennsylvania militia. Just before the battle, he was captured and paroled outside Harrisburg. In less than two days he walked almost nonstop through Confederate-held territory, a distance of thirty-six miles, to be with her.

TOP TEN CIVILIAN DEEDS AND MISDEEDS

Waking from the nightmare of battle, citizens of Adams County soon realized their hour of darkness had not yet passed. Gone were nearly all livestock and food stores. Instead they found piles of corpses, contaminated streams, decimated crops, and gutted homes. Casting the most intense shadow across this landscape were twenty-two thousand wounded—the largest such collection ever produced by combat in North America. The dying and the dead occupied schools and churches, hotels and shops, the Evergreen Cemetery gatehouse, and one out of every five private homes.

Into this flood zone came yet another tide. By the thousands, outside civilians silted into the streets until they outnumbered locals four to one. With a spectrum of motives, they came because of the wounded, the dead, and the battlefield itself. After three days of horrendous combat, Gettysburg had become a spectacle, a morgue, and a cause. Listed below are the ten main categories of civilians who swarmed into this very public scene. Much like the soldiers before them, they were a conglomeration of the brave and the monstrous, and they are ranked here by the degree to which they changed the state of existing misery, from most constructive to least.

1. RELIEF AGENCIES

When President Lincoln sanctioned the all-civilian U.S. Sanitary Commission (USSC) in the summer of 1861, authorizing it to review camps and hospitals, he casually referred to the institution as the "fifth wheel to the coach." In ramping from a peacetime strength of sixteen thousand regulars to a volunteer force nearing a million, the coach began to break down on a regular basis. The Sanitary Commission was there to pick up the pieces.[40]

With the battle of Gettysburg still in progress, wagons of donated supplies came rolling into the area, the first of a long train of assistance. "Thank God," sighed a Union surgeon, "here comes the Sanitary Commission; now we shall be able to do something."[41]

More than a week passed before Washington inquired if medical units needed anything. By that time hundreds of USSC workers were already in place, supply and distribution depots were well established,

Conspicuously superior to the Federal government's meager relief efforts, the U.S. Sanitary Commission arrived at Gettysburg before the battle was over. Evergreens were used extensively to counter the smells emanating from the battlefield.

LIBRARY OF CONGRESS

kitchens were up and running, and additional food was on its way. As rail service resumed in mid-July, USSC-chartered convoys rolled in, dripping water from their ice-laden cars, carrying tons of vegetables, eggs, fish, and poultry. Following trains were packed with stoves, dry goods, clothes, sheets, and over a thousand crutches—all private donations.[42]

In a month the USSC issued some seventy thousand pounds of bread, mutton, butter, chocolate, soup, and milk. It also brought cooks, doctors, drivers, clerks, fresh socks and shirts, medicines, and bandages. The effort nearly emptied the institution's coffers.

Yet the USSC was only the largest of many such organizations that came to the area. The Baltimore-based Adams Express Company donated rail service, provisions, and wagons. The Ladies Aid Society of Philadelphia, the New York Soldiers' Relief Agency, the pro-Union Patriotic Daughters of Lancaster, the tacitly pro-Confederate Fireman's Association of Baltimore, and others cared for soldiers largely abandoned by their own armies. Watching them in operation, a nurse professed, "They are God's blessed agencies for providing for the needy soldier.[43]

The U.S. Sanitary Commission grew to seven thousand chapters across the North. Plagued by inflation, poverty, a dying infrastructure, and enemy occupation, the Confederacy never produced an equivalent.

---

2. FAMILIES OF THE FALLEN

The Union and Confederate war machines could induce ten thousand casualties in a day, yet neither could produce an accurate casualty report in four years. If a soldier was wounded, captured, or killed, his family would be lucky to learn about it in a few weeks, if at all. Word came by way of a commanding officer, a fellow soldier, a nurse, or a newspaper account. In cases of hospitalization, sometimes the soldier himself wrote home or had someone scribe the letter for him, explaining his situation.

Counter to their governments' wishes, many relatives traveled to battle sites in search of their kin, hoping to find them still among the living. Bittersweet were reunions in hospitals. Relations were found emaciated, deformed, blind, but alive. In crowded wards siblings brushed away flies and wished away fevers. The fortunate ones were able to take their relatives to nearby homes. Col. William Colvill, who led the costly charge of the 1st Minnesota on day two, recovered from his bullet wounds with the help of his sister and the comfortable lodgings of the James Pierce residence. The Peter Myers house on West High Street at one time held several wounded enlisted and their doting mothers.[44]

More often than not, the desire to rescue a loved one meant exposing oneself to extraordinary horrors. Many wives and fiancées arrived from as far away as Wisconsin and Minnesota with letters from sweethearts in their hands, only to be informed that the patient had passed away in the meantime. Fifteen-year-old Tillie Pierce recalled a Mrs. Geenly who came to see her son, only to watch him die after an emergency amputation. In his final moments, he screamed for his mother repeatedly before succumbing. For months relatives came, knowing their husbands or sons or brothers had already perished, but they insisted on taking the remains back home. Since few resting places were well marked, searching often involved exhuming many blanket-wrapped bodies, all in progressive stages of rot, in hopes that one could be identified as their own. Despite looking and digging for weeks on end, many never found their kindred spirits.[45]

In at least one instance, parents mistakenly removed the wrong body and took it home for reburial. In this particular case, the mother and father realized their mistake when their assumed deceased son turned up alive and well.

---

3. VOLUNTEER MEDICS

Union army medical director Jonathan Letterman painted the second week of July in rather tranquil hues. "The time for primary operations had passed," he assured his superiors, "and what remained to be done was to attend to making the men comfortable, dress their wounds, and perform such secondary operations as from time to time might be necessary." Normally an honest man, Letterman was masking the fact that his medical system was on the verge of collapse.[46]

CORNELIA HANCOCK had a better view from beside the operating table: "There is a great want of surgeons here; there are hundreds of brave fellows, who have not had their wounds dressed since the battle."[47]

The source of the problem was the absence of the main armies. Lee and Meade presupposed that Gettysburg was merely the first scene of a climactic act. Consequently, nearly their entire complement of medical teams, operating equipment, and supplies traveled south with them and away from the legions of the dying. Of the Union's eleven hundred ambulances, perhaps fifty remained, and teams quickly wore out. In some instances, horses toiled and slept in their harnesses for sixty straight hours. Of 650 Union doctors, 544 went with Meade. Lee took all but 50 of his 400 surgeons and medics. Those that stayed behind would conduct surgeries into July 7 without letup. Some doctors fainted on their feet. Others became severely ill. A few completely broke down from the weight of their unprecedented burden.[48]

Forced to work with a fraction of their staff and supplies, military doctors, including those captured in gray, begged Washington for assistance. Normally critical of private practitioners, exhausted army surgeons sought any help available, and at least eighty medics responded.

Military prejudice against civilian doctors was not without reason. At the time, incompetence was a professional pandemic. On average, "doctors" had two years of academic training, little of it formal. Even the best physicians had minimal surgical experience. Fewer still had ever worked in conditions as primitive and with injuries as barbaric as Gettysburg was offering. Most who came were quickly dumbfounded by what they saw, and these were subsequently unable or unwilling to assist in any meaningful way. "They would then stroll about the hospital a couple of hours," observed a surgeon in uniform, "and leave immediately after." Of the thirty fellow practitioners the doctor spotted at the Union 2nd Corps hospital, he thought, "only four or five were really of much benefit."[49]

Then there were a few who came purely for profit, enticed by the $118 monthly stipend from the government and impatient to get more. One soldier reported that a civilian doctor stationed in a field hospital charged him $50 for an amputation.[50]

In spite of the majority, a few doctors were worthy of their title, and they meant the difference between life and death for an incalculable number of severe cases. Philadelphia native Dr. Bushrod James recalled how he and others worked nearly a week straight, "amputating limbs, probing for and removing bullets or sewing, bandaging and dressing the wounds . . . the horror of that scene I can never forget."[51]

U.S. surgeon general William Hammond, who at first rejected all volunteers, later admitted, "The suffering would have been much greater than it was but for the aid afforded the medical officers by the benevolent individuals who came to their assistance."[52]

Dr. John Shaw Billings was a civilian doctor who operated for days near the base of Little Round Top. Years later, armed with the lessons he had learned at Gettysburg and elsewhere, he helped found Johns Hopkins Medical School.

---

4. PREACHERS

Nineteenth-century Americans were predominantly spiritual but not altogether religious. A majority did not belong to a specific church, including the Union president. Those who traditionally followed precise doctrines, such as devout Quakers and foreign-born Catholics, were the exception. Most expressed varying degrees of faith through speech and behavior, though the majority would readily classify themselves as "believers."

Eruption of the Civil War, as crises often do, pushed people either to higher levels of piety or greater depths of skepticism. Accordingly, the self-proclaimed righteous often aspired to save the troubled souls any way they could. A fair choir of these well-meaning angels descended upon postbattle Gettysburg and aimed straight toward the wounded.

They distributed Bibles and Gospels and set up tents for readings and services. Clergy gave daily sermons. Priests gave absolution. The U.S. Christian Commission, established in late 1861 by the Young Men's Christian Association, sent fifty delegates to provide food and clothing as well as spiritual instruction.

Some encountered surly flocks. A man of the cloth entered a barn full of tired and bloodied members of the U.S. 11th Corps. When he fell to his knees and began delivering a sermon, he was met with a swelling chorus of "put the preacher out" and left in much haste. One pastor made the mistake of entering a hospital tent and declaring "tidings of great victory" of how "General Lee and his whole army have been intercepted before reaching the Potomac." Not only was his information false, he was shouting it to a ward full of Confederate wounded.[53]

Most were able to avoid unnecessary wrath, and some found willing converts among the impious, provided they practiced common sense and brought a helping hand or a morsel of food along with their Testaments.

The official motto of the Southern Confederacy was *Deo Vindice*—"God will avenge."

5. PHOTOGRAPHERS

Contrary to popular belief, the American Civil War was not the first military conflict to see the use of photography. That distinction goes to the Mexican War of 1846–48. Nor was a single confirmed live battle ever successfully photographed, due to cumbersome equipment and exposure times of five to ten seconds. Yet some of the most vivid recollections of Gettysburg and the war itself were taken by a handful of artists and businessmen. A few made sizable profits from their work.

First to arrive, sometime during the daylight hours of July 5, were Alexander Gardner, Timothy O'Sullivan, and James Gibson, all former employees of the famous Mathew Brady. Monopolizing their attention, and most of their wet-plate negatives, were the bloating bodies of men and animals near the Rose farm and Devil's Den south of town. As no other cameramen arrived before burial crews completed their work on July 6, Gardner and his team produced the only known images of soldiers killed in action at Gettysburg. Gardner personally knew the public impact of such visions. Brady's grisly display "The Dead of Antietam" had marked the first time Americans saw photos of combat fatalities, and many of the images were Gardner's.

Pioneers though they were, these men were not above taking dramatic license with the deceased. O'Sullivan was among the most liberal in

One of the earliest images of Gettysburg, this scene was composed by the first team of photographers to arrive on the field. The body and the rifle were posed in Devil's Den, and photographer Alexander Gardner crafted an eloquent caption about a Confederate sharpshooter.

LIBRARY OF CONGRESS

this pursuit. More than likely, the famous image of the Confederate marksman in Devil's Den was his doing. Civil War photography expert William A. Frassanito notes that the body in question appears in shots elsewhere and must have been dragged some forty yards to appear again at the foot of the stone wall. Most damning is the rifle leaning conspicuously next to the body, a common prop tactic used by cameramen to place their long-dead subjects "in the moment."[54]

Next on the scene, sometime in mid-July, was their former boss himself. Brady likely took no pictures himself, as he had become nearly blind by 1863. But his staff produced thirty timeless images, including likenesses of the cemetery gatehouse, Lee's headquarters, a portrait of local hero John Burns, and a panorama of Little Round Top. Their unquestioned masterpiece, and one of the most famous photos in American history, was the trio of captured Confederates posing on Seminary Ridge.[55]

A handful of other photographers came, shot, and went. Among them were Gettysburg residents Charles and Isaac Tyson, whose snapshots emphasized the area's natural beauty rather than its battle landmarks. Not surprisingly, the Tysons lost out on a potential fortune.

But by 1866 the market for wartime images had largely disappeared altogether. More than twenty years passed before the public wished to gaze upon such negatives again.[56]

Of some 230 photographs taken in the days and months immediately after the battle, none were of the area covered by Pickett's Charge.

---

6. MORTICIANS

Predating the era of care centers and large hospitals, most nineteenth-century Americans died at home. Conducting wakes in the parlor and funerals in the nearby church was a matter of course. Coupled with relatively high infant mortality rates and life expectancies in the midforties, death was a tragic yet familiar part of life. For many families, separation from the departed was nearly as traumatic as the loss itself. To the rescue came professional morticians, offering loved ones closure by bringing back their dead.

In addition to the few preparers already in Gettysburg, at least a dozen more arrived in the days after the battle. Doctors also practiced the craft so as to dig up some extra income. Advertising prevention of decay and deliverance from unpleasant odor, these "surgeons" charged around $5 for an enlisted man, $100 for a colonel, and $200 for a general, or about two months' income for a middle-class family. Faced with high demand, many concentrated on preserving officers and passed on the lowly privates and corporals.[57]

Though profitable, it was an unpleasant undertaking. First step was to wash the body, which was often in an advanced state of decomposition. Next, if enough tissue was present, came embalming. This usually meant pumping liquid zinc, arsenic, and chloride into the chest of the cadaver. A more permanent method involved bleeding the patient at the neck and introducing a solution of chloride and ground glass, which tended to solidify the subject. Next came dressing the body in linen, or if available, an appropriate uniform. Finally, the body would be placed in a wooden casket or metal coffin, preferably airtight.

The long train ride home required additional touch-ups, as fluids often oozed out of the eyes, nose, and mouth during the turbulent journey. After the depot clerks, casket makers, and gravediggers all received a cut, expenses could reach into the hundreds of dollars, a price many families were willing to pay. Reflecting upon the windfall of Gettysburg, one Northern undertaker said, "There won't be another such killing for a century."[58]

Approximately three thousand families never had the option of getting their loved ones back from Gettysburg. A third of all Union and more than half of all Confederate bodies were buried without being identified.

Shipping and handling the deceased were developing sciences of the war. The new practice of embalming was just one of many steps morticians and doctors used to assist—and bill— bereaved families.

LIBRARY OF CONGRESS

7. SEEKERS OF RECOMPENSE

With the exception of William Tecumseh Sherman's infamous March to the Sea, damage to civilian property in the Civil War is rarely recalled, yet destruction was frequent and widespread. From Vermont to New Mexico, noncombatants lost possessions, livestock, and homes to the four horsemen of looting, arson, arms fire, and confiscation.

To assist in personal and company losses during military operations, the Pennsylvania legislature passed a series of bills during and after the war to permit citizens to file claims. Hundreds exercised this option after Lee and friends finished their three-week tour of the Keystone State.

Some requests were plausible. The 11th Corps took Jacob Hummelbaugh's bay horse, plus his supply of wheat, corn, cabbage, and potatoes. Tate's Hotel suffered an exceptional reduction in inventory when Confederates discovered its cache of distilled spirits. Susan and Peter Rodgers lost their only horse, and their farm was almost completely destroyed.

Other claims looked highly suspect, if not trite. Businesses, schools, and individuals demanded compensation for things like napkins, window treatments, and playing cards. Henry Carr, who operated a storeroom in the basement of the WILLS HOME, insisted that unruly troops stole a fortune in stock, consisting of such items as violin strings, fishing tackle, ink, and a flute.[59]

Unable or unwilling to distinguish the suffering from the shysters, government reviewers rejected nearly every request. A few residents received compensations, but the money received was often a fraction of what was sought.

Living near the Peach Orchard, Catharine Trostle lost five steers, fifteen barrels of flour, and fifty chickens. Sixteen horses were left rotting near her doorstep. Her house was shelled, later used as a hospital, and finally ransacked—by Union soldiers. She endured all of this without her husband, who was in an insane asylum at the time.

---

8. GAWKERS

A public warning appeared in the July 15 *Philadelphia Public Ledger:* "Let no one come to this place for the simple purpose of seeing. To come here, merely to look at the wounded and dying, exhibits a most vitiated and disgusting taste. Besides, every such visitor is a consumer, and adds to the misery of the sick."[60]

To the morbidly curious, such admonitions read like midway billboards. As word spread of the enormous damage rendered around Gettysburg, untold numbers flocked toward the town, not to ease the suffering but to bask in the engrossing spectacle. Gettysburg was experiencing its first wave of battlefield tourists.

Like flies, they milled about bloated horse carcasses, rifled through shredded uniforms, or circled tents packed with the mangled and suffering, seemingly oblivious to the lingering stench and misery. While hospitalized near Little Round Top, Col. Robert M. Powell of the 5th Texas marveled at the audacity of these passersby and wondered why he and his comrades were objects of amusement for the "vast concourse of sightseers, whole families with the baby."[61]

Just as the newspapers and government had feared, gawkers came in large numbers. With excited mobility these day-trippers devoured precious necessities, especially food. Several townspeople, even the devoutly Unionist, soon found themselves far more empathetic to Southerners in butternut tatters than Northerners in black finery. As years passed, many locals found it difficult to support the idea of making Gettysburg a tourist attraction, considering the lewd behavior of those who first came to take in the sights.[62]

In the autumn of 1863, some battlefield visitors were callous enough to pick up unearthed skulls and kick them around for sport.

---

9. LOOTERS

Every Civil War battlefield looked more like a junkyard than a land of valor. In the case of Gettysburg, wagons, tents, blankets, guns, ammunition, and wandering horses covered dozens of square miles. Lost or discarded by troops, these tools of war were worth millions of dollars to the governments that paid for them.

On July 7 members of the Union Quartermaster Department and General Staff arrived to retrieve this bounty. They instead saw flocks of wagons leaving the battlefield, each loaded with plunder and driven quickly by enterprising looters. Capt. William W. Smith, in charge of the salvage operation, estimated at least three thousand people were coming to the area each day to take away souvenirs of every sort and quantity.

Smith used local newspapers to warn the citizens to return everything they took or be jailed. In the meantime he and a hundred mounted troops scoured the countryside, searching house to house for the stolen goods. They found stables full of remarkably new saddles marked "U.S," attics and haystacks filled with muskets, uniforms, and blankets, plus a cannon barrel hidden in a well. Each day, Smith and company led a loaded wagon train back to Gettysburg, yet the captain estimated his men reclaimed only around 10 percent of all that was pilfered.

Unafraid of capture, souvenir hunters hacked down trees sprayed with bullets. Farmers cut harnesses from dismembered horses. People even took personal letters from the pockets of dead men. The most infamous among the den of thieves were the "Spring Forge Looters" from York County, who scraped open shallow graves in search of personal valuables.[63]

Hired by outside vendors, children earned pennies for collecting bullets, buckles, and bayonets. Lead was a particularly abundant prize, fetching up to thirteen cents a pound (or about six dollars per pound in 2006). Young boys figured that a handful of bullets meant a handful of coins, but an unexploded shell contained a gold mine. Carefully unscrewing the blasting cap to get at the chunks of shrapnel inside, clever kids then poured in water to tame the load of gunpowder therein. Others impatiently banged the iron casing on rocks to jar the contents loose, a practice that liberated several children of limbs and lives. Others collected cartfuls of muskets for their families and collectors. In the process of carrying, cleaning, or playing with these heavy shoulder arms, a few boys discovered that many were still loaded, resulting in at least three known fatalities.[64]

Of the 27,574 muskets found on the battlefield, 24,000 were still loaded.

---

10. PROFITEERS

Union and Confederate soldiers alike soon praised the townswomen of Gettysburg for their inexhaustible kindness. Their opinions of area farmers, on the other hand, ranged from antipathy to abhorrence. Suspicions first surfaced on the march toward Adams County. Rural folk offered the passing columns bread, cakes, and water—for a fee. Pies went for a quarter, milk for fifty cents, a loaf of bread for a dollar.

Prices rose after the battle, when the troops were most desperate. Starving men, especially the severely injured, gave their last penny to oblige the peddlers, who sometimes sold bread by the slice to maximize profits or removed ropes and buckets from their wells to prevent thirsty troops from taking a single drop.[65]

Most exorbitant were ambulances-for-hire. As the wounded tried to reach field hospitals, some by literally crawling their way, locals came by with wagons and carts offering rides, so long as the patrons could afford it. Some drivers charged as much as five dollars, or nearly two weeks' pay for a Union private. A group of five severely injured men, who had not eaten in three days, handed over all the money they had—twenty-five dollars. The coachman loaded them into a springless, uncovered wagon and carted them in haste along the rutted roads, jarring their wounds open as he sped along insensibly. Three of his fare died in hospitals the following day.[66]

Area residents were not alone in their usurping. A medical inspector for the U.S. Army laid the heaviest blame on railroad companies "who got the only profit from the battle [and] alone stood aloof and rendered no aid." Charging the government full price to transport rations, supplies, or personnel, the rail system also appeared negligent in handling cargo, especially the wounded, who were loaded in boxcars with "the dung of the cattle and litter from freight often remaining to be removed."[67]

On July 3 some farmers climbed Little Round Top and informed a Union officer that a nearby hospital had taken their straw and used it as bedding for the wounded. The farmers demanded payment. The officer threatened to arrest them and burn their homes. The solicitors grudgingly left.

TOP TEN HEROINES

Of the thirty-three million Americans who endured the supreme cataclysm of their nation's history, more than half were women, yet their story is frequently a footnote to the anthology. Marginalized politically, economically, and socially, the "fairer sort" shouldered the burden, often involuntarily, of the war's bitter harvest.

Gettysburg would be little different than a Sharpsburg or Vicksburg. There was no Veterans Administration, no government pensions yet available, no disaster relief funds or medical insurance, no Social Security or American Red Cross. Left to do most of the repair work—securing the necessities of survival, rebuilding families and homes, and caring for the physically and mentally distressed—were women.

Oddly, much of the era's conventional thinking viewed such toil as something of a reward, a task befitting the "soothing and charitable" nature assumed to be inherent in the gender. As a result, many female caretakers at Gettysburg and elsewhere never saw a penny of support or recompense for their work.

Following are just a few of the countless true authors of reconstruction, who fed the hungry, sheltered the wandering, and comforted the hopeless. Listed here are the foremost heroines of just one chapter in the Civil War story, listed in order of their overall contribution to the physical, mental, and spiritual restoration of a town and the soldiers who fought there.

1. THE SISTERS OF CHARITY AND MERCY (MARYLAND AND NEW YORK)

The battle ended on a Friday. The following Sunday brought a caravan of sixteen Catholic nurses and an elderly priest from St. Joseph's Academy in Emmitsburg, Maryland. Rolling in carriages and omnibuses loaded down with clothes, supplies, and food, weaving through the mud to avoid running over corpses, the procession wept at the mass of devastation. Father Francis Burlando confessed, "We could not restrain our tears," but that did not prevent the Sisters of Charity from staying and doing the worst of the work. Their numbers soon tripled as more nuns streamed in from nearby Westminster and Baltimore.[68]

Looking otherworldly in their black, billowing shawls, bleach-white smocks, and voluminous snow-white habits, the sisters soon wore the battle hues of mud, soot, and blood. Experienced in caring for the poor and destitute, they dispersed across the Gettysburg area with calm dispatch to gather the wounded, direct food kitchens, and pray over the dead.

Their greatest contribution came through medicine. While nursing schools would not appear in the United States until the 1870s, the sisterhood had a tradition of basic medical training that reached back to the

Middle Ages. In field hospitals, homes, and warehouses, they assisted in bandaging, suturing, and amputating. They made beds out of the pews at St. Francis Xavier Church, fed convalescents at the Methodist Episcopal Church, and labored at Gettysburg College, where seven hundred patients packed its rooms and hallways and each morning revealed an average of ten new corpses.[69]

Committed to remain neutral in times of war, the sisters administered to Northerners and Southerners alike. Most of the Confederate prisoners at the Lutheran Seminary were tended by nuns. Their neutral stance evidently did not offend the wounded of either side. One soldier from Pennsylvania spoke for many when he said, "I will always hold them in grateful remembrance for the kind and loving attention they gave us while we were under their care and keeping."[70]

In receiving immeasurable help from the Sisters of Charity and Mercy, soldiers North and South unwittingly gave the sisters something in return. Many of the nuns who worked as nurses at Gettysburg became infested with fleas.

---

2. JOSEPHINE MILLER (PENNSYLVANIA, 1836–1911)

When DANIEL E. SICKLES ordered an unauthorized advance of his 3rd Corps on July 2, a lonely log farmhouse along the Emmitsburg road became part of the front line. Just before fighting commenced, a Union officer entered the home and was shocked to see a young woman alone in the kitchen, calmly baking bread and refusing to leave until her chore was done. As she looked out at the famished soldiers, she decided to stay and feed all she could. To the annoyance of that same officer, the enlisted of the 1st Massachusetts quickly aided the serious, unshakable Josephine Miller in her task. Soon she had in her possession sacks of flour, raisins, and a sheep from the 3rd Corps supply wagon.[71]

When Confederate artillery opened on their position, Josephine abruptly found safety in her cellar. But the screams of the dying pulled her out into the daylight, and she personally dragged at least ten wounded soldiers into her home. Within hours all the carpets and bedding within the house, as well as Josephine herself, were saturated with warm blood.[72]

Without instruction, she tended to the wounded throughout the night. The next day Lee's artillery deployed within a hundred paces of the house and soon set forth their deafening volleys. The doomed infantry of Pickett's Charge passed on either side of the building, only to return minutes later to populate the ground with still more broken bodies. Once again, Josephine ventured outside, carrying water, giving bread, and dragging the injured toward her home.

Months after the debacle, Josephine married and moved away, content never to see Gettysburg again. But in July 1886 the veterans of the 1st Massachusetts sent for her to help them dedicate their new regimental monument on the Emmitsburg road. Upon her reluctant arrival, the men burst into cheers and adorned her with ribbons and medals. She returned to Gettysburg several times after and became the sole female member of the Union Army 3rd Corps Association.[73]

As testament to the intensity of the fighting there, Josephine Miller's home received no fewer than nine direct artillery hits, and after the battle, seventeen corpses were removed from the house.

---

3. CORNELIA HANCOCK (NEW JERSEY, 1840–1927)

Weighed down by a slothful father, distressed by watching every good man she knew march off to war, twenty-three-year-old Quaker Cornelia Hancock vowed that, at the first opportunity, "I, too, would go and serve my country."[74]

The opportunity came when her brother-in-law traveled to Gettysburg to conduct surgeries. Cornelia went with him, and as they reached town on July 6, she recalled, "We went the same evening to one of the churches, where I saw for the first time what war meant."[75]

Every wounded man around her had not eaten for some time, days in some cases. Hancock immediately commandeered loaves of bread and jars of preserves and fed the ones who could not walk. She equated the scene with "living as sorely as if we had been a party of shipwrecked mariners thrown upon a desert island."[76]

At daylight she walked to the Union 2nd Corps field hospital, though she had never trained to be a nurse. "There was hardly a tent to be seen," she noted with indignation. "Earth was the only available bed. . . . A long table stood in this woods and around it gathered a number of surgeons and attendants. This was the operating table, and for seven days it literally ran with blood. . . . A wagon stood near rapidly filling with amputated legs and arms."[77]

For days she was the only female in the 3rd Division section of the hospital, caring for some five hundred men. Boiling gallons of soup, foraging for wine, milk, whiskey, and bread, she managed to procure food for hundreds. She also scribed letters for the sightless, the handless, and the mortally wounded.

Later transferring with her adopted 3rd Division to Camp Letterman, the main Union field hospital erected just east of Gettysburg, she stayed until September, when she no longer felt needed. Before she returned to New Jersey, Hancock received from the wounded a silver medal inscribed with her name and the words "Testimonial of regard for ministrations of mercy to the wounded soldiers at Gettysburg."[78]

Unable to remain quietly at home, Hancock returned to the 2nd Corps after the battle of the Wilderness. She remained with her troops through Cold Harbor and City Point to the war's end, when one officer christened nurse Hancock "the Florence Nightingale of America."[79]

> After the war, Cornelia Hancock founded schools for impoverished African Americans in Philadelphia and South Carolina. She also helped create the Family Society of Philadelphia and the Children's Aid Society of Pennsylvania, all of which she actively supported into her seventies.

4. EUPHEMIA "EFFIE" GOLDSBOROUGH (MARYLAND, 1836–96)

At one time engaged to seven men simultaneously, ninety-seven-pound firebrand Euphemia Goldsborough was both a flirt and a Southern patriot. Apparently no one bothered to ask if she were a Confederate when she volunteered to help at a makeshift field hospital in Gettysburg.[80]

Born of a prominent Baltimore family, Effie verified her devotion after Antietam, when she tended to Confederates wounded in the battle. Afterward she delivered food and sundries to destitute POWs languishing in the Union's Point Lookout prison on the windblown Chesapeake. In July 1863 she set out again, this time eighty miles away from home, to the bloodsoaked classrooms and corridors of Gettysburg's Pennsylvania College.

With all the power vested in her five-foot-five-inch frame, she made order of the chaos, procuring fresh food and water for the men, washing their filthy wounds, moving them to unoccupied rooms at the college, and scolding doctors who neglected to do the same. In one instance, she found an officer who had been shot through the lungs and left on a bare floor. For hours "Little Miss Effie" kept the exhausted man sitting upright, preventing him from drowning in his own blood.[81]

Later transferring to Camp Lettermen, she tended to a ward of 110 soldiers, half of them Confederates, and made sure her "boys" were not prematurely hauled to prison camps before they were fit for travel. For those lying in the blood and mud-caked rags of their once proud uniforms, Goldsborough smuggled in fresh shirts, drawers, pants, even boots under the cloak of her hoopskirt. The act was strictly forbidden, as Confederates in civilian garb would often escape undetected.[82]

Though Goldsborough watched a few of her charges walk away, many more died in hospital. The loss of one evidently broke her. For six weeks she cared for a severely wounded private of the 5th Texas Infantry Regiment, a youthful, brown-eyed amputee named Sam. Despite her unbounded diligence, he succumbed, and she subsequently left Gettysburg for good. On her return to Baltimore, Effie's sister observed, "We scarcely knew her, so worn and changed, so utterly exhausted with the sights of the battlefield. . . . In truth, she was never the same joyous girl again."[83]

The following November, Federal authorities raided her Baltimore home, suspecting her of aiding the flight of Confederate patients. Enough evidence emerged, mostly in the form of personal letters, to banish this cherished nurse to the Confederacy for the rest of the war.[84]

By the time Euphemia Goldsborough had reached Richmond in exile, she had become a celebrity. She immediately found employment in the Confederate Treasury Department by the order of one of her many admirers—Confederate president Jefferson Davis.

---

5. ELIZABETH THORN (GERMANY, 1832–1907)

There was an archway through which the living and the dead passed at Gettysburg. It still stands as one of most famous landmarks of the region: a solemn brick gatehouse marking the entrance to Evergreen Cemetery.

At the time of the battle, the structure was the residence of German immigrant and groundskeeper Peter Thorn, who had left the area to join the 138th Pennsylvania. Awaiting his return was his thirty-one-year-old German wife, Elizabeth, who cared for their three sons, her aged parents, the gatehouse, and the thirty-acre city graveyard. She was also six months pregnant. Yet it seemed safe to assume that her family was not in any danger, living so far from the war, upon the secluded and tranquil Cemetery Hill.

On the night of July 1, 1863, that placid rise became the most sought-after real estate in a newly born battle, and Elizabeth Thorn quickly found herself in the company of Maj. Gen. Oliver O. Howard and the 11th Corps of the Army of the Potomac. Rather than hide away, Elizabeth led Howard on a quick survey of the surrounding countryside, where she pointed out the major roads and ridges that were sure to be of strategic interest in the coming hours. She then prepared a meal for the general and members of his staff as they awaited the arrival of Maj. Gen. George Gordon Meade.[85]

Finally persuaded to take her leave, Elizabeth shuttled her family several miles eastward, only to return days later to see smoldering fires, countless trenches, shell craters, and her land covered with animal and human bodies in varying degrees of dismemberment. Within the scarred gatehouse, nearly all her prized possessions were gone, and in their place were more than a dozen dead and dying men.

Faced with the inescapable, the mother-to-be and her elderly father resumed their prebattle vocation—conducting burials in Evergreen Cemetery. The two of them alone dug more than one hundred separate graves for the Union dead scattered about their home. Her arduous, quiet labor granted a dignified burial to many young men, but by Thorn's own assessment, the endeavor may have harmed her unborn child. Delivering that October, "the dear little baby was not very strong," and fourteen months later Elizabeth's fears manifested in the death of infant Rosa Meade Thorn.[86]

Gettysburg hosts a single monument to all heroines of the Civil War. It is a statue of Elizabeth Thorn (pictured above).

6. DOROTHEA DIX (MAINE, 1802–87)

 She was famous long before Gettysburg, having launched a personal crusade against American and European insane asylums, where patients were often malnourished, chained, and beaten. Her soft voice yet zealous determination convinced even the most stubborn conservatives, including Queen Victoria and Pope Pius IX, to adopt humanitarian reforms.[87]

With the outbreak of civil war in her homeland, Dorothea Lynde Dix turned her focus toward the endemic incompetence of military medicine. Her valid assessment persuaded the Lincoln cabinet to name her superintendent of the U.S. Women Nurses Corps. It was the highest civil position held by any American woman at that time. With the backing of Surgeon General of the Army Dr. William Hammond, the sixty-one-year-old Dix attained the leverage of a brigadier, personally selecting and administering every female nurse in federal service. At one point she directed more than two thousand people.

Yet by mid-1863 she was losing clout, as was her chief supporter, Hammond, for routinely challenging medical practices, such as the use of mercury as a cure-all. Dix was on the verge of relegation when Gettysburg afforded her one final and lasting contribution to the common soldier.

Initially, provost guards and marshals forbade civilian travel to the embattled city. In several instances, Dix personally overruled them, demanding passage for all of her desperately needed caretakers. She also secured shipments of medical supplies, set up field kitchens, solicited donations of food and clothing, and called for additional volunteers. Altogether some forty of her nurses served in the Gettysburg area, and she frequently conducted inspections to see that the wounded were being properly accommodated. Appearances of Dix week after week ensured that the archaic medical machine would, despite itself, respect the needs of the sick and injured.[88]

In October the autocratic Dix was officially dispossessed of power, no longer permitted to select nurses or to override military hierarchy. In two years she would leave civil service altogether, returning to her role as champion of the mentally ill, many of whom included traumatized soldiers of the Civil War.

Serving the U.S. government from June 1861 and past the end of the war, Dorothea Dix traveled tens of thousands of miles, through and into several war zones, yet she never missed a day of work and refused to be paid.

7. SOPHRONIA E. BUCKLIN (NEW YORK, CA. 1834–1902)

Dorothea Dix initially rejected her, believing the schoolteacher was too young and frail for the nursing corps. Undaunted, Sophronia E. Bucklin instead volunteered for duty at a Washington hospital. When an associate from the U.S. Sanitary Commission spoke of a sudden, dire need for assistance in southern Pennsylvania, Bucklin immediately set off for the recently plagued Gettysburg.

Reaching her destination, she saw strewn upon the landscape "exposed skulls of which insects crawled—while great worms bored through the rotting eyeballs . . . bodies were flattened against the rocks, smashed into a shapeless mass, as though thrown there by a giant hand." Angered by the scene, Sophronia resolved to stay, and she served the living to the point of illness and exhaustion.[89]

In field hospitals and Camp Letterman, she fed, washed, and bandaged hundreds of men. Rarely finding time to sleep or seek a change of clothes, she marveled that her efforts saved so few, especially Southerners. Of twenty-two Confederates brought to her ward, more than half perished. Some observers jokingly said she killed more Rebels than any soldier in blue, yet her loss rate was consistent with other wards. Through diligence and determination, she insisted her patients be kept warm, clean, and well fed, no matter their military allegiance. Her common sense and endless efforts saved many who would have otherwise succumbed.

Unlike most nurses, she remained at Gettysburg for the duration, faithfully tending to the wounded on both sides until the last temporary hospital closed. Her memoir of the experience, *In Hospital and Camp*, remains one of the most explicit and detailed visions of postmortem Gettysburg.[90]

Just before she helped send off the last of the wounded and left the area, Sophronia Bucklin attended a local event. In doing so, she was one of ten thousand to personally witness Lincoln's Gettysburg Address.

8. ELIZABETH SALOME "SALLIE" MYERS (PENNSYLVANIA, 1842–1922)

The twenty-one-year-old schoolteacher hated the sight of blood. With such an aversion, Gettysburg resident Sallie Myers was definitely living in the wrong place at the wrong time. Within hours of the battle's inauguration, more than forty homes and buildings within a mile of her house, as well as her own bedroom, were transformed into field hospitals.

During the Confederate occupation, Myers walked down her block to help at the Catholic church, where every pew and aisle were filled with wounded. "I knelt beside the first man near the door and asked what I could do. 'Nothing,' he replied, 'I am going to die.'" Sallie staggered outside, sat on the front steps, and sobbed. But she returned and asked that he be brought to her two-story clapboard home. This first of her many patients did in fact die from mortal wounds to his spine and lungs, but he would spend his final hours in the serenity of Sallie's house and under her care. He was one of twelve men and officers the Myers family acquired in the following weeks, and he was the first of two to perish under their roof.

While amputees and shrapnel victims recovered in her home, Sallie returned to the larger hospitals to help the wounded, write relatives of the recently deceased, and guide visiting families to their soldier relatives living or dead.[91]

Sallie Myers continued her unanticipated work for years to come. After the war she gave birth to a son, who grew up and became a doctor. One of his most trusted nurses was his mother.[92]

After the war, Sallie Myers became a member of the National Association of Army Nurses of the Civil War, actively supported the Sons of Union Veterans, and served as national treasurer of the Grand Army of the Republic for the last two decades of her life.

---

9. SADIE BUSHMAN (PENNSYLVANIA, 1853–19??)

A cabinetmaker's daughter and the fifth of nine children, Sadie Bushman resided in the heart of Gettysburg. When Confederates came rushing in from the west, she joined the exodus eastward and headed for the presumed safety of her grandparents' house two miles away. Crossing an open field, Sadie recalled, "There came a screech and [a] shell brushed my skirt as it went by. I staggered from the concussion of it and almost fell when I was grasped by the arm and a man said pleasantly, 'That was a close call.'"[93]

The man escorted her to her grandparents', where she discovered that her refuge had by necessity become a hospital. Soon after her arrival, Sadie was deputized as a nurse, and her first assignment was to assist a doctor in an amputation: "I had to see the whole operation, and I can remember every cut as plainly today as I saw it then." Thus began what she would later call "the most fearful two weeks I ever knew." Her experience was by no means unique in the aftermath, with the notable exception that Sadie Bushman was ten years old.[94]

Her father eventually found Sadie and brought her back home. Against his wishes she returned to the fields and continued to help the soldiers and surgeons any way she could. At times working into the night, her tiny figure milling about the cots and operating tables, Sadie earnestly administered cups of water or washed grimy faces. Patients recalled how she sometimes tipped on her toes or stood on the beds to go about her work. A source of bright life among the wounded, she was often dragged back home only to escape again. Reportedly, for her willful altruism, Sadie's father repeatedly beat her.[95]

In 1898 Sadie Bushman volunteered to be a nurse in the Spanish-American War. Her services were rejected on the grounds that she, who had helped dying men as a mere child, was too old.

---

10. MARY VIRGINIA "JENNIE" WADE (PENNSYLVANIA, 1843–63)

Ballads, poems, and a museum bear her name. By many accounts she is *the* heroine of Gettysburg. Age twenty at the time, Jennie Wade attained immortality when she became the first and only civilian killed during the battle. As with most legends, Wade barely resembles the image thrust upon her, and her death, though tragic, speaks volumes on how generations have tailored Gettysburg to suit their individual interests.

What is known is this—Wade's sister Georgiana had recently given birth to a son, and Jennie stayed behind to help tend to her needs as well as to give water and bread to Union soldiers nearby. On the morning of the battle's third day, as Jennie busily kneaded dough in her sister's kitchen, a stray sniper's bullet cracked through two doors of the house and slammed into her back, killing her instantly.

Northerners immediately painted her in angelic prose, a mere child who was hurriedly baking loaves for famished soldiers whilst a deadly whirlwind of bullets swarmed about her home (indeed, the house eventually wore the pockmarks from 150 bullets and one artillery shell). Only the venomous bite of a Confederate sharpshooter could slay this picture of innocence, a savior who lost her life while serving her countrymen.[96]

Predictably, skeptics refused this rose-tinted vision. Some claimed she was a Confederate sympathizer. Others believed the loaves she was baking were intended only for her family and not for the boys in blue. A later rumor emerged that she served her troops in a much different capacity, namely, as a prostitute. All accusations were completely untrue.

Admittedly, her family did not possess a stellar reputation among the townspeople. The Wades were often impoverished, her mother may have produced an illegitimate son, and her mentally questionable father was familiar with incarceration. Little is factually known about Jennie's short life, other than its abrupt end spawned as much heartfelt admiration as heated conjecture. Regardless, she now rests in the graveyard of Evergreen, adjacent to the national cemetery, where her status overshadows many of the nearby soldiers'.[97]

Miles away, at the same moment of her death, Jennie's friend (and perhaps her fiancé) Cpl. Johnston Skelly of the 87th Pennsylvania lay severely wounded after the battle of Winchester. Nine days after Jennie's untimely passing, Skelly died. Neither knew of the other's fate.

TOP TEN PLACES LINCOLN VISITED

The names Lincoln and Gettysburg are inseparable, though the president only visited the town once, and his address never mentioned the battle by name. Of course the true taproot of his presidency was Washington: the White House, the War Department's telegraph office to which he often walked unescorted, the Soldiers' Home at the outskirts of town where the first family spent many summer weeks. He also frequented the capital's playhouses, including ten visits to Ford's Theater. Yet it was his two-day voyage to Gettysburg and a two-minute speech on its battleground that crowned his legacy.[98]

Invited to a multitude of commemorations and gatherings during his presidency, Lincoln declined almost all of them. He had reason to beg off Gettysburg as well. In the dedication of the new cemetery, the president was not the featured guest. Keynote speaker was Edward Everett, the reigning American orator as well as a former U.S. senator, president of Harvard, governor of Massachusetts, and U.S. secretary of state. Everett was in fact invited six weeks before the president. Lincoln was simply asked to provide "a few appropriate remarks" at the ceremony. Given the distance from Washington and the diminutive role assigned to Lincoln, most cabinet members assumed he would not attend.[99]

Further dissuading the president, his youngest son, Tad, fell critically ill with scarlet fever immediately prior to the event. The Lincolns had already lost two children to illness—their gifted son Willie in 1862 and three-year-old Eddie in 1850. Lincoln himself was sick, coming down with what later proved to be a strain of smallpox. But he firmly believed the dedication presented a unique opportunity. Gettysburg represented the Union's strength and yet was a place of solemnity upon which he could publicly define the war and the future of the nation.

Traced here are the footsteps of Lincoln's brief but everlasting journey to a town he had never visited before and would never see again.

1. HANOVER

The original plan was to have the president and entourage arrive at Gettysburg on the day of the event—November 19, 1863. Lincoln interceded. Rail traffic was bound to be heavy, and he could not afford the time or embarrassment to make the trip and miss the commemoration. He would travel by special train the night before, as would several cabinet members, newsmen, honor guards, and his personal secretaries, John Nicolay and John Hay.

Departing from Washington at noon on November 18, the four-car train meandered northeast on the B&O line, transferred outside Baltimore to the Northern Central Railroad, then over to the Western Maryland Railroad to head west. At one of several stops, a young girl held a bouquet up to his window and said with an endearing lisp, "Flowerth for the presthident."

Hanover was the scene of Lincoln's last of four railway transfers on his way to Gettysburg.

NATIONAL ARCHIVES

Lincoln beamed and replied: "You're a sweet little rosebud yourself. I hope your life will open into perpetual beauty and goodness."[100]

The next-to-last stop was Hanover, a town resting a dozen miles due east of Gettysburg. The trip was in its fifth hour. Tired and unwell, Lincoln intended to stay in his car, until a local Lutheran pastor boarded the train and said, "Father Abraham, your children want to see you!"[101]

Outside stood most of the town's inhabitants, including a group of women who presented Lincoln with flowers and a handmade flag. Also in attendance was Daniel Trone, the telegraph operator who on July 3 was among the first to tell the world of the Union victory at Gettysburg. Genuinely moved by the hospitality, Lincoln decided to stay for a few minutes. He struck up conversations about Hanover's own battle, fought the day before Gettysburg against Jeb Stuart's cavalry. After hearing accounts of the fight, much of which took place upon the very ground where they were standing, Lincoln gratefully bade the congregation farewell and embarked once again.[102]

> The battle of Hanover featured a young Union brigadier who led several audacious attacks against the Confederate horsemen. The recently promoted daredevil was none other than George Armstrong Custer.

2. GETTYSBURG TRAIN DEPOT

At 6 p.m., just as the sun was setting, the president and company rolled into their destination. Organizers initially believed the following day's ceremony would be small. But when Lincoln stepped off the train, he found himself among thousands of milling outsiders streaming into town. The atmosphere was part celebratory, part somber, yet far more congenial than the preceding July.

Greeting Lincoln at the station was thirty-two-year-old chairman of the cemetery board, David Wills. The ceremony and the cemetery were largely Wills's creations. He was instrumental in securing seventeen acres of ground, finding a designer for the layout, and procuring funds for re-burials. Also receiving Lincoln were sixty-nine-year-old Edward Everett and thirty-five-year-old Ward Hill Lamon, a friend of Lincoln's from Illinois and the marshal of the nation's capital. Lamon was also to be the grand marshal of the following morning's procession.[103]

Hotels and homes in the area were already filling to the rafters. Many visitors would sleep on couches and floors that night. Lincoln's appointed lodging would be far more hospitable. Along with inviting Lincoln to the commencement, Wills asked the president to stay at his residence, and the president cordially accepted.

After an exchange of pleasantries, Lincoln and his host started off for the Wills home in the center of town.

Among other cargo present at the train station were rows and rows of coffins, shipped by the War Department for the thousands of Union soldiers yet to be reburied.

---

3. THE WILLS HOME

A mansion, in effect, the largest of the houses surrounding the town square, David Wills's home reflected his young success. He was one of the wealthiest bankers in the region and a well-known figure among political bigwigs in Harrisburg.[104]

As Lincoln's black servant, William Slade, carried the luggage to the second-floor room where the president would be sleeping, Lincoln sat down to a lavish supper in the Willses' dining room. More than twenty guests were in attendance, including Secretary of State William Seward and two other cabinet members, Edward Everett, the French and Italian ministers, and several military officers. Everett and Lincoln knew of each other well, but this was the first time the two ever met face to face. Dominant in their conversation was the nearby battlefield, from which Everett had just returned.

As the evening aged, flocks of singers gathered on York Street outside the home to serenade the president. Among the songs offered was "We Are Coming, Father Abraham, Three Hundred Thousand Strong."[105]

Several people rejected David Wills's invitation to Gettysburg, including Secretary of War Edwin Stanton, Radical Republican and former Gettysburg resident Thaddeus Stevens, Maj. Gen. George Gordon Meade, and poet Henry Wadsworth Longfellow.

---

4. TOWN SQUARE

The Wills home and many like it around the plaza were adorned with flags, bunting, wreaths, and evergreen branches. Flagpoles held their banners at half-staff in honor of what the *Washington Chronicle* called "an occasion of such melancholy interest." Around 9 p.m., long after dinner had ended, the 5th New York Artillery band played in the square under a clear harvest moon, and people by the thousands gathered near. Lincoln stepped outside to acknowledge the band and the crowd. The multitude called out for a speech, which set Lincoln ill at ease, and he tactfully said as much.

He began, "In my position it is somewhat important that I should not say foolish things." Someone shouted back, "If you can help it!" A few in the crowd chuckled.

Lincoln responded, "It very often happens that the only way to help it is to say nothing at all." Which drew an eruption of laughter. He concluded, "Believing that is my present condition this evening, I must beg of you to excuse me from addressing you further." One reporter who witnessed the moment said of Lincoln, "He had said nothing, but he had said it well."[106]

The president then retired to his second-story bedroom overlooking the square and set about completing the address he would deliver the following day (see MYTHS AND MISCONCEPTIONS).

Among several vendors around the town square were opportunistic peddlers selling artifacts from the battlefield.

---

5. THE HARPER HOME

Next to the Wills estate was the home of *Gettysburg Sentinel* editor Robert G. Harper, where Seward was staying for the night. After Lincoln's short and somewhat disappointing greeting, the crowd wandered over and called on the secretary to offer an oration, which he did with pleasure.

Seward delivered a prepared statement, filled with superfluous praise for the Union and heavy criticism of slavery. The bellicose rant was typical Seward. He appeared to many Northerners as a zealot, but his words rang true in Gettysburg, where the occasion prompted a high sense of patriotism. Seward thought so highly of his little invocation that he insisted it be printed in newspapers along with Lincoln's address of the following day.

As the evening wore down, the masses wandered off in search of accommodations. At approximately 10 p.m., Lincoln stepped over to the Harper house to visit with Seward. Witnesses saw him carrying several papers, quite possibly telegrams he had received during the course of the day, including news of Tad's steady recovery and an assurance from the War Department that all was quiet along every front. Whether he brought his address with him is unknown but probable. Lincoln was nearing completion of the work, but he had yet to review it with anyone. Seward was the likely sounding board, as the secretary had previously assisted Lincoln with his first inaugural.[107]

Sometime before 11 p.m. Lincoln returned to his bedroom in the Wills home and refined the speech still further.[108]

In the 1860 Republican National Convention, Abraham Lincoln won the presidential nomination on the third ballot. He trailed in the first two ballots by a large margin, behind abolitionist front-runner William Seward.

---

6. THE BATTLEFIELD

Rain fell intermittently in the early hours and drifted away as morning approached. Daybreak came with bugle calls emanating from Cemetery Ridge, punctuated by the echoing boom of signal cannon at 7 a.m.

Having read several reports of the battle, along with hearing Everett's account during the previous evening, Lincoln was eager to see the grounds for himself. After an early breakfast, he took a tour of the fields with Seward.

The carriage started down the Chambersburg pike, the same road many Confederates used to reach the fight on July 1. Lincoln's small delegation proceeded northwest to the Lutheran Theological Seminary and into the countryside.[109]

The battle was four months past, but the touring party could clearly see remnants of the debacle. Trees were profoundly mangled, their limbs and trunks gnawed by countless strikes from shot and shell. Many horse carcasses were still present, unburned or unburied, their rib bones curling up from rotted, settling flesh. Strewn here and there were ratty blankets, torn haversacks, and bits of decomposing shoes and uniforms. Combing the ground were souvenir hunters looking for bullets, buttons, and other trinkets. Many more were on the battlefield for a very different reason, walking slowly among the thousands of shallow graves, reading the names scratched on rough slabs of jutting lumber, hoping to find lost husbands, brothers, or sons. The new military cemetery had only reinterred eleven hundred Union bodies. Thousands more still lay shallow in these fields.[110]

The morbid experience made Lincoln intensely somber. He would remain so for the rest of the day, becoming largely introspective and detached from the affairs around him.

At the time Lincoln toured the battlefield, there were still unburied Confederate remains deep in the crevices of Devil's Den.

---

7. REYNOLDS'S DEATH SITE

There is one account of Lincoln dismounting the carriage on his tour—to walk to the spot where Maj. Gen. John F. Reynolds was killed. With his back to the seminary, entering the cool morning shade of McPherson's Woods, Lincoln walked silently where the first day's battle took a decisive turn, when one of the Union's most able and respected commanders fell in the battle's early moments.

Lincoln knew the man personally. During the crisis after the battle of Chancellorsville, Reynolds went to the White House and visited with the president at length about replacing Joseph Hooker at the head of the Army of the Potomac.

Many hypothesize that Lincoln offered the post to Reynolds. The esteemed commander may have been on a short list, but no evidence has ever validated the claim. During their meeting, Lincoln told Reynolds that Hooker was still at the helm, but Reynolds's dissatisfaction with Hooker added to a growing swell of frustration with "Fighting Joe." The general instead recommended a fellow Pennsylvanian as a worthwhile replacement—Maj. Gen. George Gordon Meade.[111]

> The first family lost many acquaintances and friends in the war, including three relatives of Mary Todd Lincoln.

8.   THE PARADE ROUTE

After returning to the Wills home to dress and prepare, Lincoln emerged around 10 a.m. to thousands of people in the plaza. By this mid-November day, most of the trees had lost their leaves, but a warm sun shone through the crisp autumn air. The weather was far brighter than Lincoln's mood.

His attire was all black: a long frock coat, lanky dress pants dangling upon his bony legs, his stovepipe hat, a black crepe band at its base in memory of his son Willie. Upon his hands were bone-white gauntlets that accentuated his long and gangly arms.

People rushed him as he came forth, trying to shake his hand or catch his attention. He was cordial but focused as he made his way to his appointed horse. The color of the animal has long been a point of conjecture. Some described it as a smallish brown steed; others claimed it to be a large bay charger. An army officer swore the horse was jet black. A woman claimed it to be all white. One thing is known: Lincoln's horse was one of more than a hundred mounts for the event. Most of the dignitaries would make the half-mile trek on horseback. Coaches were dismissed as too unwieldy for the narrow procession, and the already crowded cemetery grounds provided no room to park them.[112]

The parade line formed slowly along Carlisle and adjacent streets, fifty yards north of the town square. It took more than forty minutes to situate the order. Heading the column was the Marine Corps band, followed by caissons and mounted guards and a section of infantry. Lincoln came next, followed by several governors and other notables, with the plaza crowd in tow. Several witnesses claimed the president looked awkward, his six-foot-four-inch frame loped over the steed. Others said he appeared stately and graceful, as at home in the saddle as he was at his desk. Both camps were probably close to the true picture. He rode much of the way with his head down and steady.[113]

Southward down Baltimore Street the procession went, paced by a slow funeral dirge. Turning onto the Emmitsburg road, the parade moved onto the Taneytown road and then to the new cemetery. The skies suddenly turned overcast.

When Lincoln rode to the cemetery along Baltimore Street, he passed by a stand of sycamore trees. To date, two of these sycamores are still standing.

---

9. THE CEMETERY

For all the pageantry of the preliminaries, the commencement was itself austere. Cemetery Hill, though possessing a commanding view of the surrounding countryside—including Culp's Hill, the Round Tops, and Seminary Ridge—was primarily bare. There were no audience seating, no grand trees, and no awnings. Facing east, the speakers' platform had a sparse number of banners and little else, its twelve-by-twenty-foot area full to capacity with every notable that would fit onto its limited space. In the front row of the stage, Everett sat to Lincoln's right, Seward to his left.

To the left of the platform was most of the military escort; to the right sat war widows and battle veterans. Packed tight against the stage were more than ten thousand people, with a team of newspaper reporters competing for the best vantage points. To the back of the platform, a short distance away, were the fresh graves of the new cemetery in progress.

After several songs and a lengthy prayer, Everett rose to speak. In a lecture of nearly two hours, almost all of it memorized, he performed oratory theatrics, describing the battle in detail and lacing his exposition with innumerable references to classic heroes and tales. Most observers were thoroughly absorbed, Lincoln included. But not everyone was impressed. The *Philadelphia Daily Age* proclaimed the speech as "lifeless as wax flowers."

Then Lincoln rose to the front, and the sun once again emerged from the clouds. In his hand were two sheets of paper. His hat removed, his wire-rim spectacles perched at the end of his prominent nose, he began

To reach the dedication ceremony, most of the crowd (estimated at between eight thousand and twenty thousand) walked south from town and through the gatehouse of Evergreen Cemetery to the dirt hill on which eleven hundred Union dead had already been reinterred—one-third of the total to be reburied here. Lincoln's somber procession moved slowly down the Baltimore pike just to the west.

to speak. Above the crowd he lofted his penetrating tenor voice, an intonation still strumming with its aged Kentucky accent. He was slow and deliberate, vocalizing in long sentences not of victory or slavery or enemies but of universal sacrifice. He reminded his listeners that they were part of a new and largely experimental form of governance, one that could still yet perish but was yet still alive because of that sacrifice. He finished by giving credit to all veterans North and South and by laying responsibility for the future upon all civilians, North and South.

Reviews then and in the days that followed were varied in the extreme. People had yet to truly comprehend what they had witnessed. Even the most appreciative were caught unaware. Lincoln's speech ended nearly as soon as it began. A long applause followed the president to his seat, though by many accounts, he was not pleased with his effort.

HARPER'S WEEKLY

The military cemetery Lincoln dedicated was for Union bodies only. The majority of the Confederates killed in the battle were later reburied in a mass grave in Hollywood Cemetery in Richmond, Virginia. Nonetheless, it is believed that at least eight Confederate soldiers were mistakenly buried in the Union cemetery at Gettysburg.

10. THE PRESBYTERIAN CHURCH

After a brief benediction, the cemetery dedication was declared at an end. Nearly three hours had passed. Lincoln stepped from the platform and shook hands with several veterans, some of whom had been wounded at the battle. After a few moments, the parade column reformed and escorted Lincoln and company back into town.[114]

The president and several others took in a late lunch at the Wills home, followed immediately by an hourlong informal reception in the parlor, and Lincoln personally greeted visitors as they entered the home.

He shook hands with a slew of governors, ambassadors, congressmen, and prominent citizens. But Lincoln wanted to meet one person in particular—the irascible and heralded "Old Patriot" John Burns, the only civilian from the town to fight in the battle.

Burns came to the house, still hurting from the wounds his body had sustained in July. Soon after Burn's arrival, Lincoln and Seward accompanied him arm in arm to the Presbyterian church on Baltimore Street. The trio sat together in a pew up front.[115]

The congregation was packed to the rafters. For every one person seated in the church there were ten outside wanting to get in. The guest speaker was the newly elected lieutenant governor of Ohio, Charles Anderson, who gave yet another rousing oration on the famous battle, describing the contest and the entire war as a struggle between freedom and despotism.

After the services, Lincoln hurried back to the Wills home and then proceeded almost immediately to the depot. As his train rolled out of town shortly after 6 p.m., the dog-tired president retired to his car. He reclined his long and weary body as best he could and draped a wet towel across his face in a failing attempt to tame an escalating fever. Rest would prove elusive. With several stops and transfers to come, the rattling train would not reach Washington until 1 a.m.[116]

Lieutenant Governor Anderson had a prominent relation. His brother was Robert Anderson, commanding officer at Fort Sumter during the 1861 bombardment that signaled the start of the war.

PURSUING GETTYSBURG

TOP TEN "MUST READS"

Approximately five thousand books, articles, and dissertations have been written on the subject. With the exception of June 6, 1944, no other single military engagement has received more print in English than the battle of Gettysburg. The subject has been analyzed, scrutinized, fictionalized, measured, and mapped, and yet the pace of publication steadily increases.

The first works surfaced while the war was still in motion. Most were memoirs, short and few. The country did not yet care to venerate a battle that killed one of every fifteen participants or honor a war that eradicated one of every five. Literary memorials would have to wait a score of years before civilians requested them.

While the nation tried to heal, a number of veterans chose to open old wounds, spilling ink in magazines and newspapers. Old comrades argued over who had the most blood on their hands. John B. Gordon traded accusations of foot dragging with James Longstreet. George Gordon Meade's chief of staff, Daniel Butterfield, belittled his commander's involvement. Daniel E. Sickles berated everybody.

By the twenty-fifth anniversary, however, nostalgic books emerged, mostly from writers who had not seen the elephant, alongside bound memoirs from generals who continued to bicker. As the veterans faded away, the devotees multiplied with spikes in publishing at the fiftieth and seventy-fifth anniversaries. The centennial truly fueled the presses. Chief among the many works were Bruce Catton's *Glory Road* adoring the North and Clifford Dowdey's *Death of a Nation* proclaiming Robert E. Lee the greatest general in all human history. Gradually, the overall quality and quantity of scholarly volumes have increased to the point where esteemed historians continue to dissect every facet of the battle in depth.

Following are ten outstanding nonfiction works pertaining to Gettysburg. Each has been selected for its historical accuracy, balance of coverage, cited evidence, objectivity, and appeal to the general public.

1. *THE GETTYSBURG CAMPAIGN: A STUDY IN COMMAND*
   EDWIN CODDINGTON (1984)

In spite of its age, Coddington's work remains the authoritative single-volume text on the engagement. A perennial favorite among buffs, battlefield guides, and scholars, this masterpiece is eight hundred pages of exceptional military history.

Traversing the planning stages of the raid in May 1863 to the return of the Army of Northern Virginia to its namesake six weeks later, *The Gettysburg Campaign* provides balance and coverage through a chronological weave of troop movements, statistics, letters, dispatches, and eyewitness accounts. No stones, it seems, are left unturned, from the more famous boulders on Little Round Top to the unsung but deadly rock wall along Oak Ridge.

Though Coddington is generally impartial, the Milwaukee-born, Dartmouth-educated professor openly contributes his views. He presents Meade in a favorable light, crediting the commander for making a string of sensible decisions in a rushed and traumatic environment. The author is lenient toward Jeb Stuart, suggesting the cavalry commander operated to the best of his abilities on vague orders. Longstreet does not receive a favorable review, depicted in several chapters as a gloomy and inflexible corps commander. Yet whenever Coddington offers his perspective, he is careful to include viewpoints from other historians and participants of the battle. His endnotes are invaluable on this point alone, overflowing with the divergent details and opinions unveiled over the preceding century.

Most impressive is Coddington's attention to the lower levels of command and the physical conditions of the field. Rather than paint an operatic battle of wills and male bonding, he details the roles of communication, troop strength, terrain, and timing.

If Coddington's work contains a flaw, it is the frequent practice of name-dropping. To read that Jones's, Nicholl's, and Steuart's brigades were reinforced by Daniel's, O'Neal's, Walker's, and Smith's might make sense to those already familiar with the figures, but to the general public, the Greek tragedy might simply read like Greek. Nonetheless, within its military framework, *The Gettysburg Campaign* remains the best overview available.

Coddington devoted much of his life to the study of the Civil War, and he labored on *The Gettysburg Campaign* for well over a decade. In 1967, months before his opus hit the bookshelves, he became ill and died.

---

2. *GETTYSBURG*
STEPHEN W. SEARS (2003)

For those who prefer flowing narrative to meticulous examination, Stephen Sears's *Gettysburg* is a sound choice. Whereas Coddington analyzes, Sears humanizes. Author of *Chancellorsville* and *A Landscape Turned Red: The Battle of Antietam,* Sears does not provide anything particularly new or insightful on the subject of Gettysburg, but he can paint a scene with vibrant expression.

As with Coddington, he addresses the campaign from beginning to end, but he also acknowledges the political realities of the time. For example, he elucidates the terrific pressures heaved upon the commanding generals, especially Meade, who was ordered to catch the great Robert E. Lee and simultaneously protect the civilian centers of Philadelphia, Baltimore, and Washington.

With innate awareness of his audience, Sears deftly balances orders of battle with human-interest stories. He also acknowledges that combat involves sights, sounds, and smells as well as the names of officers and regiments. As for the great what-ifs, he does not avoid them, nor does he take undue liberties. James Longstreet may have been correct, Sears suggests, that a drive to the south and east would have produced far better results than giving battle at Gettysburg, but the author acknowledges that long-term effects of such a move were ultimately indeterminable. He is generally unkind to Richard S. Ewell and R. E. Lee for their aggressive tactics over poor terrain, but he also concedes that a general lack of sound information made their every decision a difficult one.

The battle's crescendo is undoubtedly the highlight of the book. Sears treats Pickett's Charge with all the skill of a seasoned playwright. Some academic purists may view his presentation as too ornate to be considered scholarship, but Sears places the reader at the heart of the assault, and every step is verified.

> Stephen Sears has a good deal of experience writing popular history. He is the former editor of *American Heritage.*

3. *GETTYSBURG: A JOURNEY IN TIME*
WILLIAM A. FRASSANITO (1975)

In the preface of his seminal work, William Frassanito noted that many Gettysburg photographs had become renowned over the years, but none were ever truly scrutinized. Treated as iconography rather than evidence, the shots contained volumes yet unread. To correct the oversight, Frassanito embarked on an extensive search to answer the unasked questions and to develop a clearer picture of the battle.

The end result is *Gettysburg: A Journey in Time,* containing the most famous images available plus several never-before published photos. The author focuses on photographs taken between 1863 and 1866, which, he notes, marked the beginning and the end of strong public interest in Gettysburg for twenty years. Frassanito has been able to determine when the photos were taken and by whom. For instance, he finds that one team shot all of the pictures of the dead in two days over a relatively small area. He also shows, with damning evidence, that at least one of the photographers doctored scenes by rearranging muskets, body parts, and corpses for dramatic effect (see CIVILIAN DEEDS AND MISDEEDS).

Perhaps his greatest contribution is noting where photographs were taken. While some locales were obvious, such as Devil's Den and Little Round Top, many more Civil War–era shots were of unspecified or misidentified areas. By carefully studying backgrounds and rock formations within the pictures and comparing them to modern-day topography, Frassanito has been able to determine that some scenes thought to be of Herbst Woods were actually of the Rose farm, that an indistinct shot of a subtle elevation was actually a rare view of Cemetery Hill, and that the famous image of three Confederate prisoners was taken on Seminary Ridge. In addition, Frassanito places contemporary photographs of the same scenes next to the Civil War–era shots. The comparisons are stunning, as they astutely reveal how much the battlefield has changed over time.

Before becoming the leading authority on Civil War photography, William Frassanito graduated from Gettysburg College, joined the U.S. Army, and received a bronze star in Vietnam.

---

4. *GETTYSBURG: JULY 1*
DAVID G. MARTIN (1996)

Whether through the voices of *Killer Angels* or the spectacle of Devil's Den, the tendency is to overlook the events of July 1. Too often, the day's events are perceived as mere preliminaries. David Martin quickly dispels this common mistake, presenting the most detailed and engaging single volume yet written on the topic.

As Martin points out, taken by itself, the first day of Gettysburg ranks as the twenty-third largest battle of the war. Thousands of soldiers were wounded or killed, whole regiments were nearly wiped out, and a Northern town fell under the occupation of a Confederate army. Once more, the author notes, the outcome of the first day largely dictated the options and boundaries of the second and third.

To maintain clarity, Martin divides the day into locations rather than hours, concentrating on one fight at a time, such as the terrible sequence of events that sent Alfred Iverson's North Carolinians to their doom along the foot of Oak Ridge. The author also provides several detailed maps, further illuminating the size and dynamics of each individual contest.

Concerning the routed U.S. 11th Corps, Martin is unsympathetic to their poor performance north of town, placing most of the blame on the officers. Nor is he particularly tolerant of R. E. Lee's frequent use of vague orders. On whether the Confederates could have taken Cemetery Hill on the first day (see CONTROVERSIES), Martin contends an assault would have likely failed, given the exhausted condition of the Confederate troops and the Union preparations for defense already under way. As with Coddington, Martin makes sure to note differing views and refrains from falling into conjecture.

Covering topics on the American Revolution and the Civil War, David Martin has written more than twenty books in twenty years.

---

5. *GETTYSBURG—THE SECOND DAY*
HARRY W. PFANZ (1987)

Among the many scholars of the battle, Harry Pfanz stands with the elite. In *Gettysburg—The Second Day,* the eminent historian brings his precise research and encyclopedic memory to bear against what James Longstreet called the best three hours of fighting the Army of Northern Virginia had ever done.

The title misleads. Not addressed are Cemetery or Culp's hills, both of which saw extremely heavy combat on July 2. Pfanz instead focuses purely on the exceptionally complex and bloody fights that raged from 4 p.m. until sundown in and around the Peach Orchard, the Wheatfield, Devil's Den, and the Round Tops.

This is not a light read. To some the text may appear dry, like an audit. For military historians, this single volume is more like a bountiful archive. It provides biographical material on nearly every officer. Every regiment receives extended coverage. Every house and outbuilding is recognized as an added dimension to the trials of combat.

Trying to stay as close to actual events as possible, Pfanz saves his own observations for the final chapter, preferring instead to chronicle rather than critique the battle. Though noble, his practice might frustrate a Gettysburg newcomer. All the detail in the world is sometimes not as informative as a modicum of insight, and with his unmatched knowledge on the subject, Pfanz has more to offer than most.

After serving in World War II as an artillery officer, Harry Pfanz worked for ten years as a historian at the Gettysburg National Military Park and became chief historian of the National Park Service.

---

6. GETTYSBURG: CULP'S HILL & CEMETERY HILL
HARRY W. PFANZ (1993)

Viewing the engagements on the Union left and right flanks as two separate contests, Pfanz dedicates an entire volume to the latter. His commitment is a great benefit to those who want a more complete picture of Gettysburg. The mystique of Little Round Top and the Copse of Trees gather a great deal of attention, but Culp's Hill and Cemetery Hill saw far more fighting over a much longer period of time, and a definitive study on the two critical hills had never been done—until Pfanz.

Part of the challenge in writing about the peaks, aside from their complex and overlapping engagements, is the dearth of reports left behind by the Confederate participants. The author conquers this obstacle by tracking down every shred of writing available from the Southern side. He also pores over the more abundant Union accounts to triangulate the positions and actions of their opponents. The result is trademark Pfanz—chronological, exhaustive, and reliable.

Yet this work contains inherent appeal. Unlike the basics of Little Round Top and Pickett's Charge, most of the harrowing events that took place on Culp's Hill and Cemetery Hill have been shrouded in mystery. With Scotland Yard precision, Pfanz traces the evidence, step by step, until all is revealed.

> Harry Pfanz has three ancestors who served with Ohio units in the Civil War, none of whom had the pleasure of fighting at Gettysburg.

7. PICKETT'S CHARGE: THE LAST ATTACK AT GETTYSBURG
EARL J. HESS (2001)

For decades the standard treatise on the subject was George Stewart's *Pickett's Charge*, until Earl Hess produced a minute-by-minute assessment of the battle's fiery culmination. An engaging, entertaining, yet reputable read, *The Last Attack at Gettysburg* is supremely balanced, a perfect dichotomy to its topic.

Hess begins with the planning stages for the assault, recognizing that although Isaac Trimble's and James Pettigrew's divisions may have been battle-worn, so were nearly everyone else's. Proceeding to the artillery barrage, from both the Confederate and Union perspectives, the author shows an ability to challenge treasured notions. Some evaluations, including eyewitness accounts, contend that the cannonade lasted ninety minutes and more. Hess calculates through exhaustive research that the event probably lasted no more than an hour, ceasing at or near 2 p.m.

He also challenges a revisionist favoritism of Longstreet. If Lee could be accused of relinquishing responsibilities to his subordinates, argues Hess, so could his Old War Horse. Symbolic of the South Carolinian's position on the attack, the author notes, Longstreet watched much of Pickett's Charge while sitting on a fence.

Hess's intricate description of the march itself, both for the men walking through the grass fields and their enemies watching them draw near, is one of the most tangible narrations of the hour ever written. It is also recounted with a precision only attainable through the strenuous inspection of the most reputable primary and secondary sources available. Hess's use of descriptive maps and images add further dimension.

Unfortunately the book ends not unlike the charge itself—rather suddenly. Hess does not delve far into the short- or long-term reactions of survivors. This is understandable, as there appears to be little immediate evidence of soldiers on either side treating the assault as exclusive of preceding events, George E. Pickett excepted. Yet as Hess so skillfully illustrates, the great charge involved infinitely more than just Pickett. A good companion piece to the volume is Carol Reardon's *Pickett's Charge in History and Memory*, which examines the changing perceptions of the assault over successive generations.

Earl Hess's expertise stretches far beyond the charge. He has published histories on Civil War soldier life, civilian life in the North, field fortifications, the battle of Pea Ridge, and the Kentucky campaign.

---

8.   *A STRANGE AND BLIGHTED LAND—GETTYSBURG: THE AFTERMATH OF BATTLE,* GREGORY COCO (1995)

A quick glance at Gregory Coco's publications reveals his authority on Gettysburg and his focus. Among his many works are *A Vast Sea of Misery: A History and Guide to the Union and Confederate Field Hospitals at Gettysburg* (1988); *Killed in Action: Eyewitness Accounts of the Last Mo-*

ments of 100 Union Soldiers Who Died at Gettysburg (1992); and *Gettysburg's Confederate Dead* (2003). Suffice to say, Coco does not sugarcoat the bloodiest battle of the war.

His best and most comprehensive writing appears in *A Strange and Blighted Land—Gettysburg: The Aftermath of Battle,* a straightforward account of what happened to the town, the residents, and the twenty-two thousand wounded soldiers left in the wake of the engagement. With fine interconnections, Coco pieces together the shattered remnants. He begins with an assessment of the battleground, with its living and dead still present on the Emmitsburg road, Cemetery Hill, and in the Herbst Woods. After examining the hasty effort of the burial crews and the even speedier work of scavengers, the author details the operations of field hospitals filled to capacity. Ending with a synopsis of the ceremony on Cemetery Hill four months after the battle and a speech that the world would later note and long remember, he closes with Gettysburg's new birth, outlining how the killing fields would eventually become a national military park.

At times, the book's prose may seem wooden. A more flowing style can be found in Gerard Patterson's *Debris of Battle,* another fine overview of Gettysburg's collateral damage. Yet Coco's detachment is excusable, because the information presented speaks for itself. As a man of his credentials well knows, there is no need for embellishment when describing the labors of hospital angels or grave robbers.

Akin to fellow Gettysburg author William Frassanito, Gregory Coco served in Vietnam and was awarded the Bronze Star.

---

9. DEVIL'S DEN: A HISTORY AND GUIDE
GARY ADELMAN AND TIM SMITH (1997)

Microhistories can easily spelunk beyond the point of no return, reaching so deeply into every possible crevice that they lose their way. A remarkable exception is Gary Adelman and Tim Smith's exploration of Devil's Den, a life story of the most unique geological feature at Gettysburg.

Containing fifteen maps and more than one hundred images, the book begins with an overview of the den's gestation, explains how the granite came to rise and unearth itself over time. The authors follow with an impressive survey of primary documents that describe how the locals viewed the massive and mysterious lair before it became legendary. Afterward is a moving account of the den's place in the battle, detailing how troops were both spared and trapped by its fissures.

Adelman and Smith then recount a postbattle den, often viewed more as a place of bemusement than of homage, with tourists crawling over every inch of its back, scratching graffiti into its sides, and dropping tons of litter into its openings. The authors conclude by detailing the growing effort to spare the rocks. They also provide the finest touring guide of Devil's Den available so that readers can peer into the cracks of the past, regardless if they ever make it to Gettysburg.

> Timothy Smith and Gary Adelman became extremely familiar with their
> subject long before they wrote the book. Both resided in Gettysburg, were
> licensed battlefield guides, and served on the board of the Gettysburg
> Battlefield Preservation Association.

10. *GETTYSBURG: MEMORY, MARKET, AND AN AMERICAN SHRINE*
JIM WEEKS (2003)

Other authors address the battle. Jim Weeks contemplates the icon. Viewing Gettysburg as a place "where shrine and festival merge," the scholar ponders how and why the place has changed over the years, and his findings say more about the nation as whole than about its most visited national battlefield.

Weeks draws a road map from the end of the battle to its 140th anniversary, noting how Gettysburg transformed from a crash site to a vacation destination. He traces the origins of relic collecting and tour guides, which he argues were present in rudimentary form from the very beginning. Convincing is his stance that the site benefited from early promotion, mostly by way of the Gettysburg Battlefield Memorial Association. Mile-marker anniversaries also boosted visitation. Yet nothing, he contends, affected the landscape more than the gasoline engine and the nuclear family.

As the United States started to revolve around the automobile, so did the military park, insists Weeks. Footpaths and benches gave way to wide avenues and large signs. Hotels came down. Motels went up. Patrons wanted entertainment over education. The author then logs the park's return to a more somber tone, brought about by the American experience in Vietnam and an aging population.

For those who idealize Gettysburg, this book might be a bitter pill, but it is enlightening. Weeks's social criticisms are heavy-handed, and his writing is peppered with academia buzzwords, for instance, he uses the word *genteel* more than a hundred times. Yet his deconstruction can bring a devotee closer to a true understanding of what Gettysburg once was and how it came to be.

Jim Weeks knows history, and he knows Pennsylvania. He was a resident scholar with the state's Historical and Museum Commission and taught American history at Penn State.

TOP TEN CONTROVERSIES AND WHAT-IFS

At reenactments, in roundtables, through Internet chat rooms, and in print, contentious questions resonate unabated. While the North and South may have fused back together in 1865, it was a shotgun wedding. The passage of time has only granted its offspring the opportunity to debate the past at length and in depth, and the Brothers' War still raises the blood, which is to be expected. As with any family reunion, there are bound to be issues.

The present generations are simply heirs to a well-established legacy. Civil War veterans had their own mediums of deliberation—speeches, monuments, memoirs—in which they addressed problems unresolved. They bickered amongst themselves as much as with their former enemies, arguing over fault and fame, unwilling to resort to the better angels of their nature. From their time to ours, certain doubts have refused to rest quietly. As Gettysburg produced more casualties than any other battle, it is altogether fitting and proper that it created a multitude of deep-seated conundrums.

Following are the most divisive issues produced by the battle. Some concern what happened; others contest what might have been. All are nearly as old as the battle itself. Brave men may have consecrated Gettysburg, but that did not prevent others from attempting to add or detract from the questions it created.

1. "HIGH WATER MARK" OR JUST ANOTHER EASTERN BATTLE?

"It was a time of indescribable enthusiasm," said a Union officer as he and his comrades watched Pickett's Charge ebb away. Never before had the Army of the Potomac sent its opposite in full retreat. Billy Yank tossed his hat into the air and cheered as he never had before. Loyal papers were soon writing of the triumph. The *Philadelphia Journal* proclaimed, "It is a complete victory." The glory would not last, as both sides understood that a great deal of hard labor still lay ahead. Only following generations would consciously point to Gettysburg as the Confederacy's "High Water Mark," the beginning of the end.[1]

Was the battle the definitive turning point of the war? Militarily, probably not. While Gettysburg netted the Union five thousand prisoners, the Federal victory at Fort Donelson in 1862 bagged thirteen thousand prisoners plus the mighty Cumberland River and northwest Tennessee.

Gettysburg counted 2,500 residents. In April 1862 the Union captured the 180,000 inhabitants of New Orleans, an urban center larger than the next four most populous Confederate cities put together. While Gettysburg sat between Willoughby Run and Rock Creek, the Crescent City anchored the Mississippi and accounted for more commerce than all other Southern ports combined. Farther upriver, the fall of Vicksburg in 1863 gave the Union the length of the national artery plus an entire Confederate army.

Gettysburg had Pickett's Charge. At the battle of Franklin in 1864, a desperate Gen. John Bell Hood marched nearly twice as many men over twice the open ground, losing twice the casualties as Lee had at Gettysburg. Lee backtracked one hundred miles and retained two-thirds of his force. Hood retreated three hundred miles with barely a quarter of his men.[2]

Gettysburg was not a major rail link; Atlanta was. And with the fall of the Gate City in 1864 came the March to the Sea and the reelection of the Lincoln administration.

The Gettysburg campaign was neither the first nor the last Confederate incursion into Union territory. Raids of varying success entered Illinois, Indiana, Ohio, and Vermont. Border wars decimated whole cities and counties in Missouri. Initially neutral Kentucky hosted major battles from 1861 onward. In 1862 Maryland experienced the bloodiest day in

U.S. military history. Within the eastern theater itself, the monthlong Gettysburg campaign cost sixty thousand total casualties, whereas the May 1864 Wilderness campaign produced in excess of eighty thousand.[3]

Yet in terms of Southern hope and Northern frustrations, Gettysburg may have been the signal event of a great climactic change. Never had Lee's army reached so far, and never had the major cities of the Union felt so endangered. Morale between the armies had reached polar opposites. Europe again contemplated intervention. Northern antiwar movements were widespread and growing.

A wholly unexpected Federal victory reversed all of that. Lee's men began to write home of hopelessness while the boys of the Potomac started to look and act like an army capable of winning. The great Confederate general no longer appeared unstoppable, and Meade emerged from relative obscurity. By August, Confederate secretary of state Judah P. Benjamin all but gave up on foreign recognition. By October the Southern economy started to free-fall, with inflation reaching 70 percent and worse.[4]

Lincoln may have provided one of the better perspectives on Gettysburg. As he stressed repeatedly to his constituents, any victory was welcome news, but it mattered not whether a Confederate army marched through Pennsylvania or Virginia or Kentucky or Georgia; it was still an army marching through the United States. That fact alone, Lincoln insisted, was the basis of the war. In one of his long-remembered speeches, he also noted that the great task of civil war required dedication, and that any battle, no matter how great, was ultimately unfinished work.

Forced to fight increasingly on the defensive after Gettysburg, Lee actually improved his battle record. Before July 1863 he lost more engagements than he won. Afterward, he won more than he lost and bested Lt. Gen. U. S. Grant in nine out of eleven major fights.

---

2. WHAT IF LEE HAD WON?

Of all the Civil War's what-if scenarios, chief among them is the premise of a Confederate win at Gettysburg. Supposedly, such a result would have allowed Lee to attack Washington DC or any other city of his choosing. Victory in Pennsylvania might also have brought the Union to its knees, with the U.S. government begging Richmond for peace terms.

To minds modern and past, it was all very possible, even probable. Lee himself entertained the idea, as did many of his subordinates. Unionists in Baltimore constructed defenses in anticipation of an attack. Residents of Philadelphia frantically dug rifle pits, piled breastworks, and assembled militia on the assumption they would next feel the wrath of invasion. U.S. secretary of war Edwin M. Stanton made preparations for a block-by-block last stand in Washington, instructing the army to plant "batteries at the avenues of approach and at different points in the city."[5]

Of course the Confederates achieved no such conquest or occupation, with the exception of holding one town of twenty-five hundred residents for two and a half days.

But suppose Lee did push the Army of the Potomac from the heights southwest of Gettysburg. The goal was certainly achievable, considering he had previously accomplished far more with far longer odds. Would his Army of Northern Virginia have attacked Washington and marched victoriously down Pennsylvania Avenue? Judging by historical patterns, most likely not. The South had won decisively at First Manassas and did not march the twenty-five miles to the Federal capital. Lee achieved resounding success in the Peninsula campaign, yet he made no attempt to bite at the seat of the Union government. Massive fights at Second Manassas, Fredericksburg, and Chancellorsville all resulted in clear victories for the Confederacy, yet none of them produced follow-up attacks on Washington or any other major city.

Lee may have been one of the most aggressive commanders in American military history, but he never completely overcommitted himself. He was well aware that regardless of victory or defeat at Gettysburg, his army was still fifty miles from Virginia, starving for ammunition, deep in hostile territory, and vulnerable to civilian spies and Union reinforcements. Once more, if he elected to march on the District of Columbia eighty long miles away, he would be storming the most heavily armed and fortified city in the Union. Any assault on its hefty garrisons and overlapping trench works might possibly end the war—in favor of the Union.

Gettysburg's rich anthology of gallant charges, waving flags, and bursting cannon inspires the imagination. But militarily speaking, cavalier strikes and spur-of-the-moment miracles did not decide the Civil War. Lengthy and decimating struggles did. It is entirely possible that defeat in Pennsylvania actually saved Lee and his army from eventual destruction in the North, allowing him to continue fighting in the South, where indeed his army eventually broke, not in a solitary battle, but after a protracted and devastating siege.

The Union siege of Richmond and Petersburg lasted nine months. It remains the longest continuous siege in American military history.

---

3.   WHAT IF STONEWALL HAD BEEN ALIVE?

Perpetual is the lamentation among Confederate empathizers that, had Thomas "Stonewall" Jackson survived Chancellorsville, his unequalled genius and courage would have carried any hill or ridge that Lee wanted at Gettysburg or anywhere else. His countrymen and comrades certainly thought so.

J. A. Stikeleather of the 4th North Carolina deduced that Culp's Hill would have easily fallen to the South had the aggressive Stonewall been present, but "timidity in the commander [Lt. Gen. RICHARD S. EWELL] that stepped into the shoes of the fearless Jackson, prompted delay." Brig. Gen. John B. Gordon claimed that Jackson would have known precisely what to do practically everywhere on the field. "Had he [Jackson] been there, his quick eye would have caught at a glance the entire situation." If pressed, Lee might have agreed. On a visit in 1870 with his cousin, Cassius Lee, the great general allegedly said that if Jackson had been present, the Confederacy would have won at Gettysburg.[6]

Jackson's biographer James I. Robertson Jr. provides the most emphatic answer, saying that if Stonewall had been alive on July 1, there would have been no battle at Gettysburg, as Jackson and his battle-hardened troops would have reached Vermont by that date.

Yet nothing elevates a reputation like death. "Old Jack" was probably the finest combat commander in the war, but the blue-eyed evangelist was not perfect. In the Peninsula campaign, he showed no savvy and minimal initiative, perhaps because he had marched himself and his men too hard. Not unlike Joseph Hooker, he refrained from sharing any plans or information with subordinates until the last possible moment. The security measure backfired horribly at Cedar Mountain, Virginia, in 1862, when a surprise Union attack nearly forced him to retreat. Only a bold counterstroke by subordinate A. P. HILL saved the stoic Stonewall.[7]

If indeed he had lived to lead the 2nd Corps to Gettysburg, Jackson might have been as aggressive as his admirers believed he would be. Then again, he might have advised Lee to fight at another place and time, just as Longstreet did. A soldier in the 23rd Virginia, forced to charge the Union defenses again and again, said that he wished Jackson were present to correct the situation, "For it was always his policy never to assault strongholds or storm positions as impregnable as these."[8]

Theoretically, Stonewall Jackson could have been killed at Gettysburg instead of Chancellorsville. His successor, Richard Ewell, nearly was. On July 1, "Baldy" narrowly survived an artillery blast that killed his horse. On July 3, a bullet hit Ewell squarely in the leg. Luckily for Ewell it was his wooden leg, a souvenir from Second Manassas.

---

4.   JAMES LONGSTREET: CULPRIT OR VICTIM?

After Lee's death, unreconstructed Southerners beatified him as the saint of the Lost Cause—a genteel, patriarchal, flawless lord among men. When James Longstreet publicly questioned Lee's actions at Gettysburg, the once-admired corps commander was dubbed a heretic and sentenced to a firing line of accusers. Jubal A. Early and John B. Gordon pointed to Longstreet's slow deployment to the right flank on July 2, contending that it allowed the Union time to prepare against it. They also viewed his skepticism of Pickett's Charge and his refusal to send reinforcements as proof that he lacked the determination required for success. In response, Longstreet intensified the feud by suggesting that Lee's entire Pennsylvania campaign was overly aggressive and insisted his plan of moving to the southeast would have brought far better results.

Years later, during a newspaper interview, Longstreet went so far as to call Lee "too pugnacious, too willing to go on the attack, when his skills were much better suited for defense." Previously seen as a supporting actor in the tragedy, Longstreet began to look more like a pouting prima donna. Though still beloved by his old 1st Corps, other former comrades were far less receptive, and John B. Gordon made it a point never to invite Old Pete to his military reunions.[9]

It took a Pulitzer Prize–winning novel to lifeline Longstreet's reputation. Michael Shaara's *The Killer Angels* presented the corps commander as a loyal but troubled servant, unable to stop his quixotic mentor's self-destruction. The South Carolinian appears as the lone farsighted soul among the blindly devoted.

Whether Longstreet's suggestion of disengaging from Gettysburg would have ever resulted in Confederate success is unknowable. But he was undoubtedly correct in a statement he made sometime after the war: "No Southern writer dares to admit that General Lee ever made a military mistake."[10]

Postwar Southerners generally thought so little of Longstreet that they did not erect a statue of him at Gettysburg for 135 years. In 1998 his likeness was finally raised on Seminary Ridge. A fitting metaphor, the statue is slightly smaller than life-size.

---

5. SICKLES'S SALIENT: DEADLY MISTAKE OR LIFESAVING MOVE?

As it stuck out nearly a mile from the Union main line, with its flanks exposed and its tip just five hundred yards away from the Confederates, Daniel E. Sickles's tactical salient resembled a big razzing tongue. Yet a controversy revolves on whether Sickles's lone act very nearly destroyed or actually facilitated the Army of the Potomac's chances for overall victory. According to Sickles, he was a savior, having single-handedly created a breakwater against which the Confederates threw themselves.

Theoretically, he may have been partially correct. Had Sickles not taken the fight to his opposition, Lee's forces conceivably could have approached the Round Tops and the low grade of south Cemetery Ridge with much greater ease. The South may have been able to roll up the North's left flank by day three, thereby driving a wedge between Billy Yank and Washington. Then again, had Sickles remained on Cemetery Ridge in the first place, he could have simplified and solidified Meade's defenses, forcing the Confederates to attack a unified line and permitting the Union to counterattack at some point. Of course, all is conjecture.[11]

What is factual is the cost. The ensuing Confederate attack upon the salient reduced Sickles's corps by a third. To stop the onslaught, Meade had to use his 5th Corps and elements of the 2nd Corps. Overall, the fight for the salient and surrounding areas involved twice the area, lasted twice

as long, and cost the Union four times the casualties as the artillery barrage and Pickett's Charge on the following day.

For his actions on July 2, Maj. Gen. Daniel E. Sickles received the Medal
of Honor.

---

6.   COULD MEADE HAVE DESTROYED LEE?

This is arguably the North's utmost "what might have been." On July 4
Lee concluded he could not stay on the offensive. He had lost too many
men. Retracting his forces to the protection of Seminary Ridge, Lee actually waited for Meade to attack. Meade never did.

By July 5 the Army of Northern Virginia was on its way out. Through
the narrow mountain passes ten miles to their rear, Lee's haggard troops
funneled back into the safety of the Shenandoah, turned left, and headed
for home. Meade belatedly prodded his way through mountain gaps farther south but never fully engaged his adversaries on their march back
through Maryland.

When sudden rains flooded the Potomac, trapping Lee and nearly his
entire army on the Union side of the river, Meade chose not to launch an
offensive, allowing the Confederates time to fabricate ramshackle foot-
bridges. Meade told Washington that he would attack on July 13. Heeding the cautious advice of five of his seven corps commanders, Meade
changed his mind. By the end of the following day, the Confederates were
over the river and gone.[12]

To eyewitnesses, Meade's hesitation to attack was understandable. All
along the Confederate line of retreat, Lee constructed heavy earthen re-
doubts as he went, none more formidable than the ones at his Potomac
bridgehead. Meade knew the lethal risks of advancing upon strong defenses, having personally observed such recklessness in the Peninsula campaign, Fredericksburg, and for that matter, Cemetery Ridge. He had also
been in command of the Union's largest army for a mere week, and in that
time he had weathered the bloodiest battle of the war, losing nearly 50 percent more dead and wounded than had been lost at Antietam. A quarter of
his men, including his two best corps commanders, were either dead,
wounded, captured, or missing. Suffering as he had, Meade saw no reason
to placate either the White House or Lee by risking a hasty assault.[13]

Meade may have also hesitated to pursue because of Lincoln's instruction to remain between Lee and the national capital. Had the Army of the Potomac rushed to cut off the Southern path of retreat, it would have given the Army of Northern Virginia an alternate route, namely, an open avenue to Washington.

Yet it must be said that Meade did not test his opportunity to any great extent. He had reserves available, whereas Lee did not. The narrow mountain passes threatened to slow the Confederates as much as the Federals. Had Meade forced a large engagement, he may have discovered that the South only had enough ammunition to last one more day. The Pennsylvanian and his staff were also remarkably unimaginative in seeking ways to monitor or prevent the Confederate retreat across the Potomac.[14]

Foremost, as demonstrated by congratulatory remarks he made to his troops after the battle, Meade may have forgotten his ultimate responsibility—to end the Rebellion. As President Lincoln stated emphatically: "Our army held the war in the hollow of their hand, and they would not close it." Unfortunately for Lincoln, Meade made no substantial attempt to reach out and grab the Confederacy's largest army, opting instead to keep his own army safe as a tightly closed fist, one that would not move with any appreciable force until the following May.[15]

The last Confederates to cross the Potomac River into Virginia were members of Maj. Gen. Henry Heth's division, the same unit that initiated the battle of Gettysburg on July 1.

---

7. WAS CEMETERY HILL "PRACTICABLE"?

Finding their right flank turned and their thin line breaking apart, elements of the Union 1st and 11th Corps beat a hasty retreat from the north edge of town. Giving chase was Lt. Gen. RICHARD S. EWELL's 2nd Corps. Within hours, the Confederates held Gettysburg itself, plus fifteen hundred Union prisoners. Lee asked, by way of courier, if Ewell might take advantage of his good fortune and take Cemetery Hill, just south of town, "if practicable." Ewell assessed the situation and refrained.[16]

Many observers, including one of his division commanders, the brash and exaggerative John B. Gordon, viewed Ewell's hesitation as one of the biggest mistakes of the battle, if not the war. Cemetery Hill was the capstone to Cemetery Ridge, and without it the Union would likely have lost its main line of defense to the south and its primary supply artery of the Baltimore pike just to the east. Ewell eventually did try to capture the rise on July 2, at 8 p.m., against well-prepared Union defenses reinforced with scores of cannon and a dozen infantry regiments. The resulting repulse and loss of life might be viewed as proof that Ewell moved far too late.[17]

Yet would Ewell have succeeded on the first day of the battle? Given the state of affairs, perhaps not. To begin with, he could clearly see that Cemetery Hill was becoming a rallying point for the retreating Federals. Artillery pieces were visible and increasing in number. To answer, he had few cannon of his own close at hand and no good positions from which to shoot them. Looking up at the steep slope, he had no idea what lay in wait forty feet above. His own men were scattered over miles, far from organized, and dead tired. It was nearing 5 p.m., and his men had been marching or fighting since 8 a.m. Lee could offer him no assistance from the other two corps. After assessing all that his own men had achieved in the course of a single day, Ewell had neither the will nor the incentive to reward them with orders to charge up a lengthy incline and into an uncertain future.[18]

The best testimony for the defense comes from Robert E. Lee, certainly no admirer of Ewell. In his postbattle report, Lee reiterated that he had recommended an attack, but only under the right conditions and with adequate reinforcements, neither of which appeared available to Ewell on the evening of July 1.[19]

Although the Confederate 2nd Corps did not charge up Cemetery Hill on July 1, it did endure continuous fire from Union troops, much of it coming from Federal sharpshooters embedded in the town of Gettysburg.

---

8. THE CHARGE: PICKETT'S OR PETTIGREW'S?

Days after Lee's ultimate assault on Cemetery Ridge, newspapers in Richmond began to call the attack "Pickett's Charge," in part to glorify the all-Virginia division. Arbitrary and arrogant, the title slighted the other two divisions involved. Maj. Gen. James J. Pettigrew's command was a bit larger and marched side by side with Pickett's into the fray. It also contained regiments from Alabama, Mississippi, North Carolina, and Tennessee as well as Virginia. Close behind was Maj. Gen. Isaac R. Trimble's smaller division of two North Carolina brigades.

Tactful accounts referred to the advance as the Pickett-Pettigrew Assault, or the Pickett-Pettigrew-Trimble Charge. Technically, Longstreet was the chief officer on the scene, and the order to perform the assault came from Lee. Born of hubris, the Virginia christening has nonetheless endured, mostly from the weight of repetition and convenience.

Ownership aside, a much angrier debate erupted over who advanced farther: Virginia or North Carolina. The *Richmond Daily Inquirer* fueled the fight by claiming Pickett was wounded in the advance and Pettigrew's non-Virginians faltered and ran, neither of which was true. The soldiers joined in, exchanging accusations of cowardice in the face of the enemy.[20]

The foundation of the problem was the low stone wall that meandered in front of the famous copse of trees. Running straight north for a hundred yards, the barrier then stretched east, forming the famous Angle. After seventy yards, the wall turned north again. Attacking the closer stretch, Pickett's Virginians breached the stones and progressed a few hard-fought paces, but they could rightly claim to be the only ones to break through the Union line. Far to their left, with seventy more hellish paces to negotiate, Pettigrew's men never breached the far wall, but they may have marched a greater distance in the attempt.[21]

R. E. Lee assigned Isaac R. Trimble to head the former division of the wounded Maj. Gen. William Pender, despite the fact that Trimble had just arrived a few hours before the attack and was familiar with almost none of the men he was about to lead.

---

9. MEADE'S COUNCIL OF WAR: DID HE WANT TO RETREAT?

On March 11, 1864, Maj. Gen. George Gordon Meade appeared before the Joint Committee on the Conduct of the War, not to receive a commendation, but to face charges. In his testimony, Meade tersely denied "any recollection of having issued or directed to be issued, any order on the morning of the 2d of July for the retreat of the army from the enemy."[22]

Meade was facing what Lincoln called "the fire in the rear," the never-ending litany of critics and rivals that came with the burden of leadership. Far less amiable than the president and practically void of political skills, the Pennsylvanian had a difficult time courting allies. Ene-mies, however, came at him in droves, a plight verified by the fact that his finest victory was under close review before the committee.

Allegations of cowardice stemmed from statements Meade had made at the battle. After a second day of acutely intense combat, the command-ing general gathered together a council of war to discuss the situation. In attendance at the late-hour meeting, held at his field headquarters at the Leister family home south of town, were his senior staff and all seven corps commanders. Crammed into the twelve-by-twelve-foot room, the informal session opened with an assessment of remaining manpower, available supplies, and current positions on the battlefield. Meade then followed with a tactical question, stated in a most untactful way: should the Army of the Potomac retreat or stay?[23]

Meade's detractors, then and years later, considered this as evidence that the "Victor of Gettysburg" actually wanted no part in the battle. His many accusers—including his own chief of staff, Daniel Butterfield, and cavalry commander Maj. Gen. Alfred Pleasonton—also pointed to his "Pipe Creek Circular," written on July 1, calling for a concentration of forces miles south of Gettysburg, along the southern bank of Pipe Creek in Maryland.[24]

His accusers failed to point out that Meade never distributed the cir-cular. When subordinates deemed Gettysburg favorable ground for a fight, he tabled the document and moved the body of his army forward.

As for his council of war on the night of July 2, Meade's query on whether to retreat was only the first in a series of questions. Everyone present voted to stay. Also posed was the option to attack. All favored to stay on the defensive. How long, it was asked, should they wait for Lee to attack them? The majority supported waiting one day. "Such then is the decision," said Meade.[25]

The commander may have miscalculated in appearing too congenial. His findings fully coincided with theirs, but he failed to explicitly state that fact. In his effort to respect the opinions of his colleagues, Meade may have given ammunition to those who would later be jealous of his fame and hungry for his job.

Of Meade's seven original corps commanders at Gettysburg, three outranked him.

---

10. CHAMBERLAIN VS. OATES

In the fight for Little Round Top, on the extreme left of the Union line, Col. Joshua Lawrence Chamberlain of the 20th Maine went head to head with Col. William Oates and his 15th Alabama. The Southerners attacked. The Federals pushed them back. It was to be a pattern for years to come.

Exalted in Chamberlain's memoirs and immortalized in the Pulitzer Prize–winning novel *The Killer Angels,* the 20th had run out of ammunition and much of the regiment lay dead or wounded when the Alabamians came at them yet again. Refusing to surrender or pull back, Chamberlain ordered his men to fix bayonets. With a deafening battle cry, they ran downhill into the Confederates, standing "not 30 yards away," and "swept them from the valley."[26]

Years later Oates contended that his men were exhausted and were already assembling for a general retreat when the attack came. Just to reach Little Round Top, the doomed regiment had marched twenty miles without a break and had run out of water hours before their multiple, desperate assaults upon the Union line. Chamberlain dismissed the assertion as sour grapes.[27]

Then, in an attempt to commemorate the 15th Alabama, Oates returned to Little Round Top to erect a monument at the point of his regiment's farthest advance. Chamberlain protested, saying the 15th never reached as far as Oates claimed (although it likely had). After heated exchanges between the two, and an attempt by the U.S. War Department to mediate, park officials eventually sided with Chamberlain, and the monument was never built.[28]

After the war, both Chamberlain and Oates became governor of their respective states, and they never reconciled their differences over what happened at Little Round Top.

TOP TEN BEST MONUMENTS

Accommodating more than twenty-five hundred tablets, statues, and memorials, Gettysburg may be the largest collection of outdoor monuments in the world. By appearances the vast assembly of granite and bronze appears as a cohesive homage to all Americans lost in the struggle. In reality, the silent markers confess to a long and often strained evolution.

During the initial postwar years there was no urgent desire to build altars to past battles. Following a pattern consistent with most wars, veterans and civilians demonstrated little desire to recall let alone exalt such devastation. Of greater concern was the need to move on, to reestablish a sense of normalcy. Many, including Robert E. Lee, argued that erecting tributes and ornamentation to the terrible conflict was not only impractical but also distasteful. And across the country, most grave sites and battlefields lived unadorned of artillery, pillars, or commemorative statues well into the twentieth century.

Compared to other sites, Gettysburg was a relatively early host to monuments, in part because of its ever-increasing status as the preeminent site of the war. In 1867 friends and members of the 1st Minnesota placed a funeral urn at the national cemetery. Two years later came the Soldiers' National Monument facing the semicircle of Union graves. A handful of markers followed afterward.

The battle's twenty-fifth anniversary opened the floodgates. Northern states raised thousands in cash to build their own towering commemorations, resulting in a strange contest of hubris and one-upmanship. Feuds began as to who belonged where. Regiments argued over who advanced the farthest. Few could agree on where celebrated officers fell. The Gettysburg Battlefield Memorial Association (GBMA) imposed a "Line of Battle" rule, mandating that monuments were to be placed where units entered the fight, which consequently left Confederate markers far away from prestige locations such as Little Round Top, Devil's Den, and Cemetery Ridge.[29]

In spite of the politics, more than three hundred monuments went up by the turn of the century, and the total reached four figures by the mid-1900s. At the date of this publication, there is a moratorium on the placement of new memorials. Yet what stands today is an odd flock of ornamentations, many of which say more about the postwar period than they do about the battle itself.

Following are the ten most outstanding monuments in their respective categories. Each also represents the lengthy, erratic, and often controversial transformation of Gettysburg from killing field into "the grand mausoleum of our patriot dead."[30]

1. THE PENNSYLVANIA STATE MEMORIAL

 Situated in the middle of Cemetery Ridge, towering sixty-nine feet into the air, the Pennsylvania State Memorial is the largest, tallest, and most expensive statement of grandeur on the field. There are no official statistics, but it also may be the most visited and photographed. Made of concrete, sand, reinforced steel, bronze, and more than twelve hundred tons of granite, the memorial is an engineering and artistic achievement. It also represents Pennsylvania's triumph in laying special claim to the battle.

Decades after the war, seedlings of future memorials appeared in the guise of wooden signs set up around the battlefield to indicate where Pennsylvania units had fought. Somewhat alarmed by this implied monopoly, other Northern states maneuvered for similar recognition. When the names of regiments and brigades began to be written in stone, the home state suddenly lost its premier status. At one time, Massachusetts had more monuments than Pennsylvania, though the Bay State had twenty-one regiments at Gettysburg while the Keystone had seventy-three. None could keep pace with New York, which eventually had a monument for each regiment, battery, and all nineteen of its generals present at Gettysburg.[31]

But when the battle's fiftieth anniversary approached, native sons worked to create the largest, most prominent, most ornate, and most expensive structure on the premises. In 1910, after fifty designs, a budget of two hundred thousand dollars, and a year of construction, they succeeded.[32]

Atop the memorial's great dome is the goddess of victory and peace. More than twenty feet tall, she is made of bronze melted from cannons used in the war. Supporting the dome is a four-sided archway, each side representing the branches of field service present at the battle: infantry, artillery, cavalry, and signal corps. Guarding the archways are eight bronze statues: seven prominent Pennsylvanians accompanied by Abraham Lincoln. Around the entire base, scribed in bronze tablature, is the name of every Pennsylvanian who fought at Gettysburg. Despite its intent to overshadow all other monuments present, the structure is indeed a marvel to behold.

The Pennsylvania Memorial's bronze tablets contain more than thirty-four thousand names. Builders installed the final plate just hours before the official dedication in 1910. Officials soon discovered that because of inaccurate records, many of the names did not belong. Consequently, the tablets have been undergoing alterations ever since.

---

2. HIGH WATER MARK MEMORIAL

More than any other, this memorial worships the battle itself, proclaiming the great conflict, and Pickett's Charge in particular, to be the single great turning point of the American Civil War. Meant to exalt all veterans of the battle, it was the brainchild of one man. Though not a historian, author, veteran, or even a witness to the battle, John Badger Bachelder committed much of his life to elevating Gettysburg to its zenith status.[33]

Immediately after the Confederate withdrawal on July 4–5, the sometimes painter and cartographer Bachelder began collecting hundreds of personal accounts of the event. Using his interviews as his template, he created ornate maps of unit positions on the battlefield. His somewhat inaccurate but rather opulent illustrations won him many buying admirers. Although Bachelder's credentials hardly merited the distinction, he subsequently became the universally recognized authority on Gettysburg.[34]

His influence expanded even further in 1883 when he became the battlefield's superintendent of tables and legends. Overseeing every monument proposal, he designed and funded one of his own.[35]

Completed in 1892, the High Water Mark Memorial features an immense open book with its back resting against pyramids of cannonballs. On the pages are the names of Union and Confederate units involved in Pickett's Charge. The gloried manifest resides on a base eighteen feet by forty-eight feet, with two menacing artillery pieces acting as watchful sentries. Just behind the memorial stands the famous copse of trees where

Lee supposedly aimed his infantry. The tiny grove has been protected since 1887 by an iron fence (also a Bachelder idea).

Curiously, the copse was not a focal point of veterans' accounts. Post-battle photographers and tourists also took little notice of this part of the battlefield. Aside from a brief mention in *Harper's Weekly* in October 1863, Pickett's Charge was not referred to as the high tide of the Confederacy for decades, until Bachelder raised this altar. In doing so, Bachelder was part sage, part salesman, and wholly a disciple.[36]

Congress granted John Bachelder fifty thousand dollars (nearly $1.5 million in 2006 dollars) to write a definitive history of Gettysburg, although he had never published a historical work in his life. He never would. Not until the late twentieth century was his 2,550-page manuscript whittled down to three volumes and released to the public.

---

3.   THE IRISH BRIGADE MONUMENT

Among the forest of temples, certain shrines possess an enigmatic mysticism, lending to the battle's status as a spiritual as well as military event. By far the most exceptional example is the serene but simple tribute to the Irish Brigade near the Wheatfield. The monument has an inexplicable draw, magnified by its ghostly vigil within the undying shade of surrounding trees. Even the most rushed tourists cannot help but stop and admire its simple strength as it stands vigil for a brigade that nearly disappeared in southern Pennsylvania.[37]

Though the opposing armies at Gettysburg were nearly full strength, most of the brigades that made up those armies were not. Case in point, these Irish. Numbering more than two thousand at their peak, the famed boys of Erin suffered horrific losses at Antietam, Fredericksburg, and Chancellorsville. By the time the 63rd, 69th, and 88th New York, 28th Massachusetts, and 116th Pennsylvania marched into battle on July 2, the brigade was a shell of its former self, containing fewer bodies than a single emaciated regiment.

Such bloodlettings apparently failed to crack the spirit of the heavily foreign-born force. Finding the Irish Brigade in camp or bivouac was not difficult, for they were routinely the chief source of music, dance, games of chance, and bouts of fisticuffs. The somber, solemn monument at Gettysburg stands in stark contrast to their reputation for revelry, but there is reason for its melancholic tone.

Sent into the WHEATFIELD on the second day, the brigade was reduced from slightly more than five hundred men to just over three hundred in less than an hour. Gaining a few hundred yards for their sacrifice, the unit lost all the ground and more from counterattacks. On the edge of the Wheatfield stands a Celtic cross, dedicated on the twenty-fifth anniversary of that destructive day.

The cross is made of granite and inlaid bronze and stands nearly twenty feet high. At its base lies a bronze sculpture of an Irish wolfhound in mourning. At the cross's apex is a three-leaf clover, a symbol not of the old country but of the Union 2nd Corps to which the brigade belonged.

Notice that only three of the five Irish Brigade regiments are named on the statue. The 28th Massachusetts and 116th Pennsylvania did not contribute funds for construction and were thus left off. Consequently, it is sometimes referred to as the New York Irish Brigade Monument.

---

4. THE MARYLAND STATE MONUMENT

One of the last monuments erected before the park established a moratorium on construction, the Maryland State Monument best depicts the reality that this was a Brothers' War. It is the embodiment of a state's conscious remorse and its longing for domestic reconciliation.

Dedicated in 1994 to the five Confederate and six Federal units from Maryland engaged at Gettysburg, the granite structure depicts their familial struggle with brutal poignancy. There are two soldiers atop the memorial, and both are severely wounded. Stumbling forward, each cannot stand without the help of the other.

This late-twentieth-century message of humility and healing was a far cry from the sentiment prevailing from years earlier. In the 1880s, veterans of the Confederate 1st Maryland Infantry Battalion expressed a desire to honor their comrades lost on Culp's Hill (they would in fact be the only Confederate veterans group to ever build a regimental monument at the park). When the Gettysburg Battlefield Memorial Association granted permission to proceed, Union veterans protested venomously. Leading the opposition were the old members of the Union 1st Maryland Potomac Home Brigade and 1st Maryland Eastern Shore Infantry, unwilling to allow "traitors" to share their name in stone.[38]

After long deliberation, the Confederates were allowed their humble pillar, so long as they put "2nd MD. Infantry C.S.A" on the front and hide their true name on the backside.[39]

In Pardee Field south of Culp's Hill, on the morning of July 3, the Confederate 1st Maryland Infantry Battalion clashed with the Union's 1st Maryland Eastern Shore Infantry. Both had been recruited from the same counties, and cousins served as opposing color guards. In the head-to-head fight, the Confederates won.

---

5. THE VIRGINIA STATE MEMORIAL

Grand and glorious is the tribute to the sons of Old Dominion, a veritable bastion of rock and bronze. But its overall message is clear to even the most casual observer. Virginia's memorial is less about its men and more about its Marble Man. With the exception of Stone Mountain outside Atlanta, no other sculpting better represents the godlike stature of Robert E. Lee among his countrymen.

Dedicated in 1917, covering nearly a thousand square feet, a wide base of granite has clustered at its front a tightly bound team of seven men. Readying themselves to unleash a volley are a mechanic, a merchant, a farmer, young boys, and old men. Dressed in homespun cloth, standing over the debris of combat, they represent every man who heeded the state's call to arms. But above them all, perched on a great pulpit twenty-four feet high, is Robert E. Lee, mounted on his beloved steed, Traveller. In direct contrast with the haggard mortals at his feet, he is stalwart, composed, and godlike.

The care with which their hero was cast demonstrates the absolute reverence placed upon him. Lee's face, a remarkable likeness, came from diligent scrutiny of photographs and life masks. In further search for precision, sculptors even examined the skeleton of Traveller before forming the charger in bronze. As other states fought to stake their own claim to glory on the battlefield, Virginia assured they alone possessed Lee.[40]

Legend has it that the Virginia State Memorial stands where Lee stood during much of Pickett's Charge.

---

6. THE NEW YORK EXCELSIOR MONUMENT

It is among the most beautiful, and it is the finest paradox. Most every monument is an attempt to fuse symbolic expression with stately grace. In this pursuit few can match the New York Excelsior Monument, striking in its presence between the Peach Orchard and Little Round Top. And no monument at Gettysburg better represents how looks can be extremely deceiving.

Consisting of the 70th, 71st, 72nd, 73rd, and 74th New York Infantry, with the 120th New York joining soon after, the Excelsior Brigade was a product of womanizing socialite, Tammany Hall politico DANIEL E. SICKLES. Sickles's phenomenal recruiting drive created this entire brigade and landed him an officer's commission, which he astutely parlayed into a major generalship by the time of Gettysburg.

During the great battle, the brigade experienced losses of 42 percent, mostly on the second day as it tried to hold the Union line along the Emmitsburg road. Serving together until the end of the war, the original five regiments decided to build a single brigade monument upon their field of highest achievement. The result is a five-sided base supporting five finely polished columns and capped by a solid crown of granite adorned with an eagle. The Excelsior monument stands as one of the most captivating structures on the field. But the gallant image is incomplete.

Not included is the 120th New York, which fought the best and lost the most, suffering more killed and wounded than the 71st and 72nd combined, both of which broke and ran during the fight near the Peach Orchard. But since the 120th was not an original member of the brigade, it was deemed unworthy of full inclusion.[41]

Also missing, for very different reasons, is the brigade's founder. A statue of Sickles was supposed to stand at the monument's center, but money ran short. In 1912 a New York State controller discovered why. Some twenty-eight thousand dollars had been embezzled from the monument fund. After a rather enlightening investigation, officials submitted an arrest warrant for the supervisor of the fund—ninety-three-year-old, one-legged, former Union general Daniel E. Sickles. Though probably guilty, he never went to trial, and the monument's center remains empty to this day.[42]

Represented by five pillars on a pentagon, in a monument that took five years to build, the regiments of the Excelsior suffered the fifth highest number of brigade-level battle fatalities in the war—nearly nine hundred officers and men mortally wounded or killed.

---

7. THE 44TH AND 12TH NEW YORK MONUMENT

In the battle for Little Round Top, eight regiments and a battery won the actual contest. The 20th Maine harvested all the glory, but the New York 12th and 44th Infantry Regiments inherited the hill. Theirs is by far the largest regimental monument on the battlefield as well as the most blatant attempt to use a monument to elevate a unit's status.

Of the Union regiments that secured the high ground, the 44th New York Infantry and two companies of the 12th New York held the critical center. In their honor, the monument's tower is forty-four feet high, and the base of the adjoining chamber is twelve feet square. This fortress-style tribute dwarfs the two-dozen other dedications in the vicinity. In comparison, the 20th Maine monument is slightly larger than a refrigerator.

Its disproportionate size is due in large part to its rich pedigree. Daniel Butterfield, Meade's chief of staff at Gettysburg, previously led both regiments. "Boy General" FRANCIS C. BARLOW, a superpower in postwar New York law, also commanded the 44th before his promotion. The 44th itself was raised in honor of Ephraim E. Ellsworth, the first Union officer killed in the war and a close friend of Abraham Lincoln. Thus the regiment's nickname—"Ellsworth's Avengers."

When the state of New York allocated fifteen hundred dollars for construction of a monument, veterans and powerful friends raised an additional nine thousand dollars. Butterfield designed the grand edifice himself, and the regiments' central position at the apex of Little Round Top provided a platform unequalled. Dedicated in 1893, the structure held preeminent rank for nearly a century, until literature and film catapulted the 20th Maine to idol status. Yet Ellsworth's men still have a devout following. Ask any child looking up at Little Round Top, and they will say, "Let's go see the castle!"[43]

Along with having an extensive and influential military career, and designing the 44th and 12th New York Monument, Daniel Butterfield also composed the bugle call "Taps."

---

8. THE PEACE LIGHT MEMORIAL

On Oak Hill northwest of town looms a wide yet subdued structure. It was conceived on the battle's fiftieth anniversary, the largest ever reunion of the Civil War. More than forty-seven thousand of the old blue and nine thousand former grays gathered together. Their president, who in his youth wrapped bandages for Confederate troops and who became the first president from the South since Andrew Johnson, beatified the anniversary by laying the cornerstone to a future memorial to everlasting peace. The collective dream of Woodrow Wilson and his countrymen would last but a year as the largest war then in history erupted in the Balkans the following June.[44]

Not until the seventy-fifth anniversary, the last great reunion, did the memorial finally become a reality. To a crowd of a quarter million, including eighteen hundred Civil War veterans, Franklin Delano Roosevelt dedicated the Peace Light Memorial on a sun-drenched July 3, 1938. More than the memorial itself, the president held the veterans aloft, praising their return: "Brought here by the memories of old divided loyalties, but they meet here in a united loyalty to a united cause which the unfolding years have made it easier to see."[45]

The completed memorial, with its wide plaza and flame-crowned pillar, apparently made no worldly impression. Attempting to heal the strife of the bloodiest war in American history, the beacon of harmony was alight for fourteen short months before the Third Reich invaded Poland, signaling the start of the costliest war of all time, a cataclysm that killed more humans than six thousand Gettysburgs put together.

The Peace Light burned from 1938 until the energy crisis of the 1970s. Park officials doused the flame to preserve petroleum. Though later relit, the gas jet was eventually replaced with sodium vapor, and the light has been burning ever since.

---

9. THE NORTH CAROLINA STATE MONUMENT

Union memorials outnumber Confederate structures by more than fifteen to one. The reasons are manifold. Decades of slow postwar recovery left few Southerners solvent enough to construct ornate dedications. Many veterans were also reluctant to regale a loss, let alone one conducted on the "foreign soil" of Pennsylvania. Hard-line Unionists also conspired to keep the Confederate element out of a supposedly pristine picture. Over time, many Northerners recognized that a mistake had been made. Reconciliation required tributes to former foes. Even the most unforgiving Federalists realized that without Confederate markers and statues, the message of a hard-fought victory lost much of its impact. First to act was the U.S. War Department in 1895, openly inviting former Confederates to submit their monuments to the field. The Gettysburg Chamber of Commerce repeated the request decades later.[46]

Yet old wounds healed slowly. The first Confederate state shrine, the Virginia memorial, did not go up until fifty-four years after the battle. The last, Tennessee's, was not completed until 1982. In the end, all eleven Confederate states are represented at Gettysburg. Yet the North Carolina State Monument most signifies a triumph against exclusion, not only against zealous Unionists, but also against their former comrades.

Perpetually in the limelight of Old Dominion, North Carolina had nearly forty regiments and batteries serving in the Army of "Northern Virginia" during the Gettysburg campaign. The Tarheels actually lost far more troops in the battle than Virginia—sixty-one hundred killed, wounded, captured, or missing compared to forty-five hundred. Perhaps this is why the North Carolina memorial emphasizes realism, with lifelike soldiers facing an uncertain destiny and a wounded comrade urging his brethren ever forward. Adding to the human element, all the faces were modeled from actual veterans. Illustrating the state's exceptional role in the rebellion, the flag bearer has the countenance of North Carolinian Orren Randolph Smith, designer of the Stars-and-Bars Confederate national flag.[47]

The chief sculptor for the North Carolina State Monument was Gutzon Borglum. One of Borglum's more famous works is Mount Rushmore.

---

10. THE 90TH PENNSYLVANIA MONUMENT

Hands down, this is the most abstract sculpture present. Since the first monument appeared at Gettysburg, strict regulations have been in place to guard against, among other unwanted peculiarities, overly ethereal pieces. One single memorial flies in the face of this restriction.

At first glance the odd object on Doubleday Avenue appears to be a misshapen pillar. Closer inspection reveals a stalwart trunk of a once grand tree, its top and branches torn away. Climbing up the granite monolith are shoots of bronze ivy. Upon its hacked stumps hang the remnants of soldier life: a canteen, a rucksack, a rifle.

Near the top is a bird's nest with a mother and two young chicks. Lore contends that a nest was knocked from a tree in the heat of the battle, and a soldier of the 90th Pennsylvania risked his life to put it back. More than likely the tale is fictional. Far more real is the monument itself, symbolizing the loss of innocence, departed comrades, human amputation, unspoken valor, and quiet rebirth. Whereas most statuary on the grounds commemorate death, this work is arguably the most overt tribute to life.[48]

Several monument designs have been rejected as too abstract. The original plan for the 1st Minnesota Regiment featured a rifle-wielding soldier clubbing a giant, coiled serpent. Officials dismissed it because of its metaphoric look and how it blatantly equated Southerners with reptiles.

TOP TEN MYTHS AND MISCONCEPTIONS

Thick with hearsay, nostalgia, and alterations after the fact, Gettysburg has been cloaked in more yarn than a New England spinning mill. Many of the tales stemmed from eyewitnesses who could not or would not produce accurate accounts of what actually transpired. Confederate Brig. Gen. John B. Gordon swore the U.S. 11th Corps gave him "a most obstinate resistance" on day one, whereas Union Brig. Gen. Francis C. Barlow claimed, "No fight at all was made." Few agreed on how long the Confederate artillery barrage before Pickett's Charge lasted, with guesses varying from forty minutes to two hours. There are at least five "verbatim" versions of the Gettysburg Address.[49]

Many legends originated decades after, crafted by guesswork and story making, mostly in the interest of creating or confirming heroes. Wistful "histories" also worked to turn Gettysburg into an idyllic Valhalla, a battleground upon which noble warriors disemboweled each other with the utmost mutual respect.

While truth is often in the eye of the beholder, fable is often entrenched in the public mind. Following are ten among many apocryphal stories of Gettysburg, along with their origins, that persist despite the weight of evidence against them. They are listed in order of their supposed appearance in the course of events.

1.   THE BATTLE BEGAN AS A FIGHT OVER SHOES

In his memoirs, Confederate Gen. Henry Heth claimed to have sent his brigades into Gettysburg on July 1 for the sole purpose of confiscating shoes. His recollection formed the popular notion that an innocent search for brogans led to the bloodiest battle in the Civil War.[50]

In truth, 2nd Corps commander A. P. Hill ordered Heth to conduct reconnaissance in force. Critics contend Heth may have used the shoe tale to cover his missteps. His aggressive rush into Gettysburg helped bring about a major engagement, contrary to Robert E. Lee's strict orders to avoid one.[51]

If commandeering supplies was his intent, Heth had no reason to commit nearly an entire division to do so, and there was no intelligence to suggest Gettysburg held a large supply of shoes. Maj. Gen. John B. Gordon's brigade stormed through the town not five days before and made no report of any such cache.

This is not to say the Confederates were disinterested in finding new footwear. Many a Johnny Reb slogged into the North with bare feet. Thousands more wore out their soles en route as rain, rivers, and rocky soil consumed their pods in short order. After capturing a unit of Pennsylvania militia, a group of Confederates paroled them and set them free, minus their shoes. The *New York Times* noted, "A boot and shoe dealer in Mechanicsburg was completely cleaned out of his entire stock, and all he had to show for it was $4,000 in worthless rebel currency."[52]

Lee's Confederates were in fact scouring southern Pennsylvania for everything of military worth, including food, blankets, horses, mules, munitions, and anything else the strapped army could grab. During the campaign, his men confiscated more than one hundred thousand head of livestock. Several pharmacies were cleaned out. While on a poorly timed raid around the Army of the Potomac, Jeb Stuart confiscated more than a hundred wagons for the chief purpose of transporting wares back south.[53]

There were no shoe factories or warehouses in Gettysburg, though the town did have twenty-two people who listed their profession as cobbler.

---

2.   HARRISON THE SPY WAS AN ACTOR

Immortalized in the novel *Killer Angels* and the film *Gettysburg,* the stealth scout for Gen. James Longstreet was said to be a Shakespearean actor, skilled in masking his true identity while operating behind enemy lines.

Though much of his past is an enigma, it is known that Henry Thomas Harrison was not an actor. Born and raised near Nashville, Tennessee, he joined a Confederate rifle company at the start of the war and was subsequently attached to the 12th Mississippi. While his regiment was serving in Virginia, Harrison was discharged for "medical reasons." Officials quite possibly relieved him so that he could pursue a more sublime talent. Soon after his dismissal, Harrison was spying for the South on a full-time basis.

Paid occasionally by the Confederate War Department, he went on to serve in Maryland, North Carolina, the Trans-Mississippi, Virginia, and Washington DC. During the march into Pennsylvania, Harrison gave his now famous report to Longstreet and Lee that the Union army was on the move and closing in on their invasion force.

After the battle, Harrison operated primarily in the North, gathering intelligence while living in New York, never matching his great discovery in the days before Gettysburg. Historian John Bakeless later claimed that Harrison was actually a famed actor named James Harrison, but the allegation was without merit.[54]

> The notion that Henry T. Harrison had been in theater was true to some extent. Two months after Gettysburg, a friend allegedly bet him fifty dollars to walk on stage at the New Richmond Theater while a play was in progress. Never afraid of a challenge, Harrison reportedly accepted the wager, waltzed out amongst the footlights, and won the bet.

3. REYNOLDS WAS KILLED BY A SHARPSHOOTER

Senior officers stand apart in the annals of war. History paints their life and death in reverence. During the Civil War especially, reports of famous officers falling from accident or random chance did not make for exciting print. Consequently, many field commanders fatally shot were assumed to be the victims of stealthy field assassins.

It is often contended that Maj. Gen. John F. Reynolds, while commanding the Union lines in person on the first day, was struck down by a sniper hiding in a nearby tree. *New York Times* correspondent Lorenzo Crounse stated as much in his July 2 dispatch, and several postwar histories mimicked the report. Reynolds's sister Jennie corroborated the story by stating she believed the fatal bullet traveled downward from his head and into his chest.[55]

In truth, Reynolds died while on horseback not more than one hundred yards from the Confederate lines, well within rifle range. Moments before his demise, Reynolds ordered a charge, which resulted in an immediate response of heavy Confederate volleys directed toward his position.

The possibility of a Confederate sniper's shooting from a nearby tree is dubious. Federals had occupied the position for nearly a day. It is highly unlikely that a sniper could have stayed hidden or found his way into the area unnoticed. That the would-be killer would have waited so long without trying his luck against Brig. Gen. JOHN BUFORD or another high-ranking officer is impressive, and that the marksman somehow rendered his fatal blow from very short range and remained undetected afterward is downright spectacular.

Soon after the war, a story surfaced of a sniper positioned much farther away. Allegedly Benjamin Thorpe from the 26th North Carolina headshot Reynolds from eight hundred yards while perched in a cherry tree. Why he chose such a frail perch is unknown. Also not established was how he was able to see clearly through branches, which in July would have been leafed-out and bearing fruit. Lastly, his muzzle velocity must have been a bit slow, because Private Thorpe reportedly fired his weapon at 9 a.m., and Reynolds went down at 10:30.[56]

> The most prized sniper rifle among the Confederates was the English-made Whitworth, of which fewer than a hundred were procured. It could kill from a mile away and was credited for having slain Union general and Gettysburg veteran John Sedgwick at Spotsylvania.

4.   LEE ORDERED A DAWN ATTACK FOR THE SECOND DAY

Unwilling to pass judgment on Lee, many Southerners blamed others for the defeat at Gettysburg. JEB STUART was a favorite target, with his cavalry missing in action at a critical time of the battle's development. Critics also accused A. P. Hill for not capturing Cemetery Ridge early in the battle. Heavy criticism also fell on Richard "Baldy" Ewell and Jubal "Jubilee" Early for not pressing harder on the Union right flank.

First Corps commander James Longstreet, however, was largely spared of blame. That is, until 1872, nearly two years after Lee's death, when Early addressed students and faculty at Washington and Lee University on the anniversary of Lee's birthday.

Early contended that on the night of July 1, 1863, Lee ordered Longstreet to "attack at sunrise" while Union defenses were thought to be minimal. When the morrow came, Longstreet attacked, but not until early afternoon, and his men were summarily turned back with bloody losses. Had Longstreet only followed orders, Early insinuated, the battle would have been won.[57]

A year after Early's public accusation, former Confederate general William Pendleton, no friend of Longstreet's, repeated Early's assertion, adding to the growing suspicion that Longstreet was guilty of at least lethargy, if not sedition.

Certainly Gettysburg was not Longstreet's finest hour, but evidence contradicts the notion of a dawn-attack order. First, much of the morning was occupied conducting reconnaissance, by order of Lee. Due to the absent Stuart, the Union disposition was still unknown. Lee wanted to collect more information before ordering another assault. Second, Longstreet was in no position to launch a morning offensive, and Lee knew it. His 1st Corps was nowhere near the front by the end of the first day. The nearest division was three miles distant. The farthest was more than ten miles to the rear. Third, Longstreet and his division commanders confirmed after the war that none of them received any such order from Lee or anyone else to attack so soon. Still, the myth endured well into the twentieth century, cultivated by Longstreet's detractors, many of whom were highly motivated to direct attention away from their own shortcomings at Gettysburg.

After Appomattox, James Longstreet did little to endear himself with his former comrades. He joined the Republican Party, accepted posts given to him by the federal government, and wrote a history of the Civil War that was critical of many prominent Confederates, including Robert E. Lee.

---

5. ONLY THE 20TH MAINE SAVED LITTLE ROUND TOP

According to Joshua Lawrence Chamberlain, the famous charge of his 20th Maine down Little Round Top spared the Union left flank from almost certain ruin. His admirers later contended that his solitary action probably won the battle if not the war.

Chamberlain was an unquestionably brave, intelligent, and driven man. Before age twenty he had learned to read several modern and ancient languages and eventually became an accomplished professor of several subjects at his alma mater, Bowdoin College. Yet the scholarly Chamberlain often depicted the war in romantic, idealistic terms. In his quixotic eyes, his service at the head of the 20th Maine was fate, Union victory was ordained by Providence, and his charge down Little Round Top "swept the valley and cleared the front of nearly our entire brigade."[58]

In reality the Union held Little Round Top by the collective effort of eight Union regiments, one artillery battery, and a section of regular U.S. Army sharpshooters. Chamberlain's charge was just the last of many Union counterattacks as combat flowed up and down Little Round Top throughout the afternoon of the battle's second day. Although Chamberlain and his two brothers survived the fight, another regimental commander, the battery commander, and both brigade commanders stationed on the hill did not. As for the 20th Maine's immortal charge, several men of the 2nd Maine, 44th New York, 83rd Pennsylvania, and U.S. Sharpshooters also took part.[59]

In recalling the fight for Little Round Top, Col. Joshua Lawrence Chamberlain asserted that his men were outnumbered ten to one. In reality, the ratio was less than two to one.

---

6. CONFEDERATES AND FEDERALS SHARED SPANGLER'S SPRING

At the bottom of Culp's Hill, in the marshy fields wrapped around its southern base, flowed a freshwater basin known as Spangler's Spring. The story goes that in the darkness of July 2, after a brutal night of fighting on the hill, bluecoats and graybacks called an unofficial truce and filled their canteens together at the spring.

The tale was not unlike others that took root after the war. By the 1880s, many former enemies longed for reconciliation. Wilting were memories of lethal hatred and bloodshed, and growing in their place were tales of camaraderie.

Regardless of postwar revisions, there was no such brotherly love at Spangler's Spring. Both sides endured severe casualties not moments before the alleged meeting, and both were on the lookout for enemy movements. A few Union soldiers who fetched water at the basin recalled seeing what they believed to be Confederate troops standing a short distance away. But there are no accounts from either side to suggest that contact, let alone a friendly gathering, ever took place.[60]

Cordial exchanges and generosity did occur between mortal adversaries during the war, though such meetings were less frequent than is popularly imagined, and most fraternization transpired during fallow moments.

Strangely enough, spring water was just as dangerous as the enemy. Nearly a third of all Civil War deaths came from contaminated water, as it was the chief cause of dysentery, diarrhea, cholera, and typhoid. Altogether water-born diseases killed more than two hundred thousand soldiers, nearly twice the number that fell in combat.

---

7. LEE TOLD THE ENLISTED, "IT IS ALL MY FAULT"

The scene: General Lee rides out to meet his brave, battered survivors of Pickett's Charge. In a magnificent gesture, he accepts full responsibility. "It is all my fault," he tells the enlisted. His troops respond with cries to the negative, and the majority beg to launch yet another attack.

Many prominent Civil War authors suggest the incident happened, yet there is no ironclad evidence. Several soldiers claimed Lee consoled Maj. Gen. George E. Pickett directly, saying, "The fault is entirely my own." English military observer Lt. Col. Arthur Fremantle and an officer from the 5th Florida overheard Lee utter a similar sentiment to Brig. Gen. Cadmus M. Wilcox as well, commiserating over the tremendous losses inflicted upon Wilcox's brigade.[61]

As for the lower ranks, Lee's greatest concern was to ready them for a probable Union counterattack. Appropriately, his first orders were to gather up men and prepare for a defensive stand. But no verifiable account survives that has the commanding general offering a wholesale apology to his throngs of enlisted. The closest he came, according to a major in the 8th Virginia, was a statement issued to a crowd of men that had returned from Cemetery Ridge. The wording was less than apologetic: "My men, it was not your fault."[62]

Lee was not always kind to the lower ranks. Ten days after Appomattox, the general wrote to Jefferson Davis and explained that the fall of Richmond and Petersburg was due primarily to the failure of his troops, insisting, "Except in particular instances, they were feeble."

---

8. LINCOLN WROTE THE GETTYSBURG ADDRESS ON THE BACK OF AN ENVELOPE

As intriguing as the image might be of inspired words falling upon parchment moments before their arrival with destiny, the Gettysburg Address was far from a spontaneous creation. Yet Lincoln's homily was long assumed to have been written in the eleventh hour.

In 1865 the *New York Evening Post* insisted Lincoln scratched out the address just moments before the dedication. David Wills, president of the Gettysburg cemetery commission and host to Lincoln during his visit, claimed Lincoln started writing the speech the night before. The 1906 book *A Perfect Tribute* claimed the work was penciled on brown wrapping paper during the train ride into town. When the book became a classroom text in 1910, the myth embedded itself into the hearts and minds of America schoolchildren.[63]

These accounts are highly inaccurate. Invited two weeks before the event, Lincoln accepted with the intent of making a statement. His entire purpose of going to Gettysburg was to communicate that message. Pressured by the demands of the war and office, he had neither the time nor inclination to go to a cemetery commencement far away from Washington simply as an observer. Per usual, he would leave little to chance.

Lincoln disdained giving extemporaneous speeches, preferring instead the security and precision of a thoroughly polished script, with every word carefully measured for effect. As was his custom, he spent some time mentally assembling his thoughts before committing them to paper. Writing in longhand, he began at least three days before departure. Two days before he left, someone asked the president to describe his composition. He responded that it was "short, short, short. . . . Written but not finished."[64]

Lincoln wrote the first page on White House stationery in ink and the second page on different paper in lead, suggesting, as many observers contended, that Lincoln finished the work either the night before or the morning of the commencement. No verifiable account has him writing anything on the six-hour train ride to Gettysburg. The crowded cars, numerous transfers, and multiple meetings gave him no opportunity to work on the address, a fact confirmed by his attending secretaries.[65]

> Over the years, many people believed Lincoln wrote the Gettysburg Address on the top of his stovepipe hat, though no one explained how he could fit 272 words on such a small space or how he was able to read black ink on black fabric.

9. THE SOLDIERS' MONUMENT MARKS WHERE LINCOLN SPOKE

The Soldiers' National Monument stands prominently within the Soldiers' National Cemetery, its great marble pillar adorned with statuary and stationed before the semicircle of Union graves. For years many believed this sculpture marked the spot where Lincoln, Everett, and others spoke in 1863. For decades the National Parks Department assumed this to be the case, as did several prominent authors. They were working on limited information. Every newspaper and personal account of the ceremony neglected to specify the exact location of the rostrum, and no specific landmark was available at the time to provide a point of reference. Many of the recollections were contradictory, with some claiming the stage faced toward the soldiers' burial plots while most had it facing away or to the side.[66]

Later analysis of photographs taken during Lincoln's visit suggests the speakers' platform actually stood to the southeast of the eventual placement of the monument. Former park historian Kathleen Georg Harrison estimates Lincoln stood close to what is now the Brown family vault within the confines of Evergreen Cemetery adjacent to the military cemetery. At the time, that particular area of the public cemetery was void of graves, trees, shrubs, and the tall iron fence that currently separates the graveyards. Situated near the apex of Cemetery Hill, the probable spot provided the awe-inspiring backdrop of a thousand Union graves, and beyond them the evocative vista of the battlefield itself.[67]

The Soldiers' Monument has on it a statue representing peace. Unlike most renditions of serenity, this figure is a man.

---

10. NOTABLE GETTYSBURG GEN. ABNER DOUBLEDAY INVENTED THE GAME OF BASEBALL

In 1907 sports equipment mogul A. G. Spalding assembled a commission to determine the origin of America's pastime. Consisting of a U.S. senator and several distinguished members of the sporting community, but without a single historian in the lineup, the board ascertained that Abner Doubleday, former Union general of the 1st Corps at Gettysburg, had established the basic rules of baseball in Cooperstown, New York, in 1839.

Doubleday was a popular if not patriotic selection. He was viewed at the time to be a hero of Gettysburg. Also a veteran of Fort Sumter, Second Manassas, Antietam, Fredericksburg, and Chancellorsville, and hailing from a prominent New York family, Doubleday was known to have promoted the game before the war, teaching the basics to his fellow cadets at West Point.

Despite the commission's attempt to claim sole American ownership, an abundance of historical evidence places the game's birthplace in eighteenth-century England. Known then as rounders, baseball, or feeder, the sport involved a stick and ball, rotating batters and fielders, and four posts or bases (the batter sometimes stood between the first and fourth bases). Boys of the royal family were quite fond of the game.[68]

Immigrants brought rounders to the New World, where it became popular among children as "Old Cat," which used two or more bases, depending on the number of players available. In the early 1800s "town baseball" incorporated the idea of opposing teams, and by the 1830s clubs and leagues began to form. By the time Doubleday came to the plate, the use of four bases, three strikes, three outs, and other fundamentals were already part of the old ball game.

Civil War soldiers who played baseball in camp were following an American military tradition. In 1778, George Washington's men filled some of their idle hours playing a version of the game at Valley Forge.

TOP TEN AREAS OF GREATEST CHANGE

Initially a modest commercial site, Gettysburg was certainly not alone as it endured the vile intervention of battle. Before its residents ever experienced their first whiff of cannon smoke, Winchester, Virginia, had changed hands more than a score of times. Whole counties of western Missouri had been devastated by border wars. Fredericksburg had suffered through two major battles, undergone months of military occupation, and lay torched and gutted. Residents of Vicksburg, entering their fourth week of siege, were reduced to eating family pets and living in earthen bomb shelters to stay alive.

All of these communities would survive. So would hundreds more cities, towns, and townships that were yet destined to feel the war firsthand. But the Hades surrounding Devil's Den, the dreadful reaping at the Wheatfield, and the finest hour of Pickett's Charge would come to be known and visited by more Americans than any battlefield, and the reason has to do with the *way* Gettysburg survived.

Unlike Fredericksburg, Vicksburg, or New Orleans, Gettysburg hosted combatants for a comparatively miniscule period of time. Though some homes and business were damaged, every building in town remained standing, and rail service resumed within a week, as opposed to the decimation leveled later upon the Shenandoah Valley, the Georgia heartland, and the Virginia Piedmont. Large enough to accommodate outsiders, and small enough to be known foremost as a battle site, Gettysburg rested neither on the front lines nor in the western hinterlands. In short, among the principle fields of valor, Gettysburg was far and away the most accessible.

To the south, the Confederacy had several sites of glory on home soil, but there was little time or means to memorialize any one of them. While the Gettysburg Battlefield Memorial Association (GBMA) was calling to order its first meeting mere weeks after the battle had ended, towns farther south were still fighting to stay alive. Two years later, as the GBMA began buying acreages for posterity, the Confederate experiment would concede defeat and consequently cast an infinite shadow upon every triumph past.

As illustrated above, the war provided the Union, and Gettysburg, with every advantage required to build a great monument to victory.

Demonstrated below, the image of the "ultimate battle" would ultimately be less about preservation and more about reinvention. The following is a brief tour of the battlefield's key buildings and geographic features and how they have transformed over time to reveal a much different picture than what actually existed. They are ranked in descending order by the amount of physical alterations each has experienced.

1. THE TOWN

At the outset of the war, Gettysburg contained twenty-five hundred residents. Currently the population is just under eight thousand. While this might be viewed as valiant resistance against the blitzkrieg of urbanization, development has nonetheless altered the town's countenance immensely. If Billy Yank or Johnny Reb were to return and gaze upon the landscape, Seminary and Cemetery Ridge would have a vague familiarity, Culp's Hill, Devil's Den, and the Round Tops would be self-evident, but the town would seem utterly extraterrestrial.

Though a crossroads since its inception, the town of 1863 had far fewer, narrower, quieter streets than the twenty-first-century version. Pavement was still decades away. There were no posted addresses or directional signs. Still standing are the TRAIN DEPOT, the WILLS HOME, and all three residences tied to JENNIE WADE (birthplace, residence, and death site). Other structures known to have endured currently wear small brass markers stamped "Civil War Building," but most are largely updated or easily missed in the congestion. Lost are hundreds of homes and businesses. The PRESBYTERIAN CHURCH where Lincoln attended services after his Gettysburg Address was torn down and rebuilt. The Eagle Hotel and the Wagon Hotel, used by both armies, have been replaced by minimarts.[69]

For many residents, whether for or against preservation, the root word of "battlefield" was "field." Of all the areas contemplated as worthy of sparing, the town itself was last. Domiciles and buildings were altered or replaced, and new construction continued as a matter of daily life. In the interest of expanding tax revenues, outlying areas were developed acres at a time. Invigorated by the influx of cash-toting tourists, merchants catered to the whims of their customer base. For the train travelers of the early twentieth century, it was hotels, museums, and saloons. For parents driving the kid-packed station wagons of the 1950s, it was motels, playgrounds, and burger stands. For the one-child or no-child history hounds of the 1980s, it was bed-and-breakfasts, bookshops, and period restaurants.

Today the town functions as much for its permanent residents as it does for its temporary ones, with a mixture of the historical and the practical. Nearly four times its battle-era population, the city is ten times larger in area, the manifestation of a society that needs its space.

One element remains unaltered. Contemporary residents often view tourists just as their forebears viewed the Union army: as an overwhelming force, simultaneously threatening their domestic tranquility and promoting their general welfare.

Recently a log cabin was discovered within the city limits, hidden under various layers of exterior sidings. After extensive restoration, the home now proudly bears the brass marker of a Civil War building.

---

2. CEMETERY RIDGE

For preservation purists, Cemetery Ridge truly is the high water mark. No land area of the battlefield has undergone greater exploitation and recovered to a greater extent than the former backbone of the Union's defense.

The first wave of a most bizarre offensive came in 1959, when Kenneth and Thelma Dick managed to overpower the land Robert E. Lee failed to reach. On twenty-plus privately owned acres, which soon grew beyond thirty, these two kitsch-visionaries built Fantasyland, a sprawling storybook village with rides and attractions galore. Families boated on three man-made lakes, strolled through the Enchanted Forest, and caught a quick snack at the Gingerbread House. At Fort Apache, cowboys and Indians fought to the death in eight shows a day. Santa Claus summered here, along with the Old Woman in the Shoe and Little Red Riding Hood. Somewhat callous to what happened a century before, patrons rolled around the park on a diminutive choo-choo dubbed the *Cannonball Express*. Standing guard over it all was a twenty-foot-high, forty-foot-wide picture book propped along Taneytown Road. To temper the eyesore, the National Park Service opened a visitors center nearby in 1962, reminding people that Gettysburg was a battlefield before it became a recreational area.

Over time, a collective realization emerged that cotton candy and coonskin caps were grossly inappropriate given the immediate surroundings. By 1974 the U.S. government purchased the land from the Dicks. Fantasyland closed in 1980, and its contents were parceled off to other amusement parks.

While one "attraction" came down, another was already up and running. Just beyond the southern edge of Evergreen Cemetery, on six acres not yet acquired by the government, developers provided day-trippers with snack bars, viewing telescopes, a "Sutler's Gift & Souvenir Store," and canned polka—three hundred feet above the ground. Opened in 1974, weighing almost two million pounds, embedded in fifteen thousand tons of concrete, the battleship-gray, hour-glass latticework of beams and rivets could hold seven hundred gawkers in its multistoried, climate-controlled, glass-and-steel noggin. Though providing a stunning and comprehensive view of the entire battlefield, its overbearing and futuristic design was nearly as out of place as its presumptive title of "the National Battlefield Tower."

A federal fight ensued in the 1990s to acquire and dismantle the looming overlook, an attack bitterly resisted by the tower's deeply invested owners and their grateful clientele. One hostile takeover and three million dollars in compensation later, the pet project was scheduled to be put down. On July 4, 2000, as a few pounds of skillfully placed explosives shattered its legs, the transcendence tumbled over with booming ceremony.

Grading and reseeding have all but eradicated the tower's traces while another structure evolved a few hundred paces away. Yet this has a design both indigenous and ingenious, meant to welcome and engage rather than lure and siphon. The new Gettysburg National Battlefield Park Visitors Center grows off Hunt Avenue, with architecture drawn from hearty country homesteads and wide Dutch barns. When the old center to the north finally comes down—an addition-riddled blockhouse next to an obtrusive cyclorama—Cemetery Ridge will reach one step closer to its fundamental nature.

The original price tag for the new Gettysburg visitors center was less than $40 million. Design improvements and sundries eventually pushed the cost to $100 million.

---

3.   PICKETT'S CHARGE

Treated today as sacred land, the green mile from Seminary Ridge to the stone wall was once the abode of a trolley line, railroad tracks, grinding tank treads, and for a few months, latrines for members of the Third Reich.

Looking to provide an inexpensive and popular tour for the masses, the Gettysburg Electric Railway started laying down track in 1893 across the battlefield. Starting in town, the line ran southwest along the Emmitsburg road, through the Peach Orchard and the Wheatfield before looping to the Round Tops. The following year the Gettysburg and Harrisburg Railroad offered similar access from the state capital, passing west of Gettysburg proper, then southeast. The two commercial lines formed a giant X across Pickett's Charge, irreverently overlapping a few hundred yards east of the Angle and the Copse of Trees.

By 1917 the electric line had ceased operation, but the railroad would stay for two more decades. It was near this line, as it passed by the Codori farm, that the U.S. Army constructed a training camp for soldiers headed for Flanders fields. Peaking at eight thousand doughboys, including a promising young commandant named Dwight David Eisenhower, the facilities contained barracks, horse stables, firing ranges, and a chow hall. Named Camp Colt in 1918, the compound switched from time-tested infantry to the innovation of armored tanks. With gnashing tracks, six-ton, diesel-spewing behemoths roared and rolled over the paths of twelve thousand ghosts. In 1919, after the termination of "the war to end all wars," the camp was dismantled.[70]

In 1933, at the perigee of the Great Depression, the land of Pickett's Charge again became a servant to the greater good. The Civil Conservation Corps, established by the U.S. government to provide jobs for the unemployed, established a compound along the southern length of Seminary Ridge. Hundreds of laborers constructed roads, retaining walls, walking paths, and other public works in and outside the park. The complex ceased operation in 1937, but some of the barracks and concrete slabs remained.[71]

Then, in 1944, when local farmers were in dire need of farmhands, the U.S. War Department authorized the construction of a German POW stockade on the abandoned Camp Colt. Five hundred prisoners were brought in—from a Maryland facility called Camp George Gordon

Meade—to harvest apples, cherries, corn, peas, and timber. Some of the captive Wehrmacht worked at canning factories and a nearby quarry. Many spent their days maintaining the grounds of the park.

The onset of winter required more permanent housing, resulting in a transfer of prisoners to the old CCC site and its clapboard barracks. By 1946 detainees had all been returned to Germany. Years later a few came back to the park, carrying fond memories of the one battlefield that granted them safety.[72]

Few traces of the military and work camps endure, but one of them permanently left its mark. Months of tank exercises conducted at Camp Colt undoubtedly altered the topography of Pickett's Charge, but with no surviving Civil War panoramas of the area, there is no way to measure the damage.

---

4. HERR RIDGE TO SEMINARY RIDGE

The battle started upon the succession of ridges west of town. For four days Lee and his army called these rises home. They were the foundation of his operations. Yet, unlike the conspicuous Union strongholds of Culp's Hill and the Round Tops, which were spared from residential and commercial development since the very beginning, these subtle land waves had no such protectors. As a result, much of the relevant scenery and topography have been lost to newer housing, convenience stores, a nursing home, and a golf course.[73]

Knoxlyn Ridge, where Lee first set eyes on Gettysburg and determined he would stay, is currently indistinguishable. Next in is Herr Ridge. The Herr Tavern, present at the time of the battle, still exists and provides a landmark, but the rise's superior height and width is lost among housing construction. The once open view to the east is gone, except from lawns inaccessible to the general public. Only the rim of earth extending south from the seminary is still worthy of being called a ridge. Sparsely inhabited when it served as the staging area for Pickett's Charge, it presently wears busy Confederate Avenue on its back and lies prostrate from housing eating away at its southern end.[74]

Of nearly four hundred battlefields of the American Civil War, only 15 percent currently have some degree of federal protection. Of the rest, roughly 30 percent are endangered, and another 30 percent have been lost entirely to real estate development.

---

5. GETTYSBURG COLLEGE

Gettysburg resident Samuel Schmucker was an ardent abolitionist, an agent on the Underground Railroad, and the founder of the Lutheran Theological Seminary. He also established the College of Pennsylvania, known today as Gettysburg College.

The school's beginnings were modest—three buildings set upon an austere field just north of town. Classes were in session on the morning of July 1, 1863, until thudding brass cannon and crackling steel rifles interrupted lectures on rhetoric and mathematics. Peering through north-side panes of the main building of Pennsylvania Hall, students could see clouds of gun smoke lofting from the north and west. The flat land before them provided few obstructions. Union flagmen would use this prime lookout to their advantage, setting up a signal station at the college. Yet the landscape also offered few obstacles to an attacking army. Hours later, the Union 1st and 11th Corps would learn this lesson to their great terror, fleeing across the campus as they sprinted south.[75]

A day later, the college held more than seven hundred wounded, most of them Confederates. Rooms and hallways were packed. Floors were saturated with blood. For the next two months, the main building and the surrounding grounds functioned as one of the largest hospitals in the area.

In the present day, such scenarios are barely conceivable. As the city has grown, so has the college, exponentially, with more than eighty buildings spread across a half-mile diameter. Residential neighborhoods span beyond, and the open sightlines that were available to the class of '63 are long gone.

Whatever the school has lost physically, it has more than compensated academically. Gettysburg College is home to the Civil War Institute, sponsoring exhibits, granting scholarships, organizing tours, and awarding prizes to outstanding works in Civil War fiction and nonfiction. Guest lecturers have included former Supreme Court Justice Sandra Day O'Connor and historian James M. McPherson. It also directs the "Gettysburg

Semester," allowing visiting undergraduates to immerse themselves in the study of the War Between the States, covering everything from the antebellum era to, appropriately, battlefield reclamation.

Echoing the battle, Gettysburg College's athletic teams are called the Bullets. But the school colors are blue and orange, not blue and gray.

---

6. THE LUTHERAN SEMINARY

Constructed in 1832, the Lutheran Theological Seminary of Gettysburg consisted of the Schmucker house, the Knuth house, and the "Old Dorm." At the time of the battle, the institution stood far outside the limits of town and served as the virtual epicenter of the first day's fighting.

Atop the four-story, red-brick dorm perched the bright white cupola, the same vantage that would provide both Union and Confederate observers, and perhaps R. E. Lee himself, with supreme views of the surrounding landscape. Presently under the care of the Adams County Historical Society and still a functioning seminary, the building is open to the general public, but the cupola is not. Just as well. Development of the town has completely blocked off its once sweeping views to the east and south.

Enveloping the campus, modern homes and buildings also hide the fact that this was the last bastion between the HERBST WOODS to the west and the town to the east. It was here, behind a semicircle of hastily built breastworks piled near the west side of the dorm, that the Union's Iron Brigade fought their last stand (see BLOODIEST FIELDS OF FIRE). Today

The Lutheran seminary's cupola was used as an observation post by both sides. Union Gen. John Buford scanned the first assault from here, and allegedly Robert E. Lee took advantage of the perch during the battle.

LIBRARY OF CONGRESS

the area looks more like a serene suburban setting than the site of a ruinous last stand, and the location of the Blacks Hats' Armageddon remains unmarked.[76]

Founded in 1826, the seminary is the oldest continuing Lutheran seminary in the United States.

---

7. THE TREE LINES

The view south from the city has undergone a drastic, albeit natural, misshaping. The forestation of the battlefield has shifted dramatically over the years, covering some areas that were bare and thinning others that were almost impenetrable. Aside from the general development of the town, the ever-changing vegetation marks the starkest contrast to the original scene, as it is easier to look past the tourist throngs and automobile processions than it is to mentally reconstruct the location and density of foliage in 1863.

Culp's Hill to the southeast serves as a prime example. Thoroughly covered in tall thickets today, passages were generally thinner during the fight, with some areas relatively open. Far to the west of town, the HERBST WOODS, a.k.a. McPherson's Woods, was neither as large nor as dense as it is presently, explaining why Union general JOHN F. REYNOLDS was so lethally exposed to Confederate rifle fire on day one. To the south, Little Round Top was far more open on its west side. Its exposed rocks made the area appear more like hardscrabble badlands than a lush park. So, too, the northwest base of Big Round Top was open to the sky. Alabama and Georgia boys who ran through this lower stretch of Plum Run Creek were heading into a crossfire from Devil's Den to the left and Little Round Top to the right. Had they the shelter of the current wall of trees, the few who survived would have had no reason to call the area the Slaughter Pen.

In an unprecedented effort to fully reestablish the tree lines and plant life of the time, the National Park Service and the Friends of the National Park at Gettysburg have begun the long process of removing nonhistoric trees and replanting woods, crops, and orchards lost. Some of the more remarkable reclamations are the cultivation of cherry trees in the farms to the northwest, a replanting of croplands at the Trostle farm, an expansion of the Peach Orchard, and a retraction of the woods along Wheatfield Road.

Today the National Park Service and volunteer workers labor constantly to control the spread of volunteer trees. In the 1860s this work was done by cattle, contentedly grazing the acres of Adams County and thereby keeping whole areas clear of underbrush and saplings.

---

8. CEMETERY HILL

Impossible to overlook is the Soldiers' National Cemetery just south of town. Situated on a prominent knoll, this pacific scene is home to tenured trees, the towering Soldiers' Monument, and a flush semicircle of headstones resting above three thousand Union dead. Adjoining on the east side of the hill is the sprawling Evergreen Cemetery. To the west, just across the Baltimore Pike, are the hulking visitors center, the colossal cake-box cyclorama building, and rambling parking lots (all slated for dismantling). Pervasive is the sense of being away from the battlefield, but nothing could be further from the truth. Cemetery Hill was, from day one, the critical high ground of the conflict.

In 1863 this was bare land offering wide-open vistas. The civilian graveyard was a fraction of its current size. Immense shade trees that block the surrounding view were not yet present. Also absent were most nearby structures. A soldier could stand on this rise and see for miles, including the undulation of Seminary Ridge to the west, wooded Culp's Hill to the east, and stone-crowned Little Round Top to the south.

The present cannons and monuments are more than ornamental. They mark Union battery and infantry positions during the battle. It was here that the retreating 1st and 11th Corps stopped and dug in their heels on the first day, and several Union officers came to the conclusion that Gettysburg would be fine country in which to stage a fight. In the late hours of the second day, Cemetery Hill's north and east sides witnessed brutal hand-to-hand fighting. It was here on the third day that Confederate volleys smashed civilian gravestones and disemboweled men and horses while Union batteries answered in kind. From here, Pickett's Charge could be seen almost in its entirety, inspiring foot soldiers standing on this place to either slink away to the east or charge headlong to the west.

Soon the obstructions of the current park buildings and car lots are to be removed. In deference to the deceased, however, the choirs of oaks and maples will remain.[77]

The famous gatehouse on the north side of Cemetery Hill still stands, though with a large addition built on the west side in 1868 and porches added in 1896.

---

9. DEVIL'S DEN AND LITTLE ROUND TOP

Little Round Top and its bedeviled neighbor to the west were longtime protectorates of the battlefield park, but their surrounding bases were not. In the early twentieth century the locales were the endpoints of both the electric trolley and the Gettysburg and Harrisburg rail spur.

Humming in from the Wheatfield, curling around the southern side of Devil's Den, the single-car trolley made a jolly jaunt over the Slaughter Pen and up through the Valley of Death. Rather than the geographic features it traversed, the shuttle's main attraction for years was Tipton Park, a thirteen-acre recreation area in the shadow of Big Round Top, featuring a dance pavilion and refreshment stands. Also popular was its photography studio, specializing in family and military reunion portraits in front of Devil's Den.[78]

Competing for business was Little Round Top Park, situated at the northern foot of its namesake at the intersections of Sedgwick Avenue and Wheatfield Road. Fed by the terminus of the G&H Railroad, the amusement site included eateries, a dance hall, a museum, and relic vendors. In 1913 a small casino was added, attracting practitioners and connoisseurs of the oldest profession. Falling and in and out of favor, Little Round Top Park managed to stay in business until 1939, when most of the buildings were demolished and the rail tracks removed.[79]

Strangely, far greater damage to the area may have occurred through the well-intended actions of the battlefield park. In 1902, in order to accommodate a small but growing number of automobilists, the parks commission began to build roads where none had existed, including Chamberlain Avenue, which arched around the east side of Little Round Top. Ensuing years of grading, widening, and changing the routes through Devil's Den and the neighboring mounts utterly reshaped their original slopes. Later removal of Chamberlain Avenue exacerbated the problem between the Round Tops, forming a much shallower valley than the 20th Maine and the 15th Alabama ever saw. Of the thirty miles of smooth roadways running through the current park, among the most intrusive have been these ribbons wrapped through and over this southernmost section. So much manmade change has occurred that any attempt to remold the area back to its original form would be pure guesswork.[80]

> Though faint, the railbed of the Gettysburg Electric Trolley can still be seen near Devil's Den, particularly where it crosses Plum Run and heads toward Little Round Top.

10. NEILL AVENUE/LOST LANE

Bittersweet is the realization that some parts of the battlefield have survived almost untouched and yet they are unreachable. Such is the case with Thomas Neill Avenue to the east of Cemetery Ridge. Here stood the Union's extreme right flank on July 2–3. Of Meade's legendary "fishhook" formation, this represented the sharpened barb. Manning the point were regiments of the 7th Maine, the 43rd and 49th New York, and the 61st Pennsylvania. Though not heavily involved in the fighting, these infantry units of the Union 6th Corps helped prevent any Confederate flanking movements from striking their tender Federal backside.

Standing guard over this area today are granite and bronze monuments to each of these four regiments, but they are blocked from view. While the National Park Service owns the strip of land upon which the monuments stand, private property completely surrounds it all. At one time the public could walk unhindered to this area and look upon its pristine fields and pastures as if they were stepping back in time. But the pathway has been closed for years at the discretion of the protective property owners. Hence the area's nickname: Lost Lane.

> To reach the battlefield in time, Brig. Gen. Thomas H. Neill and his men from Maine, New York, and Pennsylvania marched thirty-three miles in eighteen hours.

Epilogue

AFTER HEARING OF R. E. Lee's successful escape across the Potomac, and with it the end of the Gettysburg campaign, a discouraged Abraham Lincoln exclaimed, "Great God! What does it mean?" For the Army of the Potomac it meant a brief period of rare accolades. The *Philadelphia Enquirer* compared the battle to Waterloo. The *New York Times* said the army had won "its greatest victory."

The troops were less celebratory. In forcing the Army of Northern Virginia back south, they had captured a newfound confidence but few of the tenacious Confederates. Emphasizing the magnitude of the task yet unfinished, parts of Meade's army were hurried north to quell civil unrest. Protests against the national draft had erupted in violence. Mobs in New York City, consisting primarily of poor Irish angered by the steep three-hundred-dollar commutation fee, destroyed conscription offices, looted shops, burned an orphanage, and hanged at least a dozen African Americans. Order returned only after police and the recent victors of Gettysburg fired into the crowds. Producing more than 120 dead, the riot was, and remains, the bloodiest in U.S. history.

For the people of Virginia, the operation brought a welcome respite from the Federal menace. There was also a brief liberation from hunger. Lee's prolific foragers had plucked from the North several tons of corn, ham, and wheat. Marching along with the army were some forty-five thousand cattle, forty thousand sheep, and many thousands of pigs, but most of the livestock eventually went into the bellies of their captors.

Lee's men, though heavily damaged in the three-day battle, would live to fight for nearly two more years. But they would not breach the Mason-Dixon Line again. Desertions steadily increased. The rest of 1863 would pass without a major contest, but 1864 would bring a Wilderness campaign with casualties exceeding the invasion of Pennsylvania and end in a crippling siege of their national capital.

Union cavalry commander John Buford, who doggedly stood his ground on Gettysburg's first day, would survive the battle but not the year. In November 1863 Buford went on sick leave. Weeks later he died of typhoid, one of sixty-five thousand soldiers to do so during the course of the war. On his deathbed, Buford received a promotion to major general. His body was buried at West Point.

Francis C. Barlow, the boy general of the North who made such a costly error on the first day and was left for dead, miraculously recovered from his injuries. In nursing him back to life, his caregiver and spouse, Arabella Barlow, drove herself into severe illness and died. Her husband returned to the Army of the Potomac in 1864, serving in Ulysses S. Grant's perilous Wilderness campaign. After a sabbatical due to a relapse, he returned in time to take part in the capture of Lee's army at Appomattox Court House. Barlow went on to become a successful New York attorney and one of the founding members of the American Bar Association. As New York attorney general, he prosecuted and brought down the corrupt "Boss" Tweed dynasty of New York City. Despite his poor performance at Gettysburg, a statue of Barlow stands today near Blocher's Knoll.

Barlow's superior in the luckless 11th Corps, the "Christian General" Oliver Otis Howard, ascended to the head of the Army of the Tennessee, which he led in Sherman's March to the Sea. After the war he became the first and only director of the Freedman's Bureau, and he was an outspoken if not frustrated champion of African American rights. Howard University was so named in his honor.

Daniel E. Sickles, whose costly advance toward the Emmitsburg road precipitated the fighting on the second day, remained in the military, but he never commanded in the field again. In moving his troops far in front of the Union line on Cemetery Ridge, Sickles lost a leg and earned a lifetime of speculation concerning his unauthorized action. In 1869 he was named U.S. ambassador to Spain and in 1892 was elected to Congress. As chairman of the New York State Monuments Commission, he spearheaded the move to make Gettysburg a national battlefield park, succeeding in his quest in 1895. Defiant, proud, and sour to the end of his days, he outlived every corps commander of the famous battle, dying at the age of ninety-five. He would claim until his death that he was responsible for the Union victory in Pennsylvania.

Joshua Lawrence Chamberlain, proclaimed hero of Little Round Top, served the rest of the war despite being wounded six times. He later became president of Bowdoin College. His recollections of the war, though vivid and eloquent, were immensely self-serving. Chamberlain died in 1913, yet his memory would rise again in Michael's Shaara's *Killer Angels* and its film adaptation *Gettysburg*. Vaulted to cult status, Chamberlain is today seen by many as having saved not only the Army of the Potomac but winning the war with his charge down Little Round Top.

Winfield Scott Hancock belatedly received the Thanks of Congress for his actions at Gettysburg. Also late in coming was the removal of the saddle nail that ricocheted into his body during Pickett's Charge. A team of doctors probed the eight-inch deep channel several times before they found it near his spine. A pained Hancock served in the Wilderness, Spotsylvania, and Cold Harbor until cumulative damage from his festering wound forced him to retire. Highly popular after the war, Hancock ran against and nearly defeated fellow Civil War veteran James Garfield for the U.S. presidency in 1880.

George Gordon Meade felt for the rest of his life that he did not receive adequate praise for his victory in Pennsylvania. His anguish intensified whenever a subordinate was promoted above him, which occurred a number of times. His reputation suffered further from his sour nature. "He was unfortunately of a temper that would get beyond his control," Ulysses S. Grant said of Meade. "No one saw this better than he himself, and no one regretted it more."

During Lee's surrender at Appomattox Court House, Meade was not invited to the treaty council, nor was any officer from his Army of the Potomac. The day after Lee and Grant's immortal meeting at the McLean house, Meade wrote with a heavy heart to his wife, "I don't believe the truth ever will be known, and I have a great contempt for History." Neither forgotten nor cherished, Meade nonetheless continued to serve the U.S. Army after the war. In 1872 he died of pneumonia, a mere fifty-seven years of age.

Of the Confederate class, a number of Lee's subordinates were called into question for their Gettysburg performances. Many saw their reputations compromised by those looking to absolve the commanding general.

Richard "Baldy" Ewell never attained a high level of trust from his superior officer. Defeat at Gettysburg only solidified Lee's suspicions. The following year, Ewell's corps was nearly wiped out at Spotsylvania (immediately after Lee had taken possession of Ewell's artillery). Severe illness at Cold Harbor removed "Old Baldy" from command, and Lee made it permanent. Yet those who knew him ranked Ewell among the finest generals in gray. Artillery commander E. Porter Alexander spoke for many when he said, "No man in the army, in our corps, but loved and still loves the name and memory of good old Ewell."

Assigned to defend Richmond late in the war, Ewell led his threadbare garrison ably. He was forced to retreat with the rest of Virginia's defenders when U. S. Grant pushed Lee out of Petersburg in April 1865. Captured at Saylor's Creek with six thousand of his comrades, the lieutenant general was released from prison in the summer of 1865. In the winter of 1872 he contracted pneumonia, for which he blamed his thin attire, namely a pair of U.S. Army surplus trousers he often wore. Right before he died, Ewell said, "It's strange that an old pair of infantry pantaloons should kill me at last."

Jeb Stuart's practice of riding around Union armies, once considered a trademark of his brilliance, came under severe scrutiny in post-Gettysburg evaluations. His image was somewhat spared during the Wilderness campaign, where he received a mortal gunshot wound to the abdomen while leading his men in battle at Yellow Tavern. Stuart died the following day, in excruciating pain, as his own feces slowly seeped into the rest of his body.

The Wilderness nearly claimed James Longstreet as well. Almost a year to the day and a few miles from where Stonewall Jackson had been mortally wounded, Longstreet's own men accidentally shot him in the neck. After a long recovery, Lee's "Warhorse" managed to serve all the way to Appomattox Court House. In the following years, he went from Confederate legend to persona non grata for daring to criticize Lee's performance at Gettysburg. The tarnish only darkened when he became a Republican, rekindled his friendship with Ulysses S. Grant, and accepted several government posts, including minister to Turkey. His memoirs, published at the end of the century, reiterated his criticisms and invigorated his opponents. He died in 1904, having outlived many of his comrades but not the controversy.

For George E. Pickett the war did not proceed well after Gettysburg. In late March 1865 his command was completely routed at a crossroads

south of Petersburg called Five Forks, allowing Grant's Army of the Potomac to finally turn the Confederate flank and drive Lee's forces westward. At Appomattox Court House, Pickett was one of the most senior
officers captured. After the surrender, Pickett heard a rumor that he was
under investigation for war crimes, so he fled to Canada. Enduring several years in exile, Pickett returned. He declined offers of generalship in
the Egyptian army and a marshal's badge in the U.S. government, choosing instead to become an insurance salesman.

Pickett's reputation recovered after his death when his wife, LaSalle,
published a series of his wartime letters in a book titled *The Heart of a
Soldier.* Gushing with romanticized images of battle and endless adora-
tions for his spouse, Pickett's letters also contained many facts he could
not possibility have known when he supposedly wrote them. Most of the
penmanship and vocabulary were also atypical of his prewar dispatches.
Historians eventually determined that nearly every one of his "wartime
letters" was fabricated by his wife, attempting to present him as the ideal
warrior-knight. Her failed charade only added to Pickett's reputation as a
pitiable figure, a man forever aspiring to greatness while possessing a
character too frail for the quest.

In contrast, Robert E. Lee remained the darling of Southern sympathizers, despite losing Gettysburg as well as more than half the battles he
fought. A failing heart and exhaustive campaigning caused him to age prematurely. Photographs of him before and after the war revealed a man
who had aged twenty years in four. In the Reconstruction era, fellow veterans such as John B. Gordon and Nathan Bedford Forrest worked tire-
lessly to promote the legend of the Lost Cause and the omnipotence of
Lee. In contrast, Lee avoided such nostalgia, preferring instead to look
and labor toward the future, "to obliterate the marks of civil strife and to
commit to oblivion the feelings it engendered." Invited to a Gettysburg
ceremony in 1869, he begged off, insisting he had no desire to "keep open
the sores of war." He even criticized the construction of monuments, statuary, or any other glorifications of a conflict he increasingly loathed. Ironically, his name and likeness would be the subject of more tribute and
iconography than any other military figure in the Civil War.

Turning down several business ventures and endorsements, Lee eventually accepted the presidency of modest Washington College in Lexington, Virginia, which today bears the name Washington and Lee University.

Never brought to trial for his role in the Rebellion, Lee also never re-gained his U.S. citizenship. Several times he tried to retrieve his prewar home of Arlington from the U.S. government. Months before his death, Lee finally admitted to his wife, "The prospect is not promising." The es-tate eventually became the largest American military cemetery on earth.

In 1870 Lee died at the age of sixty-four of what was believed to be a brain aneurysm. Washington and Lee is his final resting place.

For Gettysburg itself, resurrection came slowly. Three days of combat produced an unequalled army of wounded and killed. While medics and citizens worked to save the dying, burial crews labored over the dead. Residents lived with rags over their mouths and vials of peppermint oil in their hands in futile efforts to block out a heavy, nauseating, and in-escapable smell. The effluence came from rushed work. Too many bodies were laid shallow, allowing for winds, rain, and on many occasions, raven-ous hogs to disturb their graves and a relentless sun to cook their remains.

Yet from the decomposition came new life. In accordance with an 1862 act of Congress granting executive authority to buy and sell land for mass military burials, Gettysburg became eligible for a national cemetery. The Union deceased were to be reinterred just south of town, formerly the center of Federal lines during the engagement.

The graveyard would be modest in size compared to other resting places. Antietam held a thousand more souls. The massive Union plot at Vicksburg would contain more than five times the number of soldiers than Cemetery Hill. All told, seventy-six national cemeteries were created between 1862 and 1871, from Fort Leavenworth, Kansas, to Marietta, Georgia. All were intended for Union men only, though the vast majority of sites rested in the former Confederacy.

Yet Gettysburg would become the holiest of holies. Setting in stone the battle's legend, its military cemetery received widespread attention on November 19, 1863, when the country's president delivered a garland of dedicatory remarks. The words became national scripture through his martyrdom on Good Friday, 1865. In hindsight, the man had indeed de-livered a prophecy, having foretold of Gettysburg, "from these honored dead we take increased devotion."

To build the shrine took decades. Thousands of citizens gradually constructed a memory by buying a piece of the place. Like worshipers of saints, the civilian faithful longed to acquire relics, to physically possess sacred remnants of history. And few places became more sacred than the Wheatfield, the Peach Orchard, and the Round Tops. Literally tons of artifacts were mined from the soil—bullets, buttons, sabers real and fabricated, even teeth and bones of the fallen. Adding to the haul were pamphlets, sheet music, copies of the Gettysburg Address, paperweights for the desk, portraits for the parlor, stereographs for Christmas, walking canes supposedly carved from trees on the battlefield, rocks taken from the high grounds. The unprecedented hoarding gave Americans, Northern families especially, a sense of ownership. Relatively unknown before the war, Gettysburg was becoming a nationally prized possession.

Wanting to see the site firsthand, visitors came in ever-increasing hoards and quickly outnumbered veterans and families of the fallen. In turn, the area began to serve the curious more than the reverent. To accommodate sightseers, the Gettysburg Battlefield Memorial Association (GBMA) acquired land, starting with Little Round Top and Culp's Hill. By the mid-1870s wooden signs were erected to show the position of various Union forces. Adding to the military esthetic were some thirty decommissioned artillery pieces and the first Union monuments. In 1881 the GBMA built an observation tower south of town, with four more to follow. Self-appointed guides shuttled gawkers around, carefully pointing out bullet holes in homes and trees, weaving stories of harrowing acts, and generally providing entertainment in lieu of accuracy.

Notably absent among the tourists were Southerners. In the former Confederacy, Gettysburg simply did not possess the sense of pride and redemption as it did for Northerners. Lack of access was an added disincentive. Though rail service in the North steadily expanded and improved after the 1880s, the South still languished far behind, just as it had during the war. Adding weight to roadblocks was the enduring specter of poverty. Pennsylvania saw fewer than twenty military clashes during the war. Mississippi endured more than eight hundred, Tennessee more than a thousand, and Virginia more than seventeen hundred. The resulting price left many Southern states, once prosperous, as the very poorest in the nation, a rank several Deep South states retain to the present. Relative destitution left few families with the ways and means to go on holiday excursions.

One event provided a notable exception. On the battle's fiftieth anniversary, Gettysburg hosted the largest Civil War reunion ever. More than fifty thousand veterans North and South came to a vast reunion.

Regrettably, in this moment of newfound brotherhood there would again be loss of life. As in 1863, July 1913 burned like a fever. Many of the aged warriors succumbed to heat exhaustion. Nine of them died.

In 1914 a world war erupted, reducing the flow of visitors. A postwar economic boom enabled the crowds to return and grow. The tide ebbed again with the crushing tragedy of the Great Depression.

In 1933 the fiscally tapped War Department surrendered control of the battlefield to the Department of the Interior, a beneficiary of millions from the New Deal. Money poured into public works projects, such as the beautification and conservation of national parks. The erosion stopped. Country and countryside recovered, and by 1939 a million Americans were passing through Gettysburg per annum.

The return of global war turned the battlefield back into a ghost town; 1943 brought fewer than seventy thousand visitors. The following year saw similar numbers, plus a few hundred reluctant guests from Germany and Austria, obliged to camp behind barbed wire. In general, they found their stay more pleasant than their previous trip to North Africa.

By the 1950s the peacetime park resumed its role of tourist getaway, a trend greatly augmented by a growing automobile culture. Spotlighting the Pennsylvania haven, Dwight David Eisenhower bought a farm just west of Seminary Ridge, the only home he would ever own. Drawing further attention to the park, the president's stately guest list included the likes of Winston Churchill, Charles de Gaulle, Nikita Khrushchev, Bernard Montgomery, and actor-turned-governor of California Ronald Reagan.

Under increasing pressure to supply what tourists demanded—fast food, wide roads, and modern conveniences—the site soon looked more like a cash cow than a national treasure. The area seemed to take on a new mantra: "Come for the battlefield, stay for the pie."

In its centennial year, the battlefield received a new birth of freedom. Government and private initiatives began to refurbish old buildings, remove intrusive railroad tracks, and restore the landscape to its 1863 appearance. Bolstering this movement was a new kind of visitor—the history buff. Inspired by the popular writings of Bruce Catton and Shelby Foote, versed in military lore, looking for heroes in the time of the cold war, thousands of middle-aged, middle-income Civil War aficionados began to embark on annual pilgrimages. Replacing nuclear families as the park's bread and butter, they demanded history over hype, and Gettysburg responded.

In the 1970s strict zoning laws were introduced for the first time. Kitsch gave way to period, as oily filling stations, gaudy fifties motels, and greasy spoons were removed in favor of antique stores, bed-and-breakfasts, and bistros. Fort Defiance and Fantasyland were torn down. More tablets and brigade markers went up. Snake-rail fences replaced telephones poles. Park and city planners paid greater attention to views, establishing a "scenic easement" to systematically remove unsightly modern buildings and billboards from the edges of the battlefield.

Driving forward to the past, the restoration movement went into high gear in the late 1980s. The Friends of the National Park at Gettysburg formed, pledging to acquire more land, rebuild old structures, and educate the public. Its membership reached twenty thousand in ten short years.

Then in 1990 the Public Broadcasting System aired Ken Burns's eleven-hour series *The Civil War*. The artfully assembled documentary played to millions of homes and boosted park attendance by 13 percent. In 1993 the release of the epic film *Gettysburg* swelled attendance another 20 percent.

Armed with increased attention, support, and funding, the National Parks Service has renewed its assault on modernity's infiltrations, burying power lines, tearing up unessential roads, and replanting period crops such as cherry trees, peach orchards, and wheat fields.

Currently standing guard over all of this is an army of "living historians." From weekend warriors to full-time park employees, reenactors are arguably the lifeblood of Gettysburg's and the Civil War's resurrection. For a hundred years such activists were virtually nonexistent, until the war's centennial brought forth a handful of musket demonstrations and lecturers in period dress. From these humble events came a multimillion-dollar industry, featuring privates and captains, chaplains and doctors, nurses and craftsmen. Nationwide their numbers have grown to nearly equal the number of souls Lee brought to Gettysburg. Through restoration, replacement, and reenactment, individuals and organizations have come to form a more perfect union, bonding edification with entertainment.

What was once a few dozen acres of preserved land now spans more than six thousand acres, the largest and most visited of the thirty-three federally protected Civil War National Battlefields in the United States. A once modest crossroads has become a place of, by, and for the people, inspiring all emotions commensurate with a central event in history. Ravaged, rebuilt, exploited, transformed, and cherished, Gettysburg stands as the most genuine abstract of a nation that has not yet perished from this earth.

Time Line

(All clock times are estimates)

1863

May 1–4	Battle of Chancellorsville, VA (C.S. victory)
June 3	Gettysburg campaign begins—Gen. Robert E. Lee starts to march his Army of Northern Virginia west from Fredericksburg, VA.
June 9	Battle of Brandy Station, VA (stalemate)
June 12	Lee's lead elements reach the Shenandoah Valley.
June 14–15	Second Battle of Winchester (C.S. victory)
June 15	Army of Northern Virginia starts to cross the Potomac into Maryland.
June 21	Lee's army reaches Pennsylvania.
June 25	Maj. Gen. Jeb Stuart starts his cavalry ride east around the Army of the Potomac.
June 26	Confederate Maj. Gen. Jubal A. Early reaches Gettysburg and moves on to York, PA.
June 27	Lincoln replaces Maj. Gen. Joseph Hooker with Maj. Gen. George Gordon Meade.
June 28	
3:00 a.m.	Meade is notified he is in charge of Army of Potomac.
10:00 p.m.	Lee orders his army to concentrate at Cashtown and Gettysburg. Ewell is near Carlisle and York, PA. Lt. Gen. A. P. Hill and Lt. Gen. James Longstreet are near Chambersburg, PA.
June 30	Cavalry battle of Hanover, PA (U.S. victory) Union cavalry under Brig. Gen. John Buford enters Gettysburg. Confederates west of town spot Buford but do not pursue.

Army of the Potomac is mostly south and southeast of Gettysburg, from two to twenty miles away. Army of Northern Virginia is west, north, and northeast of Gettysburg, heading for Gettysburg and Cashtown areas.

July 1	Battle of Gettysburg, PA
5:00 a.m.	Maj. Gen. Henry Heth moves two brigades from Cashtown to Gettysburg.
7:00 a.m.	First sighting between opponents west of town.
7:30 a.m.	First shot of the battle—Lt. Marcellus E. Jones of the 8th Illinois Cavalry fires a carbine at the 13th Alabama Infantry. No one is injured.
8:30 a.m.	Union 1st Corps is three miles from Gettysburg. Brig. Gen. John Buford's cavalry engages Confederate infantry west of town.
10:00 a.m.	Maj. Gen. John F. Reynolds reaches the Lutheran seminary. Heth's brigades deploy with artillery.
10:30 a.m.	Reynolds falls dead from a bullet wound. Maj. Gen. Abner Doubleday takes command of Union 1st Corps.
Noon	A lull falls over the battlefield as units from both sides hurry to Gettysburg.
12:30 p.m.	Lead elements of the Union 11th Corps reach Gettysburg.
2:00 p.m.	Gen. R. E. Lee reaches the field.
2:30 p.m.	Confederates attack from west, north, and northeast of town.
4:00 p.m.	Union 1st and 11th Corps retreat through town. Maj. Gen. Winfield Scott Hancock arrives at Gettysburg.
4:30 p.m.	Union forces solidify position on Cemetery Hill.
5:00 p.m.	Longstreet reaches Gettysburg and joins Lee.
7:30 p.m.	Sunset
Midnight	Meade reaches the field.
July 2	
3:00 a.m.	Lead elements of Longstreet's 1st Corps leave bivouac for Gettysburg.

6:00 a.m.	Lee sends scouting party to reconnoiter Union left.
9:00 a.m.	Scouting party returns to Lee with report.
11:00 a.m.	Longstreet begins his movement for the afternoon attack.
Noon	Stuart reaches Lee.
4:00 p.m.	Longstreet launches his attack on Union left.
7:00 p.m.	Union loses the Emmitsburg road, Peach Orchard, Wheatfield, and Devil's Den but holds Little Round Top and Cemetery Ridge. Ewell advances on Cemetery Hill and Culp's Hill.
10:30 p.m.	Fighting around Cemetery Hill and Culp's Hill slows to sporadic fire. Union holds Cemetery Hill and higher of two crests on Culp's Hill.

July 3

4:30 a.m.	Union 12th Corps tries to take lower crest of Culp's Hill.
11:00 a.m.	Fighting around Culp's Hill comes to an end. Union holds entire area.
1:00 p.m.	Confederate artillery barrage begins against Cemetery Ridge.
3:00 p.m.	Pickett's Charge begins.
3:20 p.m.	Advance columns reach the Angle.
3:40 p.m.	Entire Confederate line retreats.
4:00 p.m.	Pickett's Charge ends.
July 4	Lee pulls his army to a defensive position along Seminary Ridge and starts to evacuate wounded to the Potomac River and Virginia.
	Vicksburg, MS, surrenders to Union army under U. S. Grant.
July 5	Lee begins his retreat with Meade following.
July 8	Port Hudson on Mississippi River surrenders to Union forces.
July 12	Lee, with his back to the Potomac River at Williamsport, MD, waits for Meade to attack. Meade does not.
July 13	Lee begins to cross flooded Potomac into Virginia—Gettysburg campaign ends.
July 13–16	New York City draft riots.

ORDERS OF BATTLE

THE ARMY OF THE POTOMAC
Maj. Gen. George G. Meade

HEADQUARTERS
Chief of Staff: Maj. Gen. Daniel Butterfield (w)
Chief of Engineers: Brig. Gen. Gouverneur K. Warren (w)
Chief of Artillery: Brig. Gen. Henry J. Hunt
Provost Marshal: Brig. Gen. Marsena R. Patrick
Asst. Adjutant General: Brig. Gen. Seth Williams
Chief Quartermaster: Brig. Gen. Rufus Ingalls
Medical Director: Dr. Jonathan Letterman
Chief Signal Officer: Capt. Lemuel B. Norton

FIRST CORPS
Maj. Gen. John F. Reynolds (k)
Maj. Gen. Abner Doubleday
Maj. Gen. John Newton

First Division: Brig. Gen. James S. Wadsworth

First Brigade: Brig. Gen. Solomon Meredith (w)
   Col. William W. Robinson
  19th Indiana: Col. Samuel J. Williams
  24th Michigan: Col. Henry A. Morrow (w)
   Capt. Albert M. Edwards
  2nd Wisconsin: Col. Lucius Fairchild (w)
   Lt. Col. George Stevens (k)
   Maj. John Mansfield (w)
   Capt. George H. Otis
  6th Wisconsin: Lt. Col. Rufus R. Dawes
  7th Wisconsin: Col. William W. Robinson
   Maj. Mark Finnicum

---

c = captured; k = killed; mw = mortally wounded; w = wounded

Second Brigade: Brig. Gen. Lysander Cutler
  7th Indiana: Col. Ira G. Grover
  76th New York: Maj. Andrew J. Grover (k)
    Capt. John E. Cook
  84th New York (14th Brooklyn): Col. Edward B. Fowler
  95th New York: Col. George H. Biddle (w)
    Maj. Edward Pye
  147th New York: Lt. Col. Francis C. Miller (w)
    Maj. George Harney
  56th Pennsylvania: Col. J. William Hoffman

> *Second Division:* Brig. Gen. John C. Robinson

First Brigade: Brig. Gen. Gabriel R. Paul (w)
    Col. Samuel H. Leonard (w)
    Col. Adrian R. Root (w,c)
    Col. Richard Coulter (w)
    Col. Peter Lyle
  16th Maine: Col. Charles W. Tilden (c)
    Maj. Archibald D Leavitt
  13th Massachusetts: Col. Samuel H. Leonard (w)
    Lt. Col. N. Walter Batchelder
  94th New York: Col. Adrian R. Root (w,c)
    Maj. Samuel A. Moffett
  104th New York: Col. Gilbert G. Prey
  107th Pennsylvania: Lt. Col. James M. MacThompson (w)
    Capt. Emanuel D. Roath

Second Brigade: Brig. Gen. Henry Baxter
  12th Massachusetts: Col. James L. Bates (w)
    Lt. Col. David Allen Jr.
  83rd New York (9th Militia): Lt. Col. Joseph A. Moesch
  97th New York: Col. Charles Wheelock (c)
    Maj. Charles Northrup
  11th Pennsylvania: Col. Richard Coulter (w)
    Capt. Benjamin F. Haines (w)
    Capt. John B. Overmyer
  88th Pennsylvania: Maj. Benezet F. Foust (w)
    Capt. Henry Whiteside
  90th Pennsylvania: Col. Peter Lyle
    Maj. Alfred J. Sellers

Third Division: Maj. Gen. Abner Doubleday
Brig. Gen. Thomas A. Rowley

First Brigade: Col. Chapman Biddle (w)
Brig. Gen. Thomas A. Rowley
80th New York (20th Militia): Col. Theodore B. Gates
121st Pennsylvania: Maj. Alexander Biddle
142nd Pennsylvania: Col. Robert P. Cummins (k)
Lt. Col. A. B. McCalmont
151st Pennsylvania: Lt. Col. George F. McFarland (w)
Capt. Walter F. Owens
Col. Harrison Allen

Second Brigade: Col. Roy Stone (w)
Col. Langhorne Wister (w)
Col. Edmund L. Dana
143rd Pennsylvania: Col. Edmund L. Dana
Lt. Col. John D. Musser
149th Pennsylvania: Lt. Col. Walton Dwight (w)
Capt. James Glenn
150th Pennsylvania: Col. Langhorne Wister (w)
Lt. Col. H. S. Huidekoper (w)
Capt. Cornelius C. Widdis

Third Brigade: Brig. Gen. George J. Stannard (w)
Col. Francis V. Randall
12th Vermont: Col. Asa P. Blunt
13th Vermont: Col. Francis V. Randall
Maj. Joseph J. Boynton
Lt. Col. William D. Munson
14th Vermont: Col. William T. Nichols
15th Vermont: Col. Redfield Proctor
16th Vermont: Col. Wheelock G. Veasey

Artillery Brigade: Col. Charles S. Wainwright
2nd Maine Light: Capt. James A. Hall
5th Maine Light: Capt. Greenleaf T. Stevens (w)
Lt. Edward N. Whittier
1st New York Light, Batteries L-E: Capt. Gilbert H. Reynolds (w)
Lt. George Breck
1st Pennsylvania Light, Battery B: Capt. James H. Cooper
4th United States, Battery B: Lt. James Stewart (w)

SECOND CORPS
Maj. Gen. Winfield S. Hancock (w)
Brig. Gen. John Gibbon (w)
Brig. Gen. William Hays

First Division: Brig. Gen. John C. Caldwell

First Brigade: Col. Edward E. Cross (w)
Col. H. Boyd McKeen
5th New Hampshire: Lt. Col. Charles E. Hapgood
61st New York: Lt. Col. K. Oscar Broady
81st Pennsylvania: Col. H. Boyd McKeen
Lt. Col. Amos Stroh
148th Pennsylvania: Lt. Col. Robert McFarlane

Second Brigade: Col. Patrick Kelly
28th Massachusetts: Col. Richard Byrnes
63rd New York: Lt. Col. Richard C. Bently (w)
Capt. Thomas Touhy
69th New York: Capt. Richard Moroney (w)
Lt. James J. Smith
88th New York: Capt. Denis F. Burke
116th Pennsylvania: Maj. St. Clair A. Mulholland

Third Brigade: Brig. Gen. Samuel K. Zook (mw)
Lt. Col. John Fraser
52nd New York: Lt. Col. Charles G. Freudenberg (w)
Capt. William Scherrer
57th New York: Lt. Col. Alford B. Chapman
66th New York: Col. Orlando H. Morris (w)
Lt. Col. John S. Hammell (w)
Maj. Peter Nelson
140th Pennsylvania: Col. Richard P. Roberts (k)
Lt. Col. John Fraser

Fourth Brigade: Col. John R. Brooke (w)
27th Connecticut: Lt. Col. Henry C. Merwin (k)
Maj. James H. Coburn
2nd Delaware: Col. William P. Baily
Capt. Charles H. Christman
64th New York: Col. Daniel G. Bingham (w)
Maj. Leman W. Bradley
53rd Pennsylvania: Lt. Col. Richards McMichael
145th Pennsylvania: Col. Hiram L. Brown (w)
Capt. John W. Reynolds (w)
Capt. Moses W. Oliver

Second Division: Brig. Gen. John Gibbon (w)
Brig. Gen. William Harrow

First Brigade: Brig. Gen. William Harrow
    Col. Francis E. Heath
    19th Maine: Col. Francis E. Heath
        Lt. Col. Henry W. Cunningham
    15th Massachusetts: Col. George H. Ward (k)
        Lt. Col. George C. Joslin
    1st Minnesota: Col. William Colvill Jr. (w)
        Capt. Nathan S. Messick (k)
        Capt. Henry C. Coates
    2nd Co. Minnesota Sharpshooters
    82nd New York (2nd Militia): Lt. Col. James Huston (k)
        Capt. John Darrow

Second Brigade: Brig. Gen. Alexander S. Webb (w)
    69th Pennsylvania: Col. Dennis O'Kane (mw)
        Capt. William Davis
    71st Pennsylvania: Col. Richard Penn Smith
    72nd Pennsylvania: Col. De Witt C. Baxter (w)
        Lt. Col. Theodore Hesser
    106th Pennsylvania: Lt. Col. William L. Curry

Third Brigade: Col. Norman J. Hall
    19th Massachusetts: Col. Arthur F. Devereaux
    20th Massachusetts: Col. Paul J. Revere (mw)
        Lt. Col. George N. Macy (w)
        Capt. Henry L. Abbott
    7th Michigan: Lt. Col. Amos E. Steele Jr. (k)
        Maj. Sylvanus W. Curtis
    42nd New York: Col. James E. Mallon
    59th New York: Lt. Col. Max A. Thoman (k)
        Capt. William McFadden
    1st Co. Massachusetts Sharpshooters: Capt. William Plumer
        Lt. Emerson L. Bicknell

Third Division: Brig. Gen. Alexander Hays

First Brigade: Col. Samuel S. Carroll
    14th Indiana: Col. John Coons
    4th Ohio: Lt. Col. Leonard W. Carpenter
    8th Ohio: Lt. Col. Franklin Sawyer
    7th West Virginia: Lt. Col. Jonathan H. Lockwood

Second Brigade: Col. Thomas A. Smyth (w)
    Lt. Col. Francis E. Pierce

14th Connecticut: Maj. Theodore G. Ellis
1st Delaware: Lt. Col. Edward P. Harris
    Capt. Thomas B. Hizar (w)
    Lt. William Smith (mw)
    Lt. John D. Dent
12th New Jersey: Maj. John T. Hill
10th New York Battalion: Maj. George F. Hopper
108th New York: Lt. Col. Francis E. Pierce

Third Brigade: Col. George L. Willard (k)
    Col. Eliakim Sherrill (mw)
    Lt. Col. James L. Bull
39th New York : Maj. Hugo Hildebrandt (w)
111th New York: Col. Clinton D. MacDougall (w)
    Lt. Col. Isaac M. Lusk
    Capt. Aaron B. Seeley
125th New York: Lt. Col. Levin Crandell
126th New York: Col. Eliakim Sherrill (mw)
    Lt. Col. James L. Bull

Artillery Brigade: Capt. John G. Hazard
1st New York Light, Battery B/New York 14th Independent:
    Capt. James M. Rorty (mw)
    Lt. Albert S. Sheldon (w)
    Lt. Robert E. Rogers
1st Rhode Island Light, Battery A: Capt. William A. Arnold
1st Rhode Island Light, Battery B: Lt. T. Frederick Brown (w)
    Lt. Walter S. Perrin
1st United States, Battery I: Lt. George A. Woodruff (mw)
    Lt. Tully McCrea
4th United States Battery A: Lt. Alonzo H. Cushing (k)
    Sgt. Frederick Fuger

THIRD CORPS
Maj. Gen. Daniel E. Sickles (w)
Maj. Gen. David B. Birney
Maj. Gen. William H. French

First Division: Maj. Gen. David B. Birney
Brig. Gen. J. H. Hobart Ward

First Brigade: Brig. Gen. Charles K. Graham (w,c)
    Col. Andrew H. Tippin
57th Pennsylvania: Col. Peter Sides (w)
    Capt. Alanson H. Nelson

63rd Pennsylvania: Maj. John A. Danks
68th Pennsylvania: Col. Andrew H. Tippin
    Capt. Milton S. Davis
105th Pennsylvania: Col. Calvin A. Craig
114th Pennsylvania: Lt. Col. Frederick F. Cavada (c)
    Capt. Edward R. Bowen
141st Pennsylvania: Col. Henry J. Madill

Second Brigade: Brig. Gen. J. H. Hobart Ward
    Col. Hiram Berdan
20th Indiana: Col. John Wheeler (k)
    Lt. Col. William C. L. Taylor (w)
3rd Maine: Col. Moses B. Lakeman
4th Maine: Col. Elijah Walker (w)
    Capt. Edward Libby
86th New York: Lt. Col. Benjamin L. Higgins (w)
124th New York: Col. Van Horne Ellis (k)
    Lt. Col. Francis L. Cummins (w)
99th Pennsylvania: Maj. John W. Moore
1st United States Sharpshooters: Col. Hiram Berdan
    Lt. Col. Casper Trepp
2nd United States Sharpshooters: Maj. Homer R. Stoughton

Third Brigade: Col. P. Régis de Trobriand
17th Maine: Lt. Col. Charles B. Merrill
3rd Michigan: Col. Byron R. Pierce (w)
    Lt. Col. Edward S. Pierce
5th Michigan: Lt. Col. John Pulford (w)
40th New York: Col. Thomas W. Egan
110th Pennsylvania: Lt. Col. David M. Jones (w)
    Maj. Isaac Rogers

        Second Division: Brig. Gen. Andrew A. Humphreys

First Brigade: Brig. Gen. Joseph B. Carr
1st Massachusetts: Lt. Col. Clark B. Baldwin
11th Massachusetts: Lt. Col. Porter D. Tripp
16th Massachusetts: Lt. Col. Waldo Merriam (w)
    Capt. Matthew Donovan
12th New Hampshire: Capt. John F. Langley
11th New Jersey: Col. Robert McAllister (w)
    Capt. Luther Martin (w)
    Lt. John Schoonover (w)
    Capt. Samuel T. Sleeper
26th Pennsylvania: Maj. Robert L. Bodine
84th Pennsylvania: Lt. Col. Milton Opp

Second Brigade: Col. William R. Brewster
    70th New York: Col. J. Egbert Farnum
    71st New York: Col. Henry L. Potter
    72nd New York: Col. John S. Austin (w)
        Lt. Col. John Leonard
    73rd New York: Maj. Michael W. Burns
    74th New York: Lt. Col. Thomas Holt
    120th New York: Lt. Col. Cornelius D. Westbrook (w)
        Maj. John R. Tappen

Third Brigade: Col. George C. Burling
    2nd New Hampshire: Col. Edward L. Bailey (w)
    5th New Jersey: Col. William J. Sewell (w)
        Capt. Thomas C. Godfrey
        Capt. Henry H. Woolsey
    6th New Jersey: Lt. Col. Stephen R. Gilkyson
    7th New Jersey: Col. Louis R. Francine (mw)
        Maj. Fred Cooper
    8th New Jersey: Col. John Ramsey (w)
        Capt. John G. Langston
    115th Pennsylvania: Maj. John P. Dunne

Artillery Brigade: Capt. George E. Randolph (w)
        Capt. A. Judson Clark
    New Jersey Light, Battery B: Capt. A. Judson Clark
        Lt. Robert Sims
    1st New York Light, Battery D: Capt. George B. Winslow
    New York 4th Independent Battery: Capt. James E. Smith
    1st Rhode Island Light, Battery E: Lt. John K. Bucklyn (w)
        Lt. Benjamin Freeborn
    4th United States, Battery K: Lt. Francis W. Seeley (w)
        Lt. Robert James

FIFTH CORPS
Maj. Gen. George Sykes

First Division: Brig. Gen. James Barnes (w)
Brig. Gen. Charles Griffin

First Brigade: Col. William S. Tilton
    18th Massachusetts: Col. Joseph Hayes
    22nd Massachusetts: Lt. Col. Thomas Sherwin Jr.
    1st Michigan: Col. Ira C. Abbot (w)
        Lt. Col. William A. Throop
    118th Pennsylvania: Lt. Col. James Gwyn

Second Brigade: Col. Jacob B. Sweitzer
  9th Massachusetts: Col. Patrick R. Guiney
  32nd Massachusetts: Col. George L. Prescott
  4th Michigan: Col. Harrison H. Jeffords (k)
    Lt. Col. George W. Lumbard
  62nd Pennsylvania: Lt. Col. James C. Hull

Third Brigade: Col. Strong Vincent (mw)
    Col. James C. Rice
  20th Maine: Col. Joshua L. Chamberlain
  16th Michigan: Lt. Col. Norval E. Welch
  44th New York: Col. James C. Rice
    Lt. Col. Freeman Conner
  83rd Pennsylvania: Capt. Orpeus S. Woodward

                Second Division: Brig. Gen. Romeyn B. Ayres

First Brigade: Col. Hannibal Day
  3rd United States: Capt. Henry W. Freedley (w)
    Capt. Richard G. Lay
  4th United States: Capt. Julius W. Adams Jr.
  6th United States: Capt. Levi C. Bootes
  12th United States: Capt. Thomas S. Dunn
  14th United States: Maj. Grotius R. Giddings

Second Brigade: Col. Sidney Burbank
  2nd United States: Maj. Arthur T. Lee (w)
    Capt. Samuel A. McKee
  7th United States: Capt. David P. Hancock
  10th United States: Capt. William Clinton
  11th United States: Maj. DeLancey Floyd-Jones
  17th United States: Lt. Col. J. Durell Greene

Third Brigade: Brig. Gen. Stephen H. Weed (k)
    Col. Kenner Garrard
  140th New York: Col. Patrick O'Rorke (k)
    Lt. Col. Louis Ernst
  146th New York: Col. Kenner Garrard
    Lt. Col. David T. Jenkins
  91st Pennsylvania: Lt. Col. Joseph H. Sinex
  155th Pennsylvania: Lt. Col. John H. Cain

                Third Division: Brig. Gen. Samuel W. Crawford

First Brigade: Col. William McCandless
  1st Pennsylvania Reserves: Col. William C. Talley
  2nd Pennsylvania Reserves: Lt. Col. George A. Woodward

6th Pennsylvania Reserves: Lt. Col. Wellington H. Ent
13th Pennsylvania Reserves: Col. Charles F. Taylor (k)
   Maj. William R. Hartshorne

Third Brigade: Col. Joseph W. Fisher
5th Pennsylvania Reserves: Lt. Col. George Dare
9th Pennsylvania Reserves: Lt. James M. Snodgrass
10th Pennsylvania Reserves: Col. Adoniram J. Warner
11th Pennsylvania Reserves: Col. Samuel M. Jackson
12th Pennsylvania Reserves: Col. Martin D. Hardin

Artillery Brigade: Capt. Augustus P. Martin
Massachusetts Light, Battery C: Lt. Aaron F. Walcott
1st New York Light, Battery C: Capt. Almont Barnes
1st Ohio Light, Battery L: Capt. Frank C. Gibbs
5th United States, Battery D: Lt. Charles E. Hazlett (k)
   Lt. Benjamin F. Rittenhouse
5th United States, Battery I: Lt. Malbone F. Watson (w)
   Lt. Charles C. MacConnell

SIXTH CORPS
Maj. Gen. John Sedgwick

First Division: Brig. Gen. Horatio G. Wright

First Brigade: Brig. Gen. Alfred T. A. Torbert
1st New Jersey: Lt. Col. William Henry Jr.
2nd New Jersey: Lt. Col. Charles Wiebecke
3rd New Jersey: Lt. Col. Edward L. Campbell
15th New Jersey: Col. William H. Penrose

Second Brigade: Brig. Gen. Joseph J. Bartlett
5th Maine: Col. Clark S. Edwards
121st New York: Col. Emory Upton
95th Pennsylvania: Lt. Col. Edward Carroll
96th Pennsylvania: Maj. William H. Lessig

Third Brigade: Brig. Gen. David A. Russell
6th Maine: Col. Hiram Burnham
49th Pennsylvania: Lt. Col. Thomas M. Hulings
119th Pennsylvania: Col. Peter C. Ellmaker
5th Wisconsin: Col. Thomas S. Allen

Second Division: Brig. Gen. Albion P. Howe

Second Brigade: Col. Lewis A. Grant
2nd Vermont: Col. James H. Walbridge
3rd Vermont: Col. Thomas O. Seaver

4th Vermont: Col. Charles B. Stoughton
5th Vermont: Lt. Col. John R. Lewis
6th Vermont: Col. Elisha L. Barney

Third Brigade: Brig. Gen. Thomas H. Neill
7th Maine: Lt. Col. Selden Connor
33rd New York: Capt. Henry J. Gifford
43rd New York: Lt. Col. John Wilson
49th New York: Col. Daniel D. Bidwell
77th New York: Lt. Col. Winsor B. French
61st Pennsylvania: Lt. Col. George F. Smith

Third Division: Maj. Gen. John Newton
Brig. Gen. Frank Wheaton

First Brigade: Brig. Gen. Alexander Shaler
65th New York: Col. Joseph E. Hamblin
67th New York: Col. Nelson Cross
122nd New York: Col. Silas Titus
23rd Pennsylvania: Lt. Col. John F. Glenn
82nd Pennsylvania: Col. Isaac C. Bassett

Second Brigade: Col. Henry L. Eustis
7th Massachusetts: Lt. Col. Franklin P. Harrow
10th Massachusetts: Lt. Col. Joseph B. Parsons
37th Massachusetts: Col. Oliver Edwards
2nd Rhode Island: Col. Horatio Rogers Jr.

Third Brigade: Brig. Gen. Frank Wheaton
Col. David J. Nevin
62nd New York: Col. David J. Nevin
Lt. Col. Theodore B. Hamilton
93rd Pennsylvania: Maj. John I. Nevin
98th Pennsylvania: Maj. John B. Kohler
102nd Pennsylvania: Col. John W. Patterson
139th Pennsylvania: Col. Fredrick H. Collier
Lt. Col. William H. Moody

Artillery Brigade: Col. Charles H. Tompkins
Massachusetts Light, Battery A: Capt. William H. McCartney
New York 1st Independent Battery: Capt. Andrew Cowan
New York 3rd Independent Battery: Capt. William A. Harn
1st Rhode Island Light, Battery C: Capt. Richard Waterman
1st Rhode Island Light, Battery G: Capt. George W. Adams
2nd United States, Battery D: Lt. Edward B. Williston
2nd United States, Battery G: Lt. John H. Butler
5th United States, Battery F: Lt. Leonard Martin

ELEVENTH CORPS
Maj. Gen. Oliver O.Howard
Maj. Gen. Carl Schurz

First Division: Brig. Gen. Francis C. Barlow (w)
Brig. Gen. Adelbert Ames

First Brigade: Col. Leopold von Gilsa
  41st New York: Lt. Col. Detleo von Einsiedal
  54th New York: Maj. Stephen Kovacs (c)
    Lt. Ernst Both
  68th New York: Col. Gotthilf Bourry
  153rd Pennsylvania: Maj. John F. Frueauff

Second Brigade: Brig. Gen. Adelbert Ames
    Col. Andrew L. Harris
  17th Connecticut: Lt. Col. Douglas Fowler (k)
    Maj. Allen G. Brady
  25th Ohio: Lt. Col. Jeremiah Williams (c)
    Capt. Nathaniel J. Manning
    Lt. William Maloney (w)
    Lt. Isreal White
  75th Ohio: Col. Andrew L. Harris
    Capt. George B. Fox
  107th Ohio: Col. Seraphim Meyer
    Capt. John M. Lutz

Second Division: Brig. Gen. Adolph von Steinwehr

First Brigade: Col. Charles R. Coster
  134th New York: Lt. Col. Allan H. Jackson
  154th New York: Lt. Col. D. B. Allen
  27th Pennsylvania: Lt. Col. Lorenz Cantador
  73rd Pennsylvania: Capt. D. F. Kelly

Second Brigade: Col. Orland Smith
  33rd Massachusetts: Col. Adin B. Underwood
  136th New York: Col. James Wood Jr.
  55th Ohio: Col. Charles B. Gambee
  73rd Ohio: Lt. Col. Richard Long

Third Division: Maj. Gen. Carl Schurz
Brig. Gen. Alexander Schimmelfennig

First Brigade: Brig. Gen. Alexander Schimmelfennig
    Col. George von Amsberg
  82nd Illinois: Col. Edward S. Salomon

45th New York: Col. George von Amsberg
 Lt. Col. Adophus Dobke
157th New York: Col. Philip P. Brown Jr.
61st Ohio: Col. Stephen J. McGroarty
74th Pennsylvania: Col. Adolph Von Hartung (w)
 Lt. Col. Alexander von Mitzel (c)
 Capt. Gustav Schleiter
 Capt. Henry Krauseneck

Second Brigade: Col. Wladimir Krzyzanowski
58th New York: Lt. Col. August Otto
 Capt. Emil Koenig
119th New York: Col. John T. Lockman (w)
 Lt. Col. Edward F. Lloyd
82nd Ohio: Col. James S. Robinson (w)
 Lt. Col. David Thomson
75th Pennsylvania: Col. Francis Mahler (w)
 Major August Ledig
26th Wisconsin: Lt. Col. Hans Boebel (w)
 Capt. John W. Fuchs

Artillery Brigade: Maj. Thomas W. Osborn
1st New York Light, Battery I: Capt. Michael Weidrich
New York 13th Independent Battery: Lt. William Wheeler
1st Ohio Light, Battery I: Capt. Hubert Dilger
1st Ohio Light, Battery K: Capt. Lewis Heckman
4th United States, Battery G: Lt. Bayard Wilkeson (k)
 Lt. Eugene A. Bancroft

TWELFTH CORPS
Maj. Gen. Henry W. Slocum
Brig. Gen. Alpheus S. Williams

First Division: Brig. Gen. Alpheus S. Williams
Brig. Gen. Thomas H. Ruger

First Brigade: Col. Archibald L. McDougall
5th Connecticut: Col. Warren W. Packer
20th Connecticut: Lt. Col. William B. Wooster
3rd Maryland: Col. Joseph M. Sudsburg
123rd New York: Lt. Col. James C. Rogers
 Capt. Adolphus H. Tanner
145th New York: Col. E. L. Price
46th Pennsylvania: Col. James L. Selfridge

Second Brigade: Brig. Gen. Henry H. Lockwood
1st Maryland Potomac Home Brigade: Col. William P. Maulsby

1st Maryland Eastern Shore Infantry: Col. James Wallace
150th New York: Col. John H. Ketcham

Third Brigade: Brig. Gen. Thomas H. Ruger
    Col. Silas Colgrove
    27th Indiana: Col. Silas Colgrove
        Lt. Col. John R. Fesler
    2nd Massachusetts: Lt. Col. Charles R. Mudge (k)
        Maj. Charles F. Morse
    13th New Jersey: Col. Ezra A. Carman
    107th New York: Col. Nirom M. Crane
    3rd Wisconsin: Col. William Hawley

Second Division: Brig. Gen. John W. Geary

First Brigade: Col. Charles Candy
    5th Ohio: Col. John H. Patrick
    7th Ohio: Col. William R. Creighton
    29th Ohio: Capt. Wilbur F. Stevens (w)
        Capt. Edward Hayes
    66th Ohio: Lt. Col. Eugene Powell
    28th Pennsylvania: Capt. John Flynn
    147th Pennsylvania: Lt. Col. Ario Pardee Jr.

Second Brigade: Col. George A. Cobham Jr.
    Brig. Gen. Thomas L. Kane
    Col. George A. Cobham Jr.
    29th Pennsylvania: Col. William Rickards Jr.
    109th Pennsylvania: Capt. Frederick L. Gimber
    111th Pennsylvania: Col. George A. Cobham Jr.
        Lt. Col. Thomas M. Walker

Third Brigade: Brig. Gen. George Sears Greene
    60th New York: Col. Abel Godard
    78th New York: Lt. Col. Herbert von Hammerstein
    102nd New York: Col. James C. Lane (w)
        Capt. Lewis R. Stegman
    137th New York: Col. David Ireland
    149th New York: Col. Henry A. Barnum
        Lt. Col. Charles B. Randall (w)

Artillery Brigade: Lt. Edward D. Muhlenberg
    1st New York Light, Battery M: Lt. Charles E. Winegar
    Pennsylvania Light, Battery E: Lt. Charles A. Atwell
    4th United States, Battery F: Lt. Sylvanus T. Rugg
    5th United States, Battery K: Lt. David H. Kinzie

CAVALRY CORPS
Maj. Gen. Alfred Pleasonton

First Division: Brig. Gen. John Buford

First Brigade: Col. William Gamble
  8th Illinois: Maj. John L. Beveridge
  12th Illinois/3rd Indiana: Col. George H. Chapman
  8th New York: Lt. Col. William L. Markell

Second Brigade: Col. Thomas C. Devin
  6th New York: Maj. William E. Beardsley
  9th New York: Col. William Sackett
  17th Pennsylvania: Col. Josiah H. Kellogg
  3rd West Virginia: Capt. Seymour B. Conger

Reserve Brigade: Brig. Gen. Wesley Merritt
  6th Pennsylvania: Maj. James H. Haseltine
  1st United States: Capt. Richard S. C. Lord
  2nd United States: Capt. T. F. Rodenbough
  5th United States: Capt. Julius W. Mason
  6th United States: Maj. Samuel H. Starr (w,c)
      Lt. Louis H. Carpenter
      Lt. Nicholas Nolan
      Capt. Ira W. Claflin

Second Division: Brig. Gen. David M. Gregg

First Brigade: Col. John B. McIntosh
  1st Maryland: Lt. Col. James M. Deems
  Purnell (Maryland) Legion, Co. A: Capt. Robert E. Duvall
  1st Massachusetts: Lt. Col. Greely S. Curtis
  1st New Jersey: Maj. M. H. Beaumont
  1st Pennsylvania: Col. John P. Taylor
  3rd Pennsylvania: Lt. Col. E. S. Jones
  3rd Pennsylvania Heavy, Battery H: Capt. W. D. Rank

Second Brigade: Col. Pennock Huey
  2nd New York: Lt. Col. Otto Harhaus
  4th New York: Lt. Col. Augustus Pruyn
  6th Ohio: Maj. William Stedman
  8th Pennsylvania: Capt. William A. Corrie

Third Brigade: Col. J. Irvin Gregg
  1st Maine: Lt. Col. Charles H. Smith
  10th New York: Maj. M. Henry Avery
  4th Pennsylvania: Lt. Col. William E. Doster
  16th Pennsylvania: Lt. Col. John K. Robison

Third Division: Brig. Gen. Judson Kilpatrick

First Brigade: Brig. Gen. Elon J. Farnsworth (k)
Col. Nathaniel P. Richmond
5th New York: Maj. John Hammond
18th Pennsylvania: Lt. Col. William P. Brinton
1st Vermont: Lt. Col. Addison W. Preston
1st West Virginia: Col. Nathaniel P. Richmond
Maj. Charles E. Capehart

Second Brigade: Brig. Gen. George A. Custer
1st Michigan: Col. Charles H. Town
5th Michigan: Col. Russell A. Alger
6th Michigan: Col. George Gray
7th Michigan: Col. William D. Mann

Horse Artillery

First Brigade: Capt. James M. Robertson
9th Michigan Battery: Capt. Jabez J. Daniels
6th New York Battery: Capt. Joseph W. Martin
2nd United States, Batteries B-L: Lt. Edward Heaton
2nd United States, Battery M: Lt. A. C. M. Pennington Jr.
4th United States, Battery E: Lt. Samuel S. Elder

Second Brigade: Capt. John Tidball
1st United States, Batteries E-G: Capt. Alanson M. Randol
1st United States, Battery K: Capt. William M. Graham
2nd United States, Battery A: Lt. John H. Calef

Artillery Reserve
Brig. Gen. Robert O. Tyler
Capt. James M. Robertson

First Regular Brigade: Capt. Dunbar R. Ransom (w)
1st United States, Battery H: Lt. Chandler P. Eakin
Lt. Philip D. Mason
3rd United States, Batteries F-K: Lt. John G. Turnbull
4th United States, Battery C: Lt. Evan Thomas
5th United States, Battery C: Lt. Gulian V. Weir

First Volunteer Brigade: Lt. Col. Freeman McGilvery
5th Massachusetts Light/New York 10th Independent: Capt. Charles A. Phillips
9th Massachusetts Light: Capt. John Bigelow (w)
Lt. Richard S. Milton
New York 15th Independent Battery: Capt. Patrick Hart (w)
Pennsylvania Light, Batteries C-F: Capt. James Thompson (w)

Second Volunteer Brigade: Capt. Elijah D. Taft
    1st Connecticut Heavy, Battery B: Capt. Albert F. Brooker
    1st Connecticut Heavy, Battery M: Capt. Franklin A. Pratt
    2nd Connecticut Light: Capt. John W. Sterling
    New York 5th Independent Battery: Capt. Elijah D. Taft

Third Volunteer Brigade: Capt. James F. Huntington
    1st New Hampshire Light: Capt. Frederick M. Edgell
    1st Ohio Light, Battery H: Lt. George W. Norton
    1st Pennsylvania Light, Batteries F-G: Capt. R. Bruce Ricketts
    West Virginia Light, Battery C: Capt. Wallace Hill

Fourth Volunteer Brigade: Capt. Robert H. Fitzhugh
    6th Maine Light: Lt. Edwin B. Dow
    Maryland Light, Battery A: Capt. James H. Rigby
    New Jersey Light, Battery A: Lt. Augustin N. Parsons
    1st New York Light, Battery G: Capt. Nelson Ames
    1st New York Light, Battery K: Capt. Robert H. Fitzhugh
    11th New York Battery: Capt. Robert H. Fitzhugh

Train Guard: 4th New Jersey: Maj. Charles Ewing

THE ARMY OF NORTHERN VIRGINIA
Gen. Robert E. Lee

HEADQUARTERS
Chief of Staff: Col. Robert H. Chilton
Chief of Artillery: Brig. Gen. William N. Pendleton
Medical Director: Dr. Lafayette Guild
Chief of Ordnance: Lt. Col. Briscoe G. Baldwin
Chief of Commissary: Lt. Col. Robert C. Cole
Chief Quartermaster: Lt. Col. James L. Corley
Engineer Officer: Capt. Samuel R. Johnston

FIRST CORPS
Lt. Gen. James Longstreet

McLaws's Division: Maj. Gen. Lafayette McLaws

Kershaw's Brigade: Brig. Gen. Joseph B. Kershaw
2nd South Carolina: Col. John D. Kennedy (w)
　Lt. Col. F. Gaillard
3rd South Carolina: Maj. Robert C. Maffett
　Col. J. D. Nance
7th South Carolina: Col. D. Wyatt Aiken
8th South Carolina: Col. John W. Henagan
15th South Carolina: Col. William DeSaussure (k)
　Maj. William M. Gist
3rd South Carolina Battalion: Lt. Col. William G. Rice

Semmes's Brigade: Brig. Gen. Paul J. Semmes (mw)
　Col. Goode Bryan
10th Georgia: Col. John B. Weems (w)
50th Georgia: Col. William R. Manning
51st Georgia: Col. Edward Ball
53rd Georgia: Col. James P. Simms

Barksdale's Brigade: Brig. Gen. William Barksdale (mw)
　Col. Benjamin G. Humphreys
13th Mississippi: Col. John W. Carter (k)
　Lt. Col. Kennon McElroy (w)
17th Mississippi: Col. William D. Holder (w)
　Lt. Col. John C. Fiser
18th Mississippi: Col. Thomas M. Griffin (w)
　Lt. Col. W. H. Luse
21st Mississippi: Col. Benjamin G. Humphreys

Wofford's Brigade: Brig. Gen. William T. Wofford
16th Georgia: Col. Goode Bryan

18th Georgia: Lt. Col. Solon Z. Ruff
24th Georgia: Col. Robert McMillin
Cobb's (Georgia) Legion: Lt. Col. Luther J. Glenn
Phillips's (Georgia) Legion: Lt. Col. Elihu S. Barclay Jr.
3rd Georgia Sharpshooters: Lt. Col. Nathan L. Hutchins Jr.

Artillery Battalion: Col. Henry Coalter Cabell
Manly's North Carolina Battery: Capt. Basil C. Manly
Fraser's Pulaski (Georgia) Battery: Capt. John C. Fraser (mw)
   Lt. W. J. Furlong
McCarthy's Richmond Howitzers, 1st Co.: Capt. Edward S. McCarthy
Carlton's Troup (Georgia) Battery: Capt. Henry H. Carlton (w)
   Lt. C. W. Motes

Pickett's Division: Brig. Gen. George E. Pickett

Garnett's Brigade: Brig. Gen. Robert B. Garnett (k)
   Maj. Charles S. Peyton
8th Virginia: Col. Eppa Hunton (w)
   Lt. Col. Norborne Berkeley (w,c)
   Maj. Edmund Berkeley (w)
18th Virginia: Lt. Col. Henry A. Carrington (w,c)
19th Virginia: Col. Henry Gantt (w)
   Lt. Col. John T. Ellis (k)
28th Virginia: Col. Robert C. Allen (k)
   Lt. Col. William Watts (k)
56th Virginia: Col. William D. Stewart (mw)
   Lt. Col. P. P. Slaughter

Kemper's Brigade: Brig. Gen. James L. Kemper (w,c)
   Col. Joseph Mayo Jr.
1st Virginia: Col. Lewis B. Williams Jr. (k)
   Maj. Francis H. Langley (w)
3rd Virginia: Col. Joseph Mayo Jr.
   Lt. Col. Alexander D. Callcote (k)
7th Virginia: Col. Waller T. Patton (mw)
   Lt. Col. C. C. Flowerree
11th Virginia: Maj. Kirkwood Otey (w)
24th Virginia: Col. William R. Terry

Armistead's Brigade: Brig. Gen. Lewis A. Armistead (mw)
   Col. William R. Aylett (w)
9th Virginia: Maj. John C. Owens (mw)
14th Virginia: Col. James G. Hodges (k)
   Lt. Col. William White (w)
   Maj. Robert H. Poore (mw)

38th Virginia: Col. Edward C. Edmonds (k)
    Lt. Col. P. B. Whittle (mw)
53rd Virginia: Col. William R. Aylett (w)
    Lt. Col. Rawley Martin (w,c)
57th Virginia: Col. John Bowie Magruder (mw)
    Lt. Col. Benjamin G. Wade (mw)
    Maj. Clement R. Fontaine (w)

Artillery Battalion: Maj. James Dearing
    Fauquier (Virginia) Battery: Capt. Robert M. Stribling
    Hampden (Virginia) Battery: Capt. William H. Caskie
    Richmond Fayette Artillery: Capt. Miles C. Macon
    Lynchburg (Virginia) Battery: Capt. Joseph G. Blount

Hood's Division: Maj. Gen. John B. Hood (w)
Brig. Gen. Evander M. Law

Law's Brigade: Brig. Gen. Evander M. Law
    Col. James L. Sheffield
    4th Alabama: Col. Lawrence H. Scruggs
    15th Alabama: Col. William C. Oates
        Capt. Blanton A. Hill
    44th Alabama: Col. William F. Perry
    47th Alabama: Col. James W. Jackson (w)
        Lt. Col. M. J. Bulger (w,c)
        Maj. J. M. Campbell
    48th Alabama: Col. James L. Sheffield
        Capt. T. J. Eubanks

Robertson's Brigade: Brig. Gen. Jerome B. Robertson (w)
    3rd Arkansas: Col. Van H. Manning (w)
        Lt. Col. R. S. Taylor
    1st Texas: Col. Phillip A. Work
    4th Texas: Col. John C. G. Key (w)
        Maj. J. P. Bane
    5th Texas: Col. Robert M. Powell (w,c)
        Lt. Col. K. Bryan (w)
        Maj. J. C. Rogers

Anderson's Brigade: Brig. Gen. George T. Anderson (w)
    Lt. Col. William Luffman (w)
    7th Georgia: Col. William W. White
    8th Georgia: Col. John R. Towers (w)
    9th Georgia: Lt. Col. John C. Mounger (k)
        Maj. W. M. Jones (w)
        Capt. George Hillyer

11th Georgia: Col. Francis H. Little (w)
    Lt. Col. William Luffman (w)
    Maj. Henry D. McDaniel
    Capt. William H. Mitchell
59th Georgia: Col. Jack Brown (w)
    Capt. M. G. Bass

Benning's Brigade: Brig. Gen. Henry L. Benning
  2nd Georgia: Lt. Col. William T. Harris (k)
    Maj. W. S. Shepherd
  15th Georgia: Col. M. Dudley DuBose
  17th Georgia: Col. Wesley C. Hodges
  20th Georgia: Col. John A. Jones (k)
    Lt. Col. J. D. Waddell

Artillery Battalion: Maj. Mathis W. Henry
  Branch (North Carolina) Battery: Capt. Alexander C. Latham
  Charleston German Artillery: Capt. William K. Bachman
  Palmetto (South Carolina) Light Artillery: Capt. Hugh R. Garden
  Rowan (North Carolina) Battery: Capt. James Reilly

Corps Artillery Reserve: Col. James B. Walton

Alexander's Battalion: Col. E. Porter Alexander
  Woolfolk's Ashland (Virginia) Battery: Capt. Pichegru Woolfolk Jr. (w)
    Lt. James Woolfolk
  Jordan's Bedford (Virginia) Battery: Capt. Tyler C. Jordan
  Brooks (South Carolina) Battery: Lt. S. C. Gilbert
  Moody's Madison (Louisiana) Battery: Capt. George V. Moody
  Parker's Richmond Battery: Capt. William W. Parker
  Eubank's Bath (Virginia) Battery: Capt. Osmond B. Taylor

Washington Artillery of New Orleans: Maj. Benjamin F. Eshleman
  Squires's 1st Company: Capt. Charles W. Squires
  Richardson's 2nd Company: Capt. John B. Richardson
  Miller's 3rd Company: Capt. Merritt B. Miller
  Eshleman's 4th Company: Capt. Joe Norcom (w)
    Lt. H. A. Battles

SECOND CORPS
Lt. Gen. Richard S. Ewell

Early's Division: Maj. Gen. Jubal A. Early

Hays's Brigade: Brig. Gen. Harry T. Hays
  5th Louisiana: Maj. Alexander Hart (w)
    Capt. T. H. Biscoe

6th Louisiana: Lt. Col. Joseph Hanlon
7th Louisiana: Col. Davidson B. Penn
8th Louisiana: Col. Trevanion D. Lewis (k)
  Lt. Col. A. de Blanc (w)
  Maj. G. A. Lester
9th Louisiana: Col. Leroy A. Stafford

Smith's Brigade: Brig. Gen. William Smith
13th Virginia: Col. John S. Hoffman
49th Virginia: Lt. Col. J. Catlett Gibson
52nd Virginia: Lt. Col. James H. Skinner (w)

Hoke's Brigade: Col. Issac E. Avery (mw)
  Col. Archibald C. Godwin
6th North Carolina: Maj. Samuel M. Tate
21st North Carolina: Col. William W. Kirkland
57th North Carolina: Col. Archibald C. Godwin

Gordon's Brigade: Brig. Gen. John B. Gordon
13th Georgia: Col. James L. Smith
26th Georgia: Col. Edmund N. Atkinson
31st Georgia: Col. Clement A. Evans
38th Georgia: Capt. William L. McLeod
60th Georgia: Capt. Walter B. Jones
61st Georgia: Col. John H. Lamar

Artillery Battalion: Lt. Col. Hilary P. Jones
Carrington's Charlottesville Artillery: Capt. James McD. Carrington
Latimer's Courtney (Virginia) Battery: Capt. William A. Tanner
Louisiana Guard Artillery: Capt. Charles A. Green
Garber's Staunton (Virginia) Battery: Capt. Asher W. Garber

Rodes's Division: Maj. Gen. Robert E. Rodes

Daniel's Brigade: Brig. Gen. Junius Daniel
32nd North Carolina: Col. Edmind C. Brabble
43rd North Carolina: Col. Thomas S. Kenan (w,c)
  Lt. Col. William G. Lewis
45th North Carolina: Lt. Col. Samuel H. Boyd (w,c)
  Maj. John R. Winston (w,c)
  Capt. A. H. Gallaway (w)
  Capt. J. A. Hopkins
53rd North Carolina: Col. William A. Owens
2nd North Carolina Bn.: Lt. Col. Hezekiah L.Andrews (k)
  Capt. Van Brown

Iverson's Brigade: Brig. Gen. Alfred Iverson
 5th North Carolina: Capt. Speight B. West (w)
   Capt. Benjamin Robinson (w)
 12th North Carolina: Lt. Col. William S. Davis
 20th North Carolina: Lt. Col. Nelson Slouh (w)
   Capt. Lewis T. Hicks
 23rd North Carolina: Col. Daniel H. Christie (mw)
   Capt. William H. Johnston

Doles's Brigade: Brig. Gen. George Doles
 4th Georgia: Lt. Col. David R. E. Winn (k)
   Maj. M. H. Willis
 12th Georgia: Col. Edward Willis
 21st Georgia: Col. John T. Mercer
 44th Georgia: Col. Samuel P. Lumpkin (mw)
   Maj. W. H. Peebles

Ramseur's Brigade: Brig. Gen. Stephen D. Ramseur
 2nd North Carolina: Maj. Daniel W. Hurt (w)
   Capt. James T. Scales
 4th North Carolina: Col. Bryan Grimes
 14th North Carolina: Col. R. Tyler Bennett (w)
   Maj. Joseph H. Lambeth
 30th North Carolina: Col. Francis M. Parker (w)
   Maj. W. W. Sillers

O'Neal's Brigade: Col. Edward A. O'Neal
 3rd Alabama: Col. Cullin A. Battle
 5th Alabama: Col. Josephus M. Hall
 6th Alabama: Col. James N. Lightfoot (w)
   Capt. M. L. Bowie
 12th Alabama: Col. Samuel B. Pickens
 26th Alabama: Lt. Col. John C. Goodgame

Artillery Battalion: Lt. Col. Thomas H. Carter
 Reese's Jeff Davis (Alabama) Battery: Capt. William J. Reese
 Carter's King William (Virginia) Battery: Capt. William P. Carter
 Page's Morris Louisa (Virginia) Battery: Capt. Richard C. M. Page (w)
 Fry's Orange (Virginia) Battery: Capt. Charles W. Fry

Johnson's Division: Maj. Gen. Edward Johnson

Steuart's Brigade: Brig. Gen. George H. Steuart
 1st Maryland Battalion Infantry: Lt. Col. James R. Herbert (w)
   Maj. W. W. Goldsborough (w)
   Capt. J. P. Crane

1st North Carolina: Lt. Col. Hamilton Allen Brown
3rd North Carolina: Maj. Willliam M. Parsley
10th Virginia: Capt. William B. Yancey
23rd Virginia: Lt. Col. Simeon T. Walton
37th Virginia: Maj. Henry C. Wood

Nicholls's Brigade: Col. Jesse M. Williams
1st Louisiana: Col. Michael Nolan (k)
    Capt. E. D. Willet
2nd Louisiana: Lt. Col. Ross E. Burke (w,c)
10th Louisiana: Maj. Thomas N. Powell
14th Louisiana: Lt. Col. David Zable
15th Louisiana: Maj. Andrew Bradey

Stonewall Brigade: Brig. Gen. James A. Walker
2nd Virginia: Col. John Q. A. Nadenbousch
4th Virginia: Maj. William Terry
5th Virginia: Col. John H. S. Funk
27th Virginia: Lt. Col. Daniel M. Shriver
33rd Virginia: Capt. James B. Golladay

Jones's Brigade: Brig. Gen. John. M. Jones (w)
    Lt. Col. Robert H. Dungan
21st Virginia: Capt. William P. Moseley
25th Virginia: Col. John C. Higginbotham (w)
    Lt. Col. J. A. Robinson
42nd Virginia: Col. Robert Withers (w)
    Capt. S. H. Saunders
44th Virginia: Maj. Norval Cobb (w)
    Capt. T. R. Buckner
48th Virginia: Lt. Col. Robert H. Dungan
    Maj. Oscar White
50th Virginia: Lt. Col. Logan H. N. Salyer

Artillery Battalion: Maj. James W. Latimer (mw)
    Capt. Charles I. Raine
Dement's 1st Maryland Battery: Capt. William F. Dement
Carpenter's Alleghany (Virginia) Battery: Capt. John C. Carpenter
Brown's 4th Maryland Chesapeake Battery: Capt. William D. Brown
Raine's Lee (Virginia) Battery: Capt. Charles I. Raine
    Lt. William M. Hardwicke

Corps Artillery Reserve: Col. J. Thompson Brown

First Virginia Artillery: Capt. Willis J. Dance
Watson's Richmond Howitzers, 2nd Co.: Capt. David Watson

Smith's Richmond Howitzers, 3rd Co.: Capt. Benjamin H. Smith Jr.
Dance's Powhatan (Virginia) Battery: Lt. John M. Cunningham
1st Rockbridge (Virginia) Battery: Capt. Archibald Graham
Griffin's Salem (Virginia) Battery: Lt. Charles B. Griffin

Nelson's Battalion: Lt. Col. William Nelson
Kirkpatrick's Amherst (Virginia) Battery: Capt. Thomas J. Kirkpatrick
Massie's Fluvanna (Virginia) Battery: Capt. John L. Massie
Milledge's Georgia Battery: Capt. John Milledge Jr.

THIRD CORPS
Lt. Gen. Ambrose P. Hill

Anderson's Division: Maj. Gen. Richard H. Anderson

Wilcox's Brigade: Brig. Gen. Cadmus M. Wilcox
8th Alabama: Lt. Col. Hilary A. Herbert
9th Alabama: Capt. J. Horace King (w)
10th Alabama: Col. William H. Forney (w,c)
  Lt. Col. James E. Shelley
11th Alabama: Col. John C. C. Sanders (w)
  Lt. Col. George E. Tayloe
14th Alabama: Col. Lucius Pinckard (w)
  Lt. Col. James A. Broome

Wright's Brigade: Brig. Gen. Ambrose R. Wright
3rd Georgia: Col. Edward J. Walker
22nd Georgia: Col. Joseph A. Wasden (k)
  Capt. B. C. McCurry
48th Georgia: Col. William Gibson (w,c)
  Capt. M. R. Hall
2nd Georgia Battalion: Maj. George W. Ross (mw)
  Capt. Charles J. Muffett

Mahone's Brigade: Brig. Gen. William Mahone
6th Virginia: Col. George T. Rogers
12th Virginia: Col. David A. Weisiger
16th Virginia: Col. Joseph H. Ham
41st Virginia: Col. William A. Parham
61st Virginia: Col. Virginius D. Groner

Perry's Brigade: Col. David Lang
2nd Florida: Maj. Walter R. Moore (w,c)
  Capt. William D. Ballentine (w,c)
  Capt. Alexander Mosely (c)
  Capt. C. Seton Fleming

5th Florida: Capt. Richmond N. Gardner (w)
    Capt. Council A. Bryan
8th Florida: Lt. Col. William Baya

Posey's Brigade: Brig. Gen. Carnot Posey
  12th Mississippi: Col. Walter H. Taylor
  16th Mississippi: Col. Samuel E. Baker
  19th Mississippi: Col. Nathaniel H. Harris
  48th Mississippi: Col. Joseph M. Jayne

Artillery Battalion: Maj. John Lane
  Sumter (Georgia) Artillery, Co. A: Capt. Hugh M. Ross
  Sumter (Georgia) Artillery, Co. B: Capt. George M. Patterson
  Sumter (Georgia) Artillery, Co. C: Capt. John T. Wingfield (w)

                Heth's Division: Maj. Gen. Henry Heth (w)
                Brig. Gen. James J. Pettigrew (mw)

Pettigrew's Brigade: Brig. Gen. James J. Pettigrew (mw)
    Col. James K. Marshall (k)
    Maj. John T. Jones
  11th North Carolina: Col. Collett Leventhorpe (w)
    Maj. Egbert A. Ross (k)
  26th North Carolina: Col. Henry K. Burgwyn Jr. (k)
    Lt. Col. John R. Lane (w)
    Capt. H. C. Albright
  47th North Carolina: Col. George H. Faribault (w)
    Lt. Col. John A. Graves (c)
  52nd North Carolina: Col. James K. Marshall (k)
    Lt. Col. Marcus A. Parks (w,c)
    Maj. John Q. A. Richardson (k)

Brockenbrough's Brigade: Col. John M. Brockenbrough
  40th Virginia: Capt. T. Edwin Betts
    Capt. R. B. Davis
  47th Virginia: Col. Robert M. Mayo
  55th Virginia: Col. William S. Christian (c)
  22nd Virginia Battalion: Maj. John S. Bowles

Archer's Brigade: Brig. Gen. James J. Archer (c)
    Col. Birkett D. Fry (w,c)
    Lt. Col. Samuel G. Shepherd
  5th Alabama Battalion: Maj. Albert S. Van de Graaf
  13th Alabama: Col. Birkett D. Fry (w,c)
  1st Tennessee (Provisional Army): Maj. Felix G. Buchanan (w)
  7th Tennessee: Lt. Col. Samuel G. Shepherd
  14th Tennessee: Capt. Bruce L. Phillips

Davis's Brigade: Brig. Gen. Joseph R. Davis
   2nd Mississippi: Col. John M. Stone (w)
      Lt. Col. David W. Humphreys (k)
      Maj. John A. Blair
   11th Mississippi: Col. Francis M. Green
   42nd Mississippi: Col. Hugh R. Miller (mw)
   55th North Carolina: Col. John Kerr Connally (w)
      Maj. Alfred H. Belo (w)

Artillery Battalion: Lt. Col. John Garnett
   Maurin's Donaldsville (Louisiana) Battery: Capt. Victor Maurin
   Moore's Norfolk (Virginia) Battery: Capt. Joseph D. Moore
   Lewis's Pittsylvania (Virginia) Battery: Capt. John W. Lewis
   Grandy's Norfolk Blues Battery: Capt. Charles R. Grandy

               Pender's Division: Maj. Gen. William D. Pender (mw)
                     Brig. Gen. James H. Lane
                     Maj. Gen. Isaac R. Trimble (w,c)
                     Brig. Gen. James H. Lane

Perrin's Brigade: Col. Abner Perrin
   1st South Carolina (Provisional Army): Maj. Charles W. McCreary
   1st South Carolina Rifles: Capt. William M. Hadden
   12th South Carolina: Col. John L. Miller
   13th South Carolina: Lt. Col. Benjamin T. Brockman
   14th South Carolina: Lt. Col. Joseph N. Brown (w)
      Maj. Edward Croft (w)

Lane's Brigade: Brig. Gen. James H. Lane
    Col. Clark M. Avery
    Brig. Gen. James H. Lane
    Col. Clark M. Avery
   7th North Carolina: Capt. J. Mcleod Turner (w,c)
      Capt. James G. Harris
   18th North Carolina: Col. John D. Barry
   28th North Carolina: Col. Samuel D. Lowe (w)
      Lt. Col. W. H. A. Speer
   33rd North Carolina: Col. Clark M. Avery
   37th North Carolina: Col. William M. Barbour

Thomas's Brigade: Brig. Gen. Edward L. Thomas
   14th Georgia: Col. Robert W. Folsom
   35th Georgia: Col. Bolling H. Holt
   45th Georgia: Col. Thomas J. Simmons
   49th Georgia: Col. Samuel T. Player

Scales's Brigade: Brig. Gen. Alfred M. Scales (w)
    Lt. Col. G. T. Gordon (w)
    Col. W. Lee. J. Lowrance (w)
  13th North Carolina: Col. Joseph H. Hyman (w)
    Lt. Col. H. A. Rogers
  16th North Carolina: Capt. Leroy W. Stowe
  22nd North Carolina: Col. James Conner
  34th North Carolina: Col. William L. Lowrance (w)
    Lt. Col. G. T. Gordon
  38th North Carolina: Col. William J. Hoke (w)
    Lt. Col. John Ashford (w)

Artillery Battalion: Maj. William T. Poague
  Albemarle (Virginia) Light Artillery: Capt. James W. Wyatt
  Charlotte (North Carolina) Artillery: Capt. Joseph Graham
  Madison (Mississippi) Light Artillery: Capt. George Ward
  Brooke's Warrington (Virginia) Battery: Capt. James V. Brooke

Corps Artillery Reserve: Col. R. Lindsay Walker

Mcintosh's Battalion: Maj. D. G. McIntosh
  Danville (Virginia) Light Artillery: Capt. R. Sidney Rice
  Hardaway's (Alabama) Artillery: Capt. William B. Hurt
  2nd Rockbridge (Virginia) Battery: Lt. Samuel Wallace
  Johnson's Richmond Battery: Capt. Marmaduke Johnson

Pegram's Battalion: Maj. William J. Pegram
    Capt. E. B. Brunson
  Crenshaw's Virginia Battery: Capt. William G. Crenshaw
  Fredericksburg (Virginia) Artillery: Capt. Edward A. Marye
  Letcher (Virginia) Artillery: Capt. Thomas A. Brander
  Pee Dee (South Carolina) Artillery: Lt. William E. Zimmerman
  Purcell (Virginia) Artillery: Capt. Joseph McGraw

CAVALRY DIVISION
Maj. Gen. James Ewell Brown "Jeb" Stuart

Hampton's Brigade: Brig. Gen. Wade Hampton (w)
    Col. Laurence S. Baker
  1st North Carolina Cavalry: Col. Laurence S. Baker
  1st South Carolina Cavalry: Col. John L. Black
  2nd South Carolina Cavalry: Col. Matthew C. Butler
  Cobb's (Georgia) Legion: Col. Pierce B. L. Young
  Jeff Davis's Legion: Col. Joseph F. Waring
  Phillips's (Georgia) Legion: Lt. Col. Jefferson C. Phillips

Fitz Lee's Brigade: Brig. Gen. W. Fitzhugh Lee
    1st Maryland Battalion: Maj. Harry Gilmore
        Maj. Ridgely Brown
    1st Virginia Cavalry: Col. James H. Drake
    2nd Virginia Cavalry: Col. Thomas T. Munford
    3rd Virginia Cavalry: Col. Thomas H. Owen
    4th Virginia Cavalry: Col. William Carter Wickham
    5th Virginia Cavalry: Col. Thomas L. Rosser

Robertson's Brigade: Brig. Gen. Beverly H. Robertson
    4th North Carolina Cavalry: Col. Dennis D. Ferebee
    5th North Carolina Cavalry: Col. Peter G. Evans

Jones's Brigade: Brig. Gen. William E. Jones
    6th Virginia Cavalry: Maj. Cabel E. Flourney
    7th Virginia Cavalry: Lt. Col. Thomas Marshall
    11th Virginia Cavalry: Col. Lunsford L. Lomax
    35th Virginia Battalion: Lt. Col. Elijah V. White

W. H. F. Lee's Brigade: Col. John R. Chambliss Jr.
    2nd North Carolina Cavalry: Lt. Col. William Payne
    9th Virginia Cavalry: Col. Richard L. T. Beale
    10th Virginia Cavalry: Col. J. Lucius Davis
    13th Virginia Cavalry: Capt. Benjamin F. Winfield

Stuart's Horse Artillery: Maj. Robert F. Beckham
    Breathed's (Virginia) Battery: Capt. James Breathed
    Chew's (Virginia) Battery: Capt. R. Preston Chew
    Griffin's (Maryland) Battery: Capt. William H. Griffin
    Hart's (South Carolina) Battery: Capt. James F. Hart
    McGregor's (Virginia) Battery: Capt. William M. McGregor
    Moorman's (Virginia) Battery: Capt. Marcellus M. Moorman

Jenkins's Brigade: Brig. Gen. Albert G. Jenkins (w)
       Col. Milton J. Ferguson
    14th Virginia Cavalry: Maj. Benjamin F. Eakle (w)
    16th Virginia Cavalry: Col. Milton J. Ferguson
    17th Virginia Cavalry: Col. William H. French
    34th Virginia Battalion: Lt. Col. Vincent A. Witcher
    36th Virginia Battalion: Capt. Cornelius T. Smith
    Jackson's (Virginia) Battery: Capt. Thomas E. Jackson

Imboden's Brigade: Brig. Gen. John D. Imboden
    18th Virginia Cavalry: Col. George W. Imboden
    62nd Virginia Mounted Infantry: Col. George H. Smith
    Virginia Partisan Rangers: Capt. John H. McNeill
    Virginia (Staunton) Battery: Capt. John H. McClanahan

Notes

CHAPTER 1: COMING TO THE CROSSROADS

1. Gary W. Gallagher, ed., *The Fredericksburg Campaign* (Chapel Hill: University of North Carolina Press, 1995), 201, 208. *Chicago Tribune* quoted, ibid., 174. Lincoln quoted in William H. Wadsworth to Samuel Barlow, December 16, 1862, Barlow Papers, Henry E. Huntington Library, San Marino, CA.

2. Margaret S. Creighton, *The Colors of Courage: Immigrants, Women, and African Americans in the Civil War's Defining Battle* (New York: Basic Books, 2005), 50–51; James M. Paradis, *African Americans and the Gettysburg Campaign* (Lanham, MD: Scarecrow, 2005), ix, 2–4, 37–38.

3. James Kelaher of the 9th New York and John Hutchison of the 15th New Jersey quoted in Gallagher, *Fredericksburg Campaign,* 192.

4. Charles Blacknall quoted in Kent M. Brown, *Retreat from Gettysburg* (Chapel Hill: University of North Carolina Press, 2005), 32; James M. Paradis, *African Americans and the Gettysburg Campaign,* 36.

5. An account of Lincoln's honorary substitute is in Webb Garrison, *The Amazing Civil War* (New York: MJF Books, 1998), 92–93; Geoffrey C. Ward, Ric Burns, and Ken Burns, *The Civil War* (New York: Knopf, 1990), 242.

6. For details on Southern food shortages and their causes, see James M. McPherson, *Battle Cry of Freedom* (New York: Oxford University Press, 1988), 384, 440; Dorothy Volo and James Volo, *Daily Life in the Civil War* (Westport, CT: Greenwood, 1998), 230–34.

7. Clement Eaton, *A History of the Southern Confederacy* (New York: Free Press, 1954), 234–35; Emory Thomas, *The Confederate Nation, 1861–1865* (New York: Harper & Row, 1979), 203–5.

8. Eaton, *History of the Southern Confederacy,* 227; McPherson, *Battle Cry of Freedom,* 616; Thomas, *Confederate Nation,* 198.

9. Hooker quoted in McPherson, *Battle Cry of Freedom,* 639.

10. Jackson quoted in Ernest B. Furgurson, *Chancellorsville, 1863* (New York: Knopf, 1992), 328.

11. Lee quoted in John M. Taylor, *Duty Faithfully Performed: Robert E. Lee and His Critics* (Dulles, VA: Brassey's, 1999), 128.

12. U.S. War Department, *The War of the Rebellion: A Compilation of the Official Records of the Union and Confederate Armies,* 128 vols. (Washington, DC: Government Printing Office, 1880–1901), vol. 27, pt. 3, 27. (Hereafter cited as *OR.*)

13. Allan Nevins, *The War for the Union: The Organized War, 1863–1864* (New York: Scribner's, 1971), 80.

14. *OR*, vol. 27, pt. 1, 50.

15. Ibid., 58.

16. Ibid., 60.

17. Ibid., pt. 3, 369.

18. *New York Times,* July 1, 1863.

19. Meade quoted in Wilmer L. Jones, *Generals in Blue and Gray,* 2 vols. (Westport, CT: Praeger, 2004), 1:291.

20. Lee's report to Richmond, July 31, 1863, *OR,* ser. 1, vol. 27, pt. 2, 307–8.

21. G. Moxley Sorrel quoted in Jeffry D. Wert, *General James Longstreet* (New York: Simon and Schuster, 1993), 237.

22. Lee's report to Richmond, July 31, 1863, *OR,* ser. 1, vol. 27, pt. 2, 307–8.

23. *OR,* ser. 1, vol. 27, pt. 2, 308.

24. Lee quoted in *OR,* ser. 1, vol. 27, pt. 2, 308.

25. Edwin Coddington, *The Gettysburg Campaign: A Study in Command* (New York: Scribner's, 1984), 9.

26. *New York Times,* July 1, 1863; Sarah Broadhead account, File 8–6, Gettysburg National Military Park Archives.

27. Davis quoted in Ward, *The Civil War,* 127.

28. McPherson, *Battle Cry of Freedom,* 627.

29. Hudson Strode, *Jefferson Davis* (New York: Harcourt, Brace, and Co., 1959), 402–3; Michael A. Palmer, *Lee Moves North* (New York: Wiley, 1998), 50; Noah Andre Trudeau, *Gettysburg: A Testing of Courage* (New York: HarperCollins, 2002), 4. Historians Herman Hattaway and Richard E. Beringer contend that Vicksburg and Chattanooga were not key factors in the Confederate high command's decision to invade Pennsylvania. Yet in making this claim, they concentrate on Lee's concerns only. Comments, letters, and dispatches from cabinet members, and primarily from Jefferson Davis, indicate that the western theater was a permanent concern for the high command before, during, and after Lee's Pennsylvania campaign. Hattaway and Beringer, *Jefferson Davis, Confederate President* (Lawrence: University Press of Kansas, 2002), 226–28.

30. Joseph B. Mitchell, *Military Leaders in the Civil War* (New York: Putnam, 1972), 64–65; Connelly, 37–38; Steven H. Newton, *Joseph E. Johnston and*

the Defense of Richmond (Lawrence: University Press of Kansas, 1998), 209; *OR*, ser. 1, vol. 27, pt. 3, 886.

31. Strode, *Jefferson Davis*, 402–5; Trudeau, *Gettysburg*, 4.

32. Strode, *Jefferson Davis*, 402–3; Michael A. Palmer, *Lee Moves North* (New York: Wiley, 1998), 50; Trudeau, *Gettysburg*, 4; Hattaway and Beringer, *Jefferson Davis*, 226–28.

33. John D. McKenzie, *Uncertain Glory: Lee's Generalship Re-examined* (New York: Hippocrene, 1997), 139.

34. Lee quoted in McPherson, *Battle Cry of Freedom*, 647.

35. For a review of how Confederate soldiers viewed their adversaries, see Bell I. Wiley, *The Life of Johnny Reb* (New York: Bobbs-Merrill, 1962), 308–21. Georgia soldier quoted in Daniel E. Sutherland, *Fredericksburg and Chancellorsville* (Lincoln: University of Nebraska Press, 1998), 193. Alexander quoted in Wert, *Longstreet*, 255.

36. Lee quoted in Stephen W. Sears, *Chancellorsville* (Boston: Houghton Mifflin, 1996), 444.

37. Lee quoted in Alan T. Nolan, *Lee Considered* (Chapel Hill: University of North Carolina Press, 1991), 85.

38. Trimble quoting Lee in McPherson, *Battle Cry of Freedom*, 655n, and in Fellman, *Making of Robert E. Lee*, 138.

39. Sutherland, *Fredericksburg and Chancellorsville*, 1.

40. *OR*, ser. 1, vol. 27, pt. 3, 881.

41. Lee quoted in Douglas Southall Freeman, *R. E. Lee: A Biography* (New York: Scribner's, 1935), 27; *OR*, ser. 1, vol. 27, pt. 2, 305.

42. Terry L. Jones, *Lee's Tigers: The Louisiana Infantry and the Army of Northern Virginia* (Baton Rouge: Louisiana State University Press, 1987), 163.

43. For greater detail on the "balance sheet" on the Confederacy in early 1863, see Nevins, *War for the Union*, 8–45.

44. Confederate soldier quoted in William Hassler, *A. P. Hill: Lee's Forgotten General* (Richmond, VA: Garrett and Massie, 1957), 150; John West quoted in Gregory A. Coco, *A Strange and Blighted Land* (Gettysburg: Thomas, 1995), 2.

45. McPherson, *Battle Cry of Freedom*, 649.

46. J. G. Randall and David H. Donald, *The Civil War and Reconstruction* (Lexington, KY: Heath, 1969), 8–10.

47. Wiley, *The Life of Johnny Reb*, 289.

48. *OR*, ser. 1, vol. 27, pt. 3, 880–82.

49. Frank L. Klement, *The Copperheads in the Middle West* (Chicago: University of Chicago Press, 1960), 73–75.

50. Early quoted in Millard K. Bushong, *Old Jube: A Biography of General Jubal A. Early* (Boyce, VA: Carr Publishing, 1955), 139.
51. *New York Times,* July 1, 1863; *OR,* vol. 27, pt. 1, 43; Henrietta S. Jaquette, ed., *South After Gettysburg: Letters of Cornelia Hancock from the Army of the Potomac, 1863–1865* (Philadelphia: University of Pennsylvania Press, 1937), 12.
52. Louisiana soldier quoted in Jones, *Lee's Tigers,* 163–64.
53. Lee quoted in Nolan, *Lee Considered,* 110–11.
54. Charles M. Hubbard. *The Burden of Confederate Diplomacy* (Knoxville: University of Tennessee Press, 1998), 23; Robert E. May, ed., *The Union, the Confederacy, and the Atlantic Rim* (West Lafayette, IN: Purdue University Press, 1995), 4–5.
55. London *Times,* May 2, 1863.
56. Howard Jones, *Union in Peril: The Crisis over British Intervention in the Civil War* (Chapel Hill: University of North Carolina Press, 1992), 227.
57. See also Jones, *Generals in Blue and Gray.*
58. See also Michael A. Riley, *"For God's Sake, Forward": General John F. Reynolds* (Gettysburg: Farnsworth House Military Impressions, 1995).
59. Ewell quoted in Donald C. Pfanz, *Richard S. Ewell: A Soldier's Life* (Chapel Hill: University of North Carolina Press, 1998), 303.
60. *OR,* ser. 1, vol. 27, pt. 2, 317.
61. Lee quoted in Gary W. Gallagher, ed., *Three Days at Gettysburg: Essays on Confederate and Union Leadership* (Kent, OH: Kent State University Press, 1999), 32.
62. Hill quoted in James I. Robertson, *General A. P. Hill: The Story of a Confederate Warrior* (New York: Random House, 1987).
63. Hill quoted in Gallagher, *Three Days at Gettysburg,* 39.
64. Buford quoted in David M. Jordan, *Winfield Scott Hancock: A Soldier's Life* (Bloomington: Indiana University Press, 1988), 83.
65. Hancock quoted in ibid., 84.
66. Early quoted in Jones, *Generals in Blue and Gray,* 2:321.
67. Lee and Longstreet quoted in Wert, *Longstreet,* 257.
68. Sickles quoted in Jones, *Generals in Blue and Gray,* 1:191.
69. Howard quoted in Coddington, *The Gettysburg Campaign,* 37.
70. *OR,* ser. 1, vol. 27, pt. 3, 463.
71. Ibid., 374.
72. Ibid., 426.
73. Robert J. Trout, *They Followed the Plume: The Story of J. E. B. Stuart and His Staff* (Mechanicsburg, PA: Stackpole Books, 1993), 28–29.

74. Mark M. Boatner III, *The Civil War Dictionary*, rev. ed. (New York: McKay, 1988), 815–16; Ezra J. Warner, *Generals in Gray: Lives of the Confederate Commanders* (Baton Rouge: Louisiana State University, 1959), 296–97.

75. Trout, *They Followed the Plume*, 16; Nevins, *War for the Union*, 448–49.

CHAPTER 2: THE BATTLE

1. Exchange between Buford and Reynolds quoted in George Sheldon, *When the Smoke Cleared at Gettysburg* (Nashville, TN: Cumberland House, 2003), 60.

2. Hill quoted in Edwin B. Coddington, *The Gettysburg Campaign: A Study in Command* (New York: Scribner's, 1984), 310; Slocum 5 p.m. report to Meade, *OR*, ser. 1, vol. 27, pt. 3, 466.

3. Meade quoted in Stephen W. Sears, *Gettysburg* (New York: Houghton Mifflin, 2003), 166.

4. All numbers are from David Martin and John Busey, *Regimental Strengths and Losses at Gettysburg*, 4th ed. (Hightstown, NJ: Longstreet House, 2005). The Union 1st Corps was also missing its largest brigade consisting of the 13th, 14th, and 16th Vermont, totaling 1,950. The Vermonters would not arrive until the second day of the battle. Their two remaining regiments in the brigade, the 12th and 15th Vermont, were left guarding trains, depriving the 1st Corps of another 1,200 men.

5. Coddington, *The Gettysburg Campaign*, 307.

6. Ibid., 305.

7. David L. Martin, *Gettysburg: July 1*, rev. ed. (Conshohocken, PA: Combined Books, 1996), 282

8. Fairfax Downey, *The Guns of Gettysburg* (Gaithersburg, MD: Butternut Press, 1985), 30

9. Reynolds quoted in Coddington, *The Gettysburg Campaign*, 269.

10. Ibid., 276–29.

11. Bradley Gottfried, *Brigades of Gettysburg* (Cambridge, MA: Da Capo Press, 2002), 644.

12. William Frassanito, *The Gettysburg Bicentennial Album* (Gettysburg: Gettysburg Bicentennial Committee, 1987), 2–3.

13. Union soldier quoted in Noah Andre Trudeau, *Gettysburg: A Testing of Courage* (New York: HarperCollins, 2002), 13.

14. Union soldier quoted in Stephen W. Sears, *Chancellorsville* (Boston: Houghton Mifflin, 1996), 432.

15. Howard quoted in Coddington, *The Gettysburg Campaign*, 32–33.

16. Sgt. Charles Wickesberg quoted in Gottfried, *Brigades of Gettysburg*, 341.

17. D. Scott Hartwig, "The Unlucky 11th—The 11th Army Corps on July 1, 1863," *Gettysburg Magazine*, no. 2 (January 1990): 49.

18. Coddington, *The Gettysburg Campaign*, 310–12.

19. Trudeau, *Gettysburg*, 212–18.

20. Coddington, *The Gettysburg Campaign*, 309–11.

21. Harry Pfanz, *Gettysburg—The Second Day* (Chapel Hill: University of North Carolina Press, 1987), 113.

22. Ibid., 119–21.

23. For critical assessments of Longstreet's attitude on the second day, see Coddington, *The Gettysburg Campaign*, 377–80; Gary Gallagher, ed., *The Second Day at Gettysburg: Essays on Confederate and Union Leadership* (Kent, OH: Kent State University Press, 1993), 68–72; Pfanz, *Gettysburg—The Second Day*, 118–20.

24. Pfanz, *Gettysburg—The Second Day*, 103.

25. Coddington, *The Gettysburg Campaign*, 378–82.

26. McLaws quoted in ibid., 381.

27. Longstreet quoted in ibid., 382.

28. See A. P. Hill's report, *OR*, ser. 1, vol. 27, pt. 2, 607–9; J. B. Robertson's report, *OR*, ser. 1, vol. 27, pt. 2, 404–6.

29. Scott Bowden and Bill Ward, *Last Chance for Victory: Robert E. Lee and the Gettysburg Campaign* (Conshocken, PA: Savas Publishing, 2001), chapter 7.

30. Coddington, *The Gettysburg Campaign*, 395.

31. Guiney quoted in Coddington, *The Gettysburg Campaign*, 446. Birney quoted in ibid., 450.

32. John Busey and David Martin, *Regimental Strengths and Losses at Gettysburg* (Hightstown, NJ: Longstreet House, 1986), 241–47, 280–94. Coddington, *The Gettysburg Campaign*, 427–36.

33. Coddington, *The Gettysburg Campaign*, 428.

34. Ibid., 427–28.

35. Ibid., 436.

36. Trudeau, *Gettysburg*, 431–32.

37. Coddington, *The Gettysburg Campaign*, 468–69.

38. Gary Kross, "True Cavalry: Jeb Stuart and George Custer at Gettysburg," *Blue and Gray Magazine*, July 1997, 50.

39. Ibid.

40. Gregory Coco, *A Concise Guide to the Artillery at Gettysburg* (Gettysburg: Thomas, 1998), 84–85; Hess, *Pickett's Charge*, 25, 117.

41. Downey, *The Guns of Gettysburg*, 133; Jeffrey C. Hall, *The Stand of the*

U. S. Army at Gettysburg (Bloomington: Indiana University Press, 2003), 190.

42. *Daily Richmond Enquirer,* July 22, 1863; *New York Times,* July 4, 1863.

43. Union soldier quoted in Philip M. Cole, *Civil War Artillery at Gettysburg* (Cambridge, MA: Da Capo Press, 2002), 283.

44. Longstreet quoted in Trudeau, *Gettysburg,* 442.

45. Coddington, *The Gettysburg Campaign,* 68; Hall, *The Stand of the U.S. Army at Gettysburg,* 185; Jeffrey Wert, *Gettysburg: Day Three* (New York: Simon & Schuster, 2001), 128.

46. Coddington, *The Gettysburg Campaign,* 11–18.

47. Alexander quoted in Glenn Tucker, *Lee and Longstreet at Gettysburg* (Indianapolis, IN: Bobbs-Merrill, 1968), 225.

48. Hess, *Pickett's Charge,* 249–51.

49. Lee quoted in Trudeau, *Gettysburg,* 460–61.

50. Hess, *Pickett's Charge,* 25, 117.

51. Longstreet quoted in Trudeau, *Gettysburg,* 459. Alexander quoted in Lesley J. Gordon, *General George E. Pickett in Life and Legend* (Chapel Hill: University of North Carolina Press, 1998), 111.

52. Coddington, *The Gettysburg Campaign,* 497–98.

53. Ibid., 497.

54. Coco, *Concise Guide to the Artillery at Gettysburg,* 84–85.

55. Gary W. Gallagher, ed., *The Third Day at Gettysburg and Beyond* (Chapel Hill: University of North Carolina Press, 1994), 115; *Augusta Daily Constitutionalist,* July 23, 1863; Lash, "The Philadelphia Brigade at Gettysburg," 104.

56. Coddington, *Gettysburg Campaign,* 490–91.

57. Ibid., 799n.

58. Wright quoted in Trudeau, *Gettysburg,* 462.

59. Confederate soldier quoted in ibid., 510. Pickett quoted in Gallagher, *Third Day at Gettysburg and Beyond,* 115.

60. Anderson quoted in Trudeau, *Gettysburg,* 510.

61. Michael Fellman, *The Making of Robert E. Lee* (New York: Random House, 2000), 190.

62. Wert, *Gettysburg,* 194–95.

63. Trudeau, *Gettysburg,* 507–8.

64. Ibid., 478, 498.

65. David G. Martin, *Gettysburg: July 1st,* rev. ed. (Conshohocken, PA: Combined Books, 1996), 487; Pfanz, *Gettysburg—The First Day,* 339.

66. Trudeau, *Gettysburg,* 383, 392–93.

67. There is a dispute whether Hancock or the Vermont brigade commander George Stannard issued the order to enfilade the Confederate first wave. Indications are that both came up with the idea at the same time.
68. Hancock quoted in Trudeau, *Gettysburg*, 500.
69. Gottfried, *Brigades of Gettysburg*, 388.
70. *OR*, ser. 1, vol. 27, pt. 2, 857.
71. Gottfried, *Brigades of Gettysburg*, 393; R.L. Murray, *A Perfect Storm of Lead* (Wolcott, NY: Benedum Books, 2002), 41–44, 57.
72. *OR*, ser. 1, vol. 27, pt. 3, 374, 426.
73. Coddington, *The Gettysburg Campaign*, 444, 448.
74. Ibid., 405.
75. Pfanz, *Gettysburg—The Second Day*, 349–50.
76. Gottfried, *Brigades of Gettysburg*, 644; Coddington, *Gettysburg Campaign*, 405.
77. Douglas Southall Freeman, *Lee's Lieutenants*, 4 vols. (New York: Scribner's, 1942), 3:179.
78. Downey, *The Guns at Gettysburg*, 79–80, 110.
79. Trudeau, *Gettysburg*, 492.
80. Edward Longacre, *The Cavalry at Gettysburg* (Cranbury, NJ: Associated University Press, 1986), 182.
81. Ibid., 188, 273.
82. Coddington, *Gettysburg Campaign*, 388–89.
83. Pfanz, *Gettysburg—The Second Day*, 224.
84. Coddington, *Gettysburg Campaign*, 394.
85. Ibid., 406–11.
86. Pfanz, *Gettysburg—The Second Day*, 254; Busey and Martin, *Regimental Strengths and Losses at Gettysburg*, 266; *OR*, ser. 1, vol. 27, pt. 2, 362.
87. Gottfried, *Brigades of Gettysburg*, 143.
88. Coddington, *Gettysburg Campaign*, 424–25.
89. Hancock quoted in ibid., 528.
90. Eric Wittenberg, *Protecting the Flank: The Battles for Brinkerhoff's Ridge and East Cavalry Field* (Celina, OH: Ironclad Publishing, 2002), 40.
91. Trudeau, *Gettysburg*, 438.
92. Wittenberg, *Protecting the Flank*, 162–64.
93. Ewell quoted in Wilmer L. Jones, *Generals in Blue and Gray*, 2 vols. (Westport, CT: Praeger, 2004), 316.
94. Longacre, *Cavalry at Gettysburg*, 148.
95. *OR*, vol. 27, pt. 3, 913, 923.
96. Coddington, *Gettysburg Campaign*, 198–201.

97. Longacre, *Cavalry at Gettysburg*, 202; *OR*, ser. 1, vol. 27, pt. 2, 321.
98. Coddington, *Gettysburg Campaign*, 344–45.
99. For situations where Lee subordinates are blamed for his defeats and his vague command style was involved, see Alan T. Nolan, *Lee Considered* (Chapel Hill: University of North Carolina Press, 1991), 59–67, 169–70.
100. Pfanz, *Gettysburg—The Second Day*, 426–27.
101. Trudeau, *Gettysburg*, 217.
102. Trudeau, *Gettysburg*, 218.
103. Barlow Papers, MHS; Pfanz, *Gettysburg–The First Day*, 231.
104. *OR*, vol. 27, pt. 2, 607; Gary W. Gallagher, ed., *The First Day At Gettysburg* (Kent, OH: Kent State University Press, 1992), 44.
105. Coddington, *The Gettysburg Campaign*, 425–26; John Pezzola, "Hill's Corps and the Failure of the Confederate Attack on Cemetery Ridge: July 2, 1863," *Gettysburg Magazine,* January 2005, 57–58.
106. Scott Bowden and Bill Ward, *Last Chance for Victory: Robert E. Lee and the Gettysburg Campaign* (Conshocken, PA: Savas Publishing, 2001), 510–11.
107. John Imhof, *Gettysburg: Day Two* (Baltimore: Butternut and Blue, 1999), 186.
108. Gottfried, *Brigades of Gettysburg*, 576
109. Trudeau, *Gettysburg*, 394.
110. Larry Tagg, *The Generals of Gettysburg* (Campbell, CA: Savas Publishing, 1998), 314–16.
111. Gottfried, *Brigades of Gettysburg*, 583; Trudeau, *Gettysburg, A Testing of Courage*, 394.
112. Jeffrey C. Hall, *The Stand of the U.S. Army at Gettysburg* (Bloomington: University of Indiana Press, 2003), 149; Busey and Martin, *Regimental Strengths and Losses at Gettysburg*, 588.
113. Trudeau, *Gettysburg*, 209.
114. North Carolina soldier quoted in Trudeau, *Gettysburg*, 211.
115. Tagg, *Generals of Gettysburg*, 286; Rodes quoted in Trudeau, *Gettysburg*, 407.
116. Coddington, *The Gettysburg Campaign*, 372; Tagg, *Generals of Gettysburg*, 372.
117. Downey, *The Guns of Gettysburg*, 117.
118. Coddington, *The Gettysburg Campaign*, 791n.
119. Tagg, *Generals of Gettysburg*, 28
120. Martin, *Gettysburg*, 180; Coddington, *The Gettysburg Campaign*, 308. Col. Rufus Dawes of the 6th Wisconsin quoted in Pfanz, *Gettysburg–The First Day*, 328. Tagg, *Generals of Gettysburg*, 28.

121. Coddington, *The Gettysburg Campaign*, 308; Mark M. Boatner III, *The Civil War Dictionary* (New York: Vintage Books, 1988), 711.

CHAPTER 3: THE LAST FULL MEASURE

1. Col. Joseph Mayo quoted in Richard Rollins, ed., *Pickett's Charge: Eyewitness Accounts* (Redondo Beach, CA: Rank and File Publications, 1994), 147. Rate of fire calculated from an estimate of three thousand functioning muskets on each side firing at a rate of two shots per minute.

2. In calculating the number of killed and wounded in the fight for the Wheatfield, adjacent areas are also factored in, including the part of Plum Run Valley that lies just south of the Wheatfield road. It was the area that the U.S. regulars and William McCandless's Pennsylvania reserves saw action.

3. One of Alexander's men heard him say "finish the whole war this afternoon" as he urged them north along the Emmitsburg road; Noah A. Trudeau, *Gettysburg: A Testing of Courage* (New York: HarperCollins, 2002), 381.

4. Harry Pfanz, *Gettysburg—The Second Day* (Chapel Hill: University of North Carolina Press, 1987), 372.

5. In this ninety-acre area, Union commanders William R. Brewster and Joseph B. Carr lost 1,430 men. Col. George Willard's regiments were involved here and in the repulse of Pickett's Charge, but it appears their heaviest losses were in this action on the second day. On the Confederate side, Wright lost 527 dead and wounded from his 1,413 men. David Perry lost 335 men here and 115 men in support of Pickett's Charge. Estimating 2,300 dead and wounded for the Union and 1,200 for the Confederacy leaves 39 men per acre. *OR*, ser. I, vol. 27, pt. 2, 476, 621; Earl Hess, *Pickett's Charge: The Last Attack at Gettysburg* (Chapel Hill: University of North Carolina Press, 2001), 335.

6. Harry Pfanz, *Gettysburg—Culp's Hill and Cemetery Hill* (Chapel Hill: University of North Carolina Press, 1993), 284.

7. Casualties are easily discernable for most of the Union regiments on Culp's Hill. But four Union regiments from the 1st Corps had also been involved in the first day's fight west of town. Two Confederate brigades, Col. Edward A. O'Neal's and Junius Daniel's, had been heavily involved also in the same fight. O'Neal did not give a breakdown of his losses while Daniel stated his first day losses were a third of his regiment, so the balance occurred at Culp's Hill. This sixty-nine-acre field of fire had a loss rate of forty-two men per acre. Estimating two hundred more men killed and wounded from O'Neal's brigade and another sixty from other Union regiments provides a final total of forty-five men per acre. Pfanz, *Gettysburg—Culp's Hill and Cemetery*

Hill, 353; *OR,* ser. I, vol. 27, pt. 2, 591, 603; James McLean Jr., *Cutler's Brigade at Gettysburg* (Baltimore: Butternut and Blue, 1987), 152–54.

8. L. R. Coy of the 123rd New York and S. R. Norris of the 7th Ohio quoted in John M. Archer, *Culp's Hill at Gettysburg* (Gettysburg: Thomas, 2002), 121.

9. Soldiers from 2nd South Carolina quoted in Trudeau, *Gettysburg,* 352.

10. Soldier from 17th Mississippi quoted in ibid., 368.

11. The Union brigades of C. K. Graham and George C. Burling took the brunt of the losses in this area. The 39th New York aided their retreat, with Union combined losses at 1,105. Southern losses are more difficult to determine. Joseph Kershaw's regiments lost 313. From Barksdale's brigade only the 21st Mississippi reached the Trostle farm. The other three turned north to take part in the fight north of the Trostle farm road. Part of William T. Wofford's brigade also came into the area, but there is no clear breakdown of their losses between this fight and the Wheatfield, though their losses were comparatively lighter than other brigades'. Barksdale's casualties for the day were 655 dead and wounded. Losses in the Peach Orchard area and eastward are estimated to be 1,754 over eighty acres. See John Busey and David Martin, *Regimental Strengths and Losses at Gettysburg* (Hightstown, NJ; Longstreet House, 1986), 245, 247, 282; Pfanz, *Gettysburg—The Second Day,* 370.

12. Losses for Scale's brigade are estimated at 545. A definitive number is not possible due to the brigade's participation in Pickett's Charge. A recent study of losses determined that Perrin sustained a loss of 522, which roughly agrees with Perrin's estimate of no fewer than 500. This would total 22 men in a fifty-acre field. Union losses cannot be discerned, but if 500 were lost for all the regiments, the final total would be 31 men per acre. See Busey and Martin, *Regimental Strengths and Losses at Gettysburg,* 292; Harry Pfanz, *Gettysburg—The First Day* (Chapel Hill: University of North Carolina Press, 2001), 319; *OR,* ser. I, vol. 27, pt. 2, 663.

13. Pennsylvania soldier quoted in Trudeau, *Gettysburg,* 314.

14. Trudeau, *Gettysburg,* 342–43.

15. Area of action in this analysis includes Devil's Den proper, the immediately adjacent portion of Plum Run Valley, and the eastern edge of Wheatfield Woods. Approximately 1,665 were lost within 56 acres, making 30 dead and wounded per acre. See Gary Adelman and Tim Smith, *Devil's Den: A History and Guide* (Gettysburg: Thomas, 1997), 7–11.

16. Pfanz, *Gettysburg—The First Day,* 280.

17. Ibid., 287.

18. Though the 19th Indiana and 24th Michigan would fight later around Culp's Hill, the majority of their losses occurred in the Herbst Woods. See Busey

and Martin, *Regimental Strengths and Losses at Gettysburg*, 239; Rod Gragg, *Covered with Glory: The 26th North Carolina Infantry at the Battle of Gettysburg* (New York: HarperCollins, 2000), 141, 209; McLean, *Cutler's Brigade at Gettysburg*, 152–54; Pfanz, *Gettysburg—The First Day*, 281.

19. Edwin B. Coddington, *The Gettysburg Campaign: A Study in Command* (New York: Scribner's, 1984), 395–96.

20. Lance R. Herdegen and William K. Beaudot, *In the Bloody Railroad Cut at Gettysburg* (Dayton: Morningside House, 1990), 211.

21. All numbers for strengths, losses, and percentages come from Busey and Martin, *Regimental Strengths and Losses at Gettysburg*.

22. Sickles's statements in Bill Hyde, *The Union Generals Speak: The Meade Hearings on the Battle of Gettysburg* (Baton Rouge: Louisiana State University Press, 2003), 33

23. Carroll quoted in Trudeau, *Gettysburg*, 409.

24. For a synopsis of the U.S. 2nd Corps war record, see Mark M. Boatner III, *The Civil War Dictionary* (New York: Vintage Books, 1988), 188–89.

25. Pfanz, *Gettysburg—The Second Day*, 153.

26. Georgia private quoted in Trudeau, *Gettysburg*, 229.

27. Gregory Coco, *A Concise Guide to the Artillery at Gettysburg* (Gettysburg: Thomas, 1998), 74–75.

28. All numbers for strengths, losses, and percentages come from Busey and Martin, *Regimental Strengths and Losses at Gettysburg*.

29. Terry L. Jones, *Historical Dictionary of the Civil War* (Lanham, MD: Scarecrow, 2002), 957.

30. Richard Moe, *The Last Full Measure: The Life and Death of the First Minnesota Volunteers* (New York: Henry Holt, 1993), 8. In total regimental losses, the 1st Minnesota ranks sixteenth due in large part to the regiment's small number at the start of the battle.

31. Richard Rollins, *"The Damned Red Flags of the Rebellion": The Confederate Battle Flags at Gettysburg* (Redondo Beach, CA: Rank and File Publications, 1997), 235.

32. Jones, *Historical Dictionary of the Civil War*, 488.

33. John D. Imhof, *Gettysburg–Day Two: A Study in Maps* (Baltimore: Butternut and Blue Press, 1999), 198.

34. *OR*, ser. 1, vol. 27, pt. 2, 632.

35. Patricia Faust, ed., *Historical Times Illustrated Encyclopedia of the Civil War* (New York: Harper & Row, 1986), 525.

36. William Marvel, *The First New Hampshire Battery 1861–1865* (Conway, NH: Lost Cemetery Press, 1985), 46–51.

37. Jones, *Historical Dictionary of the Civil War,* 107.

38. Bradley Gottfried, *Brigades of Gettysburg* (Cambridge, MA: Da Capo Press, 2002), 436–39.

39. Faust, *Historical Times Illustrated Encyclopedia of the Civil War,* 3.

40. Ibid., 500.

41. Gottfried, *Brigades of Gettysburg,* 614.

42. Faust, ed., *Historical Times Illustrated Encyclopedia of the Civil War,* 214.

43. *Report of the Joint Committee, to Mark the Positions Occupied by the 1st and 2nd Delaware Regiments at the Battle of Gettysburg* (Hightstown, NJ: Longstreet House, 1998), 15.

44. The *OR* lists Gettysburg totals as 3,155 killed, 14,529 wounded, and 5,365 missing for a total of 23,049. Confederate losses per the *OR* were 2,592 killed, 12,700 wounded, and 5,150 missing for a total of 20,442. Confederate numbers are especially fraught with errors, disagreements, missing reports, and units failing to report losses. Southerners combined mortally wounded with killed whereas Union reports did not. Historian Robert Krick, in an exhaustive study, recalculated Confederate losses as 22,198 with 4,427 dead, 12,179 wounded, and 5,592 missing. Krick acknowledges that gaps still exist. Studies of Union losses have produced new numbers showing 23,055 casualties, with 5,098 dead. See *OR,* ser. 1, vol. 27, pt. 1, 187; *OR,* ser. 1, vol. 27, pt. 2, 346; John W. Busey, *These Honored Dead* (Hightstown, NJ: Longstreet House, 1988), xi; Busey and Martin, *Regimental Strengths and Losses at Gettysburg,* 57. See also Gregory A. Coco, *A Strange and Blighted Land* (Gettysburg: Thomas, 1995), 2; Robert K. Krick, *The Gettysburg Death Roster* (Dayton: Morningside, 1981), 3; Thomas L. Livermore, *Numbers and Losses in the Civil War* (Bloomington: Indiana University Press, 1957), 75–76, 101–3; Joseph B. Mitchell, "Confederate Losses at Gettysburg: Debunking Livermore," *Blue and Gray,* May 1864, 38–40; U.S. Surgeon General's Office, *Medical and Surgical History of the War of the Rebellion, 1861–1865* (Washington DC: Government Printing Office, 1870).

45. George W. Adams, *Doctors in Blue* (Baton Rouge: Louisiana State University Press, 1996), 113–15. Union officer quoted in Gregory A. Coco, *The Civil War Infantryman* (Gettysburg: Thomas, 1996), 103; Adams, *Doctors in Blue,* 115.

46. Adams, *Doctors in Blue,* 115.

47. Henrietta S. Jaquette, ed., *South After Gettysburg: Letters of Cornelia Hancock from the Army of the Potomac, 1863–1865* (Philadelphia: University of Pennsylvania Press, 1937), 5.

48. Adams, *Doctors in Blue,* 91–92.

49. Confederate cavalry soldier quoted in Stephen W. Sears, *Gettysburg* (New York: Houghton Mifflin, 2003), 471–72.

50. Terry L. Jones, *Lee's Tigers: The Louisiana Infantry and the Army of Northern Virginia* (Baton Rouge: Louisiana State University Press, 1987), 176.

51. Bucklin quoted in Elizabeth D. Leonard, *Yankee Women* (New York: Norton, 1994), 39.

52. Gregory A. Coco, *A Vast Sea of Misery* (Gettysburg: Thomas, 1988), 101; Michael A. Dreese, *The Hospital on Seminary Ridge at the Battle of Gettysburg* (Jefferson, NC: McFarland, 2002), 167–68; Gerard A. Patterson, *Debris of Battle: The Wounded of Gettysburg* (Mechanicsburg, PA: Stackpole, 1997), 162–63.

53. Dreese, *The Hospital on Seminary Ridge,* 106, 139.

54. *OR*, vol. 27, pt. 3, 514.

55. Coco, *A Strange and Blighted Land,* 257–63.

56. *OR*, Ser. 2, vol. 6, 369, 422, 476–77, 525.

57. Lonnie R. Speer, *Portals to Hell: Military Prisons of the Civil War* (Mechanicsburg, PA: Stackpole Books, 1997), 54, 143–47, 151–54, 187–88.

58. Coco, *A Strange and Blighted Land,* 296; Gragg, *Covered with Glory,* 232.

59. Philip M. Cole, *Civil War Artillery at Gettysburg* (Cambridge, MA: Da Capo Press, 2002), 256, 282; Coco, *A Strange and Blighted Land,* 164.

60. Jim Slade and John Alexander, *Firestorm at Gettysburg* (Atglen, PA: Schiffer, 1998), 131. Robert Carter of the 22nd Massachusetts quoted in Cole, *Civil War Artillery at Gettysburg,* 257. E. Porter Alexander quoted in Cole, *Civil War Artillery at Gettysburg,* 256, 283–84.

61. Sears, *Gettysburg,* 289–91.

62. The 121st Pennsylvania reported to have gathered nearly three thousand arms from the battlefield, of which the vast majority were Enfields. Less than 10 percent were smoothbores. Union Brig. Gen. Samuel W. Crawford reported that of some nineteen hundred "enemy" shoulder arms his men gathered on July 2 and 3 (some could have been Union weapons), well over half were either Springfields or Enfields while about 10 percent were smoothbores. *OR*, vol. 27, pt. 1, 264–65, 656.

63. Dreese, *Hospital on Seminary Ridge,* 167–68.

64. Kent M. Brown, *Retreat from Gettysburg* (Chapel Hill: University of North Carolina Press, 2005), 430n.

65. Bradley M. Gottfried, "'Friendly' Fire at Gettysburg," *Gettysburg Magazine* (27): 78.

66. Ibid., 80–81.

67. Thomas L. Elmore, "The Effects of Artillery Fire on Infantry at Gettys-

burg," *Gettysburg Magazine* (5), 118; Sears, *Gettysburg*, 330. Possible origin of Hancock wound hypothesized in A. M. Gambone, *Hancock at Gettysburg* (Baltimore MD: Butternut and Blue, 1997), 268n.

68. *Medical and Surgical History of the War of the Rebellion, 1861–1865* (Washington DC: Government Printing Office, 1870).

69. Edward G. Longacre, *The Cavalry at Gettysburg* (London: Associated University Press, 1986), 33–35.

70. *Medical and Surgical History of the War of the Rebellion, 1861–1865* (Washington DC: Government Printing Office, 1870). Jeffords anecdote in Dreese, *The Hospital on Seminary Ridge at the Battle of Gettysburg*, 104.

71. Slade and Alexander, *Firestorm at Gettysburg*, 152.

72. Coco, *A Vast Sea of Misery*, 91.

CHAPTER 4: POSTBATTLE

1. J. Cutler Andrews, *The North Reports the Civil War* (Pittsburgh: University of Pittsburgh Press, 1955), 425.

2. David H. Bates, *Lincoln in the Telegraph Office* (New York: D. Appleton-Century, 1939), 155–58.

3. Lincoln quoted in ibid., 157.

4. Gabor S. Boritt, ed., *Lincoln and His Generals* (New York: Oxford University Press, 1994), 89; John Hay Diary, July 14, 1863, Hay Papers.

5. Lincoln quoted in Benjamin P. Thomas, *Lincoln: A Biography* (New York: Modern Library, 1968), 389.

6. Thomas, *Lincoln*, 389.

7. Exchange between Lee and John D. Imboden in Emory M. Thomas, *Robert E. Lee: A Biography* (New York: Norton, 1995), 301.

8. Lee quoted in Noah A. Trudeau, *Gettysburg: A Testing of Courage* (New York: HarperCollins, 2002), 550.

9. In criticizing Lee's Pennsylvania campaign, the *Charleston Mercury* wrote, "It is impossible for an invasion to have been more foolish and disastrous." Confederate secretary of war Robert Kean considered it a complete failure. Many officers and men privately said they believed the expedition to be a terrible and perhaps irreparable loss. See Michael Fellman, *The Making of Robert E. Lee* (New York: Random House, 2000), 147–49, 151.

10. Glenn Tucker, *Lee and Longstreet at Gettysburg* (Indianapolis, IN: Bobbs-Merrill, 1968), 220. Lee's postwar letter quoted in Robert E. Lee Jr., *My Father General Lee* (New York: Doubleday, 1960), 102. Lee's report to Davis quoted in Fellman, *Making of Robert E. Lee*, 190.

11. Meade-Halleck exchange in *OR*, ser. 1, vol. 27, pt. 1, 92–94.

12. Halleck quoted in David H. Donald, *Lincoln* (New York: Simon & Schuster, 1995), 447.

13. Oliver O. Howard quoted in Freeman Cleaves, *Meade of Gettysburg* (Dayton: Morningside, 1980), 185. Gabor S. Boritt, ed., *Lincoln's Generals* (New York: Oxford University Press, 1994), 83.

14. *OR*, vol. 27, pt. 2, 359–60.

15. Gary W. Gallagher, *Lee and His Generals in War and Memory* (Baton Rouge: Louisiana State University Press, 1998), 145. Longstreet quoted in Jeffry D. Wert, *General James Longstreet* (New York: Simon & Schuster, 1993), 423.

16. Longstreet quoted in Wert, *Longstreet*, 296.

17. Herman Hattaway and Richard E. Beringer, *Jefferson Davis, Confederate President* (Lawrence: University Press of Kansas, 2002), 231. Gorgas quoted in Clement Eaton, *Jefferson Davis* (New York: Free Press, 1977), 179.

18. Davis quoted in Hattaway and Beringer, *Davis*, 232.

19. Ibid., 221.

20. Ibid., 232.

21. Lesley J. Gordon, *General George E. Pickett in Life and Legend* (Chapel Hill: University of North Carolina Press, 1998), 109.

22. Pickett's lament to Longstreet witnessed by courier William Youngblood; see Gordon, *Pickett*, 115–16, 118. Pickett's complaint of lack of support quoted in Arthur C. Inman, ed., *Soldier of the South* (New York: Houghton Mifflin, 1928), 78.

23. Gordon, *Pickett*, 119, 221n. The exact words of Lee were in a dispatch dated August 4, 1863, labeled "Special Orders No. 190": "General: You and your men have crowned yourselves with glory; but we have the enemy to fight, and must carefully, at this critical moment, guard against dissentions which the reflections in your report would create. I will, therefore, suggest that you destroy both copy and original, substituting one confined to casualties merely." See *OR*, ser. 1, vol. 27, pt. 3, 1075.

24. Pickett quoted in Gordon, *Pickett*, 162–63.

25. *New York Times*, July 3, 1863.

26. *New York Times*, July 6, 1863.

27. *New York Times*, July 7, 1863.

28. *New York Times*, July 7, 1863.

29. *Richmond Examiner*, July 15, 1863; *Richmond Daily Dispatch*, July 21, 1863.

30. *Charleston Mercury*, July 16, 1863.

31. *Charleston Mercury*, July 20, 1863.

32. *Charleston Mercury,* July 22, 1863.

33. J. Cutler Andrews, *The South Reports the Civil War* (Princeton, NJ: Princeton University Press, 1970), 323.

34. William Howard Russell quoted in Philip Van Doren Stern, *When the Guns Roared: World Aspects of the American Civil War* (Garden City, NY: Doubleday, 1965), 31. Lord Palmerston quoted in Philip Guedalla, *Palmerston: 1784–1865* (New York: G. P. Putnam's Sons, 1927), 463.

35. Seward quoted in Van Doren Stern, *When the Guns Roared,* 209.

36. Sarah Broadhead account, File 8–6, Gettysburg National Military Park Archives.

37. Ibid.

38. Ibid.

39. Ibid.

40. Clement Eaton, *A History of the Southern Confederacy* (New York: Free Press, 1954), 103.

41. Union doctor quoted in Ira M. Rutkow, *Bleeding Blue and Gray: Civil War Surgery and the Evolution of American Medicine* (New York: Random House, 2005), 276.

42. Gregory A. Coco, *A Strange and Blighted Land* (Gettysburg: Thomas, 1995), 242; Rutkow, *Bleeding Blue and Gray,* 276.

43. Coco, *Strange and Blighted Land,* 240–46; Jim Slade and John Alexander, *Firestorm at Gettysburg* (Atglen, PA: Schiffer, 1998), 161.

44. Slade and Alexander, *Firestorm at Gettysburg,* 169; Coco, *A Vast Sea of Misery* (Gettysburg: Thomas, 1988), 51.

45. Slade and Alexander, *Firestorm at Gettysburg,* 161. Story of parents who exhumed the wrong body is from Gerard A. Patterson, *Debris of Battle: The Wounded of Gettysburg* (Mechanicsburg, PA: Stackpole, 1997), 122.

46. Letterman report of October 3, 1863, *OR,* ser 1, vol. 27, pt. 1, 197.

47. Henrietta S. Jaquette, ed., *South After Gettysburg: Letters of Cornelia Hancock from the Army of the Potomac, 1863–1865* (Philadelphia: University of Pennsylvania Press, 1937), 8.

48. Gregory Coco estimates about 10 percent or around a hundred Union ambulances remained behind at Gettysburg, while Gerard Patterson suggests perhaps thirty remained. See Coco, *Strange and Blighted Land,* 154, 158; Patterson, *Debris of Battle,* 110.

49. Dr. Justin Dwinnel quoted in Patterson, *Debris of Battle,* 99.

50. Coco, *Strange and Blighted Land,* 239.

51. James quoted in Patterson, *Debris of Battle,* 98.

52. Hammond quoted in ibid., 161.

53. Coco, *Vast Sea of Misery,* 248; Patterson, *Debris of Battle,* 106.

54. William A. Frassanito, *Gettysburg: A Journey in Time* (New York: Scribner's, 1975), 24–29, 32–33, 190–91.

55. Ibid., 35–40.

56. Ibid., 17, 40–43.

57. Coco, *Vast Sea of Misery,* 128.

58. Embalmer quoted in ibid., 129–30.

59. Coco, *Vast Sea of Misery,* 361–64.

60. *Philadelphia Public Ledger* quoted in Patterson, *Debris of Battle,* 116.

61. Robert Powell quoted in ibid., 118.

62. Coco, *Vast Sea of Misery,* 317.

63. Patterson, *Debris of Battle,* 73–74, 126, 130.

64. Ibid., 129.

65. Ibid., 53–55.

66. Ibid., 70–71.

67. U.S. Army medical inspector quoted from *OR,* ser. 1, vol. 27, pt. 1, 28. Anecdote of the farmers on Little Round Top from Patterson, *Debris of Battle,* 54.

68. Burlando quoted in Patterson, *Debris of Battle,* 2.

69. Coco, *Vast Sea of Misery,* 32; Sister Mary Denis Maher, *To Bind Up the Wounds: Catholic Sister Nurses in the United States Civil War* (New York: Greenwood Press, 1989), 101.

70. Maher, *To Bind Up the Wounds,* 1, 13–14, 27–29; Sister Ignatius Sumner, *Angels of Mercy* (Baltimore: Cathedral Foundation Press, 1998), xii–xiii; letter from Sr. Liguori at Matanzas, Cuba, February 25, 1898, Sisters of St. Joseph of Carondelet Archives; Pennsylvania soldier quoted in Michael A. Dreese, *The Hospital on Seminary Ridge at the Battle of Gettysburg* (Jefferson, NC: McFarland, 2002), 132.

71. Timothy H. Smith, "Josephine Miller: A Heroine of the Battle," *Blue and Gray,* Holiday Issue 2002, 22–23.

72. *Philadelphia Press,* July 4, 1888.

73. Margaret S. Creighton, *The Colors of Courage: Immigrants, Women, and African Americans in the Civil War's Defining Battle* (New York: Basic Books, 2005), 188; Smith, "Josephine Miller."

74. Jaquette, *South After Gettysburg,* 2.

75. Ibid., 4.

76. Ibid., 6.

77. Ibid., 5.

78. Roland R. Maust, *Grappling with Death: The Union 2nd Corps Hospital at Gettysburg* (Dayton: Morningside, 2001), 658.

79. Capt. Charles Dod quoted in Jaquette, *South After Gettysburg*, vii.
80. Curtis Carroll Davis, "Effie Goldsborough: Confederate Courier," *Civil War Times Illustrated*, April 1968, 29.
81. Patterson, *Debris of Battle*, 134–35.
82. Ibid., 168.
83. Goldsborough's sister quoted in ibid., 182.
84. Davis, "Effie Goldsborough," 30.
85. Creighton, *Colors of Courage*, 96, 120.
86. Thorn quoted in ibid., 154.
87. Patterson, *Debris of Battle*, 101.
88. Dreese, *Hospital on Seminary Ridge*, 131.
89. Bucklin quoted in Coco, *Strange and Blighted Land*, 20.
90. Patterson, *Debris of Battle*, 103. For an extended look at Sophronia Bucklin's life and war service, see Elizabeth D. Leonard, *Yankee Women* (New York: Norton, 1994).
91. Sallie Myers quoted in Slade and Alexander, *Firestorm at Gettysburg*, 76.
92. Slade and Alexander, *Firestorm at Gettysburg*, 179.
93. Sadie Bushman quoted in ibid., 53.
94. Sadie Bushman quoted in Creighton, *Colors of Courage*, 154, 118–19.
95. Creighton, *Colors of Courage*, 200.
96. Cindy Small, *The Jennie Wade Story* (Gettysburg: Thomas, 1981), 32.
97. For an analysis of the Jennie Wade story and whether she was a heroine or an accident victim, see Creighton, *Colors of Courage*, 194–98.
98. *Historic Structures Report: Restoration of Ford's Theater* (Washington, DC: U.S. Department of the Interior, 1963), 105.
99. Donald, *Lincoln*, 460; Thomas, *Lincoln*, 400.
100. Kent Gramm, *November: Lincoln's Elegy at Gettysburg* (Bloomington: Indiana University Press, 2001), 130.
101. The Reverend M. J. Alleman, pastor of Hanover's St. Mark's Lutheran Church, quoted in Louis A. Warren, *Lincoln's Gettysburg Declaration: "A New Birth of Freedom"* (Fort Wayne, IN: Lincoln National Life Foundation, 1964), 60.
102. Warren, *Lincoln's Gettysburg Declaration*, 60.
103. John C. Waugh, *Reelecting Lincoln* (New York: Crown Publishers, 1997), 47.
104. Garry Wills, *Lincoln at Gettysburg* (New York: Simon & Schuster, 1992), 21.
105. Waugh, *Reelecting Lincoln*, 47; Kent Gramm, *November: Lincoln's Elegy at Gettysburg* (Bloomington: Indiana University Press, 2001), 132.
106. Exchange between Lincoln and the crowd in Wills, *Lincoln at Gettysburg*, 31. Reporter quoted in Warren, *Lincoln's Gettysburg Declaration*, 67.

107. In 1901 a Colonel Yinling claimed that Lincoln showed former secretary of war Simon Cameron a draft of the Gettysburg Address in Washington before the event, though this has not been verified. Ward Hill Lamon claimed Lincoln showed him a draft in Washington on November 18, 1863, the day before the dedication, but Lamon was in Gettysburg at that time, making preparations for the president's arrival and the ceremony. See Warren, *Lincoln's Gettysburg Declaration*, 53–54; Wills, *Lincoln at Gettysburg*, 31.

108. Thomas, *Lincoln*, 400–402.

109. Gramm, *November*, 132.

110. Thomas, *Lincoln*, 401.

111. Gramm, *November*, 133.

112. Warren, *Lincoln's Gettysburg Declaration*, 81.

113. Waugh, *Reelecting Lincoln*, 48.

114. Warren, *Lincoln's Gettysburg Declaration*, 131.

115. A *New York Times* correspondent described the Burns and Lincoln trip to the Presbyterian church, but he incorrectly called Lincoln's guest "Tom Burns." See *New York Times*, November 21, 1863.

116. Warren, *Lincoln's Gettysburg Declaration*, 137–38.

CHAPTER 5: PURSUING GETTYSBURG

1. Union officer quoted in Noah A. Trudeau, *Gettysburg: A Testing of Courage* (New York: HarperCollins, 2002), 511; *Philadelphia Journal*, July 5, 1863.

2. See James Lee McDonough and Thomas L. Connelly, *Five Tragic Hours: The Battle of Franklin* (Knoxville: University of Tennessee Press, 1983).

3. For a battle-by-battle breakdown of wins and losses under commanding generals, see Philip Katcher, *The Civil War Source Book* (New York: Facts on File, 1992), 47–50.

4. Robert E. May, ed., *The Union, The Confederacy, and the Atlantic Rim* (West Lafayette, IN: Purdue University Press, 1995), 11; James M. McPherson, *Ordeal by Fire* (New York: Knopf, 1982), 377.

5. *OR*, ser. 1, vol. 27, pt. 3, 429.

6. Stikeleather quoted in Gary W. Gallagher, ed., *Three Days at Gettysburg: Essays on Confederate and Union Leadership* (Kent, OH: Kent State University Press, 1999), 29. Gordon quoted in idem, 29. Cazenove Lee's account of his father's visit with Robert E. Lee in Robert E. Lee Jr., *Recollections and Letters of General Robert E. Lee* (Garden City, NY: Doubleday, Page, and Co., 1924), 415.

7. Mark M. Boatner III, *The Civil War Dictionary* (New York: Vintage Books, 1988), 101–2.

8. Virginia soldier quoted in Trudeau, *Gettysburg,* 428.

9. James Longstreet, *From Manassas to Appomattox* (1896; repr., New York: Mallard Press, 1991), 388. Larry Tagg, *The Generals of Gettysburg* (Campbell, CA: Savas Publishing, 1998), 208–9. Longstreet quoted in Jeffry D. Wert, *General James Longstreet* (New York: Simon & Schuster, 1993), 296.

10. Longstreet quoted in Glenn Tucker, *Lee and Longstreet at Gettysburg* (Indianapolis, IN: Bobbs-Merrill, 1968), 226.

11. For a lengthy analysis of the questions surrounding this issue and others between Meade and Sickles, see Richard Sauers, *A Caspian Sea of Ink: The Meade-Sickles Controversy* (Baltimore: Butternut and Blue, 1989). See also Bill Hyde, *The Union Generals Speak: The Meade Hearings on the Battle of Gettysburg* (Baton Rouge: Louisiana State University Press, 2003), 46–50.

12. Coddington, *The Gettysburg Campaign,* 567.

13. Freeman Cleaves, *Meade of Gettysburg* (Dayton: Morningside, 1980), 186.

14. Edwin Coddington, *The Gettysburg Campaign: A Study in Command* (New York: Scribner's, 1984), 535–36.

15. Ibid., 572.

16. Ibid., 318–19.

17. Harry Pfanz, *Gettysburg–The First Day* (Chapel Hill: University of North Carolina Press, 2001), 342.

18. For an excellent discussion of all of these and other factors see Harry Pfanz, *Gettysburg—Culp's and Cemetery Hill* (Chapel Hill: University of North Carolina Press, 1993), chapter 6. Ewell's assessment of his chances are in *OR,* ser. 1, vol. 27, pt. 2, 318.

19. *OR,* ser. 1, vol. 27, pt. 2, p. 318

20. *Richmond Daily Enquirer,* July 22, 1863; W. R. Bond, *Pickett or Pettigrew* (Dayton: Morningside, 1981), v.

21. W. R. Bond, *Pickett or Pettigrew,* iv; Carol Reardon, *Pickett's Charge in History and Memory* (Chapel Hill: University of North Carolina Press, 2001), 32.

22. Meade quoted in Hyde, *Union Generals,* 326.

23. Coddington, *The Gettysburg Campaign,* 449–50.

24. Trudeau, *Gettysburg,* 151 map. Sickles actually claimed to have received the Pipe Creek Circular. His allegation is almost certainly apocryphal. See Hyde, *Union Generals,* 36–37.

25. Hyde, *Union Generals,* 127.

26. Chamberlain quoted in Mark Perry, *Conceived in Liberty* (New York: Viking, 1997), 224; Coddington, *Gettysburg Campaign,* 394.

27. Morris Penny and J. Gary Lane, *Struggle for the Round Tops: Law's Al-*

abama Brigade at the Battle of Gettysburg, July 2–3, 1863 (Shippensburg, PA: Burd Street Press, 1999), 99; Alice Rains Trulock, *In the Hands of Providence: Joshua Chamberlain and the American Civil War* (Chapel Hill: University of North Carolina Press, 1992), 147.

28. Perry, *Conceived in Liberty,* 415–19.

29. Thomas A. Desjardin, *These Honored Dead: How the Story of Gettysburg Shaped American Memory* (Cambridge, MA: Da Capo Press, 2003), 154–56.

30. 121st New York Monument Committee quoted in Jim Weeks, *Gettysburg: Memory, Market, and an American Shrine* (Princeton, NJ: Princeton University Press, 2003), 61–63.

31. Weeks, *Gettysburg,* 73.

32. Frederick Hawthorne, *Gettysburg: Stories of Men and Monuments as Told by Battlefield Guides* (Hanover, PA: Sheridan Press, 1988), 82–83.

33. Among those who credit John Bachelder with promoting Gettysburg above and beyond its actual historical significance are Desjardin, *These Honored Dead;* Weeks, *Gettysburg.*

34. Desjardin, *These Honored Dead,* 87–98.

35. Weeks, *Gettysburg,* 24.

36. Hawthorne, *Gettysburg,* 116.

37. Ibid., 66.

38. Ibid., 93.

39. Daniel Toomey, *Marylanders at Gettysburg* (Baltimore: Toomey Press, 1994), 50, 80. Anecdote of the battling Maryland units is from Stephen W. Sears, *Gettysburg* (New York: Houghton Mifflin, 2003), 370.

40. Hawthorne, *Gettysburg,* 38.

41. The 120th New York lost 186 killed and wounded at Gettysburg compared to 78 killed and wounded for the 71st New York and 86 killed and wounded for the 72nd. William F. Fox, *New York at Gettysburg* (Albany, NY: J. B. Lyon, 1900), 145. See also Bradley M. Gottfried, *Brigades of Gettysburg* (Cambridge, MA: Da Capo Press, 2002), 219–22.

42. Account of the Sickles embezzlement is in Desjardin, *These Honored Dead,* 81.

43. Hawthorne, *Gettysburg,* 54–55.

44. Gabor S. Boritt, ed., *The Gettysburg Nobody Knows* (New York: Oxford University Press, 1997), 218–19.

45. FDR quoted in Boritt, *Gettysburg Nobody Knows,* 219–20.

46. James M. McPherson, *Hallowed Ground: A Walk at Gettysburg* (New York: Crown Publishers, 2003), 67. Weeks, *Gettysburg,* 133.

47. Hawthorne, *Gettysburg*, 36.

48. Ibid., 28.

49. Gordon and Barlow quoted in Coddington, *Gettysburg Campaign*, 304–5.

50. Coddington, *Gettysburg Campaign*, 683n ; "Heth Memoirs," CWH, 8, 304. *OR*, ser. 1, vol. 27, pt. 2, 317.

51. McPherson, *Hallowed Ground*, 35–36.

52. *New York Times*, July 3, 1863.

53. James M. Paradis, *African Americans and the Gettysburg Campaign* (Lanham, MD: Scarecrow, 2005), 48.

54. Bernie Becker, "A Man Called Harrison," *America's Civil War*, November 2004, 46–52.

55. Jennie Reynolds's account of the bullet's path from Coddington, *Gettysburg Campaign*, 686–87n.

56. Coddington, *Gettysburg Campaign*, 269; Tucker, *Lee and Longstreet at Gettysburg*, 214–17.

57. Tucker, *Lee and Longstreet at Gettysburg*, 11–12.

58. Chamberlain quoted in Mark Perry, *Conceived in Liberty* (New York: Viking, 1997), 224.

59. Coddington, *Gettysburg Campaign*, 390–94.

60. For a detailed account of the Spangler's Spring story and what actually transpired there, see John M. Archer, *Culp's Hill at Gettysburg* (Gettysburg: Thomas, 2002), 136–37n; Pfanz, *Gettysburg—Culp's Hill and Cemetery Hill*, 377–78.

61. Michael Fellman, *The Making of Robert E. Lee* (New York: Random House, 2000), 142–43; Along with Fremantle, Capt. James Johnson of the 5th Florida also witnessed Lee say, "It is all my fault," to Brig. Gen. Cadmus M. Wilcox. Pvt. Charles T. Loehr of the 1st Virginia provides one of the better accounts of the postcharge meeting between Lee and Pickett. See Richard Rollins, ed., *Pickett's Charge: Eyewitness Accounts* (Redondo Beach, CA: Rank and File Publications, 1994), 165, 334–35.

62. Fellman, *Making of Robert E. Lee*, 142. Maj. Edmund Berkely of the 8th Virginia quoted in Kent M. Brown, *Retreat from Gettysburg* (Chapel Hill: University of North Carolina Press, 2005), 9.

63. Louis A. Warren, *Lincoln's Gettysburg Declaration: "A New Birth of Freedom"* (Fort Wayne, IN: Lincoln National Life Foundation, 1964), 61.

64. Warren, *Lincoln's Gettysburg Declaration*, 54.

65. James M. Cole and Roy E. Frampton, *Lincoln and the Human Interest Stories of the Gettysburg National Cemetery* (Hanover, PA: Sheridan Press, 1995), 11.

66. In the landmark volume on battlefield photography, *Gettysburg: A Journey in Time,* author William Frassanito stated the memorial marked the spot. He changed his statement in later editions of his book.

67. Newspaper reporters at the cemetery commencement either failed to mention the rostrum's location or were vague. For a breakdown of theories old and new as to where Lincoln stood, see Garry Wills, *Lincoln at Gettysburg* (New York: Simon & Schuster, 1992), 205–10.

68. *Encyclopedia Britannica,* vol. 3 (Chicago: William Benton, 1971), 226.

69. William A. Frassanito, *The Gettysburg Bicentennial Album* (Gettysburg: Adams County Historical Society, 1987), 10.

70. Barbara L. Platt, *This Is Holy Ground: A History of the Gettysburg Battlefield* (Harrisburg, PA: Huggins Printing, 2001), 33–35.

71. Ibid., 39.

72. Ibid, 45–46; *Gettysburg Compiler,* June 17, 1944; *Gettysburg Times,* July 16, 2001. See also *America's Civil War,* July 2002.

73. Coddington, *Gettysburg Campaign,* 310.

74. The authors wish to express their thanks to licensed battlefield guide Howie Frankenfield for arranging the opportunity to view McPherson's Ridge from Herr Ridge.

75. For a photo of Gettysburg College and its setting near the time of the battle, see Frassanito, *Gettysburg Bicentennial Album,* 10.

76. William A. Frassanito, *Early Photography at Gettysburg* (Gettysburg: Thomas, 1995), 185–87.

77. Photos of the area and the surrounding landscape can be in seen a series of views from Tipton and Myers taken in 1869, ibid., 185–87.

78. Platt, *Holy Ground,* 17–23.

79. Ibid., 13–14, 17–23.

80. Annual Report of the Gettysburg National Military Park Commission to the Secretary of War, 1902. For photos of how the early roads were constructed (Telford Type) see Platt, *Holy Ground,* 23.

SELECTED BIBLIOGRAPHY

PERIODICALS

America's Civil War

American Historical Review

Blue and Gray

Civil War History

Civil War Times Illustrated

De Bow's Review

Gettysburg Magazine

Hallowed Ground

History

History Today

Journal of Southern History

NEWSPAPERS

Augusta Daily Constitutionalist

Charleston Mercury

Chicago Times

Chicago Tribune

Cincinnati Gazette

Gettysburg Compiler

Harper's Weekly Illustrated

London *Times*

New York Evening Post

New York Herald

New York Times

New York Tribune

Philadelphia Inquirer

Philadelphia Journal

Philadelphia Weekly Times

Richmond Daily Dispatch

Richmond Daily Enquirer

Richmond Examiner

Richmond Sentinel

Washington Chronicle

BOOKS

Adelman, Gary. *The Early Gettysburg Battlefield: Selected Photographs from the Gettysburg National Military Park Commission Reports, 1895–1904.* Gettysburg: Thomas Publications, 2001.

———. *Little Round Top: A Detailed Tour Guide.* Gettysburg: Thomas Publications, 2000.

———. *The Myth of Little Round Top: Gettysburg, PA.* Gettysburg: Thomas Publications, 2003.

Alleman, Tillie. *At Gettysburg, or What a Girl Saw and Heard of the Battle.* Baltimore: Butternut and Blue, 1987.

Andrews, Mary Raymond Shipman. *The Perfect Tribute.* New York: Scribner's, 1906.

Archer, John. *The Hour Was One of Horror: East Cemetery Hill at Gettysburg.* Gettysburg: Thomas Publications, 1997.

Arrington, B. T. *The Medal of Honor at Gettysburg.* Gettysburg: Thomas Publications, 1996.

Baumgartner, Richard. *Buckeye Blood—Ohio at Gettysburg.* Huntington, WV: Blue Acorn Press, 2003.

Bennett, Gerald. *Days of Uncertainty and Dread: The Ordeal Endured by the Citizens at Gettysburg.* Camp Hill, PA: Gerald Bennett Publisher, 1994.

Bertera, Martin, and Ken Oberholtzer. *The 4th Michigan Volunteer Infantry at Gettysburg: The Battle for the Wheatfield.* Dayton: Morningside House, 1997.

Boritt, Gabor, ed. *The Gettysburg Nobody Knows.* New York: Oxford University Press, 1997.

Bowden, Scott, and Bill Ward. *Last Chance for Victory: Robert E. Lee and the Gettysburg Campaign.* Conshocken, PA: Savas Publishing, 2001.

Brooke-Rawle, William. *The Right Flank at Gettysburg.* Philadelphia: Philadelphia Weekly Times, 1878.

Brown, Herbert, and Dwight Nitz. *Fields of Glory: The Facts Book of the Battle of Gettysburg.* Gettysburg: Thomas Publications, 1990.

Brown, Kent Masterson. *Cushing of Gettysburg: The Story of Union Artillery Commander.* Lexington: University of Kentucky Press, 1993.

———. *Retreat from Gettysburg: Lee, Logistics, and the Pennsylvania Campaign.* Chapel Hill: University of North Carolina Press, 2005.

Busey, John W. *These Honored Dead: The Union Casualties at Gettysburg.* Hightstown, NJ: Longstreet House, 1988.

———, and David Martin. *Regimental Strengths and Losses at Gettysburg.* Hightstown, NJ: Longstreet House 1986.

Bushong, Millard K. *Old Jube: A Biography of General Jubal A. Early.* Boyce, VA: Carr Publishing, 1955.

Caba, G. Craig, ed. *Episodes of Gettysburg and the Underground Railroad as*

Witnessed by Prof. Howard J. Wert. Gettysburg: C. Craig Caba Antiques, 1998.

Casdorph, Paul. *Confederate General R. S. Ewell.* Lexington: University Press of Kentucky, 2004.

Catton, Bruce. *Gettysburg: The Final Fury.* Garden City, NY: Doubleday Press, 1974.

Chamberlain, Joshua. *Through Blood & Fire at Gettysburg: General Joshua Chamberlain and the 20th Maine.* Gettysburg: Stan Clark Military Books, 1994.

Christ, Elwood. *The Struggle for the Bliss Farm at Gettysburg, July 2nd and 3rd, 1863.* Baltimore: Butternut and Blue, 1992.

Clark, Champ, ed. *Gettysburg: The Confederate High Tide.* Alexandria, VA: Time-Life Books, 1985.

Coco, Gregory A. *The Civil War Infantryman.* Gettysburg: Thomas Publications, 1996.

———. *A Concise Guide to the Artillery at Gettysburg.* Gettysburg: Thomas Publications, 1998.

———. *Confederates Killed in Action at Gettysburg.* Gettysburg: Thomas Publications, 2001.

———. *Gettysburg's Confederate Dead.* Gettysburg: Thomas Publications, 2003.

———. *Killed in Action: Eyewitness Accounts of the Last Moments of 100 Union Soldiers Who Died at Gettysburg.* Gettysburg: Thomas Publications, 1992.

———. *A Strange and Blighted Land—Gettysburg: The Aftermath of Battle.* Gettysburg: Thomas Publications, 1995.

———. *A Vast Sea of Misery: A History and Guide to the Union and Confederate Field Hospitals at Gettysburg, July 1–November 20, 1863.* Gettysburg: Thomas Publications, 1988.

Coddington, Edwin B. *The Gettysburg Campaign: A Study in Command.* New York: Scribner's, 1984.

Coffin, Howard. *Nine Months to Gettysburg: Stannard's Vermonters and the Repulse of Pickett's Charge.* Woodstock, VT: Countryman Press, 1997.

Cohen, Stanley. *Hands Across the Wall: The 50th and 75th Reunions of the Gettysburg Battle.* Charleston, WV: Pictorial Histories Publishing Company, 1997.

Cole, James, and Roy Frampton. *Lincoln and the Human Interest Stories of the Gettysburg National Cemetery.* Hanover, PA: Sheridan Press, 1995.

Cole, Philip M. *Civil War Artillery at Gettysburg*. Cambridge, MA: Da Capo Press, 2002.

Crumb, Herb, ed. *The 11th Corps Artillery at Gettysburg: The Papers of Major Thomas Ward Osborn, Chief of Artillery*. Hamilton, NY: Edmonston Publishing, 1991.

Dalton, Pete, and Cyndi Dalton. *Into the Valley of Death: The Story of the 4th Maine Volunteer Infantry at the Battle of Gettysburg July 2, 1863*. Union, ME: Union Publishing Co., 1994.

Desjardin, Thomas. *These Honored Dead: How the Story of Gettysburg Shaped American Memory*. Cambridge, MA: Da Capo Press, 2003.

Discorfano, Ken. *They Saved the Union at Little Round Top*. Gettysburg: Thomas Publications, 2002.

Donald, David H. *Lincoln*. New York: Simon & Schuster, 1995.

Dougherty, James. *Stone's Brigade and the Fight for McPherson Farm: Battle of Gettysburg, July 1, 1863*. Conshocken, PA: Combined Publishing, 2001.

Dowdy, Clifford. *Death of a Nation: The Story of Lee and His Men at Gettysburg*. Baltimore: Butternut and Blue, 1988.

Downey, Fairfax. *The Guns of Gettysburg*. 1958. Reprint, Gaithersburg, MD: Butternut Press, 1985.

Dreese, Michael. *Never Desert the Old Flag: 50 Stories of Union Battle Flags and Color-Bearers at Gettysburg*. Gettysburg: Thomas Publications, 2002.

———. *This Flag Never Goes Down: 40 Stories of Confederate Battle Flags and Color-Bearers at Gettysburg*. Gettysburg: Thomas Publications, 2004.

Eicher, David. *Gettysburg Battlefield: The Definitive Illustrated History*. San Francisco: Chronicle Books, 2003.

Fennel, Charles. *Battle for the Barb: The Attack and Defense of Culp's Hill on July 2, 1863*. Gettysburg: Friends of the National Park of Gettysburg, 2001.

Fiebeger, G. J. *The Campaign and Battle of Gettysburg*. New Oxford, PA: Bloodstone Press, 1984.

Foote, Shelby. *Stars in Their Courses: The Gettysburg Campaign*. New York: Modern Library, 1994.

Frassanito, William A. *The Gettysburg Bicentennial Album*. Gettysburg: Gettysburg Bicentennial Committee, 1987.

———. *Gettysburg: A Journey in Time*. New York: Scribner's, 1975.

———. *Gettysburg: Then & Now—Touring the Battlefield with Old Photos, 1863–1889*. Gettysburg: Thomas Publications, 1996.

————. *The Gettysburg Then and Now Companion.* Gettysburg: Thomas Publications, 1997.

Frinfrock, Barbara, ed. *Mr. Lincoln's Army: The Army of the Potomac in the Gettysburg Campaign—Programs of the Sixth Annual Gettysburg Seminar.* Gettysburg: Gettysburg National Military Park, 1997.

————. *Unsung Heroes of Gettysburg: Programs of the Fifth Annual Gettysburg Seminar.* Gettysburg: Gettysburg National Military Park, 1996.

Gallagher, Gary W., ed. *The First Day at Gettysburg: Essays on Confederate and Union Leadership.* Kent, OH: Kent State University Press, 1992.

————. *The Fredericksburg Campaign: Decision on the Rappahannock.* Chapel Hill: University of North Carolina Press, 1995.

————. *The Second Day at Gettysburg: Essays on Confederate and Union Leadership.* Kent, OH: Kent State University Press, 1993.

————. *The Third Day at Gettysburg and Beyond.* Chapel Hill: University of North Carolina Press, 1994.

————. *Three Days at Gettysburg: Essays on Confederate and Union Leadership.* Kent, OH: Kent State University Press, 1999.

Gottfried, Bradley. *Brigades at Gettysburg: The Union and Confederate Brigades at the Battle of Gettysburg.* Cambridge, MA: Da Capo Press, 2002.

Gragg, Rod. *Covered with Glory: The 26th North Carolina Infantry at the Battle of Gettysburg.* New York: HarperCollins, 2000.

Gramm, Kent. *November: Lincoln's Elegy at Gettysburg.* Bloomington: Indiana University Press, 2001.

Hall, Jeffry C. *The Stand of the U.S. Army at Gettysburg.* Bloomington: Indiana University Press, 2003.

Hamblen, Charles P. *Connecticut Yankees at Gettysburg.* Edited by Walter L. Powell. Kent, OH: Kent State University Press, 1993.

Hamlin, Percy G., ed. *The Making of a Soldier: Letters of General R. S. Ewell.* Richmond, VA: Whittet and Shepperson, 1935.

Harman, Troy. *Cemetery Hill.* Baltimore: Butternut and Blue, 2001.

Harrison, Kathleen Georg, *The Location of Monuments, Markers, and Tablets on the Gettysburg Battlefield.* Gettysburg: Thomas Publications, 1993.

————, and John Busey. *Nothing but Glory: Pickett's Division at Gettysburg.* Hightstown, NJ: Longstreet House, 1987.

Hartwig, D. Scott, and Ann Marie Hartwig. *Gettysburg: The Complete Pictorial of Battlefield Monuments.* Gettysburg: Thomas Publications, 1995.

Hassler, Warren. *Crisis at the Crossroads: The First Day at Gettysburg.* Gaithersburg, MD: Butternut Press, 1986.

Hassler, William. *A. P. Hill: Lee's Forgotten General.* Richmond, VA: Garrett and Massie, 1957.

Hawthorne, Frederick. *Gettysburg: Stories of Men and Monuments as Told by Battlefield Guides.* Hanover, PA: Sheridan Press, 1988.

Hess, Earl. *Pickett's Charge: The Last Attack at Gettysburg.* Chapel Hill: University of North Carolina Press, 2001.

Hofe, Michael. *That There Be No Stain Upon My Stones: Lt. Col. William L McLeod, 38th Georgia Regiment, 1843–1863.* Gettysburg: Thomas Publications, 1995.

Hoisington, Daniel. *Gettysburg and the Christian Commission.* Roseville, MN: Edinborough Press, 2002.

Howard, William. *The Gettysburg Death Roster: The Federal Dead at Gettysburg.* Dayton: Morningside, 1990.

Hunt, Henry. *Three Days at Gettysburg: July 1, 2, & 3, 1863.* Golden, CO: Outbooks, 1981.

Imhof, John. *Gettysburg: Day Two: A Study in Maps.* Baltimore: Butternut and Blue, 1999.

Jaquette, Henrietta S., ed. *South After Gettysburg: Letters of Cornelia Hancock from the Army of the Potomac, 1863–1865.* Philadelphia: University of Pennsylvania Press, 1937.

Jones, Terry L. *Lee's Tigers: The Louisiana Infantry and the Army of Northern Virginia.* Baton Rouge: Louisiana State University Press, 1987.

Jordan, David M. *Winfield Scott Hancock: A Soldier's Life.* Bloomington: Indiana University Press, 1988.

Jorgensen, Jay. *Gettysburg's Bloody Wheatfield.* Shippensburg, PA: White Maine Books, 2002.

———. *The Wheatfield at Gettysburg: A Walking Tour.* Gettysburg: Thomas Publications, 2002.

Kennell, Brian. *Beyond the Gatehouse: Gettysburg's Evergreen Cemetery.* Gettysburg: Evergreen Cemetery Association, 2000

Kowalis, Jeffrey, and Loree Kowalis. *Died at Gettysburg!* Hightstown, NJ: Longstreet House, 1998.

Krick, Robert. *The Gettysburg Death Roster: The Confederate Dead at Gettysburg.* Dayton: Morningside, 1981.

LaFantasie, Glenn. *Twilight at Little Round Top: July 2, 1863: The Tide Turns at Gettysburg.* Hoboken, NJ: John Wiley and Sons, 2005.

———, ed. *Lt. Frank Haskell, U.S.A., and Col. William C. Oates, C.S.A.: Gettysburg.* New York: Bantam Books, 1992.

Lash, Gary. *The Gibraltar Brigade on East Cemetery Hill.* Baltimore: Butternut and Blue, 1995.

Leonard, Elizabeth D. *Yankee Women.* New York: Norton, 1994.

Loski, Diana. *Gettysburg Experience: A Biographical Collection.* Gettysburg: Princess Publications, 2002.

Luvas, Jay, and Harold Nelson, eds. *The U.S. Army War College Guide to the Battle of Gettysburg.* Carlisle, PA: South Mountain Press, 1986.

MacLachlan, Renae. *Our Bravest and Best: The Iron Brigade at Gettysburg.* Gettysburg: Friends of the National Park, 2001.

Marvel, William. *The First New Hampshire Battery, 1861–1865.* Conway, NH: Minuteman Press, 1985.

Maust, Roland: *Grappling with Death: The Union 2nd Corps Hospital at Gettysburg.* Dayton: Morningside, 2001.

McDonald, JoAnna. *The Faces of Gettysburg: Photographs from the Gettysburg National Military Park Library.* Redondo Beach, CA: Rank and File Publications, 1997.

McIntosh, Davie Gregg. *Review of the Gettysburg Campaign.* Falls Church, VA: Confederate Printers, 1984.

McLaughlin, Jack. *Gettysburg: The Long Encampment.* New York: Appleton-Century, 1963.

McLean, James, Jr. *Cutler's Brigade at Gettysburg.* Baltimore: Butternut and Blue, 1987.

McNeily, J. S. *Barksdale's Mississippi Brigade at Gettysburg.* Gaithersburg, MD: Olde Soldier Books, 1987.

Michigan, Gettysburg Battle Field Commission. *Michigan at Gettysburg: Proceedings Incident to the Dedication of the Michigan Monuments upon the Battlefield of Gettysburg, June 12th, 1889.* Detroit: Win and Hammond, 1889.

Motts, Wayne. *"Trust in God and Fear Nothing": Gen. Lewis Armistead, CSA.* Gettysburg: Farnsworth House Military Impressions, 1994.

Murray, R. L. *E. P. Alexander and the Artillery Action in the Peach Orchard.* Wolcott, NY: Benedum Books, 2000.

———. *"Nothing Could Exceed Their Bravery": New Yorkers in Defense of Little Round Top.* Wolcott, NY: Benedum Books, 1999.

———. *A Perfect Storm of Lead: George Sears Greene and His New York Brigade in Defense of Culp's Hill.* Wolcott, NY: Benedum Books, 2002.

———. *The Redemption of the "Harper's Ferry Cowards": The 111th and 126th New York State Volunteers at Gettysburg.* Wolcott, NY: Benedum Books, 1994.

New York Monuments Commission for the Battlefields of Gettysburg and Chattanooga. *Final Report of the Battlefield of Gettysburg.* 3 vols. Albany: J. B. Lyon, 1900.

Newton, Steven. *McPherson's Ridge: The First Battle for the High Ground.* Cambridge, MA: Da Capo Press, 2002.

Nofi, Albert. *The Gettysburg Campaign: June and July 1863.* New York: Gallery Books, 1986.

Patterson, Gerald. *Debris of Battle: The Wounded of Gettysburg.* Mechanicsburg, PA: Stackpole Books, 1997.

Pennsylvania, Fiftieth Anniversary of the Battle of Gettysburg Commission. *Fiftieth Anniversary of the Battle of Gettysburg.* Harrisburg: W. S. Ray, 1915.

Penny, Morris, and J. Gary Lane. *Struggle for the Round Tops: Law's Alabama Brigade at the Battle of Gettysburg.* Shippensburg, PA: Burd Street Press, 1999.

Perisco, Joseph. *My Enemy, My Brother: Men and Days of Gettysburg.* Cambridge, MA: Da Capo Press, 1996.

Perry, Mark. *Conceived in Liberty: Joshua Chamberlain, William Oates, and the American Civil War.* New York: Viking Press, 1997.

Pfanz, Harry W. *Gettysburg—Culp's Hill and Cemetery Hill.* Chapel Hill: University of North Carolina Press, 1993.

———. *Gettysburg—The First Day.* Chapel Hill: University of North Carolina Press, 2001.

———. *Gettysburg—The Second Day.* Chapel Hill: University of North Carolina Press, 1993.

Phipps, Michael, and John S. Peters. *"The Devil's To Pay": Gen. John Buford, USA.* Gettysburg: Farnsworth House Military Impressions, 1995.

Pinchon, Edgcumb. *Dan Sickles: Hero of Gettysburg and "Yankee King of Spain."* Garden City, NY: Doubleday, Doran and Company, 1945.

Platt, Barbara. *"This Is Holy Ground": A History of the Gettysburg Battlefield.* Harrisburg, PA: Huggins Printing, 2001.

Priest, John. *Into the Fight: Pickett's Charge at Gettysburg*. Shippensburg, PA: White Maine Books, 1998.

Reardon, Carol. *Pickett's Charge in History and Memory*. Chapel Hill: University of North Carolina Press, 1997.

Riggs, David F. *East of Gettysburg: Custer vs. Stuart*. Fort Collins, CO: Old Army Press, 1970.

Robertson, James A. *General A. P. Hill: The Story of a Confederate Warrior*. New York: Random House, 1987.

Rollins, Richard. *The Damned Red Flags of the Rebellion: The Confederate Battle Flag at Gettysburg*. Redondo Beach, CA: Rank and File Publications, 1997.

———, and David Shultz. *Guide to Pennsylvania Troops at Gettysburg*. Redondo Beach, CA: Rank and File Publications, 1998.

Roy, Paul L., compiler. *Pennsylvania at Gettysburg*. Vol 4, *The Seventy-fifth Anniversary of the Battle of Gettysburg, Report of the Pennsylvania Commission*. Gettysburg: Times and News Publishing Co., 1939.

Sauers, Richard. *A Caspian Sea of Ink: The Meade-Sickles Controversy*. Baltimore: Butternut and Blue, 1989.

Schildt, John. *Roads from Gettysburg*. Chewsville, MD: John Schildt, 1979.

———. *Roads to Gettysburg*. Parsons, WV: McClain Printing Co., 1978

Schultz, David. *"Double Canister at Ten Yards": The Federal Artillery and the Repulse of Pickett's Charge*. Redondo Beach, CA: Rank and File Publications: 1995.

Scott, James P. K. *The Story of the Battles at Gettysburg*. Harrisburg, PA: Telegraph Press, 1927.

Sears, Stephen W. *Gettysburg*. New York: Houghton Mifflin, 2003.

Selcer, Richard. *Faithfully and Forever Your Soldier: Gen. George E. Pickett, CSA*. Gettysburg: Farnsworth House Military Impressions, 1995.

Shue, Richard S. *Morning at Willoughby Run: July 1, 1863*. Gettysburg: Thomas Publications, 1995.

Slade, Jim, and John Alexander. *Firestorm at Gettysburg: Civilian Voices, June–November 1863*. Atglen, PA: Schiffer Publishing, 1998.

Small, Cindy L. *The Jennie Wade Story*. Gettysburg: Thomas Publications, 1991.

Smith, Timothy. *John Burns: The Hero of Gettysburg*. Gettysburg: Thomas Publications, 2000.

———. *The Story of Lee's Headquarters: Gettysburg Pennsylvania*. Gettysburg: Thomas Publications, 1995.

Storrick, W. C. *The Battle of Gettysburg*. Harrisburg, PA: J. Horace McDonald Co., 1953.

———. *Gettysburg: The Places, the Battles, the Outcome*. Harrisburg, PA: J. Horace McFarland and Company, 1932.

Stouffer, Cindy, and Shirley Cubbison. *A Colonel, a Flag, and a Dog*. Gettysburg: Thomas Publications, 1998.

Symonds, Craig. *Gettysburg: A Battlefield Atlas*. Baltimore: Nautical and Aviation Publishing Company of America, 1992.

Tagg, Larry. *The Generals of Gettysburg*. Campbell, CA: Savas Publishing Company, 1998

Thomas, Benjamin P. *Abraham Lincoln: A Biography*. New York: Modern Library, 1968.

Tilberg, Frederick. *Gettysburg National Military Park Pennsylvania*. Washington DC: National Park Service Historical Handbook Series, 1954.

Toney, B. Keith. *Gettysburg: Tours and Tales with a Battlefield Guide*. Shepherdsville, KY: Publishers Press, 1994.

Toomey, Daniel. *Marylanders at Gettysburg*. Baltimore: Toomey Press, 1994.

Trudeau, Noah. *Gettysburg: A Testing of Courage*. New York: HarperCollins, 2002.

Tucker, Glenn. *Lee and Longstreet at Gettysburg*. Indianapolis, IN: Bobbs-Merrill, 1968.

Tucker, Phillip. *Storming Little Round Top*. Cambridge, MA: Da Capo Press, 2002.

U.S. Surgeon General's Office. *Medical and Surgical History of the War of the Rebellion, 1861–1865*. Washington DC: Government Printing Office, 1870.

Valuska, David, and Christian Keller. *Damn Dutch: Pennsylvania Germans at Gettysburg*. Mechanicsburg, PA: Stackpole Books, 2004.

Venner, William. *The 19th Indiana Infantry at Gettysburg: Hoosiers' Courage*. Shippensburg, PA: Burd Street Press, 1998.

Walker, Paul. *The Cavalry Battle That Saved the Union: Custer vs. Stuart at Gettysburg*. Gretna, LA: Pelican Publishing, 2002.

Warren, Louis A. *Lincoln's Gettysburg Declaration: "A New Birth of Freedom."* Fort Wayne, IN: Lincoln National Life Foundation, 1964

Wasel, Bob, and Mimi Johnson-Bosler. *A Soldier's Grave: Original Burial Sites on the Gettysburg Battlefield*. N.p.: Quick and Dirty Publications, 2000.

Waugh, John C. *Reelecting Lincoln*. New York: Crown Publishers, 1997.

Wert, Jeffrey. *Gettysburg: Day Three.* New York: Simon & Schuster, 2001.

Wheeler, Richard. *Witness to Gettysburg.* New York: Harper & Row, 1987.

Wills, Garry. *Lincoln at Gettysburg.* New York: Simon & Schuster, 1992.

Wilkinson, Warren, and Steven Woodworth. *A Scythe of Fire: A Civil War Story of the Eighth Georgia Infantry Regiment.* New York: HarperCollins, 2002.

Wills, Garry. *Lincoln at Gettysburg: The Words That Remade America.* New York: Touchstone, 1992.

Wittenberg, Eric. *Gettysburg: Forgotten Cavalry Actions.* Gettysburg: Thomas Publications, 1998.

———. *Protecting the Flank: The Battles of Brinkerhoff's Ridge and East Cavalry Field: Battle of Gettysburg, July 2–3, 1863.* Celina, OH: Ironclad Publishing, 2002.

Young, Emma. *They Will Remember: The Rupp Family, House and Tannery.* Gettysburg: Friends of the National Parks at Gettysburg, 2004.

Young, Jesse Bowman. *The Battle of Gettysburg.* Dayton: Morningside, 1976.

Index